African Enclosures?

The Social Dynamics
of Wetlands in Drylands

African Enclosures?

The Social Dynamics
of Wetlands in Drylands

Philip Woodhouse
Henry Bernstein
David Hulme

WITH

PIPPA TRENCH
ANDREW CLAYTON
EDWARD LAHIFF
CHRISTOPHER SOUTHGATE
MOUSSA DIT MARTIN TESSOUGUÉ

JAMES CURREY
OXFORD

AFRICA WORLD PRESS
TRENTON, NJ

DAVID PHILIP
CAPE TOWN

EAEP
NAIROBI

James Currey
73 Botley Road
Oxford
OX2 0BS

David Philip Publishers (Pty) Ltd
208 Werdmuller Centre
Claremont 7708
Cape Town

Africa World Press
P.O. Box 1892
Trenton
NJ 08607

EAEP
PO Box 45314
Nairobi

British Library Cataloguing in Publication Data

Woodhouse, Philip
  African enclosures? : the social dynamics of wetlands in drylands
  Trench ... [et al.]
  1.Wetlands – Africa 2.Community development – Africa
  I.Title II.Bernstein, Henry III.Hulme, D.
  IV.Trench, Pippa
  307.1′4′096
  ISBN 0-85255-415-X (James Currey cloth)
       0-85255-416-8 (James Currey paper)

Library of Congress Cataloging-in-Publication Data
available on file at the Library of Congress
  ISBN 0-86543-937-0 (Africa World Press cloth)
  ISBN 0-86543-938-9 (Africa World Press paper)

Typeset in 10½/12 Bembo by Saxon Graphics Ltd, Derby
Printed & bound in the United Kingdom by Antony Rowe Ltd, Chippenham, Wiltshire

Contents

List of figures — vii
List of maps — ix
List of tables — xi
List of boxes — xiii
Acknowledgements — xv
List of contributors — xvii

1
Africa's 'Wetlands in Drylands'
From Commons to Enclosures? — 1
PHILIP WOODHOUSE, HENRY BERNSTEIN & DAVID HULME

2
A Very Decentralized Development
Exploiting a New Wetland in the Sourou Valley, Mali — 29
PHILIP WOODHOUSE, PIPPA TRENCH &
MOUSSA DIT MARTIN TESSOUGUÉ

3
Uncommon Property
The Scramble for Wetland in Southern Kenya — 73
CHRISTOPHER SOUTHGATE & DAVID HULME

4
Modernizing Communal Lands
Evolving Resource Use in the Shoshong Hills, Botswana — 119
ANDREW CLAYTON & PHILIP WOODHOUSE

5
The Mutale River Valley
An Apartheid Oasis — 155
EDWARD LAHIFF

6
Whose Environments?
Whose Livelihoods? — 195
HENRY BERNSTEIN & PHILIP WOODHOUSE

7
Governance & the Environment
Politics & Policy — 215
DAVID HULME & PHILIP WOODHOUSE

Index — 233

Figures

2.1 Mali: GDP, contribution of livestock production, agriculture & the
    whole rural sector   34
2.2 Mali: production of cereals   35
2.3 Average monthly rainfall in Bankass & San, 1975–86   36
2.4 Mean monthly values for rainfall, evapotranspiration & temperature at San 37
2.5 Aerial photographs of the Sourou valley in the vicinity of Baye, taken in
    1992 & 1996   42
2.6 Comparison of vegetation cover in aerial photographs taken in
    1992 & 1996   43
3.1 Mean monthly rainfall & spring discharge in Loitokitok   80
3.2 Population change in Kajiado District   81
3.3 Territorial levels of Maasai natural resource management   83
3.4 Simplified diagram of Kisonko clan relations   93
3.5 A chronology of natural hazards in Maasailand   99
3.6 Cattle & human population in Kajiado District, 1942–94   100
3.7 Grazing areas used by Kimana Maasai during the dry & wet seasons
    of 1994   102
3.8 Land tenure in Loitokitok   104
3.9 Streams flowing into & out of Kimana Swamp   108
4.1 Annual rainfall, 1917–94   125
4.2 Rainfall distribution: Mahalapye monthly average, 1917–94   126
4.3 Livestock population, 1983–90   138
5.1 Annual rainfall in the upper & lower Mutale River valley   160
5.2 Average monthly rainfall, Thohoyandou   160
5.3 Flow records for the Mutale River   164
5.4 Livestock numbers in Venda, 1982–9   177

Maps

2.1	Mali: regions & location of case-study	30
2.2	Mali: principal rivers & approximate rainfall isohyets	31
2.3	The Sourou valley	32
3.1	Kenya: principal rivers & rainfall in Kajiado District	75
3.2	Loitokitok Division	78
3.3	Kimana Group Ranch	91
4.1	Botswana: location of case-study	120
4.2	Shoshong Hills	124
4.3	Dams & boreholes in the case-study area	134
5.1	Ex-Bantustan areas in South Africa	156
5.2	Venda & the Mutale valley	159
5.3	Irrigation in Tshiombo, upper Mutale valley	162
5.4	Irrigation in the lower Mutale valley	163

Tables

1.1   A social dynamics framework for analysing changing resource use   24
2.1   Classification of vegetation cover in the *cercle* of Bankass   33
2.2   Population change in the *arrondissements* of Bankass *cercle*, 1976–96   40
2.3   Population census in different years: Songoré & Oula villages   46
2.4   Summary of distribution of rice plots & area between different types of cultivator in Songoré and Oula   47
2.5   Overall distribution of rice harvest   56
3.1   Mean monthly rainfall at three stations in Loitokitok Division   79
3.2   Group ranches in Loitokitok Division   87
3.3   Environmental management in Loitokitok Division: the institutional framework   88
3.4   Summary of land transactions in Loitokitok Division during 1994 & 1984   89
3.5   Furrow group leaders in the Kimana/Tikondo irrigation schemes   93
3.6   Leaders of formal organizations in Kimana, 1996   95
3.7   Grazing areas used by Kimana Maasai during the dry & wet seasons of 1994   101
4.1   Distribution of population between rural & urban areas in Botswana   122
4.2   Population of villages in the vicinity of Shoshong Hills   126
4.3   Summary of water points used by Mmutlane villagers   135
5.1   Combined landholding at Tshiombo, per household   172
5.2   Distribution of cattle among households at Tshiombo   177
5.3   Estimated crop value per household at Tshiombo, all lands   182

Boxes

3.1   The group ranch model   86
3.2   The commoditization of grazing resources   90
3.3   The battle for control in Maasailand   96
3.4   The story of William Karanja   97
3.5   The politics of resource access: cultivation in Kimana Swamp   98
3.6   Singh's story   105
3.7   Economic accumulation: case-studies from Kimana/Tikondo   110

Acknowledgements

The authors wish to acknowledge with thanks the help given to this research by many individuals, not least those in the four case study areas who contributed their time, views and knowledge. In addition, Professor Bill Tordoff was a key contributor to the research in its early stages and in designing the Botswana case study, to which Richard Werbner, Martin Reynolds, Sandy Grant, Isaac Mazonde and Cornelius van der Post also made valuable contributions. Nigel Cross and Duncan Fulton at SOS Sahel, and their colleagues Mary Allen, Aly Bacha Konaté, and Mamadou Diakité at the *Projet Protection de l'Environnement de Bankass* provided vital support to the Mali case study. We wish to acknowledge also the important contribution of the late Lawrence Phala to the work undertaken in Venda.

This research was funded by the Global Environmental Change Programme of the Economic and Social Research Council of the United Kingdom, and its publication was funded by the Department for International Development of the United Kingdom. However the Department for International Development can accept no responsibility for any information provided or views expressed.

List of Contributors

Henry Bernstein
is Professor of Development Studies in the University of London at the School of
Oriental and African Studies. He has published widely in the political economy of
agrarian change, was joint editor with T.J. Byres of the *Journal of Peasant Studies* for
fifteen years, and is founding editor, again with T.J. Byres, of the new *Journal of
Agrarian Change*.

Andrew Clayton
trained as a social anthropologist and undertook his doctoral research in Tanzania.
After his work for IDPM in Botswana for this study, he worked for four years with
the International NGO Training and Research Centre (INTRAC), where he wrote
and edited a number of publications including *NGOs, Civil Society and the State*
(INTRAC 1996). He currently works as Senior Policy Officer for Asia with
Christian Aid.

David Hulme
is Professor of Development Studies at the Institute for Development Policy and
Management, University of Manchester. He has worked extensively on rural development and poverty-reduction strategies in South Asia, Africa and the Pacific. In
recent years he has been researching on local environmental management in Africa
with a particular focus in East Africa. His publications include *Governance,
Administration and Development* (with M. Turner), *NGOs, States and Donors* (with M.
Edwards), *Finance Against Poverty* (with P. Mosley) and *African Wildlife and Livelihoods:
the Promise and Performance of Community Conservation* (with M. Murphree)

Edward Lahiff
is a Senior Lecturer in Land and Agarian Studies at the University of the Western
Cape. Prior to that he spent three years as Research and Policy Coordinator with
Nkuzi Development Association, a land rights NGO based in South Africa's
Northern Province. He holds a PhD in Development Studies from the School of
Oriental and African Studies, London.

Christopher Southgate
is a lecturer in Environmental Management at the University of Central Lancashire.
He has been undertaking research in Maasailand for six years, and holds a PhD from
the University of Manchester.

Moussa dit Martin Tessougué

is a postgraduate geography researcher with the Institut Supérieur de Formation et de la Recherche Appliquée (ISFRA) in Bamako. He has undertaken field research for the *Projet Protection de l'Environnement de Bankass* and is currently completing his doctoral studies at the Laboratoire Population-Environnement at the Université de Provence, France.

Pippa Trench

works for SOS Sahel (UK) where she is leading a project on Shared Management of Common Property Resources in a number of Sahelian countries. She trained as a biologist and anthropologist, and has previously worked in Kenya. She holds a PhD from University College, London.

Philip Woodhouse

is a Senior Lecturer in Environment and Rural Development at the Institute for Development Policy and Management, University of Manchester. He worked for a number of years as a soil scientist in Mozambique, and for the past decade has been researching land and water management in Africa, particularly in Southern Africa and francophone West Africa.

1

Africa's 'Wetlands in Drylands' From Commons to Enclosures?

PHILIP WOODHOUSE, HENRY BERNSTEIN,
& DAVID HULME

Introduction

While focused on Africa, this book originated in a research programme on global
environmental change. The wider debate of global environmental change today is
structured by two principal perspectives as far as issues of development and developing countries are concerned. The first, characterized as the 'conventional wisdom'
or dominant narrative (Leach and Mearns, 1996), is that increasing poverty is caused
by declining productivity of the biophysical resource base (land, vegetation, water) –
'environmental degradation' – itself largely attributable to demographic pressure. A
second perspective, associated with the more optimistic prospectus of Agenda 21 set
out by the United Nations Commission on Environment and Development
(UNCED) at the Rio Summit in 1992, is that effective environmental management
driven by local initiative and participation can, and should, provide the key to
reducing rural poverty, as well as conserving the natural resource base.

Both these perspectives are derived from and applied to research and debate on
environmental change in Africa with particular intensity, including selection of
appropriate policy and institutional reforms. Recent innovative empirical research
investigates the practices and institutional forms of resource use and management by
resource users (arable and livestock farmers, forest users and fisherfolk) and seeks to
develop policy prescriptions based on its findings. At the same time, the results of
much of this work tend to be limited by its notions – rudimentary at best, absent at
worst – of how wider social, economic and political forces influence natural resource
use and regulation, including the decisions and practices of (differentiated) resource
users. Consequently, many proposals for policy and institutional reform of environmental management in Africa rest on typically idealized visions of 'community' or
the imposition of externally derived models of 'good governance' as part of aid
conditionality, or perverse combinations of both.

This book presents case-studies of natural resource management in four very different African 'wetlands in drylands', based on fieldwork conducted in 1994–6, to identify socio-economic and political dynamics operating locally and more widely in the societies concerned, and to explore their connections. Our title for the book signals our conclusion that these 'dynamics', allowing for their unevenness and contradictory effects and for the specificities of different cases, do suggest a discernible direction of social change towards greater commoditization and (*de facto* as well as sometimes *de jure*) 'privatization' of land and water, a conclusion captured in the metaphor or analogy of 'enclosure'. This in turn raises issues of the politics of policy objectives and instruments that may affect the direction of change, and hence the future character of society and environment and their interactions in Africa.

This introductory chapter seeks to do four things:

- To provide an overview of themes that link environmental with economic, political and development issues within a periodization of modern (colonial and independent) African history.
- To assess an emergent and increasingly influential agenda for policy and institutional reform concerning environmental management.
- To sketch the location of 'wetlands in drylands' in African ecologies.
- To explain the analytical framework and approach used in the chapters that follow.

Environment and development in Africa: themes and periods

We touch on four overlapping themes here, cross-cutting all of which are the contentious, and contested, issues of land tenure and property rights, to which special attention is due. The themes are discourses of 'development' in the sense of economic growth, discourses of the state and governance, discourses of agricultural production/productivity and rural livelihoods and discourses of environmental degradation/conservation and sustainability. We locate these discursive themes in four historical 'moments', broadly periodized as follows: the period of colonial establishment and consolidation (1880s–1930s); 'late colonialism' with its 'developmental' thrust (1940s–1950s); independence and the 'developmental state' (1960s–1970s); and the era of structural adjustment (1980s–present). One significant aspect of this periodization – generally accepted by historians of Africa (inasmuch as anything is) – is its correspondence to key moments of world history. The first period corresponds to the first 'golden age' of 'globalization' from the 1870s to 1914, during which the 'scramble for Africa' took place (along with European colonization of the other major remaining imperial frontiers in western and south-eastern Asia), followed by the unsettled postwar conditions of the 1920s and then the Great Depression of the 1930s. The (Keynesian and other) expansions of state activity and regulation, initiated from the 1930s, greatly expanded in wartime conditions and then adapted to the tasks of postwar reconstruction in Europe, had profound effects for 'late colonialism' and its 'developmental' aspirations in the second period of the 1940s and 1950s. The third period is that of the developmental state after independence, which both further expanded and refashioned that of late colonialism, with its apogee in the 1960s at the peak of an unprecedented cycle of growth of the world economy. The downward turn of that cycle of growth into worldwide recession in the 1970s generated a new (our fourth and current) period of international economic and political turbulence, of which exposure to acute foreign debt combined with structural adjustment lending was common to many poor countries but perhaps experienced most intensely by those in Africa.

These observations are an important dimension of setting the historical stage and the succession of dramas enacted on it in Africa. At the same time, they indicate the need to exercise caution. To sketch them thus is not to suggest any simple or single set of effects for African societies, peoples and environments in the manner of crude versions of 'world systems' approaches. Nor is it to succumb to types of generalization about 'Africa' (or 'sub-Saharan Africa') that essentialize the attributes of its societies and cultures and/or of its 'nature' (ecologies, land-scapes) – typically a feature, explicit or implicit, of the discourses we review in this section. Our review is without any pretensions to completeness; its purpose is illustrative and (we trust) suggestive. We hope that its propositions will be tested and elaborated by further scholarship in environmental history that embraces the perspectives of political economy (largely lacking until now, according to Beinart, (1996:71)), and is able to do so with the sophistication of Vaughan's illuminating essays (1991) on colonial power and its discourses of illness and practices of medicine in Africa.

Colonial establishment and consolidation (1880s–1930s)

A defining feature of the modern historical experience of Africa is that compre-hensive colonial rule was established in most of the continent relatively late in the long history of European overseas expansion. As the late Julius Nyerere remarked (in a speech at the University of Dar es Salaam in the 1970s, attended by one of the authors): 'for Lenin imperialism was the last stage of capitalism, but for us in Africa it was the first'. By the late nineteenth century, not only were the principal European colonial powers in Africa (Britain and France) industrialized countries, but the 'second industrial revolution' from the 1870s (Hobsbawm, 1987) generated a massive growth of demand for agricultural and mineral raw materials, including those tropical products that it was the role of colonial economies in an expanding (and shifting) international division of labour to supply.

At the same time, as African colonial economies were organized to produce tropical agricultural products (and minerals) for export to world markets, this activity was also expected to yield the revenues to pay for colonial administration. The formation and functioning of colonial states was marked by what Berry (1993) calls 'hegemony on a shoestring', which is also a theme in the most important analysis of colonial state formation for many years, that by Mamdani (1996), who emphasizes the 'decentralized' despotism of its indirect rule. Under indirect rule, the lowest tier of state administration in the countryside was allocated to the authority of chiefs and headmen governing by the ostensibly 'customary law' of particular 'tribes', to which rural people were subject on the basis of their 'tribal' identity, as perceived and legislated by colonial rulers.

While the powers of chiefs were thoroughly subordinated to those of colonial state authority (e.g. in relation to duties of tax collection and labour recruitment for military and public works, and ultimately in terms of the deposition and replacement of chiefs), they were often greatly increased in relation to their subjects. Political relations in precolonial African societies often had 'pluralist' features, which countered and contained tendencies to the consolidation and exercise of strongly hierarchical authority (and not only in 'stateless' societies), including that associated with the spread of 'conquest states' in the nineteenth century in the course of Sahelian jihads and the southern African *mfecane*. Mamdani (1996) suggests that colonial indirect rule increased hierarchical and authoritarian tendencies in pre-existing political systems at the expense of the latter's forms of 'pluralism' and 'checks and balances'. He argues that the colonial refashioning of chieftaincy (with the active participation of many chiefs and their allies) in effect fused executive, legislative and judicial powers of 'customary' authority as the exercise of indirect rule in the countryside.

This had particular and potent effects for land tenure and use (as for other areas), which connect with issues of emergent forms of agricultural production and their commoditization, in turn associated with integration in world markets and divisions of labour (see above). There is widespread recognition that, through the institution of indirect rule, the 'customary' in Africa – in relation to land as well as political status – was refashioned (or even 'invented') by colonial interventions (Colson, 1971; Platteau, 1992; Berry, 1993; Peters, 1994; Mamdani, 1996). In areas under customary jurisdiction, the development of land markets was suppressed (see further below), and existing 'ascriptive' forms of kinship (through which individuals could leave one settlement and be 'adopted' as kin within another) were replaced by more rigid 'tribal' definitions of community membership, as a condition of rights to land under 'customary' or 'communal' tenure.

In most of sub-Saharan Africa, with the exception of areas where (white) settlement was encouraged, 'peasant' farmers (including pastoralists) were not dispossessed but 'encouraged' by various means to enter the monetary (commodity) economy as producers of agricultural commodities and/or labour power (especially for colonial plantations and settler estates, where these were established). While these various means typically involved 'forcible commercialization' initially (as Bharadwaj (1985) termed it in the context of colonial India), some African farmers pioneered commodity production for export by mobilizing land and labour through customary means and without, or despite, the actions of colonial states (e.g. the 'classic' case of cocoa production in Ghana, analysed in the seminal study by Hill (1963)).

The processes outlined were accompanied by various perceptions of, and concerns with, 'nature' in Africa, from idealized conceptions of a pre- (or non-) industrial 'Eden' (Anderson and Grove, 1987) to the bracketing of a savage and dangerous 'nature' and 'culture' (Vaughan, 1991) to more pragmatic concerns with the destructive and 'wasteful' (mis)use by natives of the fragile resource endowments of their habitats through 'shifting cultivation' and pastoralism (see the essays by Scoones, Swift and Cline-Cole in Leach and Mearns (1996)). These early currents, together with links between scientific investigation of Africa's physical environments and conservation as an element of 'native policy', became more central to the colonial agenda, with a more concentrated impetus to state intervention in the 1930s. In some respects, this reflected the impact of scientific and policy response to the problem of 'dust bowls' in the USA – a key moment in the formation of applied environmental science as we know it today and one that had many international repercussions, including in colonial Africa (Anderson, 1984). In other respects, this more intense concern with conservation was one feature, among others, of a conjuncture in which colonial rule was consolidated at a time when the Great Depression of the 1930s occurred, with its manifold – and characteristically disturbing – effects for a range of economic, political and social ideas and practices, not least those of the colonial project in Africa and how its inherent contradictions were perceived and acted on by both colonial rulers and subjects.

The central contradiction of that project for its architects and engineers – as identified by Phillips (1989), Cowen and Shenton (1991a, b, 1996: ch. 6) and Grischow (1998) and, more implicitly, by Mamdani (1996), among others – was how to develop commodity production in the African colonies without generating the social (especially class) divisions and tensions of (industrial) capitalism in Europe, and moreover to do so within the political constraints of 'hegemony on a shoestring'. Indirect rule, together with its comprehensive discursive formations that naturalized/essentialized African 'culture', 'community' and 'tribe' within the responsibilities and demands of 'trusteeship' and 'respect' for native 'custom' and 'tradition', exemplifies this contradiction very clearly. It was, in vital respects, not only an attempt to exercise political domination at low cost to imperial exchequers, but also to prevent, limit or otherwise manage dynamics of class differentiation, for example, by returning migrant workers to their (solidary) tribal 'communities' and the benign patriarchal authority of their chiefs, and also to prevent chiefs and others (merchants, entrepreneurs, those acquiring western education) from emerging as a distinct class of accumulators. 'Detribalization' was such a potent expression of this contradiction of the colonial project because it was typically (if not exclusively) a code word for the formation of a working class, and above all an urban working class.

Cowen and Shenton (1991a) coined the suggestive term 'Fabian colonialism' for that set of ideas and practices, consolidated by the 1930s, in which the central motif of the colonial project was to 'protect' the natives from the costs of capitalism while gradually allowing them to share in its benefits. The former required prevention (or at least postponement *sine die*) of such mixed blessings of bourgeois civilization as private property rights in land and ease of access to commercial credit for African entrepreneurs. As well as the responsibilities and demands of prophylactic regulation, the Fabian impulse also sanctioned more proactive interventions to 'advance' Africans as well as 'protect' them. In the 1930s, this was expressed in a number of areas of economic and social policy, including land use planning and environmental conservation, which were to move centre stage in the postwar moment of 'colonial welfare and development'. Similarly carried forward (and developed) in this second period were the many expressions of contradictions between the colonial project and its subjects. These were manifested in the 1930s in the rising activism of African workers and peasant 'strikes' and other actions against the falling crop prices of the Depression decade, but also in a range of less dramatic and overt processes and contestations, through which Africans – and different groups of Africans, from labour migrants to chiefly and other emergent accumulators – sought to evade, deflect or otherwise turn to their advantage the institutions, forms and practices of colonial rule, with their many ambiguities and tensions.

Late colonialism (1940s–1950s)

Ideas and practices of economic development and of the role of government in promoting it were changed profoundly by the effects of the Depression, followed by the Second World War and postwar reconstruction (not just of Europe and Japan and its former colonies in East Asia, but also by the new 'Bretton Woods' institutions established to create and maintain stability in international monetary and trade relations). The commanding economic role of government in wartime and postwar reconstruction, coupled with booming primary commodity markets in the 1950s and the adoption of Keynesian macroeconomic policies, resulted in state-provided or sponsored investment in physical and social infrastucture and in increasing production. This was true of the colonies under the rubric of 'colonial welfare and development' as well as of the metropolitan countries, if on a suitably more modest scale (in terms of imperial expenditure and concern) but not necessarily an insignificant one relative to colonial economies. The marketing boards of the Depression years now took on more 'developmental' (rather than simply fiscally extractive) functions, and other parastatals – various forms of development corporations and schemes – were established.

During the 1950s, at least some European colonies in Africa were being 'prepared' for independence through measures to implement reform of their governance. In many British colonies, indirect rule through customary authority was partly replaced by belated efforts to institute representative local government in the form of municipal, township and rural councils with legislative powers to discharge specific functions, to raise part or much of their revenue and to recruit and manage their own staff. The partial, uneven and hence ambiguous character of such reforms – and the activists they attracted into local politics (typically younger, better-educated and/or entrepreneurial men) – often added additional layers of complexity and tension to those of indirect rule and the claims and counterclaims of chiefly authority (which was challenged rather than necessarily extinguished).

The combinations of new economic and political discourses and initiatives in the postwar period were especially marked in relation to agriculture and agricultural and conservation policies, in ways that qualified but also reproduced aspects of the earlier versions of the colonial project and its antinomies. An important example of this dynamic was the new desire to establish a class of 'progressive' or 'yeoman' African farmers. These 'family' or petty capitalist farmers, typically specialized in the production of higher-value export crops using 'modern' inputs and techniques on government-managed schemes, were to serve as a vanguard of technical modernization and agricultural productivity growth, as exemplars of cultural modernity, and as a force for civic responsibility and social stability. This vision, and the means of realizing it, raised difficult issues about 'customary' or 'communal' land tenure; one of the foundations of indirect rule and chiefly authority (and sources of rural 'stability'), this was now seen as an obstacle to agricultural modernization/development, which required a basis of private property right and incentive (albeit under state supervision). Significantly, perhaps the most important attempt at 'land reform' – land allocation combined with individual title – in the late colonial period was the Swynnerton Plan in Kenya's Central Province in the wake of the armed rebellion of Mau Mau. This was subsequently extended to embrace African pastoralists as nascent 'ranchers', with the provision of land titles, credit and improved cattle breeds.

The other side of the coin of such agricultural modernization, and linked by growing investment in and attention to agricultural and environmental research, was the growing concern with soil conservation and land use planning. While efforts were made to promote the specialized and modernized production of higher-value crops, fertilizer use and mechanization on 'progressive' farmer schemes, this was also the moment when notions of the 'carrying capacity' of particular environments for human and livestock populations were 'operationalized' (the military term 'operations' being a characteristic, if not novel, feature of the discourses of the time) in settlement and resettlement schemes. Implementing such schemes to establish 'model' small-scale mixed arable and livestock farming units often involved some coercion: 'betterment' in South Africa, the Swynnerton Plan in Kenya, resettlement in Northern Rhodesia (Zambia), *encadrement* by the Compagnie Française pour le Développement des Textiles (CFDT) cotton-growing schemes in francophone West Africa. Coercion was particularly pronounced in the least 'developed' colonies, where market incentives were lowest and the political compulsion to cash cropping and labour migration still operative, as in the Belgian Congo and the Portuguese territories.

Parastatal development corporations and (export) crop marketing, land use planning and conservation regulations, and rudimentary macroeconomic planning and project/scheme state investment and management were all to prove among the many legacies of late colonialism to the moment of independence.

Independence and the developmental state (1960s–1970s)

The late colonial model of state-led economic development was largely assimilated by newly independent African governments, albeit reinforced and reconfigured in some cases by more comprehensive Soviet-inspired planning and accumulation and the commitment to 'nation-building' as a political and social project. The outcome was to greatly increase the scale of state investment in both economic and social sectors and, in relation to the former, to direct much of it to import-substituting industrialization and major infrastructural projects (in communications, power generation, water), as well as primary production (agriculture, mining, timber), typically through the formation of parastatal companies (in manufacturing, finance and public utilities, agricultural inputs and services). Foreign aid agencies were heavily involved in the funding, the design and (through technical assistance) even the operation of many of these ambitious ventures of state developmentalism in the initial, and optimistic, period of independence. While the 1960s saw the largest rate of growth of agricultural exports since the 1920s, during the 1970s the African version of a fiscal crisis of the state was gathering, experienced with increasing intensity as worldwide recession dealt a series of 'external shocks' to all African economies (except oil exporters and, in the case of Botswana, a newly established diamond exporter).

Concerning governance, and as the above implies, independence witnessed a major growth of the state in terms of its economic and social ambitions, its expenditure and share of gross domestic product (GDP) and employment and its political and administrative centralization. All these features were considered necessary to, or at least justified by, the demands of 'national development' and 'nation-building', after the enforced underdevelopment of colonial rule and exploitation (as was the prevalence of one-party states, in *de jure* or *de facto* forms; increasingly frequent military coups and regimes similarly claimed their legitimacy in the failure of civilian governments to deliver on the promise of development). Where institutions of decentralized government had been promoted, notably in the later years of British colonial rule, they were widely perceived after independence as inefficient and conducive to ethnic and regional rivalries subversive of development and nation-building. They were progressively abolished, or otherwise rendered gestural through loss of control of budgets and staff appointments, with the tasks of development now located strongly in central government and its necessary concentration of resources and expertise (Kasfir, 1993). Mamdani (1996) identifies two post-independence outcomes of the legacy of the late colonial state: what he terms 'conservative' states (e.g. Kenya, Botswana, Nigeria) retained a key place for chiefs (and therefore 'tribal' identity) in the structures of local administration in the countryside, while 'radical' states (e.g. Tanzania, Mozambique and, to a lesser extent, francophone West African states, such as Guinea, Mali and Senegal) abolished customary authorities, but reproduced 'centralised despotism' through the 'commandist' practices of local cadres, both political and administrative, towards rural subjects (of which the implementation of Tanzania's villagization 'campaigns' – another appropriately military metaphor – in the 1970s can be seen as emblematic).

State-led modernization policies in agriculture continued after independence. In some instances, the scale of intervention increased, particularly in the form of large irrigation projects. These and similar state rural development interventions involved increasing appropriations of land by the state, often within a wider constitutional assertion of state land ownership, which took over or extended the provisions of colonial government. Otherwise, land tenure remained largely unchanged from the colonial period to that following independence: where colonial government had initiated land titling to establish freehold tenure (e.g. Kenya), this tended to continue; where customary tenure was recognized under colonial rule, explicitly or by default, this tended to continue. In other ways, there were significant shifts from colonial antecedents – for example, in a more central emphasis on overcoming rural poverty as a goal of development policies, by raising farm incomes through agricultural schemes and household welfare through social consumption of public/merit goods (clean water, education, health care).

Marketing boards and other parastatal corporations, in both export crops and food staples, were often refashioned as proactive agencies of vertical integration along their respective commodity chains, providing everything from inputs, credit and extension services to marketing (and storage and distribution of food staples). In the political conditions of independence, however, there was probably a reduction in attempts at environmental regulation and conservation – because they were subordinated to imperatives of agricultural production (and productivity) growth, and because their imposition and policing by colonial states had generated popular resistance in the countryside, which made its own contribution to popular anticolonialism (e.g. Tiffen et al., 1994:257; Stocking, 1996:337) and the legitimacy of the nationalist parties that demanded independence.

In the 1970s, the optimism and aspirations – and indeed some of the achievements, patchy as these were – of the first decade of postcolonial state-led development became subject to increasing strains, partly owing to their intrinsic contradictions and certainly compounded by adverse trends in world markets and the global economic restructuring and political realignments that followed. This generated a flood of discourse centred on the pathology of African states, hence state-led development, in a moment when environmental themes (degradation, conservation, 'limits to growth') were reinserted at the centre of concerns, not least because the 1970s added dramatic images of drought and famine in Africa to the ensemble of manifestations of African 'crisis'.

The era of structural adjustment (1980s–present)

The ambitious spending plans and commitments of state-led development after independence, combined with the rising costs of oil imports (and other strategic imports) after the Organization of Petroleum Exporting Countries (OPEC) price increases of the 1970s, led to escalating foreign borrowing by African governments (encouraged by European and American banks with vast quantities of petrodollars to lend). The debt that resulted was intensified by recession in industrialized economies, with downward pressure on primary commodity prices, reducing the foreign exchange earnings of many African countries and undermining their ability to service loans, and by rising interest rates. The incidence of major droughts in many parts of Africa (Warren, 1996:342) compounded foreign exchange shortages by increasing the need for food imports. In a growing number of countries (Ethiopia, Somalia, Mozambique, Sudan, Liberia), these pressures were dramatically aggravated by warfare and insecurity. Through combinations of these factors, virtually every country on the continent entered into negotiations with international financial institutions (the International Monetary Fund (IMF) and World Bank) to seek debt rescheduling and other financial support in return for adopting and implementing 'structural adjustment' policies.

The price for such support was the introduction of comprehensive (if unevenly implemented) 'structural adjustment' reforms to economic (macroeconomic and microeconomic) and social policies and to public institutions. The main lines of such reforms are well known, as is ongoing fierce debate on their results. The first phase of structural-adjustment lending (SAL) emphasized 'rolling back the state' in order to 'get the prices right', that is, to allow 'the market' (or market mechanism) to do its job of achieving allocative efficiency by removing the myriad sources of price 'distortion' resulting from government intervention. At the macroeconomic level, this centred first and foremost on devaluation (overvalued exchange rates were held to be the principal bias favouring imports, and importers, against the producers of export goods), combined with internal and external trade liberalization, sharp reductions in public spending (and employment), the privatization of state-owned industries and services, and so on. A second phase of SAL added to the first a concern with 'capacity-building' of government/public institutions, when it was appreciated that restoring economic growth and welfare in Africa required states that were not only 'leaner' but more efficient. A more generalized discourse of 'good governance' is incorporated in what may or may not be a third phase of SAL, informed by what is claimed (and contested) as a 'post-Washington consensus', marking the demise of earlier more virulent (and triumphalist) neoliberal ideas.

An especially comprehensive codification of 'good governance' was presented in the World Bank's annual *World Development Report* for 1997. Here the recognition of minimal functions for any effective government (and its role in processes of development) is combined with a discursive expansion that centres on 'civil society' and the possibilities – and desirability – of a range of 'partnerships' between government, the private sector and civil society. The benefits of such partnerships and their complementarities are to diffuse responsibility for positive social outcomes (and the resources they require) and thereby to enhance efficiency, as well as to promote participation and accountability and the like as both conditions and outcomes of good governance.

Some (e.g. Moore, 1999) argue that the emphasis on, and exemplification of, 'bad' governance and its effects by the World Bank (1997) is particularly marked with reference to state pathologies in sub-Saharan Africa and the measures proposed to remedy them. Among the latter, the theme of decentralization is especially resonant, not least because of its various meanings and how they can blur into each other, which we illustrate briefly. First is the more conventional inherited usage of decentralization to mean one or another form of devolution from central to local government, whether administrative and/or political (representative local government), held to increase efficiency, accountability and a democratic civic culture. Many African countries, including Botswana and Kenya, had some form of decentralized government in this sense by the 1970s. Second is decentralization understood as privatization: selling off state assets and enterprises and/or contracting out the provision of public goods to private providers, paid from public budgets or by the users of their services. If this second sense corresponds to devolution from state to market, a third (sometimes overlapping) sense is decentralization understood as devolution of function and activity from government to the agency of 'civil society' in the form of non-governmental organizations (NGOs), 'communities' or other appropriate forms of association. This third sense is especially pertinent to discourses of the 'local', 'indigenous', 'communal', and so on, in environmental management and sustainability, as we shall see.

The general thrust of SAL concerning agriculture is, of course, to encourage agricultural exports in line with the 'comparative advantage' of African economies (and their resource and factor endowments) in international trade, so as to revive the engine of economic growth and restore and maintain macroeconomic stability. This is to be achieved, as appropriate, by the rehabilitation of historic export crops (whose production had deteriorated in the 1970s and 1980s) and/or the promotion of (relatively) high-value 'non-traditional' exports aimed at global niche markets – typically horticultural products, including cut flowers and ornamental plants, usually grown through contract farming arrangements and requiring highly organized and efficient marketing.

Juxtaposed (rather than integrated) with this 'export platform' strategy of agricultural revival and productivity and income growth is the concern with environmental degradation and conservation, which resumed a centrality in the 1980s comparable to that of the 1930s, now linked also with discourses of food security, rural poverty and livelihoods. The onset of prolonged drought in the 1970s in the Sahel and elsewhere (north-east Africa in the 1970s and 1980s, southern Africa in the early 1980s and again in the early 1990s) revived colonial perceptions of African land users as agents of environmental destruction. While alternative interpretations linked Sahelian destitution to patterns of commoditization, which encouraged expansion of arable cultivation into more drought-prone areas (Franke and Chasin, 1981), these were largely over-shadowed by the dominance of the neo-Malthusian narrative in much European and North American environmental thought, referred to earlier: that increasing poverty and recurrent famine crises in rural Africa are linked to declining productivity of the biophysical resource base (land, vegetation, water), a process of 'degradation' (of which 'desertification' is emblematic) generated by population pressure on fragile ecologies (Cleaver and Schrieber, 1994).

This narrative, of course, assimilated and concentrated with particular force ideas of older provenance (not least those of Malthus himself!), including a long-running and inconclusive debate about land tenure in Africa. The centrality of land tenure to management and sustainability of land use was reinforced by Hardin's (1968) metaphor of the 'tragedy of the commons', with its emphasis on the importance of private property rights in land to resource conservation, and the more generalized neo-Malthusian environmentalism of the 'limits to growth' (Meadows et al., 1972). The complex histories of colonial and postcolonial land law and tenure practices remain as contested by scholars as they are in many African countrysides (Peters, 1999) and provide a key link between the social and environmental dimensions of agrarian change. For conventional economics (as for Hardin, 1968), the status of land as an alienable commodity is theoretically necessary to the functioning of *Homo economicus*: without its real costs established through markets for land, the private efficiency of different uses of land cannot be known properly (nor can their social efficiency on a market-derived calculus of environmental externalities). On the other hand, whether establishing *de jure* private property rights in land in Africa is advisable, given its legal and institutional compexities and likely political sensitivity, or whether the same (beneficial) end might result from spontaneous evolution of *de facto* property rights exercises the World Bank and new institutional economists (e.g. Bruce and Mighot-Adholla, 1994; Platteau, 1996).

The antinomies of land tenure/property rights apart, the environmental view of rural crisis in Africa – from the Sahelian droughts of the 1970s to subsequent crop failures in Ethiopia and southern Africa – as the consequence of overcultivation and degradation of 'fragile ecosystems' by rapidly increasing and poverty-stricken rural populations remains potent today. While variants of this narrative also attribute blame to incompetent or predatory African governments, which exacerbate rural poverty through distorting agricultural markets, the essential neo-Malthusian paradigm persists in the policy documents of international development agencies. Thus the World Bank (1996a:22–5) characterizes as 'shifting cultivation' farming in the Sudano-Sahelian region, where 'one of the most rapid annual population growth rates of the continent … has resulted in a downward spiral of extensive land degradation and fuelwood shortage … increased water scarcity, and loss of natural habitats'. Similarly, the International Fund for Agricultural Development (IFAD, 1994:10) refers to 'a vicious cycle of negative synergies', in which:

> Unable to increase yields, increasing numbers of poor people put pressure on the environment – mining soils, destroying forests, and depleting wildlife stocks … And because the poor tend to have high fertility rates … population growth rates remain elevated and the destructive cycle recommences.

Environmental change and policy: an alternative agenda

The enduring and compound 'crisis' of sub-Saharan Africa – of 'development', of poverty and famine and of governance, punctuated by wars and the ravages of acquired immune deficiency syndrome (AIDS) and compounded by ecological 'disaster' – has made it virtually open terrain for a wide spectrum of intellectual positions, diagnoses and prognoses, including the recycling of what may be called 'primordial' narratives of African 'exceptionalism': that is, the root problem of Africa is its African-ness (e.g. Hyden, 1983; Chabal and Daloz, 1999). In short, there can be no realistic (or responsible) claim to intellectual or ideological innocence for anyone attempting to investigate, assess or interpret the deeply contradictory and often savage social realities of contemporary Africa. This applies equally to approaches and arguments we may find more sympathetic, like those which seek to challenge the dominant narrative (and explanation) of environmental 'crisis' outlined above.

Over the last two decades, that narrative has been increasingly challenged by research that argues that, in many cases, European scientists misunderstood not only the rationale of African farming practice (Sandford, 1983; Richards, 1985; Reij et al., 1996), but also the dynamics of African ecosystems, particularly in dryland areas (Scoones, 1994; Thomas and Middleton, 1994; Scoones et al., 1996). Further, these misunderstandings of African land use and ecology acquired the status of received or conventional wisdom, which was not significantly modified even when contradicted by the research findings and experience of successive generations of scientists and administrators in Africa (Fairhead and Leach, 1995; Leach and Mearns, 1996; Swift, 1996).

The alternative paradigm generated by this research affirms the competence of African resource users as environmental managers, demonstrated in pastoral grazing strategies

(Behnke et al., 1993), soil conservation techniques (Reij et al., 1996) and tree management (Cline-Cole, 1996; Fairhead and Leach, 1996). Further, the spectre of neo-Malthusian disaster has been challenged by longitudinal studies showing large increases in rural population combined with environmental improvements and increased agricultural productivity (Tiffen et al., 1994; Raynaut et al., 1997). The focus of much of this research has also expanded from an initial preoccupation with technical aspects of the ('indigenous') management of land, water, trees and pasture to incorporate and emphasize the social or institutional aspects of resource management systems. In particular, interest has centred on the role of 'indigenous', 'customary' or 'traditional' (hence 'local') institutions in regulating access to, and use of, natural resources.

In contrast to the 'crisis narratives' that view African land users as agents of destruction, the alternative discourse argues that resources such as land, forests, fisheries and pasture were efficiently and equitably managed under local 'customary' (or 'traditional', 'indigenous') institutions that were subsequently undermined by outside forces, variously identified as those of colonial government, post-independence 'centralizing' African states or markets. The effect is to weaken local control of resources, as outsiders can no longer be excluded and common-property regimes have become 'open access' and subject to overexploitation and degradation (the 'tragedy of the commons'), which then generates arguments for privatization or state control. In response, proposals for decentralized management of land and water envisage re-establishing local authority over resource access and use, which is expected to be more legitimate the more it is based on traditional or customary values and institutions. Moreover, interpreting customary criteria and practices of resource allocation as representing use value/usufruct, kinship or other group rights suggests that this particular form of decentralization will achieve more equitable as well as more efficient resource use – hence the key place of decentralization in the linked agendas of poverty alleviation and environmental conservation central to Agenda 21 and the Convention to Combat Desertification (CCD).

While oversimplifying somewhat, our summary encompasses key elements of the framework of 'human ecology' or 'political ecology' approaches (Peet and Watts, 1996), which provide an intellectual rationale for the 'community-based' resource management projects from the 1990s. These have found support from a number of different quarters. As well as fitting the rhetoric of Agenda 21, the 'community-based natural resource management' approach is attractive to the minimal government stance of international aid agencies, which could be formulated as: not state but market, and if not market then 'civil society' or 'community' (Rihoy, 1995).

By the 1990s, the influence of the alternative paradigm was widely apparent, notably in the United Nations' CCD, negotiated following the Rio Summit in 1992 and ratified in 1997. Although global in reach, the CCD was designed for priority implementation in Africa. Under the Convention, African governments commit themselves to national action plans (NAPs), which should include measures to improve institutional design and performance, identified as:

1. defining the roles and responsibilities of central government and local authorities within the framework of a land use planning policy;

2. encouraging a policy of active decentralization, devolving responsibility for management and decision-making to local authorities, and encouraging initiatives and the assumption of responsibility by local communities and the establishment of local structures;

3. adjusting, as appropriate, the institutional and regulatory framework of natural resource management to provide security of land tenure for local populations.

(CCD, 1995)

In terms of the themes traced in the previous section, this discourse of environment and development formulates conservation and sustainability as local community resource management, good governance in terms of decentralization and rural livelihoods in terms of property rights (land tenure). Unstated, but implicit, is an acceptance of broadly market-led economic development. Next we interrogate each of these three main components of the new discourse and its policy agenda/prescriptions.

'Community-based natural resource management'

Although central to contemporary analysis and prescription for the African environment, 'community [is] one of the most vague and elusive concepts in social science ...' (Shore, 1993) and '... unlike all other terms of social organisation (state, nation, society etc.) it seems never to be used unfavourably' (Williams, 1976:76). This combination of ambiguity with virtue has made the term popular with policy-makers and planners everywhere, but in Africa, as discussed below, its appeal is associated with images of 'tribal' community governed by 'tradition'.

Conceptions of community-based natural resource management commonly contain three important assumptions: that a 'community' is readily defined; that it will produce consensus rather than conflict over the use of local resources; and that the community's knowledge is sufficient to manage their environment.

On the first, the International Institute for Environment and Development (IIED, 1994) identifies criteria for demarcating communities as spatial: 'groupings of people who physically live in the same place'; as socio-cultural: 'people who derive a unity from common history and cultural heritage, frequently based on kinship'; or as economic: 'groupings who share interests and control over particular resources'. The combination of these criteria produces:

> the archetypal notion of the African village composed of founding lineages who have stewardship and control over a bounded set of resources within a territory, lineages who have married into the community, and more recent settlers, all of whom inter-marry, who speak the same language and who practise the same way of life.

(IIED, 1994:5)

– an archetype its authors acknowledge is largely divorced from reality, where 'problems arise when we try to apply this ideal-type model ... across contemporary Africa' (Barrow and Murphree, 2001). The processes of social and economic change we outlined earlier, often involving migration and (re)settlement and significant social differentiation, produce socio-cultural 'communities' that are spatially dispersed (e.g. between urban and rural areas) and spatially defined 'communities' that are culturally or economically heterogeneous – for example, combining 'customary', 'state' and 'market' forms of power and authority over natural resources.

On the second assumption, confidence that communities can generate self-governing institutions for regulating local natural resource use has been encouraged by a number of empirical studies of successful common property management regimes (Netting, 1981; Ostrom, 1990; McKean, 1992). For policy-makers and development agencies in Africa, the CAMPFIRE programme of 'community-managed' wildlife areas in Zimbabwe has been a particularly influential, if flawed, example (Hulme and Murphree, 2001). Also fundamental to the wider acceptance of 'community-based' management is the theoretical development of the new institutional economics, which claims to identify the conditions of success of common-property regimes by the (ideologically acceptable) calculus of individual rational choice. Its application in African contexts to assess the feasibility of regulating resources such as forests by local 'self-governing' institutions has emphasized a requirement for:

1. legal recognition and authority for local institutions;
2. an 'enabling' environment provided by decentralized government;
3. 'social capital' (shared culture and social values) to ensure agreement within local communities on rules to govern resource management (ARD, 1992).

These conditions raise issues of relations between resource users and the state, and between different resource users within the 'community', which, we would argue, are better addressed within a framework of political economy of the kind indicated in the previous section (and further explored in Chapter 6), rather than the rational choice individualism of institutional economics. A substantial political economy literature on agrarian change in Africa shows that 'communities' are commonly differentiated by inequalities of social class, gender, generation and ethnicity – even if 'in invisible and unarticulated ways' (Peters, 1994:210) – and demonstrates how tensions and conflict are generated by the goals and interests of different groups within communities.

The third assumption – that local people's knowledge and knowledge-creation processes are adequate to ensure sustainable management of the resources they control – has been an important element in the political ecology literature. Earlier assumptions about rural communities in 'balance' or 'harmony' with nature have been criticized (Leach et al., 1997b): socially differentiated communities interacting with nature in ecologies that are also highly differentiated, with multiple rather than a single 'equilibrium' point, must inevitably produce new and unpredictable patterns of landscape. Baland and Platteau (1996:199) are somewhat more sceptical of local resource users' resource management capabilities – that is, as consciously directed towards, and efficacious in, conserving resources – and they quote McNicholl and Cain's (1990) view that people are 'error-prone, partially informed, culturally-blinkered to varying degrees, and somewhat arbitrarily mixing short and long term considerations in their decisions'. Such findings have been used in arguments for a model of 'comanagement' of local resources rather than the privileging of 'community'.

Decentralization and the local state

The promotion of community responsibility and initiative is commonly accompanied by proposals for decentralization within state structures as a means to more effective environmental management. While attractive to many aid agencies wishing to support 'good governance' as part of rural development, such proposals often leave poorly defined the role to be allocated to local administrations or authorities. At the very least, as indicated above, the local state must recognize and uphold the legitimacy of community control over resources and must be able to resolve conflicts that community organizations cannot. Recent experience of 'pluralist' service provision in rural areas (Carney and Farrington, 1998) also suggests a necessary regulatory role for state agencies: in enforcing the terms of contracts between commercial and 'community' organizations, and in ensuring compliance with environmental standards (e.g. in relation to pesticide use, pollution) by food producers, forest users and others. Moving beyond this, some have argued that the local state could continue to take a ('developmental') role in providing technical advice for resource users (Moris, 1991).

Concerning issues of the character of decentralization and of the (benign and effective) local state it aspires to create, a first observation is that current proposals for decentralization in Africa are mostly ahistorical, viewing African states as 'in transition' to more decentralized governance, in the same way as they are 'in transition' to multiparty democracy and a liberalized market economy. This view is strikingly at variance with the historical importance of decentralized governance in Africa (benign or otherwise), indicated in the previous section, particularly since indirect rule was instituted and consolidated by colonial administrations throughout the continent (Mamdani, 1996).

The design and implementation of benign models of government decentralization since independence has proved highly problematic in practice. Beyond a 'deconcentration' of central state executive agencies, whose local officials are accountable to their superiors at national level, little effective decentralization has taken place (Crook and Jerve, 1991). Carney and Farrington (1998) identify a number of reasons for this. First, current decentralization proposals sidestep, rather than confront, the inherent contradiction of expecting state agencies, already characterized by poor technical and decision-making capacities (Tordoff and Young, 1994), to achieve more with fewer resources (owing to tighter budgetary constraints). Pressure on managerial capacity includes demands to undertake more complex tasks, such as regulatory functions, in a more institutionally differentiated ('pluralist') environment and consultation and decision-making involving expanded numbers of stakeholders. In West Africa, as elsewhere, devolved local government has failed to generate the bottom-up planning expected by its architects, because local planning proposals prepared by inadequately qualified staff lack credibility with central government (Manor, 1995).

Secondly, devolution is, above all, a transfer of power and requires widespread political support for its success. Lack of enthusiasm for decentralization by senior politicians and civil servants leads them to treat reforms as concessions they have to make, and which they manage as administrative, rather than democratic, changes.

Typical of such measures is the delegation of operational responsibilities to local officials (deconcentration), who remain accountable to central government ministries. A possible exception might be the 'burden shedding' evident in state withdrawal (*désengagement*) from service provision in rural areas, in the expectation that people can be made to pay for alternative non-government services (*responsabilisation paysanne*). Otherwise, resistance to any dilution or concession of their powers by central authorities is hardly surprising. Apart from considerations of individual self-interest among officials of central state agencies (the usual explanation of rent seeking), there may be other reasons for their resistance to decentralization or other measures that they consider compromise the integrity and sovereignty of the central state – the principal gain of the struggle for independence from colonial rule. Indeed, a formula of devolution of power to customary authorities/local communities, combined with shrinkage of the powers, finances and personnel of the central state under the pressure of SAL, might plausibly appear as a reversal of national self-determination and reassertion of external control.

A third problem widely identified in the public administration literature (UNDP, 1993; Carney, 1995; Manor, 1995) is that decentralization is prone to 'élite capture': 'Government that is, in principle, more accessible to the poorest because of its proximity is also more accessible, and often more often accessed, by the richer members of society' (Carney and Farrington, 1998:100–1); '(it is) unrealistic to expect decentralization to enhance the effectiveness of government institutions in alleviating poverty and assisting vulnerable groups' (Manor, 1995:84). On the one hand, then, the promise of pluralism and civil society so often encompassed in visions of benign decentralization, relocates issues of inequality within the entities and spaces of local government (including those of 'community', as noted above) to a different institutional terrain rather than resolving them. On the other hand, the notion of (local) 'élite capture' and its dangers can be deployed highly opportunistically, for example, when national government adopts a policy favoured by important aid donors but implementation of which is frustrated by local government (on the compelling example of the World Bank and the tribal lands grazing policy in Botswana, see Peters (1994)).

The kinds of pluralist institutional landscape envisioned in the contemporary public administration literature are inhabited by the state/public sector, non-profit organizations (NGOs), membership (grass-roots or community-based) organizations and the commercial/private sector. In debate on government decentralization, there is a presumption that the legitimacy of governance should derive from democratic processes. Reference to the 'customary' is here far less explicit, presumably subsumed under 'grass-roots' or 'community-based' organizations, in contrast to the weight of the customary in proposals for local or community-based natural resource management. An interesting exception summarizes the role of indigenous institutions 'born of the culture and traditional values of the African past' thus: 'Both formal and informal institutions are needed in Africa, but in a more flexible and adapted form. Formal institutions need to be adapted to the local culture/context, *in order to build the legitimacy needed for enforceability*' (Dia, 1996:1, emphasis added). Leaving aside what is being enforced and why, this indicates a continuing dualism, in which Africans are best governed according to 'indigenous' values (with its resonance of discourses of colonial indirect rule).

It is difficult to overemphasize the significance of this dualism, whether overt or concealed. In particular, the common opposition of 'customary' organization, legitimacy and authority to the state needs to be treated with caution. To what extent are they independent of the state (as both formal structure and real functioning) rather than elements of it, and to what extent do 'traditional institutions' constitute alternatives to existing practice? Advocacy of customary resource allocation supported by decentralized ('local') management needs to be able to theorize the issues disclosed by such questions, as well as to investigate them empirically.

Property relations and land tenure

The continuing dualism of, and tension between, 'customary' and 'modern' is most striking in discussions of property relations, and particularly of land tenure. Here a historical perspective is similarly important for current debate on how best to improve security of access for African users of land, water, pastures or forests.

We noted the ambiguities, tensions and shifts of colonial discourses of, and policy and practice towards, African land tenure, ranging from suppression of market transactions in land in favour of 'customary' ('communal') tenure to promotion of individualized freehold title and hence land markets, and including attempts to juggle both simultaneously. Such ambiguities and tensions (and the confusions they generate) continue to permeate current discussions on land tenure in Africa in relation to both agricultural growth and resource conservation. The counter-argument to the neoliberal predilection for the allocation of land via market exchange to more efficient producers is that freehold tenure exposes smallholders to loss of their land through debt and distress sales. Given the scale of rural poverty and stress in contemporary Africa, even the World Bank recognizes trade-offs between the 'efficiency' effects of land markets and the equity and conservation concerns highlighted by current development and environment discourses (World Bank, 1996b).

An intense debate about the future of land tenure in Africa took off (or resumed in a new context) in the 1990s (Platteau, 1992, 1996; Hesseling and Ba, 1994; Lane and Moorehead, 1994; Swift, 1994; IIED, 1996, 1999; Quan, 1997), of which the principal axes are summarized in the following.

Market value of land is increasing and pressure is growing for land alienation through market transactions (Platteau, 1992). Under conditions of increasing demand for land, customary tenure does not provide adequate protection for land users vulnerable to appropriation of land by the state for entrepreneurial development (for Nigeria, Mortimore, 1997) or to sale by customary authorities to outside investors (for Tanzania, Shivji, 1994; for southern Africa, Quan, 1997). Under such conditions, more formal assertion of land rights may be necessary (IIED, 1999:34). However, it is also argued that different types of resource are best managed under different forms of tenure (Hesseling and Ba, 1994; IIED, 1996).

The debate remains marked by a strong dualist dichotomy between customary and modern (or statutory) tenure systems, often used as proxies for non-market and market allocation criteria, respectively (Lane and Moorehead, 1994; IIED, 1996). Advocates of 'customary tenure' argue that it is more appropriate for shared (common property), non-exclusive, management regimes from both equity and conservation standpoints (Swift, 1994), and more generally advantageous in allowing greater flexibility in allocating resources to meet social need (Platteau, 1992; Quan, 1997). This is linked to a perception of common property in pastures and forests as having important welfare functions, but at the same time being subject to encroachment and privatization by individual users, with consequent threats to both conservation and equity (Platteau, 1992; Lane and Moorehead, 1994). There are also calls for the reform of customary tenure by authors who caution that idealization of customary tenure may encourage instances of despotism and abuse of human rights (Hesseling and Ba, 1994:46).

Finally, there is widespread agreement among researchers that a critical point has been reached, because current dualism in land tenure in Africa is unsustainable while the principal alternative on offer in the current moment – enclosure, private property right and market allocation – is unpalatable on grounds of both environmental sustainability and social equity.

This summary overview suggests that current policy proposals that seek to hand back control to 'rural people' are concerned, at least in part, to support customary tenure as an escape from market-based access to resources and consequent growth in inequality and, possibly, landlessness. However, constructions of the 'customary' (including its non-market identity) are largely the result of a century of (colonial and independent) state intervention, with all its complexities and confusions. Unravelling the latter entails 'fundamental questions about the nature of the state and of governance at local level' (Quan 1997:10), which, in turn, require critical exploration of the realities of the 'customary' and its relationships with the 'modern', the 'state' and the 'market', and of the local and its relationship to the non-local. These are areas which, in our view, the new counternarrative that challenges 'conventional wisdom' is mostly silent about, and where the theoretical ideas and methods of political economy are necessary to advance understanding of historical processes that are socially, as well as environmentally, complex and dynamic.

Comanagement, institutional pluralism and partnerships

Current emphasis on decentralization and community-based management, incorporating some form of non-market or 'customary' allocation of land and other resources, may represent at least a temporary accommodation with the dominant narrative, although (with some echoes of a new 'indirect rule') leaving unclear how decentralized natural resource management fits into the wider relations of power manifested in the global environmental agenda of 'the international community'. Instead, recent policy proposals on management of resources and delivery of services have sought ways to construct positive relationships between different types of organization and social institutions. These come under a variety of labels: comanagement (Baland and Platteau, 1996); multi-agency partnerships (Carney and Farrington, 1998); synergy (Robinson and White, 1997); diverse and dynamic institutions (Leach et al., 1997a); and interorganizational linkages (Robinson et al., 2000). While some of these ideas emerge from inductive work (Leach et al., 1997a), many have normative roots in the proposition that effective management of development is not achievable through prioritizing a single sector ('state', 'market' or 'community'), or even by pairing the 'best' sectors, in the manner of the 'public action' (state and community) that Drèze and Sen (1989) advocate or the 'private action' (market and community) that underpinned World Bank (1992) thinking in the 1980s and early 1990s. Instead, they propose an eclectic approach entailing a 'complex and dynamic' mix of state, market and community organizations and institutions, the nature of which is case-specific and depends on goals, contexts and capacities. While there is an evident truism to such propositions, there is also an absence of theorization of the underlying dynamics that create linkages and interdependencies between the supposedly separate entities of 'state', 'market' and 'community'. Such a theorization is needed if there is to be any hope of understanding the nature of 'partnerships', and, as we suggest above, the key to this lies in critically assessing the boundaries of categories such as 'local', 'market', 'community' and 'state'.

The four case-studies in this book (Chapters 2 to 5) provide one means of interrogating the discourses and assessing the claims of current proposals for policy and institutional reform. The case-studies all examine aspects of the interplay of different factors in their locales, including local and wider influences on land and water use. Chapters 6 and 7 then provide broader reflections on the dynamics revealed by the case-studies. Chapter 6 illustrates the relevance and utility of the political economy of commoditization to understanding processes and trajectories of socio-economic change. Chapter 7 explores the political choices (and their constraints) in policy and institutional reform of the management of land and water resources in African countrysides today.

The remainder of this chapter sets out a framework for the case-studies, first in terms of our understanding of 'wetlands in drylands' and their significance as a focus for study of land and water management, and secondly in terms of the conceptual framework we apply to the social and political dynamics of land and water use.

Land, water and productivity in African savannas

'Savannas' cover some two-thirds of the African continent (Adams, 1996). South of the Sahara, savanna ecology predominates to the north, south and east of the equatorial forest belt. This wide extent is in part the result of a loose definition of savannas as 'tropical/subtropical ecosystems characterised by continuous ... cover of ... grasses that show seasonality related to water, and in which woody species are significant but do not form a closed canopy ...' (Adams, 1996:196). Across the continent, this definition covers a great range of grassland types with widely differing densities of trees, the classification of which reflects the principal underlying influences of rainfall and soil fertility. At the wetter end of rainfall gradients (800–1200 mm annually) are 'savanna woodlands'. North of the equator these are characteristic of 'Sudanian' vegetation, while south of it they include the 'Miombo' systems in Tanzania, Zambia, Zimbabwe and northern Mozambique and mopane woodlands in Namibia and the Limpopo basin (Botswana, southern Zimbabwe and the northern Transvaal). Where rainfall is less, trees tend to be more sparse and dominated by *Acacia* species, as in 'savanna parklands' (e.g the West African 'Sudano-Sahelian' zone: 600–800 mm) or 'low tree savanna' (e.g. the 'Sahelian' zone: 400–600 mm). Broad classifications based on rainfall are heavily modified by underlying geology and its influence on soil fertility and by the climatic effects of altitude. At a smaller scale still, variations in topography cause differential drainage and accumulation of water within the landscape, forming a mosaic of patches of different levels of productivity. The effects of greater water availability in low-lying patches of the landscape may vary, in some instances giving rise to dense 'gallery' forest along river-banks, but in others creating waterlogged conditions resulting in grasslands in which tree growth is suppressed altogether.

Historically, the balance of tree and grass species has been profoundly shaped by cultivators and herders, whose management has taken many forms, increasing tree cover in some circumstances and reducing it in others. In the nineteenth century, pastoralists' herds were important in suppressing trees (and thus tsetse infestation) in East African savannas (Richards, 1985; Adams, 1996). Conversely, expansion of settlement and cultivation in parts of the West African savanna has been associated with an increase of tree cover (Fairhead and Leach, 1995, 1996). In drier savannas in southern and eastern Africa, heavy grazing is believed to encourage the replacement of grasses by woody shrubs or 'thicket' (Adams, 1996). The extent of historic human intervention in the formation of African landscapes has been recognized by outside (notably European) researchers only comparatively recently, prompting far-reaching reassessments of the 'crisis' in the African countryside (Leach and Mearns, 1996).

One reason why outsiders fail to identify the extent of human intervention in savanna ecology is that the diverse forms of human activity and its outcome interact with natural sources of variability present at different scales not only spatially, as noted above, but also over time. Accumulation of meteorological records and of evidence of climate change before such records (notably from the levels and sediments in the Great Lakes) show historical shifts and cycles, producing wetter or drier periods (Hulme, 1996), which some authors have linked to changes in global climate processes, such as the El Niño events in the Pacific. Within these longer-term climatic changes, savanna ecosystems are subject to an extreme year-to-year variation in rainfall. This means, first, that overall biomass productivity varies greatly from one year to the next – so much so that ecologists have suggested these may be ecosystems that never reach 'equilibrium' but are naturally in a state of adjustment between drought and wetter conditions (Behnke et al., 1993). This signifies high levels of uncertainty for crop or livestock production dependent on rainfall, and recent research has emphasized how cultivators and herders on the African savannas confront this using risk-minimizing and 'opportunistic' management strategies, in which production 'tracks' the variation in productive potential determined by rainfall (Scoones, 1994, 1996; Reij et al., 1996).

Secondly, variation in rainfall will affect the relative productivity of the different patches of the savanna. For example, higher parts of the landscape will be more drought-prone in dry years, but lower-lying patches may experience flooding in wetter years. However, since water is the main factor limiting plant productivity in savannas (and rainfall is restricted to 4–5 months of the year), the potential biomass production over any given year tends to be higher in the wetter patches of the landscape. These 'wetlands in drylands', relatively small-scale resources in predominantly dry landscapes, are key resources for production strategies in African savannas (Scoones, 1991a and b). They include river valleys and lower-lying areas, which may be waterlogged for part or most of the year, giving rise to soils with high levels of organic matter: the *fadamas* or *bas-fonds* of West Africa, the *dambos, vleis* and *machongos* of southern Africa. They may be modified by human activity through excavation of wells or construction of small dams to store water. They are key resources in the sense that, in most years, they permit production (either grazing or crops) during the dry season and, in dry years, may provide the only productive areas, as they concentrate the little water available. Therefore, although relatively small in terms of area, in many years wetland patches may provide critical grazing and watering resources in the dry season or may provide crop-growing opportunities during the dry season, which deliver an early harvest when stocks harvested from the main growing season are running low.

For all these reasons, wetland patches are often subject to multiple and possibly conflicting uses (Scoones, 1991b). The relatively greater certainty of moisture avail-ability at these sites also signifies less risk attached to investments to intensify crop production. Hence, where growth or diversification of agricultural markets offers new opportunities, these elements of the savanna patchwork may be expected to experience fastest change in patterns of land and water use. It is this aspect of 'wetlands in drylands' that prompted the selection of the four case-studies in the chapters that follow, for, where patterns of land and water use are changing, and especially where change is contested and conflictual, opportunities arise to investigate why change has taken particular forms and directions, and to draw conclusions about the social processes – both local and non-local – that shape change in contemporary management of land and water in these locations.

A framework for analysis

The four case-studies in this book are of the Sourou River valley in the Samori, Mali (Chapter 2); the Kimana Swamp in Kajiado District, Kenya (Chapter 3); village dams in the Shoshong Hills, Botswana (Chapter 4); and the Mutale River valley in Northern Province (formerly the 'homeland' of Venda), South Africa (Chapter 5). The case-studies provide contrasts, in both environmental and social terms, which influence how each chapter is structured and presented. However, their presentation and analysis is informed by some common basic issues. First, we attempt to examine critically the evidence for *change* both in natural resource profiles (land, water, vege-tation) and in local society and economy. To facilitate this, each chapter establishes a historical perspective on its case-study area, as far as documentary sources allowed. While seldom enabling straightforward or direct comparison between different periods, these sources allow us to test current perceptions of the nature of change in terms of their compatibility with data and accounts from earlier periods.

Secondly, each case-study seeks to explore the nature of 'local governance', under-stood in terms of the following elements: the structures and processes of power and authority, cooperation and conflict that govern decision-making and dispute resolution concerning resource access and use, through the interaction of local government and non-governmental, formal and non-formal, organizations and social institutions. This definition of 'local governance' recognizes the importance of practices of informal institutions, which may parallel or interact with formally defined institutions, including those of the state (see Berry, 1993; Leach et al., 1997a). The exploration of moments of conflict and their outcomes is particularly useful for illuminating how power is exercised and by whom, through both formal and informal institutions and their interconnections.

The analysis of change and governance, while seeking to understand decision-making by individuals and groups, also identifies two sets of broader 'dynamics' within and outside government: the socio-economic and political. These may converge or diverge, reinforce or contradict one another, and operate at different scales: local (including 'household' and 'community'), national and international. Consequently, our research and its findings, while focused on four instances of local governance and its effects for resource access, use and management, also examines national processes and policies relevant to each case-study.

Our use of the term 'dynamics' marks a different emphasis in our analysis from much other contemporary work in this field. First, more attention is paid to 'structural' factors shaping power relations. Secondly, these structural factors are understood to shape (if not predetermine) particular patterns and directions of change: individuals make decisions in (differentiated) conditions of constraint and opportunity. For example, both constraint and opportunity may encompass the ways in which socio-economic and political dynamics converge or diverge (and for whom), but our analysis is sufficiently 'structural' to contest those approaches, which posit a 'fluidity' of social relations so open-ended as to preclude identifying patterns or directions of change. Central to our analytical concerns with the governance of land and water, then, are issues that we have suggested are largely neglected (to date) in other work on environmental change in rural Africa: problematizing notions of the 'customary' and 'community' in the light of issues of commoditization (and social differentiation), issues of socio-economic and political sources of unequal power (and whether and how they converge or diverge) and issues of the constitution of locale within broader socio-economic and political spaces and processes.

The notions of governance and of socio-economic and political dynamics outlined are applied in the case-studies to relations, processes and practices of access to and use and management of land and water resources. By 'management' we mean regulation of access to and use of resources to achieve their conservation or 'sustainability'. This is summarized in matrix form in Table 1.1.

The elements of this framework are as follows.

Resource access

The socio-economic dynamics of resource access include:

- demand for the resource, typically driven by demography and the development of markets;

Table 1.1 A social dynamics framework for analysing changing resource use.

	Socio-economic dynamic	Political dynamic
Resource access	Demand, competition (conflict) for resources: • Demography • Markets • Historical patterns of settlement and market integration	• Institutions of property • Institutions of authority to allocate land and water • The politics of resource access at both national and local levels
Resource use	Production systems: • Technical aspects • Social relations	• Services to production • Regulation/control of resource use • Politics of resource use
Resource management	Sustainability: • Productivity trends • Equity trends	• (Central) government environmental policy • Local resource management goals

- competition, reflecting demand intensity (and possibly developing into conflict);
- historical patterns of settlement, typically shaped by specific patterns of commoditization (themelves affected by colonial and postcolonial state formation and practices);

The political dynamics of resource access include:

- institutions of property, *de jure* and *de facto,* including various types of 'customary' tenure and 'modern' tenure;
- institutions of authority to allocate land and water, often linked with specific forms of tenure;
- the politics of resource access at both national (policy and legislation) and local (local government and 'customary' authority) levels.

The interplay between these socio-economic and political dynamics is manifest in differentiated access to resources, which each case-study explores along lines of ethnicity, gender, generation and class.

Resource use

The socio-economic dynamics of resource use are manifested in production systems, characterized by their:

- technical aspects, notably their use of resources of land and water, and the productivity achieved;
- social aspects – patterns of commoditization of farming and of its conditions of production, e.g. land, pasture and water sale and leasing, sharecropping and labour hiring, as well as labour migration and other sources of non-farm income.

The political dynamics of resource use include:

- policies and practices affecting provision of services to production (e.g. technical advice, input subsidies);
- regulation of resource use (as distinct from resource access) by government and non-government authorities;
- the politics of resource use contested between discourses, agents and practices of 'modernization', on the one hand, and of 'livelihood security' and indigenous technical knowledge, on the other, and likewise between those of 'centralized' and 'local' control of resource use.

Resource management (sustainability)

Under this rubric of the conceptual framework, the case-study chapters first identify trends in physical resource use and productivity and assess the extent of environmental degradation. That is, they seek to assess the extent to which current patterns and dynamics of land and water use are 'sustainable'. Secondly, the case-studies seek to analyse the effects and implications for resource management of the processes of environmental and social change they identify, and to evaluate the character and impact of particular policies and forms of state action and their implications for different models of environmental management.

In the four case-studies that follow, this framework is used as a guide to identify structures and processes of socio-economic and political change within (or against) which individuals and groups devise their strategies of land and water use. We emphasize the use of the framework as a guide, rather than a rigid grid, to enable the structure of each chapter to reflect the special features of the case-study concerned. The utility of the framework is that it allows comparable analysis of changing resource use in four quite different contexts.

References

Adams, M. (1996) 'Savanna environments'. In: Adams, W., Goudie, P. and Orme, A. (eds) *The Physical Geography of Africa*. Oxford University Press, Oxford, 196–210.

Anderson, D.M. (1984) 'Depression, dust bowl, demography and drought: the colonial state and soil conservation in East Africa during the 1930s'. *African Affairs* 83 (332), 321–43.

Anderson, D. & Grove, R. (eds) (1987) *Conservation in Africa*. Cambridge University Press, Cambridge.

ARD (1992) *Decentralization and Local Autonomy: Conditions for Achieving Sustainable Natural Resource Management. Decentralization: Finance and Management Project*. USAID/Associates for Rural Development, Burlington, Vermont.

Baland, J.-M. & Platteau, J.-P. (1996) *Halting Degradation of Natural Resources. Is There a Role for Local Communities?* Clarendon Press, Oxford.

Barrow, E. & Murphree, M. (2001) 'Community conservation: from concept to practice'. In: Hulme, D. and Murphree, M. (eds) *African Wildlife and Livelihoods: The Promise and Performance of Community Conservation*, James Currey, Oxford.

Behnke, R., Scoones, I. & Kervan, C. (1993) *Range Ecology at Disequilibrium*. Overseas Development Institute, London.

Beinart, W. (1996) 'Environmental destruction in Southern Africa'. In: Leach, M. and Mearns, R. (eds) *The Lie of the Land*. James Currey, Oxford, 54–72.

Berry, S. (1993) *No Condition is Permanent: The Social Dynamics of Agrarian Change in Sub-Saharan Africa*. University of Wisconsin Press, Madison.

Bharadwaj, K. (1985) 'A view on commercialisation in Indian agriculture and the development of capitalism'. *Journal of Peasant Studies* 12, 47–25.

Bruce, J. & Mighot-Adholla, S. (eds) (1994) *Searching for Land Tenure Security in Africa*. Kendall/Hunt, Dubuque, Iowa.

Carney, D. (1995) *Management and Supply in Agriculture and Natural Resources: Is Decentralisation the Answer?* Natural Resource Perspectives 4, Overseas Developement Institute, London.

Carney, D. & Farrington, J. (1998) *Natural Resource Management and Institutional Change*. Routledge/Overseas Development Institute, London.

CCD (1995) *United Nations Convention to Combat Desertification. Text with Annexes*. Information Unit for Conventions, UN Environment Programme, Geneva.

Chabal, P. & Daloz, J.-P. (1999) *Africa Works. Disorder as Political Instrument*. James Currey, Oxford.

Cleaver, K. & Schrieber, G. (1994) *Reversing the Spiral: The Population, Agriculture, and Environment Nexus in Sub-Saharan Africa*. World Bank, Washington, DC.

Cline-Cole, R. (1996) 'Dryland forestry: manufacturing forests and farming trees in Nigeria'. In Leach, M. and Mearns, R. (eds) *The Lie of the Land*. James Currey, Oxford, 122–39.

Colson, E. (1971) 'The impact of the colonial period on the definition of land rights'. In: Turner, V. (ed) *Colonialism in Africa, 1870–1960*, Vol. 3. Cambridge University Press, Cambridge, 193–215.

Cowen, M.P. & Shenton, R.W. (1991a) 'The origin and course of Fabian colonialism in Africa'. *Journal of Historical Sociology* 4 (2), 143–74.

Cowen, M.P. & Shenton, R.W. (1991b) 'Bankers, peasants and land in British West Africa, 1905–1937'. *Journal of Peasant Studies* 19 (1), 26–58.

Cowen, M.P. & Shenton, R.W. (1996) *Doctrines of Development*. Routledge, London.

Crook, R. & Jerve, A. (1991) *Government and Participation: Institutional Development and Decentralisation and Democracy in the Third World*. C. Michelson Institute, Bergen.

Dia, M. (1996) *Africa's Management in the 1990s and Beyond: Reconciling Indigenous and Transplanted Institutions*. Directions in Development Series, World Bank, Washington, DC.

Drèze, J. & Sen, A. (1989) *Hunger and Public Action*. Clarendon Press, Oxford.

Fairhead, J. & Leach, M. (1995) 'False forest history, complicit social analysis: rethinking some West African environmental narratives'.. *World Development* 23 (6), 1023–35.

Fairhead, J. & Leach, M. (1996) 'Rethinking the forest–savanna mosaic: colonial science and its relics in West Africa'. In: Leach, M. and Mearns, R. (eds) *The Lie of the Land*. James Currey, Oxford, 105–21.

Franke, R. & Chasin, B. (1981) 'Peasants, peanuts, profits and pastoralists'. *Ecologist* 11, 156–68.

Grischow, J. (1998) 'Corruptions of development in the countryside of the Northern Territories of the Gold Coast 1927–57'. *Journal of Peasant Studies* 26 (1), 139–58.

Hardin, G. (1968) 'The tragedy of the commons'. *Science* 162, 1243–8.

Hesseling, G. & Ba, B.M. (1994) *Land Tenure and Natural Resource Management in the Sahel. Experiences constraints and prospects*. CILSS – Club du Sahel, Paris.

Hill, P. (1963) *The Migrant Cocoa Farmers of Southern Ghana*. Cambridge University Press, Cambridge.

Hobsbawm, E. (1987) *The Age of Empire 1870–1914*. Weidenfeld & Nicolson, London.

Hulme, D. & Murphree, M. (eds) (forthcoming 2001) *African Wildlife and Livelihoods: The Promise and Performance of Community Conservation*. James Currey, Oxford.

Hulme, M. (1996) 'Climate change within the period of meteorological records'. In: Adams, W., Goudie, P. and Orme, A. (eds) *The Physical Geography of Africa*. Oxford University Press, Oxford, 88–102.

Hyden, G. (1983) *No Shortcuts to Progress: African Development Management in Perspective*. Heinemann, London.

IFAD (1994) *A Dialogue on Capitol Hill. Workshop on Land Degradation and Poverty in Sub-Saharan Africa. Challenges and Opportunities*. International Fund for Agricultural Development, Rome.

IIED (1994) *Whose Eden? An Overview of Community Approaches to Wildlife Management*. International Institute for Environment and Development, London.

IIED (1996) *Managing Land Tenure and Resource Access in West Africa. Proceedings of a Workshop Held at Gorée, Sénégal, 18–22 November, 1996*. International Institute for Environment and Development, London.

IIED (1999) *Land Tenure and Resource Access in West Africa: Issues and Opportunities for the Next Twenty-five Years*. International Institute for Environment and Development, London.

Kasfir, N. (1993) 'Designs and dilemmas of African decentralization'. In: Mawhood, P. (1993) *Local Government in the Third World: Experience of Decentralization in Tropical Africa*. Africa Institute of South Africa, Pretoria, 24–48.

Lane, C. & Moorehead, R. (1994) 'New directions in rangeland and resource tenure and policy'. In: Scoones, I. (ed.) *Living with Uncertainty: New Directions in Pastoral Development in Africa*. IT Publications, London, 116–33.

Leach, M. & Mearns, R. (eds) (1996) *The Lie of the Land. Challenging Received Wisdom on the African Environment*. James Currey, Oxford.

Leach, M., Mearns, R. & Scoones, I. (1997a) *Environmental Entitlements: A Framework for Understanding the Institutional Dynamics of Environmental Change*. IDS Discussion Paper 359, Institute of Development Studies, Brighton.

Leach, M., Mearns, R. & Scoones, I. (eds) (1997b) 'Community based sustainable development: consensus or conflict? *IDS Bulletin* 28 (4), 4–14.

McKean, M. (1992) 'Success on the commons: a comparative examination of institutions for common property resource management'. *Journal of Theoretical Politics* 4 (3), 247–81.

McNicholl, G. & Cain, M. (eds) (1990) *Rural Development and Population Institutions and Policy*. Oxford University Press, New York.

Mamdani, M. (1996) *Citizen & Subject. Contemporary Africa and the Legacy of Late Colonialism*. James Currey, Oxford.

Manor, J. (1995) 'Democratic decentralization in Africa and Asia'. *IDS Bulletin* 26 (2), 81–8.

Meadows, D.H., Meadows, D.L., Randers, J. & Behrens, W., III (1972) *The Limits to Growth*. Earth Island, London.

Moore, D. (1999) 'Sail on, O Ship of State: neo-liberalism, globalisation and the governance of Africa'. *Journal of Peasant Studies* 27 (1), 61–9.

Moris, J. (1991) *Extension Alternatives in Tropical Africa*. Overseas Development Institute, London.

Mortimore, M. (1997) *History and Evolution of Land Tenure and Administration in West Africa*. IIED Drylands Programme Issue Paper No. 71, International Institute for Environment and Development, London.

Netting, R. (1981) *Balancing on an Alp: Ecological Change and Continuity in a Swiss Mountain Community*. Cambridge University Press, Cambridge.

Ostrom, E. (1990) *Managing the Commons*. Cambridge University Press, New York.

Peet, R. & Watts, M. (eds) (1996) *Liberation Ecologies*. Routledge, London.

Peters, P. (1994) *Dividing the Commons: Politics, Policy and Culture in Botswana*. University Press of Virginia, Charlottesville.

Peters, P. (1999) 'The limits of negotiability: security, equity and class formation in Africa's land systems'. Draft paper (cited with author's permission).

Phillips, A. (1989) *The Enigma of Colonialism*. James Currey, London.

Platteau, J.-P. (1992) *Land Reform and Structural Adjustment in Sub-Saharan Africa*. FAO Economic and Social Development Paper 107, Food and Agriculture Organization of the United Nations, Rome.

Platteau, J.-P. (1996) 'The evolutionary theory of land rights as applied to sub-Saharan Africa: a critical assessment'. *Development and Change* 27, 29–86.

Quan, J. (1997) *The Importance of Land Tenure to Poverty Eradication and Sustainable Development in Sub-Saharan Africa*. Natural Resources Institute, Greenwich University, Chatham.

Raynaut, C., Grégoire, E., Janlin, P., Koechlin, J. & Lavigne-Delville, P. (1997) *Societies and Nature in the Sahel*. Routledge, London.

Reij, C., Scoones, I. & Toulmin, C. (eds) (1996) *Sustaining the Soil. Indigenous Soil and Water Conservation in Africa*. Earthscan, London.

Richards, P. (1985) *Indigenous Agricultural Revolution*. Hutchinson, London.

Rihoy, E. (ed.) (1995) *The Commons Without the Tragedy? Strategies for Community-based Natural Resources Management in Southern Africa*. US Agency for International Development, Lilongwe.

Robinson, D., Hewitt, T., & Harriss, J. (2000) *Managing Development. Understanding Inter-Organizational Relationships*. Sage, London.

Robinson, M. & White, H. (1997) *The Role of Civic Organisations in the Provision of Social Services: Towards Synergy*. Research for Action Paper 37, UNU/WIDER, Helsinki.

Sandford, S. (1983) *Management of Pastoral Development in the Third World*. Wiley/Overseas Development Institute, London.

Scoones, I. (1991a) *Wetlands in Drylands: The Agroecology of Savanna Systems in Africa*. Part 1 *Overview – Ecological, Economic and Social Issues*. Drylands Programme, International Institute for Environment and Development, London.

Scoones, I. (ed.) (1991b) *Wetlands in Drylands: The Agroecology of Savanna Systems in Africa*. Part 3 *Case Studies*. Drylands Programme, International Institute for Environment and Development, London.

Scoones, I. (ed.) (1994) *Living with Uncertainty: New Directions in Pastoral Development in Africa*. IT Publications, London.

Scoones, I. (1996) 'Range management science and policy: politics, polemics and pasture in southern Africa'. In: Leach, M. and Mearns, R. (eds) *The Lie of the Land*. James Currey, Oxford, 34–53.

Scoones, I. and others (1996) *Hazards and Opportunities. Farming Livelihoods in Dryland Africa*. Zed Books, London.

Shivji, I. (1994) *Report of the Presidential Commission of Inquiry into Land Matters*. Vol. 1 *Land Policy and Land Tenure Structure*. Government of the United Republic of Tanzania and the Scandinavian Institute of African Studies, Uppsala.

Shore, C. (1993) 'Community'. In: Outhwaite, W. and Bottomore, T. (eds) *The Blackwell Dictionary of Twentieth Century Social Thought*. Blackwell, Oxford.

Stocking, M. (1996) 'Soil erosion'. In: Adams, W., Goudie, P. and Orme, A. (eds) *The Physical Geography of Africa*. Oxford University Press, Oxford, 326–41.

Swift, J. (1994) 'Dynamic ecological systems and the administration of pastoral development'. In: Scoones, I. (ed.) *Living with Uncertainty:* IT Publications, London, 153–73.

Swift, J. (1996) 'Desertification: narratives, winners, and losers'. In: Leach, M. and Mearns, R. (eds) *The Lie of the Land*. James Currey, Oxford, 73–91.

Thomas, D. & Middleton, N. (1994) *Desertification: Exploding the Myth*. Chichester, Wiley.

Tiffen, M., Mortimore, M. & Gichuki, F. (1994) *More People, Less Erosion: Environmental Recovery in Kenya*. Wiley, Chichester.

Tordoff, W. & Young, R. (1994) 'Decentralization and Public Sector Reform in Zambia'. *Journal of Southern African Studies* 20 (2), 285–99.

UNDP (1993) *Human Development Report 1993*. Oxford University Press, Oxford.

Vaughan, M., (1991) *Curing Their Ills. Colonial Power and African Illness*. Polity Press, Cambridge.

Warren, A. (1996) 'Desertification'. In: Adams, W., Goudie, P. & Orme, A. (eds) *The Physical Geography of Africa*. Oxford University Press, Oxford, 342–55.

Williams, R. (1976) *Keywords: A Vocabulary of Culture and Society*. London, Fontana.

World Bank (1992) *World Development Report*. World Bank, Washington, DC.

World Bank (1996a) *Toward Environmentally Sustainable Development in Sub-Saharan Africa: A World Bank Agenda*. World Bank, Washington, DC.

World Bank (1996b) *Findings*. Africa Region, No. 56, Africa Technical Department, World Bank, Washington, DC.

World Bank (1997) *World Development Report*. World Bank, Washington, DC.

2

A Very Decentralized Development
Exploiting a New Wetland
in the Sourou Valley, Mali

PHILIP WOODHOUSE, PIPPA TRENCH
& MOUSSA DIT MARTIN TESSOUGUÉ

Introduction

This chapter focuses on changes in land use in the valley of the River Sourou, in the *cercle* of Bankass (Mopti region) in southern Mali, near the frontier with Burkina Faso (Maps 2.1 and 2.2). Since 1988, the construction of a dam downstream in Burkina Faso has caused a rise in the level of the Sourou, which has extended upstream into Mali and presented Malian cultivators with an opportunity to supplement their staple dryland millet crop with an additional rice harvest. This opportunity has been taken up rapidly, resulting in the clearance of much of the riverine forest in the Sourou floodplain for rice cultivation. Largely the result of local initiatives, these developments in the Sourou valley took place following the overthrow of the government in Mali in 1991 and during a programme of constitutional reform establishing more decentralized government by elected local councils. This chapter examines the relationship between this government-led decentralization process, existing village-level governance of land and water and non-governmental organization (NGO)-managed environmental conservation projects.

The study is based on field research undertaken in the Sourou valley in January–May 1996. The most detailed work was undertaken in the villages of Songoré and Oula, located, respectively, at the northern end of the Sourou valley and to the south adjacent to the frontier with Burkina. Work in these villages involved a census of rice plots and a structured survey of a 20 per cent sample of rice cultivators, including 'outsiders' from other settlements in the surrounding area. Additional information was obtained from semi-structured interviews with pastoralists and with a range of authorities and interest groups in the villages of Songoré, Oula, Bankass and Baye. The research built upon earlier work in the area by the *Projet Protection de l'Environnement de Bankass* (PPEB) managed by the NGO SOS Sahel. Interpretation of aerial photographs of the Sourou

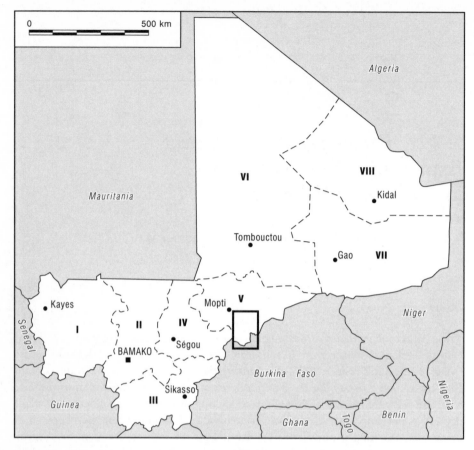

Map 2.1 Mali: regions & location of case-study

valley, taken in 1992 and 1996, allowed an assessment of overall change in land use, and particularly in the extent of rice cultivation. Further fieldwork details are given in Chenevix-Trench et al. (1997).

Context

The Republic of Mali stretches from deep in the Sahara (25° N) to the transition between Sudanian and Guinean vegetation zones (11° N). Thirty per cent of the country is desert and 59 per cent has annual rainfall less than 400 mm (Maiga et al., 1995:17). The Sahelian (400–600 mm) and Sudano-Sahelian (600–800 mm) zones together account for almost a quarter of the country, with the remainder covered by the savanna woodlands of the Sudanian (800–1200 mm) zone in the south. The Sahelian zone running east–west through the centre of the country is dominated by the Niger River, whose flow eastwards makes a loop northwards into the Sahara,

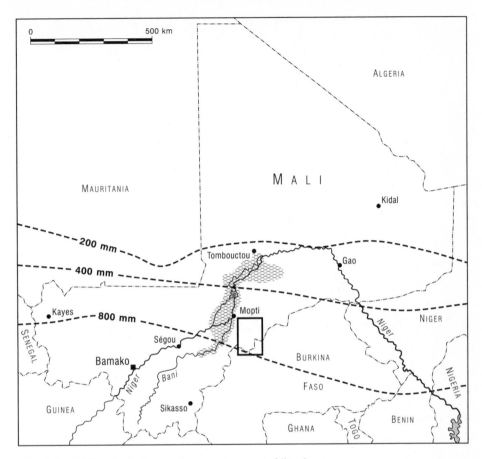

Map 2.2   Mali: principal rivers & approximate rainfall isohyets

associated with a major wetland complex – the interior delta of the Niger – before flowing south-east into Niger and Nigeria (Map 2.2). The Sourou valley lies within the Sudano-Sahelian rainfall zone, separated from the interior delta of the Niger by the Bandiagara plateau (400 m altitude) and the Seno plain and bounded to the south-east by the Yatenga plateau in Burkina Faso (Map 2.3).

The modern state of Mali dates from 1960, but society and culture in Mali have a strong identification with a history stretching back 2,000 years. Until the seventeenth century, the area was governed by a series of powerful states, whose wealth was based on control of trans-Saharan trade, particularly between the Mediterranean and the gold-producing areas of the Guinean zone. The most commonly identified of these ancient states are the Ghana empire (fifth to eleventh century), ruled by the Soninké, the Mali empire (thirteenth to fourteenth century), whose Islamic rulers are identified as 'Mande' or 'Marka', and the Songhai empire (fifteenth to sixteenth century), centred at Gao. Destruction of Songhai imperial authority in 1591 disrupted trans-Saharan trade and began a 300-year period of instability in the region, which

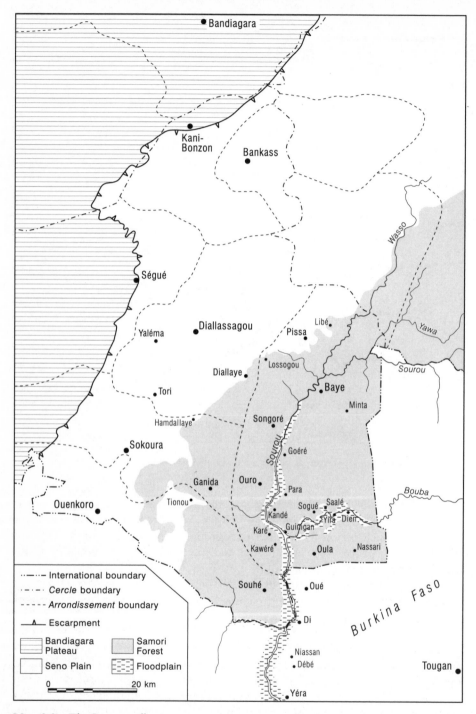

Map 2.3   The Sourou valley

coincided with the growth of European-controlled maritime trade from the West African coast. During this period, the area was dominated successively by the pagan Bambara kingdoms, centred on Ségou (1670–1810), the Islamic Fulani state, centred on Macina (1810–1863), and the Islamic Toucouleur empire, which stretched from Senegal to Tombouctou (1863–1896). The French successfully exploited continuing hostilities between these entities to bring the area under their control during the 1890s, although armed resistance from some groups, such as the Tuareg pastoralists, continued throughout the period of French administration.

Under colonial administration, two key features of the modern Malian economy – population migration and agriculture – took shape. The institution of taxation (poll tax) by the colonial authorities, coupled with increased access to markets for agricultural commodities, such as cocoa, oilseeds and cotton, provided both motive and opportunity for Malians to generate cash from agriculture or from migration to the plantations, mines or coastal cities to the south and west. Migration pressures intensified with the unreliability of commodity markets, such as during the 1930s Depression, when Bambara villagers walked to Senegal in search of wages to meet tax obligations (Toulmin, 1992:26). In the postwar period, the colonial administration invested in intensification of African smallholder production through the Office du Niger, which developed water control for rice and cotton on 54,000 ha allocated to settlers in the interior delta of the Niger in the 1950s (Maiga et al., 1995:55), and the Compagnie Française pour le Développement des Textiles (CFDT), which supplied inputs and marketing facilities for cotton producers in the higher-rainfall (Sudanian) region around Sikasso and Koutiala. Assisted by two decades of relatively high rainfall in the 1950s and 1960s (Maiga et al., 1995:21), this policy achieved an increase in output of seven principal crops by 40 per cent in volume terms between 1945 and 1959. By independence, Mali was the leading exporter of cereals in the Sahel, with 20,000 t of millet and 5,000 t of rice exported in 1959 (Lecaillon and Morrison, 1986, quoted in Davies, 1996:79). Over the same period, a doubling in the number of livestock, reared largely under conditions of transhumance between the main river valleys and the drier hinterlands (Davies, 1996:313), fed exports to the urban and mining centres in the coastal countries to the south.

Following independence from France in 1960, the 'First Republic' of Mali, proclaimed by Modibo Keita's socialist government, was soon ended by a military coup in 1968. The 'Second Republic' was governed as a single-party state by the coup's leader, General Moussa Traoré, whose Union Démocratique du Peuple Malien (UDPM) held power until 1991. Post-independence Malian governments maintained the agricultural policies and development agencies inherited from the French administration: the Office du Niger became a Malian parastatal, and the CFDT became (in 1972) the Compagnie Malienne pour le Développement des Textiles (CMDT) – a Malian–French joint venture (Maiga et al., 1995:46). In addition, from the 1970s, they established a number of loan-funded rural development agencies (*opérations de développement rurales* (ODR)) to promote agricultural and livestock extension for specified areas or products. However, in the 1970s, the Sahelian region entered a prolonged period of lower rainfall, including a series of severe droughts in 1972–3, 1984–5 and 1993. The impact of lower rainfall on agriculture and livestock output was compounded by the rise in oil prices in the 1970s, precipitating an economic crisis. By 1980, the Malian government was compelled to seek support from international funding agencies (the International Monetary Fund (IMF), the US Agency for International Development (USAID) and the World Bank), whose support was conditional on agreement to implement a number of 'stabilization and adjustment' measures to liberalize prices and trade, particularly in agricultural inputs and cereals, to reduce government budget deficits and improve the financial performance of parastatals, and to disengage government agencies from production and commercial activities (Maiga et al., 1995:42).

For much of the 1980s, the economy stagnated (Fig. 2.1). Livestock exports to traditional markets in Côte d'Ivoire were held back by competition from cheaper imports from Argentina and the European Union (de Frahan and Diarra, 1987; Maiga et al., 1995). By the late 1980s, agricultural output was growing (Fig. 2.2). Food imports fell from 15 per cent of food production in the 1970s to around 10 per cent in the 1990s, and food aid declined from 50 to 30 per cent of food imports over the same period (Davies, 1996:86). Much of this increase resulted from an expansion in cultivated areas, but there were significant productivity gains, particularly in the Office du Niger and CMDT areas (Maiga et al., 1995:49, 57). However, these improvements were insufficient to reverse a 'lost decade' in the 1980s, characterized by large movements of population: southwards from the increasingly drought-affected areas of the north; from countryside to towns; and out of Mali altogether. Mali's population (7.7 million in 1987) is growing annually at only 1.8 per cent overall, but during 1980–92 it declined by 5 per cent in the northernmost regions (Republic of Mali, 1994), while growing 2.3 per cent in southern regions (Davies, 1996:85). Similarly, in the 1980s, urban population increased by 4.6 per cent per year, compared with rural population growth of only 1.3 per cent, so that in 1995 urban residents were estimated to be more than a quarter of the total living in Mali (Republic of Mali, 1994). Finally, the 1987 census estimated that 24 per cent of Malians were living abroad, a figure rising to 28 per cent (3.5 million) for 1992,

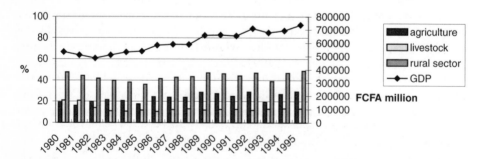

Figure 2.1   Mali: gross domestic product (GDP) (constant 1987 prices), contribution of livestock production, agriculture & the whole rural sector (includes fishing and forestry)

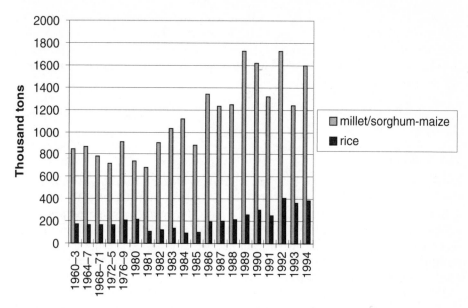

Figure 2.2 Mali: production of cereals (from Republic of Mali, 1994; Davies, 1996)

including 2.5 million in West Africa, 800,000 elsewhere in Africa, and 80,000 in Europe (Maiga et al., 1995:41).

The economic strains during the 1980s, from destitution in the drought-hit north to unemployment among educated urban youth, excluded after 1983 from automatic civil service recruitment (Hall et al., 1991:22), translated into increasing political opposition to the UDPM government, in the form of Tuareg insurrection and guerrilla activity in the north, and calls elsewhere in the country for multiparty democracy. Violent government repression of student protests in March 1991 was followed by a general strike and a military revolt, which resulted in the imprisonment of Moussa Traoré and the establishment of a multiparty constitution for the 'Third Republic'. Elections held in 1992 resulted in victory for the Alliance pour la Démocratie au Mali (ADEMA) and the installation of its leader, Alpha Oumar Konaré, as president. A referendum in 1992 confirmed a new constitution, in which a commitment to decentralization was a central feature, most immediately as the basis for a series of pacts between the Tuareg and the new Malian government, which, by 1994, had restored peace to the north of Mali in return for a degree of regional self-government (Thompson and Coulibaly, 1994:39).

The economic outlook remains bleak. Economic growth adjusted for inflation averaged only 2.5 per cent between 1980 and 1995, and is dependent on agri-culture for around 40 per cent of gross domestic product (GDP) (Fig. 2.1), for around three-quarters of exports (Maiga et al., 1995:35) and for three-quarters of employment (85 per cent of male employment) (UNDP, 1994:36). Between 1992 and 1994, the value of exports covered between 49 and 53 per cent of the cost of imports (Republic of Mali, 1994:13), leaving the government dependent on continued external financial support. Finally, in January 1994, the Malian currency, the Franc Communauté Financière Africaine (FCFA), was devalued by 50 per cent, adding very considerably to the costs of inputs for agricultural intensification (Maiga et al., 1995).

A 'wetland in dryland'

The dryland environment

The Sudano-Sahelian climatic zone, in which much of the Sourou valley lies, has a rainy season from June to September and a dry season from October to May (Fig. 2.3). Within the dry season a cool period, *Fonené* (November–February), precedes a hot period, *Tilimiya* (March–May) (Fig. 2.4). Table 2.1 summarizes the main agro-ecological zones in the vicinity of the Sourou, the Bandiagara plateau, the Seno plain and the Samori forest, and their distribution across the seven administrative subdivisions (*arrondissements*) of Bankass *cercle* (Map 2.3).

The plateau is dominated by broken rocky terrain. Occasional areas of soil in depressions and faults provide opportunities for cultivation on less than 10 per cent of the surface (PIRT, 1983). These have been exploited since the eighteenth century by Dogon communities, which developed a particularly intensive form of fruit and vegetable farming, often involving irrigation, in isolated valleys within the plateau (Gallais, 1975; Critchley, 1991).

The Seno plain is derived from old and eroded sand dunes. The area has been extensively cultivated since the turn of the century. Analysis of satellite images in 1987 (DNEF, 1990; PIRL, 1990) suggests that, in *arrondissements* that fall completely

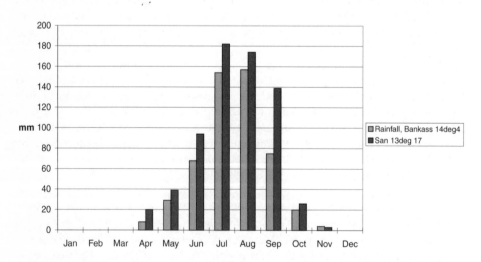

Figure 2.3   Average monthly rainfall in Bankass & San, 1975–86 (from DNEF, 1990)

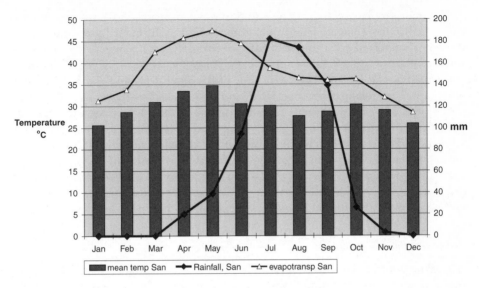

Figure 2.4 Mean monthly values for rainfall, evapotranspiration & temperature at San (Ségou region)

within the Seno plain (e.g. Bankass and Diallassagou), land under cultivation and short fallow amount to 82 and 69 per cent of the total land area, respectively (Table 2.1), and the wooded savanna dominated by *Combretum* spp. and *Pterocarpus lucens* has been largely replaced by fields, cultivated principally for millet, *wanzou* (*Voandzea subterranea*, 'Bambara groundnut'), *niébé* (*Vigna unguiculata*, cowpea) and groundnut. The cultivated area supports a dispersed tree cover, constituted principally by baobab (*Adansonia digitata*), *Acacia albida*, tamarind (*Tamarindus indica*), *nere* (*Parkia biglobosa*) and, in the more southern parts, the shea nut (*Vitellaria paradoxa*) (DNEF, 1990).

Table 2.1 Classification of vegetation cover in the *cercle* of Bankass (from DNEF, 1990).

		Distribution of *arrondissement* land area between agroecolological zones (%)					
		Plateau		Seno		Samori	
Arrondissement	Land area (1000 ha)	Cultivated	Not cultivated	Cultivated	Not cultivated	Woodland	Flood-plain
Bankass	28.6	0	0	82	15	0	0
Kani–Bonzon	59.7	1.7	15	60	22	0	0
Ségué	138.0	2.7	74	14	7.1	0	0
Diallassagou	106.3	0	0	69	24	6.7	0
Sokoura	82.7	0	21	23	23	30	0
Ouenkoro	84.6	0	0	14	31	50	2.7
Baye	161.4	0	0	9.3	4.4	75	4.3

The boundary between the Seno and the Samori is marked by transition to soils with a higher clay content. The natural vegetation for well-drained parts of the zone is savanna woodland – the 'forest of Samori' (Konaté and Tessougué, 1996) – with patches of dense gallery forest (principally *Anogeissus leocarpus, Mitragyna inermis, Pterocarpus santalinoides*) on black clay soils of the alluvial plain of the Sourou, and more open woodland (*Acacia seyal, P. lucens, Combretum micranthum, Dalbergia melanoxylon, Ziziphus mauritiaca*) on sandy clay soils. Close to the river, there are also poorly drained areas of grassland (*Vitiveria* spp. and *Pannicum* spp.) with little woody vegetation. There was, until recently, little cultivation in the Samori. It is one of the most important woodlands in Mopti region (Konaté and Tessougué, 1996), and plans since 1948 to designate 72,000 ha of this area a forest reserve (*forêt classée)* have meant that land use surveys (Table 2.1) have tended to ignore potential or actual cultivation in the Samori (see below and Chenevix-Trench et al., 1997).

Settlement and demography

According to oral history, the Sourou valley and its surrounding area has been popu-lated for 800 years, the Sourou forming a natural boundary between two sets of original settlers: 'Marka' and Bobo migrating from the west, and Mossi and Samogo (or Pana) people migrating from the south and east. The settlements around the Sourou identify three historical hierarchies centred on the villages of Oula (Ouladougou) and Dien (Diendougou) on the east bank and on Tionou (Tiondougou) on the west bank. Together, Diendougou and Ouladougou are referred to as the Panadougou. Despite continuity of settlements, such as those at Songoré and Oula, stretching back hundreds of years, the area was peripheral to many of the historic states in Malian history, particularly from the seventeenth to the late nineteenth century, when the area was subject to slave raiding by Mossi from the south and Peulh (Fulani) from Macina, and was also a battleground for forces of the Islamic state of Macina and its opponents, including renegade Peulh groups based at Libé. During this period of insecurity, the ancient villages of the Samori survived as enclaves in the relatively inaccessible wooded areas, while the agricultural population of the Seno took refuge on the Bandiagara plateau, where they developed the pattern of fortified villages, strong clan identity and intensive agriculture characteristic of the Dogon people (Gallais, 1975). Conquest by the Toucouleur in the latter part of the nineteenth century brought Panadougou, Tiondougou and Dogon under a single authority and order to the area, enabling the Dogon clans to begin recolonizing the Seno plain. This process gained impetus under French administration after 1905, spurred on by shortage of land and susceptibility to famine in the villages of the plateau, some of which lost over half their population in the 'Kittangal' famine of 1913–14. Between 1900 and 1914, forty-three new villages were created on the Seno plain (Gallais, 1975).

Processes of migration and settlement in some instances produced culturally distinct villages, such as those of Dogon cultivators and Peulh pastoralists in the Seno. In other cases, immigrants joined existing settlements and intermarried. In the Samori, for example, intermarriage between Dogon, Pana, Marka and Mossi produced a culturally hybrid group speaking a version of Bambara, known as 'Dafing' (Konaté and Tessougué, 1996). As a result, in communities along the Sourou where people would have called themselves 'Pana' or 'Samogo' at the turn of the century, most identified themselves as 'Dafing' by the end of the half-century of French rule.

Economy and livelihoods

In the latter half of this century, the economy of the Seno and Samori has been dominated by dryland agriculture, livestock and migration. Bankass *cercle* accounts for 20–30 per cent of the area planted with millet and sorghum in Mopti region. In a pattern widespread in the Sahel, the crops are sown each year on 'infields' (*lara*) close to the village, manured by household waste and by village livestock or visiting herds grazing the stubble, and on 'outfields' (*baracoum*), where 2–4 years of cultivation is rotated with 3 years of fallow grazing. The head of an extended household (*gua-tigi*) directs the available adult household labour force in the production of the family millet crop (*foroba*), which feeds the extended household during the farming season and on family occasions. He also allocates land for *djonforo* crops cultivated by individual adult men and women within the household for their own use or to feed their immediate 'nuclear' family during the dry season. The *lara* is typically occupied by *foroba* millet, often intercropped with *niébé*, while the *baracoum* may contain *foroba* fields as well as *djonforo* crops of *fonio*, millet and *niébé,* groundnut, *wanzou*, sesame, or *dah* (*Hibiscus sabdariffa*). Although Peulh pastoralists make up 15 per cent of the Seno population (de Frahan and Diarra, 1987: 4), Dogon and Dafing cultivators in the Seno and Samori, respectively, are believed to own most – up to 80 per cent (de Frahan and Diarra, 1987:36) – of the livestock, as an important form of savings as well as a source of meat, milk and manure. Herding is often contracted out to Peulh pastoralists, and may involve local transhumance between village lands in the dry season and the plateau or Samori woodlands in the wet season, or long-distance transhumance to the Niger inner delta for the dry season.

The dryland farming system of the Seno is commonly described as being in crisis owing to 'excessive' population pressure, resulting in a decline in trees on cultivated fields and shortages of wood fuel (de Frahan and Diarra, 1987:12; Ruthven and Koné, 1995). Evidence to support this is equivocal, however. In relation to land productivity, the scarce data available suggest millet areas in Bankass *cercle* increasing annually between 1974 and 1986 by 2 per cent but with yield unchanged at about 550 kg/ha (de Frahan and Diarra, 1987:33). Population growth in the Seno is estimated at less than 1 per cent per year. This may be owing to long-established patterns of emigration, historically to Accra, more recently to Abidjan and, increasingly, to smaller urban centres within Mali, so that 75 per cent of households in Seno villages count at least one migrant among their members (Ruthven and Koné, 1995). However, depletion of the agricultural workforce through migration appears to have been compensated in some households by switching from hand cultivation to donkey-drawn ploughing and weeding and to animal-drawn carts for transport. This mechanization may be one cause of a decline in trees in fields through a reduction in tree seedling survival. Another explanation is the strong disincentive to maintain trees on fields resulting from state forestry officials' predatory and illegal imposition of fines on farmers for cutting trees on their own fields (McLain, 1991; McLain and Sankaré, 1993).

While a simple 'crisis' mechanism is difficult to establish, the poverty of many in the Seno and Samori is clearly apparent: they form part of the poorest zone in Mali, with 90 per cent of people classified as 'poor' (annual expenditure less than FCFA 100,000) and 60 per cent as 'very poor' (expenditure less than 50,000) (Meyer et al., 1993:17), and health and education services are worse than in other parts of Mali. In many villages of the Samori, such as Songoré, there is no school and illiteracy is the norm. It is also clear that rainfall conditions have worsened: as in the rest of the Sahel, where average rainfall for the period 1961–90 was 30 per cent lower than for 1931–60 (Hulme, 1996:92), local rainfall data for Bankass *cercle* (Veeneklaas and Stol, 1989; DNEF, 1990; Gosseye et al., 1990) indicate a drop of 100 mm in annual average rainfall for 1977–86 compared with 1922–80, so that since the 1970s the 600 mm isohyet has effectively moved southwards from the latitude of Baye to the latitude of Ouenkoro (de Frahan and Diarra, 1987:11–12).

It is perhaps unsurprising, therefore, that the 'pioneer front' of Dogon settlement, which had advanced southwards across the Seno since the turn of the century, and which during the 1970s had appeared stalled by heavier soils and lack of good water supplies in the Samori (Gallais, 1975:121), was on the move again by the early 1990s. In addition to Dogon cultivators, migrants to the Samori included fifteen new fishing communities of Bozo, from the inner delta of the Niger, and Bellah and Foulankriabé pastoralists from the Gourma, to the north. As a result, although the population for Bankass *cercle* increased by only 8 per cent between 1987 and 1996, increases of 54 and 21 per cent were recorded over the same period in the Samori *arrondissements* of Baye and Ouenkoro, respectively (Tables 2.1 and 2.2).

One important trigger for Dogon settlement in the Samori may have been the reduction in policing of the forest by state forestry service (Services des Eaux et Forêts

Table 2.2 Population change in the *arrondissements* of Bankass *cercle*, 1976–96.

Arrondissements	Population*		
	1976	1987	1996
Bankass	20,969	21,519	21,165
Kani-Bonzon	14,765	17,298	17,443
Ségué	15,971	17,275	18,524
Diallassagou	47,989	48,102	48,435
Sokoura	19,780	22,279	22,945
Ouenkoro	10,047	11,618	17,945
Baye	17,252	17,908	21,634
Total	146,783	155,999	168,091

*Data for 1976 and 1987 from census (DNSI, 1980, 1990), data for 1996 from *recensement administratif* (Bankass *Cercle* Administration, 1996).

(SEF)) officials, pending a reform of SEF instigated after the 1991 *coup d'état*. A further incentive was the greatly enhanced opportunities for livestock, fishing and crop production offered by the rise in the water level of the Sourou after 1989.

The 'wetland' resource

The Sourou River is the largest surface-water resource in Bankass *cercle*. Outside the valley, apart from villages close to seasonal streams flowing off the Bandiagara escarpment, the population of the *cercle* is dependent on infrequent small lakes (*marés*), which occur in the Seno, or groundwater at a depth of between 35 and 85 m in the Seno and between 35 and 65 m in the Samori (PIRT, 1983).

Upstream of Baye, the head of the Sourou valley is constituted by three tributaries: the Yawa, flowing from the south-east, the Wasso from the north-east and the Wonvosso from the north. Downstream of Baye, the principal tributaries joining the Sourou are the Yirèkèrè from the west, just north of Songoré, the Bouba from the east, at Guinigan and the Kossin, which forms the frontier with Burkina Faso, from the west. Between Goéré and Oula, the Sourou floodplain is relatively narrow, but it becomes more extensive in the region of Souhé and to the south in Burkina Faso.

There are no stream-flow data for the Sourou in Mali but, according to local tradition, the Sourou was historically subject to a cycle whereby seven wetter years, in which the river flowed throughout the year, were followed by seven dry years, in which the flow stopped before the end of the dry season.

The water level of the Sourou River rose significantly in 1989 with the construction of a new dam at Lery, in Burkina Faso, with funding from the European Union, to enable the irrigation of 30,000 ha of gravity-fed and pumped irrigation for market gardening, rice and cotton production in the floodplain of the Sourou and its seasonal tributary, the Débé, in the area south of Di in Burkina Faso. The dam is located downstream of the confluence of the Sourou with the Mouhoun (formerly Volta Noire), and has effectively diverted water from the Mouhoun up into Mali, where the Sourou valley forms the northern extremity of the dam's reservoir. As a consequence, the Sourou in Mali has changed from a seasonal river to a perennial watercourse with an annual flood. The flood level of the Sourou is subject to the considerable year-to-year variations in annual rainfall, although no data are yet available on the fluctuations of the water level. The annual flood cycle begins when the water starts to rise from July, reaches its highest level in September at the end of the rains and starts to decrease from the end of October, reaching its lowest levels again in March (Gana, 1995).

In 1996, a total of 3,000 ha, 10 per cent of that planned, was under irrigation in Burkina from the reservoir created by the Lery dam. In addition to irrigation, managers of the dam are obliged to maintain a minimum dry-season flow for downstream hydroelectric power generation and irrigation in Burkina Faso and Ghana. The impact of the Lery dam on the Sourou valley in Mali appears not to have been foreseen by the dam's designers and no irrigation was planned in Mali. However, comparison of aerial photographs of the Sourou valley for 1992 and 1996 indicated that at the northern end of the valley (Baye–Goéré) there had been a rapid increase (48 per cent per year) in land cleared for rice cultivation, mostly at the expense of woody vegetation (Figs 2.5 and 2.6). Overall, land cleared for cultivation (mainly for rice) in the floodplain of the Malian part of Sourou valley, from Baye to the Burkina frontier, was estimated at over 6,000 ha in 1996 (Chenevix-Trench et al., 1997). Most of this area had been cleared since the dam's completion in 1989. The governance of access, use and management of land and water in this development of rice production is the subject of the remainder of this chapter.

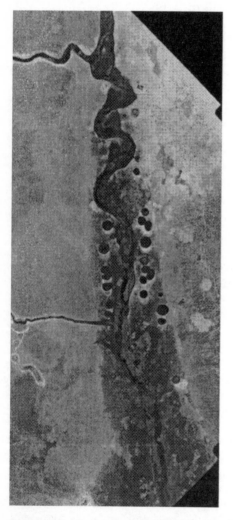 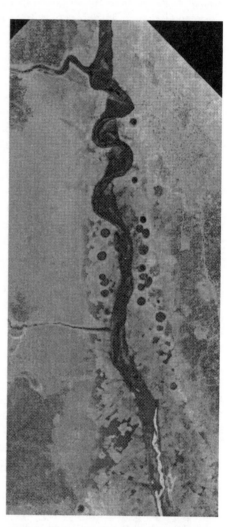

Figure 2.5 Aerial photographs of the Sourou valley in the vicinity of Baye, taken in 1992 (left) and 1996, showing reduction in tree cover (dark tones) as a result of clearing for rice cultivation

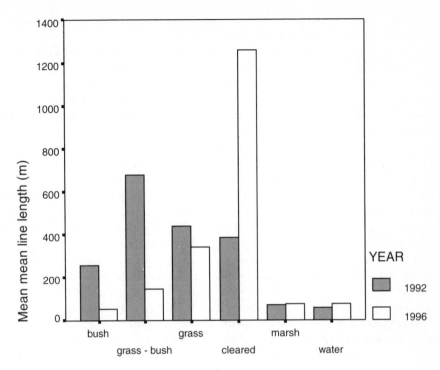

Figure 2.6 Comparison of vegetation cover in aerial photographs taken in 1992 & 1996, using a line-intersect method (Chenevix-Trench et al., 1997)

Institutional frameworks in the Sourou valley

Throughout the historical changes in the Malian state, the village appears as the basic unit of governance throughout Mali, with the exception of the most mobile of the pastoralist groups in the Sahara, and village authority derives from the same basic roots: religion, kinship, age and conquest. Religious authority derives from animist traditions, in which the first to clear land using axe or fire has necessarily established a special relationship with the spirits of the land, and descendants of the first cultivator are thus uniquely placed to seek the spirits' favour, and hence the land's fertility, on behalf of present users of the land.

Kinship authority is that of the oldest male member of a lineage over all members of that lineage. Lineage authority governs rights to land and other resources. Lineages are traced back to the founders and early settlers of the village, and often constitute separate wards (*quartiers*) of the village. More recent arrivals in a village may form new *quartiers* or may attach themselves to existing *quartiers*, by forming alliances with, or negotiating membership of, existing lineages (Crowley, 1991:24). The authority of older lineage members over younger ones is paralleled by the age set system. All youths in the village within a 5–10-year age-group constitute an age set, and older age sets have authority over younger ones, principally in the sphere of 'public works' activities of collective interest to the village.

Authority from conquest may, at its simplest, refer to the subjugation of one village by a neighbour or by small invading groups, whereby the conquerors establish themselves or their nominees as the village authority, though this does not always include appropriating religious authority held by the lineage of the land's first cultivator, leaving the possibility of a more diffuse power structure within villages. In Songoré and Oula villages in the Sourou valley, for example, oral history discriminates between the *Zora,* who represents the original founding lineage, and the *Massa (chef de terre),* who has formal authority over all resources to which the village lays claim and whose lineage, in some oral accounts, usurped the control of the *Zora.* In practice, the formal authority of the *Massa* over village land is conditioned by the more immediate control of land and labour by lineage leaders, many of whom are formal advisers (*conseilleurs*) of the *Massa.* Lineage control of land, although formally allocated by the *Massa,* is inherited and, as such, strongly skewed towards lineages of earlier settlers.

Conquest on a larger scale brought the need for representation between village and centralized state authority. In the Samori and Seno, incorporation in the Toucouleur empire in the 1860s brought the institution of the *chef de village* as the representative of the *Massa* to the Toucouleur administrative authority in Bandiagara. Nominated by village elders, but paid by government, the *chef de village* was strengthened under French administration to secure tax collection and the provision of *corvée* labour, and continues to this day as the primary element of the state, with responsibility for rural tax collection and resolution of disputes at village level. The relationship between different sources of authority, particularly that between *Massa* and *chef de village,* varies according to the specific historical and present circumstances of a village. Animist traditions in relation to the land persist, but are heavily modified by Islamization and an acknowledgement of the role of the state in conflict resolution.

In the Samori, the supra-village entities of the Tiendougou and Ouladougou appear to have originated in the capacity of their leading villages to both withstand raiders during the eighteenth and nineteenth centuries and assert authority over neighbouring villages. With the establishment of French administration at the turn of the century, the area was governed from the *cercle* at Bandiagara under a European administrator (*commandant*), but left African authorities at the level of village and the intermediate *canton,* which grouped a number of villages. However, the colonial boundaries of the nineteen *cantons* covering the Seno and Samori were drawn to cut across the existing supra-village and ethnic allegiances. In particular, the Ouladougou, along with the other Pana entity, the Diendougou, were mostly incorporated, with Peulh (Fulani) settlements at Libé and Nassari and the Dogon village of Pissa, in the *canton* of Pana, under the leadership of the village authorities of Baye – a comparatively recent and non-Pana settlement.

After independence in 1960, the 'first republic' reorganized administration into the present hierarchy of *régions,* subdivided into *cercles,* in turn subdivided into *arrondissements.* In the Seno and Samori, the *cercle* of Bankass was established and the *canton* of Pana, together with a number of villages on the west bank of the Sourou (Karé, Woro, Dian, Niamia), became the *arrondissement* of Baye, still with Baye as its administrative centre, although the villages of Oula and Dien continued to command cultural importance as the centres of the historical entities of the Panadougou.

While the origins of formal administration in conquest and colonial rule are often contrasted with those of 'customary' village authority, the two appear closely intertwined in the formation and legitimation of new villages during the rapid expansion of settlement in the Seno and Samori since the end of the nineteenth century. All land in the Seno and Samori, no matter how sparsely settled, is notionally claimed by existing villages, so that all new settlements need the agreement of the village authority claiming jurisdiction over the settlement's location. In general, such agreement – symbolized by permission to dig a well at the new settlement – is conditional on the settlers' recognition of the prior land rights of the 'mother village' on whose land they have established themselves. A new settlement's subordinate status in terms of customary rights over land is further reinforced by local administrators' treatment of a new settlement as a part of the 'mother village' for tax collection purposes and hence the responsibility of the *chef de village*. Conversely, when growth of a new settlement eventually made appointment of its own *chef de village* necessary, the administration effectively changed the status of the settlement from a satellite of the 'mother village' to an 'official' village in its own right, simultaneously weakening its subordination under customary land rights. The process of 'recognition' of new villages by the administration may therefore have profound effects on customary land rights. Before recognizing new villages as separate tax collection entities, administrators therefore normally seek the agreement of the relevant customary authorities. These, in turn, would seek to counterbalance the new village's 'independence' by strengthening kinship links of customary authority and, where necessary, by installing one of their own members as *Massa* – customary authority over land – in the new village.

The role of settlement in materializing claims over land is evident in the current process of migration to the Samori. The areas for the planned forest reserve (*forêt classée*) were marked with posts (*bornage*) in 1989, bringing closer the prospect of their permanent exclusion from settlement or cultivation. That this was followed, in 1991, by the democratization of the Malian state, including the relaxation of the punitive controls that the forestry service had exercised over forested areas, may have signalled to villagers and migrants in the Samori and Seno a 'window of opportunity' to establish cultivation rights throughout the Samori. From this perspective, establishing new settlements in the forest served the interests of both migrants and local village authorities in asserting their claims against those of the state. Further, in contrast to earlier migrants, such as those fleeing the famines of 1913–14 and 1927–30, who were mainly absorbed into existing villages, the migrants of the past 20 years have settled in satellite settlements, or 'farming hamlets' (*hameaux de culture*), within the territory and under the authority of an existing 'official' village. Konaté and Tessougué (1996) report that, of 86 *hameaux* they identified in the Samori, 63 had been established since 1970 and 42 had been established since 1985. They observed that this pattern of settlement offers short-term advantages to both settlers and their hosts. For settlers there are opportunities to avoid taxation (the poll tax or *minimum fiscale*): members of a *hameau* may be registered under their original villages or the village in whose territory the *hameau* is installed, but many are not registered under either. For their hosts, *hameaux* installed in the 'grey' area at the boundary between lands of two villages serve to assert ownership of land under conditions of increasing demand and where there are no clearly defined boundaries.

Access to land and water in the Sourou valley: demand, competition and conflict

Many villages of the Sourou have recent memories of food shortage, when house-holds had empty granaries from June to October and, lacking cash to buy millet, survived on millet bran and whatever wild grains (*oseille de Guinée*) and leaves they could gather. The clearance by hand of over 6,000 ha for rice cultivation within 6 years is an indication of the strong demand for increased agricultural output in a very poor area. Much of this demand is for better food security.

Widespread recognition of the productivity of rice cultivation has prompted culti-vators from outside the Sourou villages to seek access to land on the Sourou flood-plain. In villages of the Samori, such as Ganida, Tionou, Diallaye, Minta and Sogué, which identify themselves as Dafing, people have sought to strengthen and multiply ties with friends and relatives in the riverside villages. Villagers in Ganida, for example, identified a total of 65 rice plots they cultivated in the floodplain, on land belonging to the villages of Songoré (26 plots), Woro (20), Souhé (11), Goéré (4), Kawéré (3) and Karé (1). Many have been attracted from even further afield, notably Dogon from the Seno and plateau, to seek a rice plot of their own or work on someone else's.

Increasing competition for land is also indicated by rapid increases in population, particularly at the northern end of the valley, where Dogon settlers have established a number of *hameaux de culture* close to the river at Tiron (or Tollé) on the territory of Songoré, Yara and Boila within the territory of Baye, Djimouté and Bissan on the territory of Goéré, and Leré on the territory of Woro. Yara, established by six Dogon families in 1989, had grown to 72 families by 1996. In some instances, settlers in the *hameaux* outnumber the residents of the 'mother village' within whose jurisdiction they have settled. This appears to be the case in Songoré (Table 2.3), where eleven *hameaux* have been established since 1976, five of them in the last five years. While settlers are registered by government census as part of Songoré village, our research shows that, for the village proper, the population is only half that registered by government, so the remainder are likely to be settlers. This contrasts with the village of Oula, in the south of the valley, where immigration pressure is less and population figures are influenced more by emigration.

Table 2.3 Population census in different years: Songoré & Oula villages.

Census year	1933	1948	1976	1987	1996	Present study (main village only) – 1996
Songoré	708	913	1,155	1,301	1,408	730
Oula	824	984	732	953	910	943

Greater assurance of water, coupled with the grazing available on harvested rice fields, has also made the Sourou more important as a dry-season resource for livestock and an attractive alternative for herds that might have travelled to the inner delta of the Niger for the dry season. This, together with the increased numbers of animals purchased with the proceeds of rice sales and increasing use of the Samori by Bellah and Foulankriabé goatherds from the north, implies a larger livestock population in the Sourou valley than in the past and further competition between pasture and encroaching cultivation.

Under pressure of immigration, the customary authorities in the Samori have generally allowed outsiders access through the establishment of new hamlets on dryland sites, but have tightened their control of access to the flooded lands of the Sourou valley since the advent of highly profitable rice cultivation.

This can take a number of forms. One is how inheritance rights of families who are absent have been 'forgotten' – allowed to 'lapse'. This applies particularly to families in Baye and Songoré, who in the past left to establish hamlets in sandy areas, which offered better prospects for cultivating millet – in the Seno lands of Lossogou, Korossogou, Minta and Hamdallaye. Where they are not simply forgotten in the allocation of rice land, they find themselves classified as outsiders with no customary land rights in the flooded area.

The comparatively small extent of flooded land, coupled with a pattern of land-holding shaped by the history of settlement, means that inherited access to rice fields is uneven, both within and between villages. The dense web of marriage and extended-family ties within and between villages gives rise to an ever-growing demand for those with inheritance rights to loan rice fields to cousins, nephews and so on. There is evidence, however, of a growing reluctance of lineage heads to allocate rice-growing land to local villagers except close relatives, as the status and influence such loans confer are outweighed by risks that after a few years borrowers will claim hereditary rights to the plots, in conflict with the lender's rights.

The great value now attached to rice plots makes those who control them unwilling to risk future difficulties in reclaiming them from borrowers. As a result, the holders of customary rights over rice-growing land are more likely to loan it to

Table 2.4 Summary of distribution of rice plots & area between different types of cultivator in Songoré and Oula.

	No. of rice fields (%)		Mean area (ha) per field		Total area of rice fields (%)	
	Songoré	Oula	Songoré	Oula	Songoré	Oula
Total	483	372			629 ha	568 ha
Cultivated by:	%	%			%	%
Households	36	51	2.02	1.95	55	65
Individual men	13	19	0.53	0.76	5	10
Married women	25	15	0.52	0.63	10	6
Settlers (hamlets)	11	3	1.47	2.58	13	4
Seasonal cultivators	15	12	1.44	1.84	16	15

outsiders than to members of their own village. This is illustrated by an exchange in Baye, while the research team was explaining the procedure for the field census. One villager observed straight away: 'Our relatives have forgotten the spirit of help to families who do not have hereditary land rights. They prefer to offer all the land to the Dogon who come from far away.' This brought an immediate response: 'It's my ancestors' land, and I'll only give it to those who can work for me and those who are useful to me.' A poignant example was provided by the case of one villager telling his brother, during a particularly heated discussion, that he would never give him land to cultivate rice, preferring instead to give it to a stranger, from whom he could get the land back whenever he so wished.

The importance of land loans varies between villages. In Songoré, villagers had inheritance rights on 84 per cent of the rice fields they cultivated, and only 9 per cent were entirely dependent on borrowing land for the main household (foroba) rice crop. In Oula, only 57 per cent of villagers' fields were inherited, and 31 per cent of households relied entirely on borrowing land for their foroba crop. Land loaned to outsiders (settlers and seasonal cultivators) accounted for 26 per cent of rice plots in Songoré, more than double the number loaned to local villagers and 70 per cent of all loaned rice plots in Songoré (Table 2.4). By contrast, in Oula two-thirds of loaned plots were cultivated by local families and only a third by outsiders. The principal difference between the two villages is the much higher immigration pressure in Songoré.

Competition for rice land has led to increasingly contested interpretations of customary tenure. In Oula, where immigration pressure is low, village authorities have restricted settlement to the hamlet of Guinigan, where customary rights are claimed by the Koné lineage of Kindiasso quartier in Oula, on the grounds that their lineage ancestors fled to Oula from an earlier settlement on the site of the new hamlet. Consequently the settlers in the hamlet, who include Dogon from the Seno, Mossi from Burkina Faso and Bellah pastoralists, all cultivate land loaned to them by the Koné lineage. The loans are long-term, with only token gifts offered to the land-holding lineage by cultivators, on the understanding that their descendants will never be proprietors of the land they cultivate: 'No matter how long a log floats in the river, it will never become a cayman.' In Songoré, immigration pressure is high, and attempts by Dogon in the hamlet of Tiron to strike a similar long-term understanding with holders of customary rights over rice land have failed, with the notable exception of some fifty rice plots they cultivated on the land of an old man, Anlè Doumèrè, with few children of his own. Despite the settlers' best efforts to recip-rocate the old man's goodwill with gifts and by providing labour to plough and harvest his fields, they lost their rice plots when he died and his brother reclaimed his land. Elsewhere in the northern end of the valley, those with few family ties to land-holding lineages, such as Dogon settlers, must renegotiate access to rice plots each year under increasingly onerous terms. Settlers in Yara hamlet complain that the Togokina lineage on whose land the hamlet stands have repeatedly reclaimed rice plots after only a year or two of cultivation, requiring the settlers to clear more woodland, each time further from the river and with less prospect of sufficient flooding to grow rice. The insecurity of access to loaned plots is not restricted to settlers, though they appear to be the most vulnerable group, with 40 per cent having had their rice plots reclaimed by landholders in Songoré, compared with 19 per cent for all borrowers of rice plots in the same village.

Although land borrowers often offer gifts to the holders of customary rights over their rice plots (42 per cent of cases where there are no family ties between borrower and lender), the predominant interpretation of customary tenure is that such trans-actions are not formally monetized. However, under a different interpretation of custom, more formal sharecropping arrangements are being used to allocate land to seasonal cultivators, particularly by holders of customary land rights in the village of Baye. They justify their practice with references to coffee and cocoa plantations in Côte d'Ivoire, where many themselves went in their youth as migrants seeking work and found that plantation workers earned a third of the harvest for a season's work. Comparing their rice land with property for rent in urban areas, they assert their right to offer access to the highest bidder. A senior member of the Togokina said:

> I see nothing wrong in claiming part of the harvest from those who come to borrow our land. They keep their paddy when they return to the Seno. Anybody who doesn't agree with the prin-ciple of sharing the harvest can stay at home. We didn't ask them to come here. As far as I'm concerned, I prefer my land to stay uncultivated and burned if necessary, rather than lend it to an outsider who gives me nothing after harvest.

Another added:

> The land stays where it is, for God and for us. Can you tell me that someone who rents a house in town shouldn't pay the rent? Here, if the Dogon want to cultivate rice and are happy with our conditions, they can have land, but if not they can stay at home. It's a favour we are doing them, because they keep their share of the harvest.

The increasing competition for rice land highlights the greatly enhanced power of customary (lineage) landholders to appropriate a larger share of agricultural output than previously. This trend has been met with a number of attempts to reforge non-market relationships in access to floodplain land. As noted above, these include attempts by those without direct access to the floodplain to strengthen and multiply family and friendship links with those that do. This may involve new forms of reci-procity, particularly for residents of the *cercle* administrative centre of Bankass, whose rapidly changing status from villagers to townspeople leaves them well placed to exchange urban services for access to rice land in the Sourou valley.

For those without such possibilities, and particularly the Dogon in hamlets such as Yara, maintaining access to rice plots is a continual battle of wits to retain the goodwill of the customary proprietor of the land, through offering several days' work with the ox-team or several bags of rice after the harvest. Those who lose this game, through misjudgement or misfortune, risk losing their rice plot and being forced into the increasingly unrewarding work of clearing yet more woodland further from the river. For these immigrants, the hope for the future is outside intervention to develop (*aménager*) the Sourou valley. They hope that a state or commercial organization that takes over management of the flooded land will suspend customary proprietors' rights, and thereby the threat of eviction from their plots.

In contrast, for many landholding lineages, any intervention by government or other 'outside' agencies is perceived as a threat to their customary land rights. Given government administrators' role in ratifying the establishments of new settlements, it is possible for them to be seen not as arbitrators but as supporters of the settlers' case. In this, the deep mistrust of written records as a means of undermining customary (oral) authority is evident. The Dogon immigrants of Yara have a document formally recording the founding of the hamlet in 1992, and identifying the founding families, signed by the *chef d'arrondissement* of the time at Baye. It is clear that this document is regarded by the residents of Yara as an important safeguard with which to counter threats of eviction, veiled or otherwise, by the customary landholders at Baye. Equally, it appears to landholding lineages as evidence of state collusion in supporting the immigrants' ultimate aim of usurping customary rights to the land. Such tensions were evident even in villages that collaborated in this study. Thus, in Songoré an early response to proposals to undertake a field census was:

> You want us to make a census of our rice fields. But is this a good idea, when some have not inherited their fields in the flooded zone? In whose name will such fields be recorded? As far as I'm concerned, it would be wrong to record those fields in their names, because the fields are on loan to them. And you, with your white people, everything you put on paper today is difficult to deny tomorrow because the writing doesn't get lost like the spoken word.

This type of concern meant that the field census was conducted in such a way that a clear distinction was drawn between inherited and borrowed land. The definition of the latter was necessarily comprehensive and explicit: All plots which you have cleared or ploughed after consulting someone who is not of your lineage, and who does not manage your lineage's customary land rights. Plots, therefore, that you cannot leave to any of your descendants.

In the climate of tension that pervades the relationship between settlers and their hosts, all intervention by agencies of the state and any outsider identified with them (as, to some extent, were the present research team) is assessed primarily in terms of whether they are likely to strengthen settlers' land rights. We return later to the issues this raises for current policy proposals for resource management.

Aspirations to institutional transformation of existing tenure contrast, however, with the individual basis on which land loans are arranged. With few exceptions, village-level authorities (the *Massaké* and the administrative *chef de village*) have little direct involvement in individuals' access to rice fields. The exceptions are when access is sought by more organized groups. The customary authorities at Oula, for example, granted a site on the banks of the Sourou for the Panadougou Village Development Association (Association pour le Développement des Villages du Panadougou (ADVP)), based at Saalé, to establish an agricultural training centre for Ouladougou youths. Village-level authorities are also involved in decisions about the establishment of new settlements (see above) or access for pastoralists seeking grazing and water (see below), as well as responsible for negotiating access with neighbouring villages. There are instances when this has generated a climate of mutual support. For example, 19 per cent of rice plots borrowed by villagers in Oula were on the territory of the neighbouring village of Souhé. This may extend across the international frontier, as in the case of the Burkinabé villages of Donon and Niasseri, whose inhabitants cultivate a total of eight rice plots loaned by proprietors of land at Oula. More commonly, however, the advent of rice growing has provoked discord, as village authorities seek to increase their access to floodplain land by reasserting claims seldom used before the rise in the level of the Sourou. The following cases illustrate the issues.

The dispute between Para and Sogué

The floodplain land now claimed by the authorities of Para originally belonged to the much older village of Sogué, which occupied the current site of Para before moving many years ago to its present location – perceived as healthier – away from the river. The customary authorities at Sogué originally established the villages of Woro and Para as its dependencies to assert its continuing claim to land on both sides of the river, and cultivators from Sogué retained fields on the river bank for maize and sorghum. Sogué also claimed control of the water in this stretch of the Sourou, which, until the rise in the level of the river in 1987, conferred the privilege of controlling the start of the fishing season and allowing members of the village a day's fishing before people from neighbouring villages (Para, Kandé, Woro) were allowed to fish.

From 1987, villagers from both Para and Sogué began clearing land to cultivate rice. The authorities at Sogué wished to reassert their historic rights in order to allocate rice plots to all the households of Sogué, but, recognizing the more recent and continuous occupation of the area by Para, sought an agreement for joint management of the floodplain. This was refused by the authorities at Para, who now assert exclusive control over this part of the floodplain. Excluded from customary rights, villagers from Sogué borrowed rice plots from neighbouring villages. In 1990–1 these totalled 47 plots on loan from individual proprietors in Oula (22), Kandé (6), Goéré (2) and Para itself (17). The growing tension between the two communities has resulted in the eviction of Sogué villagers from five of these plots in Para and growing resentment in Sogué:

> People from Para don't want us in the flooded zone. They take our plots away and hand them over to people from Minta, to the Peulh pastoralists ... In Para they just don't want to understand, they consider us a nuisance. We had our maize and sorghum fields there ... we were on the banks of the Sourou well before Para. That's why we had control over Para's rights on the river. We know how profitable rice is and we are not prepared to let Para alone benefit from it. This problem could break out into the open any moment between Para and Sogué. God save us from that.
>
> (Administrative chief at Sogué)

This anxiety to avoid both open conflict and arbitration by government officials, despite the intense frustration felt by the authorities at Sogué, is paralleled in other disputes, for example between Songoré and Baye. It stems from experience of an earlier dispute over control of the Sourou floodplain, between Karé and Kawéré.

The dispute between Karé and Kawéré

The village of Karé was founded in precolonial times by the authorities at Oula to assert their claim to territory on the west bank of the Sourou. However, the colonial administration included Karé in the *canton* of Diallaye, not that of Pana, to which Oula belonged. The separation of the two villages increased when a dispute between them in 1945–7 resulted in the colonial administration restricting the limits of Oula's jurisdiction to the east bank of the Sourou. In effect, this gave Karé authority over a strip of the west bank and its floodplain, extending southwards as far as the territory of Souhé. By 1948, Karé authorized a settlement by Mossi at Kawéré, a little to the south of Karé itself. Curiously, this settlement on the west bank was considered part of the *canton* of Pana, on the east bank, and the authorities in Oula seized an opportunity to reassert their claims to the west bank by installing one of their own lineages as chief of Kawéré. Kawéré was subsequently recognized as a village with full authority over land within its jurisdiction to the south of Karé.

With the advent of rice production, the village authorities at Karé, seeking to clear and cultivate land on the floodplain to the south, found themselves hemmed in by land controlled by Kawéré. They sought to create an enclave to the south of Kawéré's jurisdiction, but found their right to do so contested by the authorities at Kawéré, who (allegedly at the instigation of Oula's authorities) now laid claim to all the floodplain southwards to Souhé. In the 1994–5 agricultural season, members of the two villages competed to cultivate the disputed area: some ploughing where others had cleared, some sowing where others had ploughed. Government officials, alerted to the growing tension, attempted to mark a boundary between the territories of the two villages. Since this exercise was guided by the customary authorities of Oula, it was inevitable that their old adversaries at Karé found the boundary unacceptable and destroyed the marker posts. At the time of harvest, the contest between the two sets of villagers rapidly escalated into armed confrontation, at which point the administration in Bankass despatched government security forces to the area, sequestered the disputed harvest and prohibited any further cultivation on the disputed area pending a negotiated settlement of the conflict.

Despite numerous attempts to bring the sides together by the customary authorities of the historic Ouladougou entity, by the *cercle* administration at Bankass and by the regional judicial authority at Mopti, the dispute remained unresolved in mid-1996, amid some confusion about which government agency is responsible. In the meantime, the economy of Karé and Kawéré has been crippled by their exclusion from cultivating the floodplain, their most productive resource: 'War exterminates the able-bodied, but legal processes are also costly' (Dogon proverb). This has had a salutary effect on the many other disputes between villages engendered by the rapid transformation in land use in the Sourou floodplain. Few wish to suffer the fate of Karé and Kawéré, and disputes tend to be promptly brought under control by village authorities and lineage heads.

Relations between villages and pastoralists

Before rice farming started, problems over land were rare. The tensions of recent years among the Dafing villages are above all due to the rice-fields. In the past every village in the Samori had its place, and it was the two ancient villages Tionou and Oula who controlled the land. These villages (who now claim land) like Ganida, Karé and Kawéré are only recent. We, the Peulh, if only we were more sedentary, we too could have had a village on the bank of the Sourou and would today be masters of a large domain in the floodplain.

(Pastoralist from Nassari Peulh)

Before the rise of the level of the Sourou, the floodplain provided dry-season grazing and water for herds from the Seno and from the Peulh settlements on the margins of the Samori (Libé, Nassari and Minimankanda). During most of the year, herds grazed in the large area of surrounding woodland in the Samori and some were watered during the dry season from wells dug in the dry Sourou river bed. The water and grazing which the Sourou offered for this *'petite transhumance'* was limited, however, and most herds made the *'grande transhumance'* to the more distant but richer *bourgou* pastures of the inner delta of the Niger.

The rise in the level of the Sourou greatly increased the quantity and quality of dry-season water and grazing resources, and prompted increasing numbers of herders in the Samori to switch to the *petite transhumance*. However, pastoralists found their access to the river increasingly blocked by the strip of rice fields along both banks and areas of pasture increasingly encroached by rice cultivation. The period of greatest difficulty is between November and January, when the ponds on the Samori pastures begin to dry up and the rice harvest has not yet begun, and pastoralists find themselves in increasing conflict with the village authorities that control the use of the floodplain.

Nowadays it is the fields that are chasing the cattle. The cattle can stay where they are but the fields come after them. If as a herder you let your herd stray onto a rice field, no matter how poorly flooded or poorly germinated, they'll say you have damaged a good harvest and the administration will fine you.

(Herder from Libé)

The growing problems confronting pastoralists are recognized by government officials in the *arrondissement* and *cercle* administration, who have attempted to guarantee access to the river for stock. These efforts have not met with much support from village authorities.

In the area controlled by Oula, where herders previously had three points at which to cross the river, they are now confined to one. Although the authorities at Oula have agreed to preserve a corridor for pastoralists to reach this remaining crossing point and access to a dry-season watering area on the Bouba tributary, they rejected attempts by the government livestock service to mark the corridor with posts in 1995. The corridor has none the less remained open to the pastoralists since then.

The jurisdiction of Baye contains a large dryland area known as Koroo, historically reserved for rainy-season pasture for the herds belonging to the Peulh at the neighbouring village of Libé. In 1993, the government livestock officer at Baye *arrondissement* attempted to persuade the customary authorities of Baye village to create a corridor to allow the herds on the Koroo to water at the Sourou during the dry season. The villagers accused him of bias in the pastoralists' favour and refused to grant access. Similarly, Peulh from Minimankanda complained to the government administrators at Bankass *cercle* that encroachment of rice cultivation on their grazing lands, known as Siri, Welou Houki and Bakoma, which lie in the territory of the villages of

Baye, Songoré and Lossogou, prevented their herds from reaching the river. The *cercle* administration upheld the pastoralists' complaint by limiting any further establishment of hamlets by Dogon immigrants in the area. However, this has not prevented the expansion of rice fields by local villagers from Songoré, Baye and Lossogou, which continue to block pastoralists' access to the Sourou and its backwaters in the area.

The Peulh recognize the customary rights over land exercised by the authorities of the Dafing villages of the Sourou valley, and have sought a share of the rice output by loaning draught animals to those cultivating rice, or by financing the clearing, ploughing and harvest of rice on land loaned from local landholders. However, the survey of rice cultivation in Songoré and Oula revealed no fields cultivated by Peulh, and, at the very least, pastoralists' involvement in rice cultivation appears localized and dependent on specific conditions of pastoralist–villager relations in each locality.

Land and water use in the Sourou valley

The rice production system

The rice now cultivated in the Sourou is of the 'floating' type, which grows rapidly as the water level rises and matures as the water levels fall again. Long cultivated on the inner delta of the Niger, it was introduced to the Sourou in 1989 (the year after the level of the river first rose), reputedly by a group of young migrants from the *cercle* of Koro, living at Kandé on the east bank. People in villages near the river recall their early experimentation with the new crop. Using seed bought in Di (Burkina Faso), they tried to sow the floating rice in the same way they had the upland (non-flooded) rice, with which they were familiar – a few seeds in a hole made with a hoe. The crop failed owing to weeds, and some tried to control weed growth by hoeing the ground before broadcasting the seed. Early success with this approach was swiftly followed by substitution of the hoe by the plough and a rapid expansion of the area planted. Three varieties of rice are currently identified: Mali Sawn (3–71–20) or *Malo ba*, Khao-Gaew (92–5–23) or *Malo mensin*, and RM40 (Gana, 1995). *Malo ba* is a slower-maturing variety preferred for fields closest to the river where the flood is deepest. *Malo mensin* and RM40 are faster-maturing varieties planted where the flood is shallower and likely to retreat earlier. Selection of rice variety and field site is practically the sole means of managing water in the production process, for the flood level is completely uncontrolled and varies considerably from one year to the next. This means that fields at the margin of the flooded area may be subject to crop failure in drier years, as happened in the 1995/6 season when the flood failed to reach the unprecedented high level achieved the previous (1994/5) season. The 1996 survey showed that on fields classified by villagers as poorly flooded, rice yield averaged only 232 kg/ha, compared with 1,500 kg/ha on well-flooded fields.

Between 1992 and 1996, the cultivated area increased from 20 per cent to 64 per cent of the northern part of the floodplain (between Baye and Goéré). Three-quarters of this increase involved the clearance of wooded land, so that, for many cultivators, growing rice involved a first stage of labour-intensive clearing of woody vegetation to ground level. Larger trees are often cut at around a metre above ground or burnt where they stand, the dead trunk and roots left in place. The cleared material is stacked and burnt. Fields may be cleared up to a year before planting, to allow the first flood to clear debris from the site. At the start of the season, during April and May, fields are cleared of the previous year's residues by burning. Rice seed, saved from the previous year or purchased from fellow villagers, is broadcast before any tillage, and then covered using a plough drawn by oxen or donkeys or by hand with a hoe. Sowing and ploughing are dependent on the start of the rains, but generally take place from early July to late August. If the timing is right, the seed germinates shortly before the rising flood, which kills most of the weed competition, and there is little work to be done on the crop until harvest, which begins in December/January, when water levels have dropped. Where water levels remain high, harvesting may be done from *pirogues* (canoes). All harvesting is by hand: the crop is cut using sickles, threshed using poles, and winnowed before transport from the field in sacks on carts drawn by donkeys or oxen.

With the exception of sorghum, previously grown on 27 per cent of the rice fields surveyed in Songoré and Oula, the expansion of rice cultivation does not appear to have displaced other crops: 63 per cent of rice plots were on previously uncultivated land (Figs 2.5 and 2.6). While the rice harvest has greatly increased the demand for agricultural labour during the dry season, it only commences after – and therefore does not compete with – the harvest of the staple millet crop. However, both crops are sown at around the same time, and 22 per cent of rice cultivators have reduced their millet areas in order to use labour to plant rice. However, a further 10 per cent said they had increased their areas of other crops, because income from rice had allowed investment in animal draught. The ownership of draught oxen is a key criterion that villagers use in ranking households' wealth, and is associated with the cultivation of larger areas of rice and higher productivity. Fields ploughed with oxen yielded an average of 1,509 kg/ha, against 839 and 707 kg/ha, respectively, for fields ploughed using donkeys or hoed by hand. At the northern end of the Sourou valley, at Songoré, ownership of draught oxen is high among both local villagers (68 per cent) and seasonal cultivators from the Seno and Samori (82 per cent), the latter having been the main providers of draught power in the early years of rice culti-vation. The large number of ox-teams in the area also means that oxen can be fairly readily hired by those without oxen or needing additional teams. Thus women, who own no oxen, hired ox-teams on 34 per cent of their *djonforo* fields, and Dogon settlers, whose draught animals are predominantly donkeys and only 30 per cent of whom owned oxen, used hired teams to plough 23 per cent of their rice fields. In contrast, in Oula, at the southern end of the valley, not only was oxen ownership lower among both villagers (57 per cent) and seasonal cultivators (50 per cent), but the proportion of cultivators hiring ox-teams tended to be lower, and overall average yields in Oula (716 kg/ha) were markedly lower than in Songoré (1,689 kg/ha).

Rice in the local economy

The rice harvest brings large numbers of seasonal labourers into the Sourou valley, and in the majority of plots in Songoré (75 per cent of *foroba* and 60 per cent of

djonforo) rice is cut and threshed with hired labour. Among settlers and seasonal cultivators and among village households in Oula, the proportion of rice producers hiring
labour for harvest varies but is generally lower (30–50 per cent) than for villagers in
Songoré. Harvest labour, including that used for winnowing and transport, is paid in
kind, and accounts for between 8 per cent of the total rice harvest in Songoré and 4
per cent in Oula. Overall, 'outsiders' to the Sourou valley (seasonal cultivators and
labourers) obtain 22 and 15 per cent of the harvest in Songoré and Oula, respectively,
with settlers taking 11 per cent in Songoré but only 3 per cent in Oula. Residents of
the two villages take 74 and 85 per cent of the harvest in Songoré and Oula, respectively, but married women control a much higher proportion (12 per cent) of the rice
crop in Songoré than in Oula (Table 2.5).

For farmers, whether resident in Songoré and Oula, settlers in hamlets or seasonal
migrants, the principal goal of rice cultivation appears to be improved food security,
since all these groups sell on average a third or less of their rice harvest. Food
shortages in the area, once commonplace, have diminished. In 1996, villagers in
Songoré and Oula identified 17 and 29 per cent, respectively, of village households as
having food deficits. However, all households in these villages were cultivating rice,
and village elders in both Songoré and Baye remarked that they had not seen any
famine since the start of rice farming.

For 65 per cent of rice cultivators, rice has also become their principal source of
income. In particular, rice from *djonforo* plots, controlled by individual men or
women, is mostly sold (72–79 per cent). For some groups, the increased cash
income has quickly translated into higher expectations of consumption. One
woman in Songoré observed: 'Growing rice for sale makes money. We no longer
worry about what to wear at Ramadan or Tabaski. At festivals like these we are so
well-dressed we hardly recognize one another from a distance.' A youth in the same
village adds:

> Buying a bicycle is no longer a problem. I would want at least a mobylette, but people here are
> becoming less interested in mobylettes. To make a good impression in the village, a young guy
> these days has to be able to buy a big Yamaha or Honda motorbike. As far as cassette-radios are
> concerned, most young people around the village are using those with at least six batteries, since
> even women and kids have got ones powered by four batteries.

Table 2.5   Overall distribution of rice harvest.

	Songoré	Oula
Estimated total harvest (t)	846	389
Percentage harvested by:		
Household units	57	76
Individual men	5	7
Married women	12	2
Settlers in 'hamlets'	11	3
Seasonal cultivators	14	11
Of which, percentage paid in kind to labourers	8	4

It is commonly asserted that high cash returns obtainable from growing rice on *djonforo* plots has reduced the number of men leaving the villages of the Sourou valley to find work in urban areas. There is some evidence to support this: the proportion of men between ages 15 and 60 absent for at least 3 months was only 15 per cent in Oula and 10 per cent in Songoré, compared with 31 per cent in other Samori villages. However, urban migration remains the first or second most important source of income for 27 per cent of men with *djonforo* rice plots in Oula and Songoré, and 23 percent used the money from their rice sales to travel or to finance small commercial activities in towns.

Rice cultivation has also generated cash income for those heads of landholding lineages in riverine villages who have established sharecropping arrangements with seasonal cultivators from the Seno or further afield, generating substantial surpluses of rice for sale. It is probably too early to determine whether rice cultivation patterns will result in widening differences in wealth among households of the Sourou valley villages. There are no clear differences in productivity between local villagers and settlers or seasonal cultivators, although within these categories there are groups with fewer assets and lower productivity, such as the settlers at Guinigan. However, the potential for increasing differentiation is indicated by the advantages of households identified by villagers as wealthy, who not only own oxen, but appear more likely to have well-flooded (i.e, favourably located) rice plots and greater average rice yields (1,180 kg/ha) than those (504 kg/ha) of households identified as poor. In addition, wealthier households cultivate, on average, 4.58 ha of rice, compared with 2.8 ha for the poor. In Songoré the poor accounted for 17 per cent of village households, but in Oula it was 53 per cent.

Land and water management: sustainability of rice cultivation in the Sourou valley

A striking feature of the development of rice cultivation in the Sourou valley is that it has been achieved with no input from state technical agencies Although officers of the government agricultural services work at *cercle* and *arrondissement* level, their roles are primarily administrative, in the collection and compilation of statistics. Extension work on rice in Bankass *cercle* is restricted to small-scale irrigated areas at the base of the Bandiagara escarpment, since, for much of the rainy season, the several thousand hectares of rice in the Sourou valley are inaccessible from Bankass.

The national research and extension programmes of the Institut pour l'Economie Rurale (IER), based at the regional capital, Mopti, have had a similarly negligible impact on the development of rice cultivation the Sourou valley. Research policy is to seek higher returns by focusing on irrigated (*inondation contrôlée*) rice, rather than the floating rice grown under variable flood regimes, which predominates in the inner delta of the Niger and now in the Sourou valley. Moreover, IER rice research appears to be restricted to the testing of new rice varieties – often as part of inter-national programmes. Two such trials undertaken in the Sourou valley for the first time in the 1995 season, at Baye and Goéré, failed to produce usable data: the seed sown in the experiment at Baye failed to germinate, while that at Goéré was damaged by fish. No research is being undertaken in the Sourou valley on other aspects of rice cultivation or on its impact on the wider farming system of the area.

When asked where they thought the water came from to change the level of the Sourou, people in the Sourou valley usually say that it came from Burkina Faso, and some that it resulted from a dam in Burkina, whose construction they attributed to the presidency of Thomas Sankara. Peulh pastoralists also confirm that the water came from the south, beginning to rise in the lower valley at Souhé and Oula, two years before it did at Baye in the upper valley. One consequence is a sense that rice cultivation depends on events in Burkina Faso for the continuation of the annual flood. There are two reasons to suppose that present water levels of the Sourou in Mali are likely to be maintained in the future. First, the water in the valley is supplied by rainfall not only in the Sourou catchment but also by that in the much wetter Mouhoun catchment to the south. This should make levels of water in the Sourou less variable than the rainfall in its catchment in Mali. Secondly, the irrigated areas in Burkina which the dam was designed to serve are upstream of the dam, so that, to avoid increases in pumping costs for these irrigation schemes, water levels would need to be maintained. It is none the less the case that any reduction in water levels behind the dam would be felt most acutely at the upper end of the Sourou valley, in the area of Baye, Songoré and Goéré.

Beyond this, however, many in the Samori have observed the rapid clearance of the land covered by the present level of flooding, and recognize that, even if the water is maintained at its present level, future access to rice cultivation may depend on increasing further the area covered by the flood. This is of particular interest to those who live in villages at some distance from the river, and some have begun publicly seeking support for infrastructure to improve their access to the Sourou flood. The villagers of Ganida, for example, are seeking funding from development agencies for works that would allow more water into a branch of the Sourou valley that reaches on to their village's land and would retain the water there for longer. They have sought alliances with other villages, notably Karé and Diallaye, to help press their case. Another 'grass-roots' initiative to modify the flood regime is the proposal by the ADVP to construct a small dam on the Bouba tributary, near Oula, to extend the area of rice cultivation along the banks of the Bouba to the east of the main Sourou valley. The ADVP, based in the village of Saalé, represents a group of about ten villages in the eastern Samori and is involved in a number of initiatives to create schools, health centres and agricultural training for youths. The proposal for a dam on the Bouba has been blocked by objections from Peulh herders from Nassari, who have been allocated the Bouba as a watering area and corridor for herds to reach the Sourou. The competing claims on the Bouba are ultimately in the hands of the customary village authority at Oula, within whose jurisdiction the lower reaches of the Bouba fall.

These initiatives suggest that, to increase their returns from rice growing, villagers are seeking ways to extend the flooded area. Our analysis of productivity of rice cultivation in the Sourou valley indicates that, in the longer term, as opportunities for area expansion become more scarce, returns from rice cultivation are going to depend on improving the yield per unit area. Improved water control is critical to increased rice yields for two reasons. First, the depth of flooding is one of the most important determinants of yield: poorly flooded fields produced on average only 15 per cent of the harvest on well-flooded fields. Secondly, the growing problem of perennial weeds (especially *Oryza longistaminata*) associated with rice-growing areas will, if not controlled, take some fields out of production completely. Control requires thorough tillage, which is possible only if the land is drained for at least part of the year.

For all these reasons, the need for some form of water management in the Sourou valley will grow in the next few years, if the prosperity based on rice is to continue. International investment is available, in principle, in the form of a project to be funded by the Fonds d'Equipment des Nations Unies (FENU). This projected an expenditure of US$9 million over five years (1996–2000) in the *cercles* of Bankass and Koro (FENU, 1992), mainly on support to improving village land management in about 80 villages, subcontracted to NGOs and other development agencies. In addition, the project will build a culverted causeway (*digue-ponceaux*) across the Sourou at Baye and construct a laterite road from Baye to Oula, thus opening up year-round road access to the Sourou valley in Mali. Finally, as part of land management improvement for villages in the valley, the project envisages the construction of small water management works.

FENU project documents are cautious about how much water management infra-structure will be built, stressing the need for further studies and consultation with the villages concerned, but they indicate a number of possibilities, including a system of sluices incorporated into the causeway crossing at Baye. This would permit the rising flood to move upstream but then to be retained (and augmented by streams feeding the upper reaches of the Sourou) by closing the sluices. A potential storage of 3.8 million cubic metres is estimated to be feasible behind such a structure, allowing longer and more extensive submersion of the upper end of the Sourou valley. The potential for smaller-scale submersible dykes to regulate water levels in the many backwaters of the Sourou floodplain has also been noted in project documents. Interventions of this kind would clearly meet the needs of villagers seeking more rice land, such as those in Ganida. However, our research suggests that any discussions of infrastructure for water control are likely to inflame the tensions over land rights between immigrants and customary landholders.

Fears and expectations attached to *aménagement*, stemming largely from their observation of the Office du Niger system in the Niger delta, are openly and exten-sively voiced in the Sourou valley. Holders of customary rights over land fear that outside investment to improve water management will bring the extinction of their control over land and its transfer to a project management over whom they will have little influence compared with outsiders from administrative or commercial centres, such as Bankass, Diallassagou or even Mopti. The suppression of customary rights which most associate with *aménagement* is viewed equally with dismay by land lenders and with hope by land borrowers. Of the latter, those with most to gain are settlers, particularly Dogon, but also Bellah and Peulh, seeking income from rice, who have no kinship ties with local landholders to exploit but who are locally resident and thus perceived by landholders to threaten long-term claims over land which they cultivate on loan.

A climate of uncertainty and rumour has been fed by uncoordinated actions among different development agencies. The present study team were viewed with deep mistrust in Baye from the start, particularly by individuals who felt that they had been the object of criticism by SOS Sahel researchers in the past. During our fieldwork, a research team from the United Nations Development Programme (UNDP) undertook an intensive study on poverty in Baye, and the *Projet National de la Vulgarisation d'Agriculture* had carried out a census of rice fields in Yara two weeks previously. Not surprisingly, it was very difficult for local people to distinguish between all the various 'research teams', and a certain amount of scepticism was evident. As one village leader in Songoré put it:

> When we were hungry and needed help, no one was interested in coming here. Now that we have some prosperity, don't come here and measure us up to tell us how much of our land we need to feed our families.

Politics and the governance of land and water

To summarize: since 1990 cultivators in the Sourou valley have cleared about 6,000 ha, mostly to grow rice. Based on a sample of 20 per cent of fields in two villages, this study produced an estimate of average paddy yield of 1.3 t/ha, giving overall annual production conservatively assessed at 5,276 tons (with a value of US$1.2 million). This has been achieved without reducing dryland production of the staple millet crop in the area, and thus represents a net gain to cereal production in the Samori. The development of rice cultivation has been achieved by the initiative of local villagers and immigrants to the Sourou valley. Decisions about access to and use of the flood-plain land have been controlled by customary authorities at village level: the *Massaké* (*chef de terres*) and the leaders of lineages with hereditary customary rights to land. Neither government technical services nor NGOs had had any significant input to the development of rice production up to the time of this study (1996).

The study identifies a number of problems that those cultivating the floodplain will have to address in the near future, and which can be grouped under two main headings: first, the need for investment to introduce some form of water management to increase the reliability of rice yields, maximize the area available for rice cultivation and allow the growing threat of perennial weeds to be contained; and, secondly, the need to resolve mounting tensions that land allocation under customary tenure creates, in relation to land distribution within village jurisdictions and also between villages and between villages and pastoralists. A key factor linking these problems, which raises questions about the nature of future intervention by government and non-government agencies, is that of customary land tenure.

The study examined the operation of customary tenure in relation to the flood-plain land, and found that the rights and obligations of those with hereditary control over land were subject to different and contested interpretations. This suggests a need to look more carefully at what is meant by 'customary tenure' and its significance in policy discourse in Mali.

Custom and modernization

In general terms, customary tenure may be interpreted as incorporating a legacy of precedent, which includes rules imposed by past states but interpreted in response to current economic and social constraints and opportunities. For example, the subjugation of the fishing and cultivating villages of the interior delta of the Niger by the pastoralist Fulani in 1820 was accompanied by the establishment of the Dina, an administrative code defining pasture rights implemented by centrally appointed officials (*dioro*), who levied grazing fees and governed herd movements between grazing areas. Under Toucouleur administation in the 1860s, the cohesion of the Dina was weakened by the breakup and exile of Fulani authority. Thirty years later, the French administration reinstated exiled Fulani and recognized the Dina code, but modified it to allow outsiders, such as Tuareg, Bellah and Maure, access to the pastures of the delta during the severe droughts of 1913–19 (Riddell, 1982:42), and to accommodate the colonial policy of expanding rice cultivation. The nature of the Dina code had undergone profound changes in the hundred years since its inception.

Within policy debates, 'customary tenure' is commonly identified with oral tradition, as opposed to 'modern' or written forms of tenure introduced under French colonial rule. The latter include two changes that remain important in the framework of access to land and water in Mali. These are: first, the direct claim of ownership of all 'unoccupied' land – '*terres vacantes et sans maîtres*' (Ould Sidi Mohamed, 1992:183) – by the colonial state, manifested, for example, through establishing forest reserves (*forêts classées*); and, secondly, the introduction of private (exclusive) ownership with the prospect of a market in land. The dichotomy between customary and modern tenure was strengthened following independence by extension of state ownership claims to all the national territory and the abolition of what were perceived to be exploitative elements of customary tenure, such as sharecropping (Crowley, 1991:54) and grazing fees (Moorehead, 1989:32). Under the Second Republic direct involvement of the state in controlling access to land increased: through suspension of customary land rights and land allocation by government officials in areas under the jurisdiction of 'national' rural development projects (ODRs) (Cissé, 1985:151); and through the SEF policing of woodcutting and grazing within both forest reserves and 'protected forests' – effectively, all forests except those planted by their owner (Ribot, 1995:16–17).

The 1986 *Code Domanial et Foncier* (CDF) attempted to harmonize tenure rights deriving from a number of historical periods within a single legislative framework. It recognized the precedence of customary tenure over claims by individuals to register land as private property, but also its subordination to any claims the state might make on land 'in the national interest' (Ould Sidi Mohamed, 1992:179–81). In two respects, the CDF is ambiguous in its support for customary authority over access to land. First, it does not make clear whether holders of customary tenure rights have the legal authority to exclude outsiders. This is critical, because of the large numbers of migrants seeking land, particularly in the interior delta or in the higher-rainfall CMDT areas in southern Mali. The need of local administrative officials to settle migrant populations often conflicts with the desire of local village authorities to control encroachment by outsiders (Ould Sidi Mohamed, 1992:184). The imprecision in the law means that outcomes can rest on the relative capacity of settlers or village authorities to bribe government officials (Toulmin, 1992:202–3) or on realizing *de jure* rights through *de facto* occupation – for example, in CMDT areas, where holders of customary rights have expanded the areas ploughed 'to occupy all the land they possess under customary law so as to prevent other farmers from taking it over' (Maiga et al., 1995:51).

Secondly, the CDF failed to define a role for customary rights in future natural resource management, maintaining instead the French colonial view of eventual conversion of customary rights into private property rights through a process of registration (*concession rurale*) and development (*cahier des charges*), involving fencing and other investment. This demands literacy and finance, which effectively restricts private property (*titre foncier*) in Mali to residential and business premises in urban areas (Riddell, 1986:115), while an estimated 90 per cent of cultivated land remains under customary tenure (Maiga et al., 1995:30).

Within the discourse of environmental conservation, the status of 'customary tenure' has been elevated in the past two decades. Whereas President Moussa Traoré was able to represent to international funding agencies the punitive policing of tree cutting as proof of his government's environmental credentials (Ribot, 1995:32), environmental degradation and conflict are now more commonly attributed to the weakness of local customary authority in the face of state appropriation or outside encroachment. This, coupled with continued expansion of opportunities for cash cropping (of which food crops are often the most important), coincides with trends of increasing individualization of control over land and labour and of substitution of reciprocal by exclusive rights of access to land and water. In the interior (Niger) delta, Moorehead (1989:265–7) and Crowley (1991:31) reported that *dioro* and other powerful individuals or groups have increasingly asserted exclusive rights over the use of or rent from the more productive grazing areas. Elsewhere, reports of land sales and of intervillage disputes over land provide evidence of further contestation of customary tenure (Soumaré et al., 1995).

Such findings may be interpreted as contested transformations of 'customary tenure', as indicated in our research on the Sourou floodplain, where historically settlements were relatively isolated both locally, because of the Samori woodland, and regionally, because of their location at the periphery of the states based at Ségou or Macina. The Tiondougou and Ouladougou entities of the Samori concentrated authority at the level of the village. Yet present-day village communities in the Sourou, for the past half-century at least, have been closely linked through migration to urban centres in Mali and throughout West Africa. This has an impact on village society, socially, economically and culturally.

This is manifest to some extent in the testimony of villagers' aspirations as consumers, but also in interpretations of 'customary' hereditary rights as the landlord's right to charge rents – justified by explicit reference to commercial practice in towns and plantations. The opportunity to charge rent arises because floodplain land is limited but has become very productive, and hereditary rights over it are rather narrowly distributed in comparison with the number of its users. In Songoré, only 9 per cent of households had no hereditary rights to land in the floodplain, but the large number of immigrants and seasonal cultivators in this part of the Samori cultivated 36 per cent of the village's floodplain land in 1995. In Oula, there are fewer immigrants, but 31 per cent of village households have no hereditary rights on the floodplain. The study provided evidence that holders of customary land rights are inclined to substitute 'obligations' to loan land to kin or fellow villagers by more market-orientated sharecropping arrangements with outsiders from the Seno or beyond. More generally, the trend towards loaning land on an annual, rather than an indefinite, basis was considered to be exploitative by many borrowers. Since the terms of land transactions suggest that even indefinite loans involved substantial 'considerations' (in the form of labour or part of the harvest) offered by the borrower to the lender of the land, what the annual loan introduced was not the principle of payment but the insecurity of competition, with the threat of needing to find a new plot for next year inflating levels of payments.

Rather than addressing the nature and consequences of such changes in the interpretation of 'custom', current proposals for reform reproduce a dichotomy between 'modern' and 'customary', which effectively questions the legitimacy of both. The existence of 'customary' tenure emphasizes the external imposition of colonial (and by implication post-independence) government, whereas the existence of 'modern' (private) tenure suggests an unfinished process of transformation of 'customary' tenure. This dichotomy can be perceived in plans to reform the governance of land and water by decentralization, which leave intact all the ambiguities of relations between 'modern' elected government and 'customary' hereditary authority.

Decentralization and the state

An important plank in the reforms promised by the Third Republic in its new constitution, approved by referendum in 1992, is democratization and decentralization. The latter is presented as a necessary reversal of the centralization of power since independence: the First Republic's replacement of 'customary' chiefs of *cantons* by centrally appointed *commandants* in charge of *arrondissements*; and the 'deconcentration' of government ministries, enacted in 1981, consolidating central authority at *cercle* and *arrondissement* levels (Hall et al., 1991:10–11).

By 1996, two areas of reform were in progress: the reform of government departments responsible for natural resource management in rural areas, and the transfer of powers and resources to elected *Collectivités Territoriales* (CT) at the level of *région, cercle* and *commune* – the latter replacing the *arrondissement* level of administration. Under the *Code des Collectivités Territoriales* of 1995, each CT is a legally recognized entity (*personalité morale*), with fiscal authority to levy local taxes and charges for services, and to enter loan or other funding agreements with development agencies. Moreover, the legislation states that no CT has control over another, so that *communes* are not subordinate to *cercles* or *régions*, but have different areas of responsibility. The first elections to the councils of the *communes*, originally scheduled for 1996, eventually took place in 1998, and the operation of decentralized government in practice remains unclear in some details.

Three important issues are, first, the balance of authority between the elected council and mayor, on the one hand, and, on the other, local officers of central ministries (e.g. education, health) answering to a centrally appointed official (*délégué*) responsible for ensuring the rule of law and observance of the national interest in the activities of the elected council of the *commune*. Secondly, while elected councils are now to be responsible for providing primary education, health services and water supply within their *communes*, it is unclear how existing tax income, notably from the *minimum fiscale* (poll tax) and livestock tax, which are collected by *chefs de village* but accounted as national revenue (Hall et al., 1991), will be divided between *communes* and central government. Finally, the reform of local government has left the lowest tier – the village – untouched, and the interface between customary (village) authority and the elected council of the *commune* is unclear. In the proposed *communes rurales,* the *chef de village* will continue to be nominated by the (central) state representative (*délégué*), not by the elected council. The lack of clarity in the relationship between *commune* and village is compounded by confusion over the role of decentralized authorities in matters of land tenure: some sources claim that land tenure reform is part of the decentralization process, while others locate it in the redrafting of the CDF undertaken by the Ministry of Finance – a process much delayed and still incomplete at the time of writing.

In Bankass at the time of fieldwork, the first phase of defining the new *communes* had been completed prior to elections for their new councillors. Two members of the *cercle* administration had attended a training programme in Mopti. On their return, they organized a workshop for all *chefs d'arrondissement* and *notables* (usually prominent customary authorities) from the *arrondissements* of Bankass *cercle* to establish a boundary commission (*commission de découpage*) and teams to disseminate information to villages about the choices they needed to make about joining a *commune*. In practice, the existing *chefs d'arrondissement* provided almost half of the membership of the boundary commission, and participation by non-government entities was minimal. In contrast to other parts of Mali, public discussion of decentralization issues was limited, being excluded from local-language broadcasts by the local Bankass radio station, for example.

Five of the existing seven *arrondissements* were proposed for simple conversion into *communes*. Of the other two, Diallassagou, with a total of 76 villages, was split into four future *communes*, of which at least two (Tori and Lessagou) effectively reconstituted the jurisdiction of colonial *cantons*, while Kani-Bonzon was split into two *communes*. One of these, grouping 35 villages centred on the ancient village of Djimbal, reconstituted a precolonial entity concerned with tree and forest management, the *Alamodiou* (Konaté and Tessougué, 1996). Whether more time for discussion of these opportunities would have prompted more villages to reconfigure *commune* boundaries differently from those of the *arrondissements*, and whether this would have had a positive impact on land disputes in the Sourou valley, for example, remains an open question. Late in the process, it was rumoured that Songoré had joined Pissa in a bid to form a new *commune* that would have reduced its administrative ties with its neighbour Baye.

In the event, the *arrondissement* of Baye is to become a *commune* with no change of the existing boundaries. Among local administrative officials, there is some scepticism about the impact of decentralization. One said he felt the political culture in the Samori was 'not mature', contrasting local institutions with those in other parts of Mali, such as the CMDT zone, where he said the management of significant resources by the *associations villageoises* had fostered the development of a more democratic local culture. Others had reservations about the capacity of *communes* in relatively poor areas such as Bankass to generate sufficient tax revenue to support the services for which they would be responsible.

An important part of the government's decentralization programme is democratization through the electoral process. The dominance of the state by single parties in the First and Second Republics meant that the general secretary of the party often wielded as much, if not more, authority at *cercle* and *arrondissement* level than the *commandant*. Moreover, party and kinship often overlapped so that party committees at village level provided links between the *chef de village* and party secretaries in the *cercle* and *arrondissement*. The multiparty elections for *députés* to the National Assembly of the Third Republic in 1992 already presented a stark contrast to earlier elections. Instead of the presentation of candidates in a single delegation accompanied by the *commandant* of the *arrondissement*, villagers were now subject to many visits from competing candidates, none accompanied by officials.

In the event, Bankass's two elected *députés* in 1992 were from the Parti pour la Démocratie et le Progrès (PDP), mainly because one of the candidates was known to and endorsed by *chefs de village*, having been elected in the previous election as a candidate for the ruling UDPM. One of the two then switched allegiance to the ruling ADEMA party and, in the 1997 election, all candidates elected (increased from two to three) were from the ruling party, ADEMA. In this and other respects, little appears to have changed from the days of the Second Republic. Those elected were a teacher in Bankass, a retired teacher in Diallassagou and an employee in a Bamako publishing enterprise, originally from Sokoura. Of thirteen candidates elected since 1979, all but two were current or retired public employees (teachers, nurses, administrators) and only one is described as a peasant; all were born within Bankass *cercle*, except one from the Bandiagara plateau, although two lived in Bamako. In 1997, the failure of any one candidate to win the endorsement of *chefs de village* in some cases resulted in a split in village loyalties, often along lines of lineage (*quartier*), which was a source of continuing animosity after the election, manifest in increasingly acrimonious disputes over land rights, among other things. It is unclear at this stage whether party political differences in Mali provide any electoral consequences at village level beyond factional advantage, but clearly they have the potential to introduce a new dimension to the interplay between 'modern' administrative and 'customary' village authorities.

Our study of rice cultivation in the Sourou valley indicated that government agencies had no involvement in allocating land and played little role in decisions about changing resource use, such as the clearing of forest in the Sourou valley for rice cultivation. Indeed, although the state is the nominal owner of the land in the Sourou valley, the state's representative, the *chef d'arrondissement* at Baye, had to obtain his rice field as a loan from the customary authorities of the village.

The role of state agencies is more visible in regulating relationships between different groups of resource users. Instances of this included the following:

- Ratification of proposals for establishing new hamlets under the jurisdiction of existing villages.
- Redesignation of a 'hamlet' as an official village (i.e. with a *chef de village* responsible for tax collection) – rare in recent years.
- Intervention to prevent armed confrontation between villagers of Karé and Kawéré over disputed land rights in the floodplain.
- Fines applied to pastoralists for encroachment of herds on rice fields.
- Assistance to pastoralists seeking to maintain access to the river by negotiating with village authorities to define corridors for herds to move through zones occupied by rice fields.
- Action to restrain encroachment of cultivation on established grazing areas by refusing authorization for new cultivators' hamlets.

These instances make it clear that the role of local administration is largely one of policing, with the aim of maintaining order and ensuring that the rural population is fully registered for taxation purposes. Interventions to restrain one group of resource users from encroaching on another seem limited to these goals, and the role of state agencies is therefore largely reactive, with little evidence of engagement by research and extension agencies, for example, with the nature or purpose of changes in rural resource use.

Decentralization is an important element in the reform of government services, which has grouped all aspects of natural resource management in rural areas under a single Ministry of Rural Development and the Environment. This is visible in the reform of the Forest Code in 1994, which received considerable priority given the manifest hostility to the forestry service in rural areas as a result of abusive levy of fines under Moussa Traoré's government. While retaining forest reserves under direct management of the Direction Nationale des Eaux et Forêts (DNEF), the new code allocates 'protected forests' – most of the remainder of wooded areas – to the control of CT. It thereby offers the prospect of a *commune* sharing with DNEF revenues for woodcutting permits in woodland within the *commune*'s jurisdiction (Ribot, 1995), and also allows up to 60 per cent of revenue from such permits to be retained by locally appointed woodland management bodies (*structures rurales de gestion*) who could be local village authorities (Dennison and Thomson, 1992; McLain and Sankaré, 1993; Konaté and Tessougué, 1996). However, as noted above, the current decentralization programme does not define relations between the *commune* council and village authorities. The only legally recognized village authority is the administrative chief (*chef de village*), whose appointment will continue to be negotiated between the customary village authority and the local delegate of the central government. The decentralization programme excludes from legal recognition the principal authorities governing natural resource use: the *Massaké* and lineage leaders who hold customary hereditary land rights. Conversely, although the *commune* is to have authority over resources (notably forest) within its 'domain', it is unclear whether this includes land claimed by customary village authorities.

Village-level governance: gestion de terroir villageois

Since 1991 there has been an interregnum between the withdrawal of active policing of natural resource management by the (central) government's forestry service and the devolution to *communes rurales*. Over this period, the standing of village authorities has been enhanced by internationally funded approaches to supporting agricultural production through *gestions et aménagements de terroir villageois* and by the many NGO actions in the Samori and Seno focused on village-level organization. The largest such intervention is the *Programme de Gestion de Ressources Naturelles* (PGRN), funded by the World Bank within the Ministry of Rural Development and the Environment. The programme's main actions are implementing a methodology of village-level land management, widely known as the *aménagement de terroir/gestion de terroir* (AT/GT), or GT, approach. An earlier programme in Mali, Gerenat, funded by the German agency GTZ, used the same methodology and the two programmes were merged.

The GT approach uses a model of decentralized management (*gestion*) and improvement (*aménagement*) of resources at the level of *terroir*: 'a socially defined space, containing a bundle of resources and associate rights within which a community is assumed to satisfy most of its needs' (Toulmin, 1994:3). The approach aimed to provide a way of linking local-level action with broader environmental policy goals; to integrate sectoral aspects of resource use (water, forestry, agriculture and livestock); to ensure voluntary participation of local populations at all stages; to use a long-term planning time frame; and to recognize security of land rights as a prerequisite for local investment in natural resource management (Evers, 1994:7).

The PGRN in Bankass started in 1993 and is based at the local offices (*cantonnement*) of the DNEF. It is implemented by a *cellule locale*, made up of local (*cercle*) directors of government services for agriculture, livestock and cooperatives, and chaired by the *cercle* director of DNEF. In addition to these government officials, the *cellule* is advised by a programme officer: the *Chargé d'Appui Technique* (CAT). The PGRN pays the salary of the CAT, and also for motorcycles, fuel and expenses for fourteen staff of government livestock, agriculture, cooperatives and health services in selected *arrondissements* (Baye, Ouenkoro, Ségué and Bankass-central). The role of the *cellule locale* is to support the development of village-level resource-management plans: *terroir* is thus taken as equivalent to the jurisdiction of the customary village authorities. The methodology used (PGRN–Gerenat, 1993) is organized in four principal steps:

1. *Préparation*: identifying villages for the programme; initial consultations with villagers and creating a committee of villagers (*Comité Villageois de Gestion de Ressources Naturelles*); identifying a multidisciplinary team to work with the villagers.
2. *Diagnostics*: initially separated into parallel villagers' and technical diagnostic activities to identify and map village resources and resource-management priorities.
3. *Elaboration de plan de gestion de terroir*: a series of planning steps involving mapping where particular actions are required (*schema d'aménagement*), and a plan for

implementing them (*plan d'aménagement de terroir*), including supporting actions such as training and funding, and a plan for subsequent management (*plan de gestion de terroir*).

4. *Exécution*: implementing the planned actions, and monitoring and evaluation.

In early 1996, the first two steps had been completed in six villages selected by the *cellule locale,* and work on the *plan d'aménagement de terroir* was in progress for two of them.

The work of the diagnostic stage, based on the francophone version of participatory rural appraisal (*méthode accelerée de recherche participative* (MARP)), was supported by the provision of enlarged aerial photographs of the village lands. A written report of the MARP findings for Baye (PGRN, 1993) suggests that the methodology is effective in identifying the broad outline of resource use in the village and priority problems. However, the MARP report makes no mention of land tenure issues, or even of cultivation of land within the *terroir* by outsiders, even though our study showed this to be a key factor governing land management. In moving from diagnostics to planning, moreover, the PGRN in Bankass confronts a number of problems.

The first concerns the interpretation of 'participation' in the programme. The MARP in Baye involved an interdisciplinary team of six working with villagers for six days. The development of the *schema d'aménagement* involves further consultation with villagers, but the subsequent steps appear to be more centralized (the documentation of the *schema d'aménagement* is sent to PGRN in Bamako for processing, as the Bankass team have difficulty allocating sufficient time and do not have the information technology (IT) capability considered necessary), more technical and more prescriptive. A second issue of the extent of 'participation' concerns the composition of the *Comité Villageois de Gestion de Ressources Naturelles*. In Baye, this committee was effectively the same as the customary authority of the village. In the light of our findings, this evidently excludes representation of the interests of many existing resource users, such as pastoralists, settlers and sharecroppers.

Many of these observations confirm experience of implementation of GT elsewhere (Evers, 1994). This indicates a failure to deal adequately with differentiation within rural communities, with consequent under-representation of those with secondary rights of access to resources and entrenchment of local hierarchies on the *Comité Villageois de Gestion de Ressources Naturelles*. An important further limit to the impact of PGRN in Mali is that the GT programme is not linked to the wider programme of government decentralization. Thus, the GT focuses on decision-making structures at village level, which have no legal standing (except for tax collection) within the framework for decentralized government, in which the *commune* is the smallest representative unit. This presents the problem that while the resource-management decisions of the *Comité Villageois de Gestion de Ressources Naturelles* remain outside the constitutional framework of decentralized government, it is unlikely that such decisions will be defended by the state as legally binding. This seriously weakens the credibility of GT as a means of improving local governance of natural resources in Mali.

The 'pluralist' village model: democracy and legitimacy

Since the mid-1980s a number of internationally funded NGOs – SOS Sahel in the *cercle* of Bankass, and the Cooperative for American Relief to Everywhere (CARE) International and the Near East Foundation (NEF) in the neighbouring *cercles* of Koro and Doenza, respectively – have been active in funding and implementing a regional network for improving local resource management in the Seno and Samori. Decentralization, begun by the new government in 1993, has provided further scope for this work, and a series of workshops in 1993 and 1994 explored an institutional analysis and design framework for developing local institutions for resource management (ARD, 1992; CARE/Mali, 1994; Thompson and Coulibaly, 1994). Three features of the approach are important here. First, the approach seeks legal recognition for rural local resource-management organizations, whether village-level or supra-village entities, such as the customary tree and woodland management authorities, the *Alamodiou, Ogakana* and *Waldé Kelka*. Recognition of these organizations would include allowing them to set rules of access (e.g. to woodland) and to make arrests and apply sanctions for infractions. Possible routes to legal recognition under existing legislation include the constitution of these organizations as cooperatives (1988 legislation) or as private associations (1959 legislation). Either way, the right to fine or otherwise punish transgressors is likely to be seen as problematic – a form of 'private justice' to which state authorities would be opposed.

A second theme to emerge from the 1994 workshop is that the definition of decentralized collective entities (*la délimitation des collectivités dites 'décentralisés'*) should be 'adapted to the local socio-economic conditions'. This means that, where appropriate, the village should be legally recognized as a *collectivité*. In this way, the NGO approach addresses the problem exposed by the GT experience: that customary (village) authorities that control natural resource use have no legal recognition within the decentralized system of government.

A third theme, essential to support the proposed recognition of villages as *collectivités*, addresses issues of power within them. Villages consist of many institutions, which each exercise some power. Effectively, therefore, the village is a plural entity, with no one group or individual monopolizing power, and the role of the village chief is to coordinate and arbitrate. This, it is argued, provides a structure that can control abuses of power and provide alternative pathways by which villagers can seek recourse against what they see as injustice within the village.

This conceptualization of the village as a plural entity offers scope for NGOs concerned with equity to engage in partnership with social groups for whom rights are fundamentally hierarchical, rather than universal. While acknowledging that village institutions currently do not adequately represent the interests of certain groups (women, pastoralists), it allows the possibility that a plural village power structure can permit innovation to enable its institutions to become both more effective and more inclusive in managing natural resources.

The main tasks for NGOs to emerge from this approach are to mediate between government and rural organizations in order to secure legal recognition for the latter, and to encourage the evolution of village organization towards the plural model. Some progress has already been made towards the former, with the signature of local natural resource management 'subcontracts' between the local officials of DNEF and local woodland management groups. In each case, an NGO (CARE/Mali in Koro and SOS Sahel in Bankass) has been a third signatory to the agreement, effectively offering some guarantees to the government side.

It is too early to say how successful this approach will be, but it is perhaps significant that its principal exercise to date focuses on tree and woodland resources, and particularly on regulating the clearing of woodland in the Samori for agricultural expansion. The relevance of the approach to issues identified in rice cultivation in the Sourou valley may be limited, because flooded areas for rice-growing are much more limited and much more easily subject to individual control than woodland resources. Our study indicates that this approach faces considerable obstacles where the governance of floodplain resources is concerned. In particular, the village *terroir* may contain large numbers of immigrant cultivators, who are a majority of the population within the jurisdiction of some villages of the Sourou valley. These immigrants, together with pastoralists whose grazing lands are claimed by village authorities, are unrepresented within the customary authority of the village and their rights are subordinate to hereditary customary rights. Moreover, one of the most valuable resources, the floodplain land used for rice cultivation, is held by a minority who, in some villages, show an inclination to allocate it according to market criteria rather than those of community solidarity.

For the 'pluralist' model of village governance to work requires either full representation within the village councils of the interests of those, such as immigrants and pastoralists, who are currently excluded, or their consitution as separate *collectivités* with autonomy to manage their own land. The conflicts described above show that this is an extremely sensitive area, and one in which existing government structures have proved ineffective in resolving (as opposed to containing) disputes or in providing assistance for negotiated reform. It appears inescapable that future intervention, whether by *communes* or by NGOs, must deal with the need for reform of land tenure. This is most urgent on rice-growing lands, where a climate of mistrust constitutes a barrier to any reform of hereditary rights in favour of cultivator's rights.

It is possible that linking tenure reform to investment in improved water control, such as that envisaged by FENU, might be a means of creating a 'win–win' scenario, in which hereditary landholders give up certain rights in return for improved productivity and the opportunities for diversification that investment in water control could bring. This may be optimistic, however, as the experience of imposed tenure reform under state development schemes (ODRs) elsewhere in Mali led to the general view that *aménagement* is a zero-sum game, in which those with hereditary rights lose and those without such rights (such as immigrants and seasonal cultivators) win. Failure to achieve negotiated reform threatens the legitimacy of outcomes and their subversion by a continuing 'deeper' legitimacy of 'customary' rights.

References

ARD (1992) *Decentralization and Local Autonomy: Conditions for Achieving Sustainable Natural Resource Management*, Vols I and II. USAID/Associates in Rural Development, Burlington, Vermont.

CARE/Mali (1994) 'Actes de l'atelier sur les institutions locales et la gestion des ressources naturelles renouvelables'. 22–25 February, Sevaré, mimeo.

Chenevix-Trench, P., Tessougué, M. & Woodhouse, P. (1997) *Land, Water and Local Governance in Mali: Rice Production and Resource Use in the Sourou Valley, Bankass Cercle*. Rural Resources Rural Livelihoods Working Paper No. 6, Institute for Development Policy and Management, University of Manchester, Manchester.

Cissé, S. (1985) 'Land tenure and development in the Niger delta of Mali'. In: Hill, A. (ed.) *Population, Health and Nutrition in the Sahel*. KPI, London, 140–51.

Critchley, W. (1991) *Pour protéger nos terres: conservation des eaux et du sol en Afrique sub-Saharienne*. Oxfam, Oxford.

Crowley, E. (1991) *Resource Tenure in Mali: An Anthropological Analysis of Local Institutions*. Club du Sahel and OECD, Paris.

Davies, S. (1996) *Adaptable Livelihoods. Coping with Food Insecurity in the Malian Sahel*. Macmillan Press, Basingstoke.

de Frahan, B. & Diarra, M. (1987) *Résultats de l'enquête préliminaire en Cinquième Région du Mali. La Plaine Seno et le Plateau de Bandiagara*. Institut de l'Economie Rurale, Bamako.

Dennison, S. & Thomson, J. (1992) *Decentralization and Natural Resources Management: Mali Field Report. Decentralization and Local Autonomy: Conditions for Achieving Sustainable Natural Resource Management*, vol. II. Decentralization: Finance and Management Project. USAID/Associates in Rural Development, Burlington, Vermont.

DNEF (1990) *Notice de cercle*. Cercle de Bankass, Région de Mopti, PIRL, Direction National d'Eaux et Forêts, Bamako.

DNSI (1980) *Recensement général de la population 1976, résultats définitifs*. Vol. III. *Repertoire de villages*. Direction National de Statistique et de l'Informatique, Bamako.

DNSI (1990) *Recensement général de la population 1987, résultats définitifs*, Vol. 2. *Repertoire de villages*. Direction National de Statistique et de l'Informatique, Bamako.

Evers, Y. (1994) *Local Institutions and Natural Resource Management in the West African Sahel: Policy and Practice of 'Gestion de Terroir' in the Republic of Mali*. Rural Resources Rural Livelihoods Working Paper No. 5, Institute for Development Policy and Management, University of Manchester, Manchester.

FENU (1992) *Mission d'identification du programme du Fonds d'Equipement des Nations Unies. Rapport Provisioire*. FAO/Investment Centre, Rome.

Gallais, J. (1975) *Pasteurs et paysans du Gourma: la condition sahélienne*. Mémoires du Centre d'Etudes de Géographie Tropicale du Centre National de la Recherche Scientifique, Paris.

Gana, D. (1995) *Etude sur l'exploitation rizicole dans la vallée du Sourou: contraintes et stratégies d'amélioration*. Mémoire de fin d'étude, Institut Polytechnique Rural de Katibougou, Bankass.

Gosseye, P., Veeneklaas, F. & Stol, W. (1990) 'Pluviométries et zones pluviométriques'. In: Cissé, S. and Gosseye, P. (eds) *Compétition pour les ressources limitées: le cas de la cinquième région du Mali. Rapport I: Ressources naturelles et population*. CABO, Wageningen, ESPR, Mopti, 9–31.

Hall, R., Magassa, H., Ba, A. & Hodson, J. (1991) *Decentralisation, Service Provision, and User Involvement: Local-level Options in the Republic of Mali. Final Report*, Vol. II. Studies on Decentralization in the Sahel, OECD, and Associates in Rural Development, Burlington, Vermont.

Hulme, M. (1996) 'Climate change within the period of meteorological records'. In: Adams, W., Goudie, P., and Orme, A. (eds) *The Physical Geography of Africa*. Oxford University Press, Oxford, 88–102.

Konaté, A.B. & Tessougué, M. (1996) *La Gestion des ressources naturelles renouvelables dans la Forêt du Samori*. Vol. I: *Eléments de reconnaissance de la forêt du Samori*. Rapport préparé pour le Projet de Protection de l'Environnement, Bankass, SOS Sahel (GB), Bankass.

McLain, R. (1991) *Forest Agent Survey Report No 4. Land Tenure Project Mopti, Mali*. Land Tenure Center, University of Wisconsin, Madison.

McLain, R. & Sankaré, O. (1993) *Decentralized Management of the Segue Forest: Institutional Analysis*. Agriculture and Natural Resources Technical Report Series. CARE International in Mali, Koro.

Maiga, A., Teme, B., Coulibaly, B., Diarra, L., Kergna, A., Tigana, K. & Winpenny, J. (1995) *Structural Adjustment and Sustainable Development in Mali*. Working Paper 82, Overseas Development Institute, London.

Meyer, P., Sacko, B. & Dembele, A. (1993) *Mali profil de pauvreté*. Direction Nationale de la Statistique et de l'Informatique, Bamako.

Moorehead, R. (1989) 'Changes taking place in common-property resource management in the inland Niger delta of Mali'. In: Berkes, F. (ed.) *Common Property Resources*. Belhaven Press, London, 256–72.

Ould Sidi Mohamed, Z. (1992) 'Mali: une réforme à reformer'. In: Le Roy, E. (ed.) *La Mobilisation de la terre dans les stratégies de développement en Afrique noire francophone*. Laboratoire d'Anthropologie Juridique de Paris, Université de Paris I, Paris, 178–96.

PGRN (1993) *Rapport MARP exploratoire de Baye*. Projet de Gestion des Ressources Naturelles, Ministère de l'Environnement, Bamako.

PGRN–Gerenat (1993) *Elaboration d'un plan d'aménagement/plan de gestion des terroirs. Manuel de planification*. Projet de Gestion des Ressources Naturelles, Ministère de l'Environnement, Bamako.

PIRL (1990) *Carte de l'occupation agricole de terres, 1 : 200,000, Coupure 13 Tougan–Ouahigouya. Projet inventaire par télédétection des ressources ligneuses et de l'occupation agricole des terres au Mali*. Cellule d'Inventaire Direction National d'Eaux et Forêts, Ministère de Développement Rurale et de l'Environnement, Bamako.

PIRT (1983) *Projet inventaire des ressources terrestres au Mali*. Vol. 1 *Atlas*. TAMS, for USAID and Government of République du Mali.

Republic of Mali (1994) *Comptes économiques du Mali. Series revisées 1980–91, Résultats provisoires 1992–93–94, Résultats prévisionnels 1995*. Direction Nationale de la Statistique et de l'Informatique, Bamako.

Ribot, J. (1995) *Forestry Sector Policy Report: Mali. Review of Policies in the Traditional Energy Sector (RPTES) Africa Regional Study*. Africa Technical Division, World Bank, Washington, DC.

Riddell, J. (1982) *Land Tenure Issues in West African Livestock and Range Development Projects*. LTC Research Paper 77, Land Tenure Center, University of Wisconsin, Madison.

Riddell, J. (1986) *Country Profiles of Land Tenure*. LTC Research Paper 127, Land Tenure Center, University of Wisconsin, Madison

Ruthven, O. & Koné, M. (1995) 'Bankass, Mali'. In: David, R. (ed.) *Changing Places? Women, Resource Management and Migration in the Sahel*. SOS Sahel UK, London.

Soumaré, S., Traoré, O. & Dolo, O. (1995) *Rapports d'évaluation des séminaires régionaux sur le foncier rural. Partie 1 Aspects organisationnels, administratifs et techniques*. Projet Observatoire du Foncier au Mali, Cellule de Planification et de Statistiques, Ministère du Développement Rural et de l'Environnement, Bamako.

Thompson, J. & Coulibaly, C. (1994) *Decentralisation in the Sahel – Regional Synthesis*. CILSS and Club du Sahel, Paris.

Toulmin, C. (1992) *Cattle, Women and Wells: Managing Household Survival in the Sahel*. Clarendon Press, Oxford.

Toulmin, C. (1994) *Gestion de Terroirs: Concept and Development*. United Nations Sudano-Sahelian Office and International Institute for Environment and Development, London.

UNDP (1994) *Enquête nationale sur les activités économiques (enquête secteur informel)*.Vol. 2: *Synthèse*. Dispositifs Permanents d'Enquêtes auprès des Ménages (PADEM), Direction Nationale de la Statistique et de l'Informatique, Bamako.

Veeneklaas, F. & Stol, W. (1989) *Rainfall data of the 5th Region (Mali)*. CABO/ESPR Document de Travail No. 3, CABO, Wageningen.

3

Uncommon Property
The Scramble for Wetland
in Southern Kenya

CHRISTOPHER SOUTHGATE & DAVID HULME

Introduction

This study explores the dynamics of environmental and social change in southern
Kajiado District, Kenya, and in particular in Loitokitok Division. Loitokitok's
savanna and 'wetland in dryland' areas lie at the foot of Mount Kilimanjaro and
comprise one of the 'classic' landscapes that have fostered the 'myth of wild Africa'
(Adams and McShane, 1992). Both this environment and its users have undergone
profound change in recent times, as the region has been increasingly incorporated
into the Kenyan state and the global economy. The dominant narrative of these
changes has been of environmental degradation (Leach and Mearns, 1996): growing
human populations and herds, which destroy the soil and displace wildlife.
Inevitably, such narratives disguise the complexity of environmental change (Roe,
1995) and misrepresent much of what is happening. A complex web of institutions –
'customary', induced community organizations, local state, national state and private
sector – are involved in determining who has access to the area's resources, how they
are utilized and how use is coordinated and regulated (or not).

The policies of colonial and independent governments have influenced both environmental and social change. However, in Kenya, as elsewhere, there is an extreme
dissonance between policies as officially documented and state practices; inevitably
the latter are inflected by the interests of the powerful and the struggles of the weak.
Fieldwork has repeatedly revealed that policies, plans and institutional frameworks
documented in Nairobi often have very little relationship to what happens 'on the
ground' in Loitokitok. The National Environmental Action Plan (Government of
Kenya, 1994) illustrates this situation: it comprises 14 volumes of detailed
prescription, which has minimal influence over what happens in Kenya's drylands.

While pastoralism remains an important activity in this region and the Maasai remain
the most numerous group, resource access and use have been very complex in recent
decades. Cultivators have migrated into the region, tourism has become an important

activity and the provision of rural services (by both public and private agencies) has become important. Increased competition for resources has fuelled the politics of age grade and clan among the Maasai and, in addition, Maasai–incomer relations have become very politicized and, on occasion, fractious. While competition for resources occurs at the local level more remote actors, especially politicians and businessmen in Nairobi, have a keen interest in and considerable influence on this process.

Research for this study was conducted in 1994, with short follow-up visits in 1995, 1996 and 1998. Data collection focused on the Kimana Group Ranch and included in-depth interviews of 75 household heads (selected to reflect occupational and ethnic diversity within the ranch) and some 30 'key informant' interviews in Kimana, Loitokitok, Kajiado and Nairobi. A wide range of published and unpublished documents were also consulted (for further details, see Southgate and Hulme, 1996c).

The national context

Kenya (Map 3.1) straddles the equator, its very arid northern regions bordering Sudan and Ethiopia (4° N), while its southern border with Tanzania stretches from Lake Victoria to the coast near Pemba Island (5° S). Its topography, with several ranges over 4,000 metres, and the influence of the intertropical convergence zone (ITCZ) mean that it experiences a variety of climates. These range from the hot and humid coastal zone to the temperate central highlands to the vast arid and semi-arid lands of the north and east, and of the south of the country. While population is concentrated in the moister areas, where conditions are favourable for agriculture (central highlands, the undulating plateau of the west of the country and the coast), the bulk of the country's land mass is classified as semi-arid (87,000 km^2 or 15 per cent), arid (127,000 km^2 or 22 per cent) and very arid (226,000 km^2 or 46 per cent) (Darkoh, 1990). Rainfall in these arid areas is unpredictable and there is a cyclical occurrence of prolonged drought (Ottichelo et al., 1991). In addition, the soils in these areas generally have low fertility and a poor capacity to retain water.

At the time of colonial intrusion in the late nineteenth century, Kenya was populated by a variety of different groups, subsequently categorized as distinct 'tribes'. The Bantu speakers had (and continue to have) the largest populations and relied heavily on agriculture – the Kikuyu, Meru, Gusii, Embu, Akamba, Luyha and Mijikenda. The Nilotic language groups – Maasai, Turkana, Samburu, Pokot, Luo and Kalenjin – had a greater focus on cattle-rearing and commonly occupied more arid areas.

During the early colonial period, there were considerable doubts whether East Africa offered the commercial opportunities that Britain had found in other parts of its empire. The perception of a 'barbarous, unmanageable populace … and the absence of any valuable articles of trade that cannot be got vastly cheaper and easier in other parts' (Thomson, 1886:77) meant that little interest was shown in the region. However, around the turn of the century, the commercial potential of Kenya's highlands became more apparent to British government officials.

The bulk of legislation during the early decades of colonial rule focused on property rights within the economically valuable highlands where 'white' settlement was

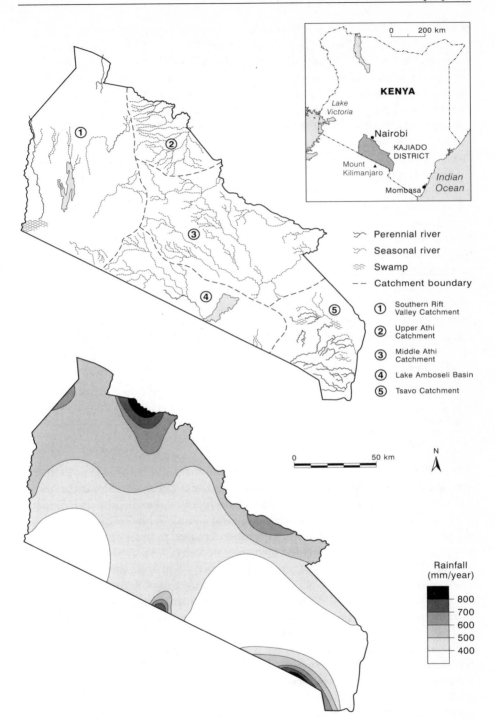

Map 3.1   Kenya: principal rivers & rainfall in Kajiado District

promoted but 'organized opinion' in African-inhabited areas posed a political threat to the administration and settler population (Okoth-Ogendo, 1991). The provision of secure tenure within the 'native reserves', adjudicated on the basis of perceived 'tribal' identities, was seen as a way of appeasing growing discontent. Within the twenty-four 'tribal' reserves demarcated in the early twentieth century, Africans continued to be denied formal property rights and remained 'tenants at will of a demanding and unsympathetic landlord', i.e. the colonial state (Ghai and McAuslan, 1970:90).

Much of Kenya's most productive land was alienated to European settlers. The 'white highlands' comprised less than 4,000 farms and estates covering 3 million hectares of high potential land. Africans were confined to non-scheduled areas, where populations grew relatively rapidly and land became increasingly scarce. By the 1940s, land pressure was believed to be causing economic hardship in the reserves. It posed an increasingly severe political problem for the colonial government (Kitching, 1980) and contributed to the Mau Mau revolt of 1952. A two-pronged plan, presented by Swynnerton (1954), sought to ameliorate land scarcity by reforming the tenure system and intensifying agricultural production in the native reserves.

Central to the Swynnerton Plan was the contention that 'sound agricultural development is dependent upon a system of land tenure which will make available to the African farmer a unit of land and a system of farming ... [requiring] ... security of tenure through an indefeasible title' (Swynnerton, 1954:9). This envisaged individual land ownership, the consolidation of fragmented landholdings and measures to prevent further subdivision through the creation of 600,000 farming units:

> Once registered, farmers will be able to buy and sell land, amongst other Africans only, and to mortgage titles to land against loans from Government or other approved agency ... able, energetic or rich Africans will be able to acquire more land and bad or poor farmers less, creating a landed and a landless class.
>
> (Swynnerton, 1954:9–10)

This, in turn, would lead to employment opportunities and economic growth, in line with the prevailing 'modernization' paradigm of late colonial 'developmentalism'.

As land became increasingly scarce in Kenya's highland districts, arid and semi-arid lands (ASAL) became a focus for agricultural expansion. While definitions vary, the ASAL are generally regarded as having a ratio of rainfall to open pan evaporation of less than 50 per cent (for a detailed discussion of Kenya's ASAL, see Southgate and Hulme, 1996a). Under this definition, 22 districts lie at least partially within the ASAL and comprise some 88 per cent of the total land area of Kenya. Policies specifically aimed at intensifying ASAL production first emerged after the Second World War, initially through the African Land Development Board (ALDEV), established in 1946. ALDEV focused on water development and rangeland management by reducing herd sizes within controlled grazing schemes. Extensive pastoralism remained, in the eyes of the colonial administration, intrinsically harmful to the environment and a constraint on social and economic improvement. Plans to intensify cattle production through the provision of boreholes, cattle dips and veterinary services, supported by research into improving pasture usage, were proposed by central government and development agencies (Rutten, 1992).

The concept of 'group ranching' emerged in the 1950s but was not legislated until after independence in 1963. Group ranches conferred formal property rights on a collective of landowners, represented by an elected committee, while group ranch members retained individual rights over livestock. By introducing formal property rights (each group ranch was awarded a single title), the state introduced the concept of land ownership, replacing indigenous systems of rights limited to access to resources for specific groups and individuals. A Registrar of Group Representatives was appointed to administer group ranches and appropriate legislation was introduced through the Land (Group Representatives) Act, 1968. Group ranches were formed in Kajiado, Narok, Samburu, Kwale, Pokot, Laikipia and Baringo Districts, with populations from thirty to 450 pastoral households (Rutten, 1992).

Over the past three decades, much of the more productive areas within the ASAL, such as the upland peripheries and wetland niches, have fallen under individual control, as Kenya's land registration programme has been implemented (albeit unevenly). The evolving land market in these areas has made land available to cultivators from more densely populated upland districts. Rift Valley Province (within which Kajiado District lies) has witnessed particularly rapid rates of population increase. Much of the land lost to cultivation here long provided dry-season grazing for livestock and wildlife, consequently intensifying pressure on remaining rangelands.

While the highlands dominated the land policy agenda for most of the colonial era, a rapidly growing population, the expansion of cultivation and attempts to commercialize pastoralism brought Kenya's ASAL to the forefront of development policy from the 1960s. Some six million Kenyans (and particularly the least well-off) are today dependent on natural resources in the ASAL. The ASAL also support Kenya's tourist industry, which has replaced agriculture as the country's largest earner of foreign exchange. The 'wetland in dryland' oases in the ASAL and their upland fringes now have considerable economic value for arable agriculture and tourism, besides their great intrinsic ecological value.

The contemporary context for effective environmental management in Kenya is highly problematic. The country's population of 28 million people is growing at more than 3 per cent each year, increasing the pressure on natural resources. Inequality continues to rise and, while a small number of 'big men' accumulate fortunes, some 46 per cent of the population is classified as living in poverty (Government of Kenya, 1999). The mismanagement of the economy and political chicanery by the Moi regime discouraged foreign investment, led to the regular suspension of International Monetary Fund (IMF) and World Bank loans, and persuaded several bilateral aid agencies (including that of the UK) to cease operations with the Kenyan government during the 1990s. MPs, and particularly ministers, use their political status to seize economic opportunities, and corruption has become endemic in the government, the police and the public sector. Worse still, politicians have sought to retain their power and influence by 'playing the ethnic card', which fuels interethnic conflict, especially over access to natural resources. Hopes that the multiparty elections of 1992 and 1997 would usher in an era of 'good governance' faded. Many Kenyans today see the country as on the brink of a political abyss, with an elderly, authoritarian leader finding it difficult to control the dominant KANU party, an opposition characterized by disunity and the ethnic genie let out of the bottle.

Wetlands in drylands: Loitokitok Division (Map 3.2)

The physical environment

Nowhere are the pressures on 'wetland in dryland' areas greater than in Kajiado District (Map 3.1). The district occupies 21,105 km² on the southern slopes of the Kenya highlands and the Rift Valley. Its climate is typical of other semi-arid districts

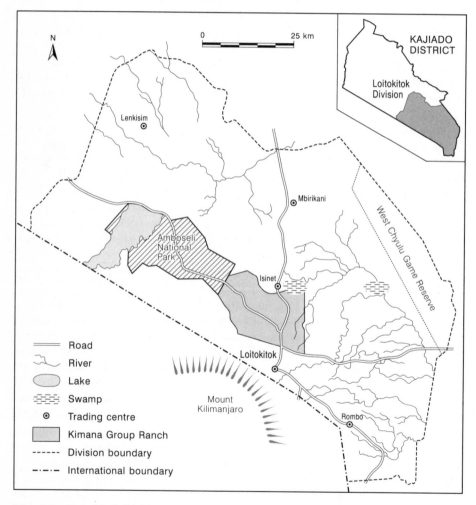

Map 3.2 Loitokitok Division

in Kenya, with temperature and rainfall varying significantly, both spatially and temporally. During the cool months of July and August, average minimum temperatures range between 10°C in Loitokitok and 23°C in Magadi, while maximum mean temperatures during the warmest months of February and March rise to 21°C and 35°C, respectively (KDDP, 1989). Average annual potential evaporation ranges from 1,700 mm to approximately 2,500 mm for the respective stations.

Annual rainfall in the district is generally bimodal, varying from 810 mm at Loitokitok town on the foothills of Mount Kilimanjaro to consistently below 400 mm on the plains only 25 kilometres to the north. Patterns of aridity are determined by topography, with more elevated areas around the Ngong Hills, Mount Kilimanjaro and the Machakos highlands receiving more rainfall. The 'long rains' generally run from March to May, but there appears to be a cycle of years of low rainfall (Lema, 1990). The Maasai in this district recall the 'great famines' of 1934 (*Olomeyu Looloyik*), 1943 (*Eboot Enkurma Nanyokie*) and 1960 (*Eboot Enkurma Sikitoi*).

While Kajiado has a significant area of medium- to high-fertility soils (Ecosystems, 1992), the rainfall–temperature regime allows soil fertility to be utilized only in a limited area. Surface-water resources within Kajiado District are limited, with few perennial watercourses, although the Amboseli basin is characterized by a number of swamps and the permanent Amboseli Lake. The abrupt climatic and physical variations mean that the agricultural potential of Kajiado District varies considerably. Approximately 56 per cent of the land area is marginal for cultivation and 36 per cent has low potential. Only 8 per cent has medium (or greater) arable potential, and cultivation has been economically insignificant until recently.

While the pattern of rainfall in Loitokitok Division, like the rest of Kajiado District, is highly seasonal (Table 3.1), a number of perennial streams and swamps have long provided the Maasai and their livestock, and wildlife, with essential sources of water, pasture and salt during the long dry season. These 'wetland in dryland' environments owe their existence to complex hydrological phenomena. Rainfall and snowmelt on Mount Kilimanjaro infiltrate the porous volcanic rock and emerge from numerous springs on the mountain foothills and in the rangelands below. Spring yields are much more consistent than rainfall patterns (Fig. 3.1). In sum, Loitokitok is characterized by stretches of arid rangeland unsuited to cultivation, broken by intermittent oases of high potential arable land around springs, streams and swamps.

Table 3.1 Mean monthly rainfall at three stations in Loitokitok Division.

	Rainfall (mm)												
	Jan	Feb	Mar	Apr	May	June	July	Aug	Sept	Oct	Nov	Dec	Total
Kimana	58.4	3.2	13.1	13.6	3.5	0.1	0	0.1	0	12.8	23.9	26.0	154.7
Ol Tukai	21.2	23.5	25.1	52.0	12.4	0.4	0.1	0	0	15.4	71.6	58.2	279.9
Loitokitok	61.2	27.6	79.8	140.8	23.0	1.3	2.1	1.7	1.3	54.7	222.9	138.6	755.0

Source: Southgate and Hulme (1996c:4).

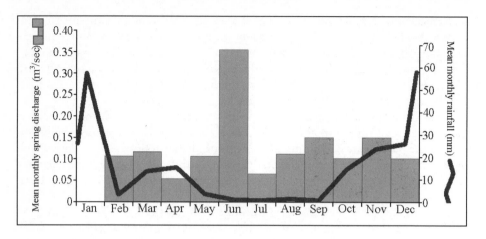

Figure 3.1   Mean monthly rainfall & spring discharge in Loitokitok

Population dynamics

Historically, Kajiado District was home to a predominantly Maasai population. Probably during the eighteenth century, Maa-speaking groups radiated south-westwards across Loita, Mara and Serengeti and south-eastwards across Kajiado as far as the foothills of Kilimanjaro (Sutton, 1993). By the end of the nineteenth century, the Maasai occupied a considerable portion of East Africa, stretching 800 km north to south and over 300 km east to west. It was during these two centuries that modern Maasai social organization is believed to have been formed, with its territorial and age-based forms of resource management. The Maasai in Loitokitok today are members of the Kisonko 'section' (*olosho* sing., *iloshon* pl.), which numbers some 100,000, most of whom are resident in Tanzania.

The population of Kajiado District grew almost eighteen times between 1927 to 1989, and was projected to be 382,495 in 1996 (Republic of Kenya, 1994). This was partly through natural increase and partly, since the 1950s, by the immigration of cultivators from neighbouring districts (Fig. 3.2). Kikuyu from Central Province, Kamba from Machakos and other non-Maasai Kenyans moved into the district in large numbers. This is expected to continue as more land becomes available for acquisition (Republic of Kenya, 1996). The intercensal increase in the population of non-Maasai between 1969 and 1979 of 28,503 represented an annual rate of 7.6 per cent (compared with an official annual increase of Maasai of 4.7 per cent). While the proportion of urban population has been steadily increasing, 89 per cent of Kajiado's population was classed as rural in 1989.

The immigration of non-Maasai into Loitokitok Division gained momentum after the Second World War, when Kikuyu and Luo government officials assigned to the administrative post in Loitokitok Town invited relatives to the area and started clearing small plots for cultivation. Between 1962 and 1989, the proportion of Maasai in the district's population decreased from 78 per cent to 57 per cent, and it is likely

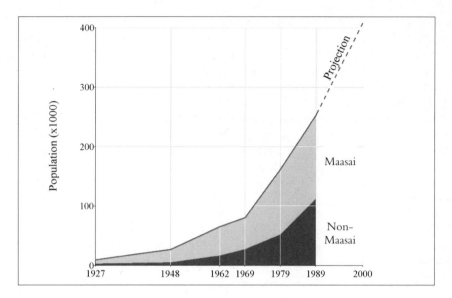

Figure 3.2   Population change in Kajiado District

that now Maasai no longer comprise the majority in Kajiado District. Despite temporary and permanent outmigration (Rutten, 1992), population densities have risen sharply. The population density for Kajiado District in 1979 averaged 7.1 persons per km², while projections for 1996 put the figure at 18.1 persons per km² (Republic of Kenya, 1994). An increase from 7.5 to 18.0 persons per km² was projected for Loitokitok Division over the same period.

The contemporary economy

While cattle-keeping remains the area's most important activity, the economy has diversified greatly in recent decades. For Kajiado District as a whole, livestock 'income' dropped from 34 per cent to 24 per cent of total income between 1987 and 1992, while the share of cultivation rose from 38 per cent to 53 per cent (Republic of Kenya, 1989, 1994). Thirteen of Kajiado District's sixteen small-scale, farmer-managed irrigation schemes fall within Loitokitok Division, covering 1,256 ha farmed by 3,219 families and making Loitokitok Division the third largest irrigation area in Kenya after Mwea Division (Kirinyaga District) and Bura Division (in Tana River District) (IDB, 1994). Onions and tomatoes grown in Loitokitok supply an estimated 70 per cent of the markets in Mombasa and Nairobi. The significance of irrigated horticulture in Loitokitok is also evident from the export revenues of chillies, okra and *karella*: KSh 72 million, KSh 47 million and KSh 50 million, respectively, in 1992 (MALDM, 1993).

There has also been a marked growth in the provision of 'services' – transport, bars, 'hotels', retail shops, sale of firewood – and a number of tourist facilities (hotels and camps) have been established for wildlife viewing. With Amboseli National Park attracting in excess of 200,000 visitors in 1990 and generating over KSh 30 million annually (Western, 1994), the service industry associated with wildlife tourism has become an important source of wage employment. Tourism, however, is poorly integrated in the local economy and much of the wealth, jobs and demand for products it creates accrue outside Kajiado.

As throughout Kenya, there is growing economic inequality, associated with individuals and households increasingly pursuing 'multiple livelihood' strategies. For successful entrepreneurs, this means managing irrigated lands, running transport businesses, trading, operating retail shops, keeping some cattle and perhaps renting out property. In contrast, poorer households attempt to patch together livelihoods from small herds of cattle, gathering natural resources, casual labouring and remittances from relatives in urban areas. For many people life is hard. At the time of initial fieldwork in 1994, government officers in the area believed that many households lacked the means to acquire food, and food relief was being distributed in rural parts of Loitokitok Division.

Management of land and water: the institutional framework

Access to land and water in Loitokitok Division is determined by a complex, and often confused, interplay of customary, state and market institutions. Both colonial and independent governments sought to introduce new institutional forms intended to improve productivity and efficiency. These initiatives have commonly been absorbed into pre-existing institutions, rather than replacing them, adding both complexity and ambiguity to the institutional framework (for detailed examinations of the institutional framework in Kajiado and Loitokitok, see Southgate and Hulme, 1996b, c).

Precolonial and customary authority

Historically, access to natural resources in Maasailand was secured through complex institutional arrangements based on geographical territories, a socio-political age-grade system and kinship. Indicative of the function such arrangements play in mitigating risk in an environment marked by cyclical drought and disease, membership of a particular age set gave every household rights of access to key resources far beyond the locale of its domicile. Such arrangements are vital to the semi-nomadic form of pastoralism practised by the Maasai (Jacobs, 1963).

A hierarchy of resource management organizations can be identified (Fig. 3.3). The Maasai never had a unified political authority. Maasai society consists of 16 or so *iloshon*, many appearing as self-contained ecological units (Spencer, 1990) and each with its own political, social and cultural identity (Evangelou, 1984). Eight *iloshon* lie within the administrative borders of Kajiado District. Within each *olosho*, a secondary tier of organization is based upon *inkutot* (sing. *enkutoto*) or 'localities'. Each *enkutoto* has its own elders' council and socio-political organization and serves as the most important tier of local governance. An *enkutoto* also represents a distinct ecological

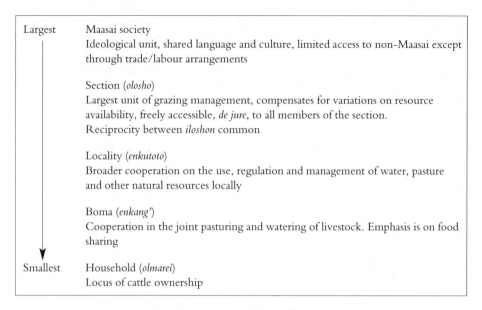

Largest	Maasai society Ideological unit, shared language and culture, limited access to non-Maasai except through trade/labour arrangements
	Section (*olosho*) Largest unit of grazing management, compensates for variations on resource availability, freely accessible, *de jure*, to all members of the section. Reciprocity between *iloshon* common
	Locality (*enkutoto*) Broader cooperation on the use, regulation and management of water, pasture and other natural resources locally
	Boma (*enkang'*) Cooperation in the joint pasturing and watering of livestock. Emphasis is on food sharing
Smallest	Household (*olmarei*) Locus of cattle ownership

Figure 3.3 Territorial levels of Maasai natural resource management

and economic unit encompassing permanent water sources and defined areas of wet- and dry-season grazing. Historically, 'individual families secured rights to the communal resources only by common residence within the same locality over long periods of time and by regular participation, involving specific obligations, in local age-set activities' (Jacobs, 1975:415).

At a more local scale, natural resource management is organized on a residential basis. Maasai reside in thorn-enclosed circular encampments, often referred to by their Swahili name *boma* but locally as *inkangitie* (sing. *enkang'*). Each *enkang'* usually comprises several domestic groups, each consisting of the male head of household and his wives, along with their dependant children and relatives. As an organizational unit, the *enkang'* is dynamic, with domestic groups freely leaving and joining. Resource management within this domestic group is complex and cannot be explored further here.

Customary Maasai resource management is also based upon non-territorial forms of organization, particularly in terms of age sets, which allow greater mobility and provide means of access to distant lands. Each age set represents a 14-year cohort of males, who enter into *murran*hood (or warriorhood) and collectively pass through successive age grades. Age sets form the basis of political and military organization and assume responsibilities for specific economic activities. Males are graded as follows: uncircumcised boys, *ilayiok* (sing. *olayoni*), circumcised young men, *ilmurran* (sing. *olmurrani*), adult men, *ilmoruak* (sing. *olmoruak*), and old men, *iltasati* (sing. *oltasat*). While the latter two categories are often collectively referred to as 'elders', the two grades have different roles and responsibilities.

While the *ilmurran* are more conspicuous than more senior age sets – as a result of their physical appearance and duties associated with livestock herding – resource control rests predominantly with the male elders. Decisions regarding where to graze livestock during the dry and wet seasons are made by councils of elders. Similarly, daily decisions are made by the elder members of the individual *enkang'*. Yet the relationship between power and age is not linear. Control over livestock peaks during the *ilmoruak* age grade and diminishes with ascent into the most senior age grades, whose livestock are distributed among relations (Ndagala, 1992).

Maasai society is also divided along two broad lines of patrilineal decent, the *Orok-kiteng* and the *Odo-mongi*, traced from the two wives of the first Maasai ancestor (Bekure et al., 1991). Each line is divided into seven major clans. Kin and territorial organization can overlap and it is possible to find all clans represented within any one *olosho*. While serving an important role in certain areas of dispute resolution, the clan otherwise has a relatively minor economic and political role. The Kisonko of Loitokitok comprise primarily members of the *Ilaiser*, *Ilaitayok* and *Ilmolelian* clans. As in other areas (Fosbrooke, 1948), the *Ilaitayok* are somewhat different from other clans, with many distinctive ceremonies and rituals.

Resource tenure among the Maasai is based on the interplay of territorial, age- and kin-related forms of social organization, facilitating access to key resources in an environment where survival has long depended upon mobility and reciprocity. The institutions that govern individuals' rights and duties in respect to key pastoral resources – livestock, pasture and water – are equally complex. As Rigby (1985:123) writes:

> such factors as 'private versus communal ownership' of the herds, 'rights in' grazing and water, notions of 'private and individual property', and so on … [result] in considerable semantic confusion and error which tend to leave the debate at what may be called an ideological level.

Galaty (1981:70) likewise suggests that 'the notion of "ownership" often does violence to relations of production in pastoral societies and fails to provide an adequate account of the agency involved in the link between persons and material objects'. Prestige and political power lie not in the ownership of livestock – over which Maasai have limited exclusive individual rights – but in control over its disposal and exchange. Thus ownership rights – to the extent that they occur – are less important than rights of control. Maasai social relations are inextricably linked to resource exchange, and honour and status customarily reflect an individual's propensity and ability to give (Galaty, 1981).

Colonial policies

During the twentieth century, Maasai institutions were systematically eroded. Colonial officials first perceived little economic or political utility in gaining control of the Maasai or Maasailand, but soon prioritized sedentarization of the Maasai. In 1904, the Maasai were confined to two reserves – one to the north on the Laikipia plateau and one to the south of Nairobi – thus denying them access to what had been their most productive land. In 1911, the Maasai inhabiting the northern reserve were relocated to an enlarged southern reserve (Sandford, 1919); again, much of the land lost was of relatively high productivity. During these two 'moves', an estimated 10,000 Maasai, 200,000 head of cattle and 500,000 small stock were relocated (Sandford, 1919). Following the 'moves', the Maasai had access to few perennial sources of water or pasture, with almost all permanent watercourses under European settler control (Sindiga, 1984), and much of the rangeland in the reserves was uninhabitable owing to tsetse infestation (Lewis, 1934).

A number of late colonial ranching schemes were established in Kajiado under ALDEV, but by 1960 all such schemes had failed (Sindiga, 1984:30). One of the largest sectional grazing schemes was introduced in the Kisonko section of Loitokitok on some 650,000 hectares. Grazing controls were enforced by grazing committees, based on existing clan-based organization. However, drought in 1956 resulted in the scheme being abandoned. Indeed, the colonial administration itself acknowledged that 'owing to the vagaries of the rains it cannot be expected that an even pattern for grazing control will ever be achieved in Il Kisongo' (KDAR, 1957:16).

Concerns over wildlife conservation also shaped land and natural resource policy during the colonial era and have continued to do so to today. The creation of wildlife conservation areas further denied the Maasai access to key resources. Following the National Parks Ordinance of 1945, Maasai were restricted from entering Nairobi and Tsavo National Parks and, since its establishment in 1975, Amboseli National Park has developed into one of Kenya's foremost wildlife attractions. Access to Amboseli has become the subject of a highly charged debate between the Maasai, the Kenya Wildlife Service (KWS) and Olkejuado County Council (which earned 75 per cent of its income from hunting and booking fees prior to the park's nationalization in 1972). Relations between communities surrounding Amboseli and KWS have fluctuated markedly over the past two decades in response to the government's changing stance towards 'community conservation' (Western, 1998).

Policies since independence

The post-independence era introduced further major institutional changes in Maasailand, and particularly so in Kajiado District. Unlike local government in neighbouring Narok District – which has retained control over the Maasai Mara and the revenues it generates – Olkejuado (Kajiado) County Council now plays a minor role throughout Kajiado District. Since losing its income from Amboseli National Park, the county council's activities have been reduced and, as in much of Kenya, the county council has become an 'appendage of the central government' (Oyugi, 1983:123).

The District Focus for Rural Development policy, introduced in 1983, provides the framework of decentralized government. Sectoral departments are officially represented throughout the hierarchy of district, divisional and locational administrative units. In reality staff from the Ministries of Environment and Natural Resources, Agriculture, Livestock Development and Marketing, and Land Reclamation, Regional and Water Development rarely have the resources or motivation to venture outside their divisional compounds in Loitokitok Town. The National Environment Secretariat and the Permanent Presidential Commission on Soil Conservation and Afforestation, key agencies of national environmental policy, have limited impact on environmental management in rural Kenya. State presence at the local level is most conspicuous in the activities of chiefs and their assistants, responsible for promoting 'the effective and efficient operation of government' (KDDP, 1994:189). Chiefs are government appointees and their authority is often subordinate to that of customary leaders.

Access to land in Loitokitok since independence has been much less affected by changes in the local state than by the creation of a unique organizational structure: the group ranch. At independence, the question of 'appropriate' land tenure in the rangelands began to dominate policy discussions, given mounting concerns over the perceived 'destruction' of Maasailand (Glover and Gwynne, 1961). The Lawrence Mission of 1965–6 proposed the creation of group ranches to overcome the problem. Leland Fallon, the range management adviser to the influential US Agency for International Development (USAID), supported the proposal: 'the era of unregulated and free use of the land resources in the Kajiado District should be terminated as soon as possible through the formation of Land Use Commissions, Cooperatives or Corporations under proper legal authority' (quoted in Rutten, 1992:269). Fallon, like many foreign advisers, clearly failed to recognize or understand the regulatory institutions developed by the Maasai over several centuries.

The first group ranches in Kenya were established in Kajiado District in 1968 under the Kenya Livestock Development Project (KLDP), sponsored by the World Bank. The concept of group titling required new legislation in the form of the Land (Group Representatives) Act and the Land Adjudication Act. Believing that common property led to overgrazing, inefficient use of resources and low levels of investment, policy-makers assumed that the group ranch, as a form of collective private property, would stimulate the development of a 'modern' ranching sector (Galaty, 1992). The *modus operandi* of group ranch development is summarized in Box 3.1.

The first and second phases of the KLDP (1968–74 and 1975–8) established twenty-eight group ranches, supported by World Bank loans for infrastructural development, particularly water supply. While 'relatively little attention was paid to the existing, traditional herd management system and the need for mobility in times of drought' (Grandin et al., 1989:245), the concept of group ownership was generally popular among the Maasai (Campbell, 1986; Munei, 1991). Above all, it provided security at a time when, following independence, many Maasai feared the loss of rights over their remaining land.

Box 3.1 The group ranch model

- Extending freehold tenure to each ranch, with a single title held by group representatives.
- Registering members, who were to be excluded from other ranches.
- Allocating grazing quotas, based on calculated carrying capacities for each ranch.
- Developing infrastructure through the provision of loans secured against the land title.
- Individualizing livestock production and providing loans for stock improvements.
- Creating a committee to enforce grazing quotas and maintaining the integrity of group ranch borders (Bekure et al., 1991).

At the same time as government promoted the group ranch model, a policy of converting communal lands to individual holdings was pursued under the auspices of the land registration programme. This focused on lands that were most productive for cultivation or commercial ranching. In Loitokitok, over 16,000 ha were allocated to Maasai leaders and government officials (Campbell, 1978). The creation of individual ranches gained momentum following disastrous stock losses during 1960 and 1961, and by the early 1970s some sixty individual ranches, averaging 600 ha, had been titled in Maasailand (Evangelou, 1984). The educated, the wealthy and those close to the loci of power staked their claims to the largest, more productive plots through opaque transactions shaped by personal networks and bribery (Galaty, 1992).

This process of individualization has been pervasive, and pastoralists have seen access to rangeland dwindle as group ranches have been subdivided, exacerbated by the alienation of areas for conservation. Thus:

> It is now clear that the major problems of livestock development in Kajiado District [are] no longer those of management of group ranches but those of coping with the breakdown of group ranches. In particular, the subdivision of group ranches, further subdivision of resultant parcels by owners and eventual sale of land [are] emerging as more urgent problems.
>
> (Munei, 1991:2)

It is increasingly common for individualized plots to be fenced, thus confining and concentrating movements of cattle and wildlife. While many group ranches have yet to proceed with subdivision, spontaneous, illegal individualization of land is increasingly common. Within the group ranches of Loitokitok (Table 3.2), members have voted in favour of subdivision. While this has not formally commenced, much of the upland and wetland areas are being 'claimed' by individuals, fenced and managed in much the same way as those areas formally registered to individuals (e.g. Isinet, Namelok, Kisanjani and Olorika). Fifty per cent of Rombo Group Ranch, for example, has already been divided in this way and leased to Chagga cultivators from Tanzania. Wherever land is perceived to have greater potential value than that attainable from group ranch arrangements, individuals assert exclusive private property rights over group ranch land.

The institutional framework for environmental management has diversified over the past three decades, and today management of land and water is subject to the

Table 3.2   Group ranches in Loitokitok Division.

Name	Area (ha)	Number of members 1982	Number of members 1999
Rombo	38,365	512	3,665
Kuku	96,000	544	3,625
Kimana/Tikondo	25,120	167	843
Mbirikani	125,893	210	3,600
Selenkei	74,794	150	3,497
Olgulului	147,050	1,031	4,100

Source: Rutten (1992) and D. Lovatt-Smith (personal communication).

often conflicting objectives of state agencies and both customary and modern forms of local organization, as depicted in Table 3.3.

Access to land and water in Loitokitok Division: demand, competition and conflict

The institutional changes outlined above, the increasing demand for land and water generated by a rapidly growing population, new forms of resource use arising from commoditization and increasing integration in the national economy have had a profound impact on the dynamics of resource access in Loitokitok. Following the adjudication of land into group ranches and private plots in the 1960s and 1970s, the

Table 3.3 Environmental management in Loitokitok Division: the institutional framework.

	Divisional Level	Locational Level
State institutions		
• Office of the President	District Officer	Chief
• Ministry of Lands and Settlement	Divisional Land Control Board	n/a
Sectoral departments		
• Environment and Natural Resources	Divisional Water Officer Divisional Forester	Local water bailiff n/a
• Agriculture	District Agricultural Officer	Front-line extension staff
• Livestock Development	Divisional Rangeland Management Officer	Front-line extension staff
Parastatal agencies		
• Kenya Wildlife Service		
• National Environment Secretariat		
• Permanent Presidential Commission on Soil Conservation and Afforestation		
• Regional Development Authority		
Formal local institutions		
• Olkejuado County Council		
• Group ranches		
• Amboseli and Tsavo Group Ranches Conservation Association		
Non-governmental organizations		
• Group Ranch Education Programme (development)		
• World Vision (relief and development)		
Customary organizations		
• Elders' councils		
• Grazing committees, territorial organizations (section, locality, *boma*, household)		
Community organizations		
• Irrigation groups		
• Self-help and women's groups		
Private sector		
• Lodge owners and tour operators		

Source: Southgate and Hulme (1996b:23).
n/a, not applicable.

'Maasai gained individual title, land values escalated and appreciable land was sold to outside cultivators with greater market sophistication and awareness of the future value of those regions' (Galaty, 1980:162). Customary institutions of resource access have been systematically weakened by public policy, and richer residents of Loitokitok increasingly seek to acquire land by purchase or by fencing group ranch land.

Records available for 1984 and 1994 (Table 3.4) suggest that, by 1984, non-Maasai were heavily involved in the official land market, as buyers and sellers of land. Of 106 land transactions recorded in 1984, 88 (83 per cent) involved the purchase of land by Kikuyu, compared with 12 (11 per cent) by Maasai (Southgate, 1998). One decade on, the number of recorded transactions had risen to 221, evidence of increasing activity in the formal land market (Table 3.4). Of those acquiring land in 1994 (whether by gift or purchase), 126 were Kikuyu (57 per cent), 56 Maasai (26 per cent) and 21 Kamba (10 per cent), suggesting relatively greater levels of involvement in the formal land market by Maasai than ten years earlier.

Despite increased activity in the land market, the total land area sold during 1994 amounted to little more than one quarter of that traded ten years earlier, reflecting the diminishing mean size of landholding traded. Commonly, those who acquire individual title to land have immediately subdivided it, selling off some portions while leasing out other portions and/or using some of the land themselves (Southgate, 1998).

The claim that 'The Maasai people ... do not understand the value of land. Land in their perspective is like air, something available and accessible to everybody, given by God' (van Klinken and ole Seitah, 1990: Appendix 2) no longer holds true. For many Maasai, as for others migrating to Loitokitok, commoditization has opened new channels of access to land and water (Box 3.2).

Commoditization goes with increased competition between resource users and aspiring users, and between resource users with competing economic interests, resulting in conflicts over access to land and water. The ways such conflicts are resolved – or allowed to fester – depend upon the specific nature of the problem.

Table 3.4   Summary of land transactions in Loitokitok Division during 1994 & 1984.

Type of transaction	Number of transactions 1994 (1984)	Total land area sold* (ha) 1994 (1984)	Number of of 'gift' transactions 1994 (1984)	Mean sale* price (KSh/ha) 1994 (1984)
Non-Maasai – Non-Maasai	66 (67)	67 (355)	19 (6)	67,207 (6,734)
Maasai – Maasai	52 (11)	203 (1,132)	31 (7)	43,844 (3,053)
Maasai – Non-Maasai	99 (27)	176 (113)	5 (2)	37,213 (4,023)
Non-Maasai – Maasai	4 (1)	1 (5)	0 (1)	117,732 (–)
TOTAL	221 (106)	447 (1,605)	55 (16)	43,564 (4,022)

Source: Southgate and Hulme (1996c:8).
*Excluding gifts.

> **Box 3.2**   The commoditization of grazing resources
>
> Crop residue provides an important supplement to rangeland pasture for ole Mikoki's livestock. Ole' Mikoki comes from Mbirikani, and can use grass and crop residue in Kimana at a cost of KSh 200–KSh 300 for the few cows each plot can support. Otherwise he will go to the Entonet area (on Kilimanjaro), where he has 16 hectares of land, given to him by his father. This is the area where his family used to graze cattle before land tenure was individualized. He leases out the land, at an annual rent of KSh 3,000 per hectare, to Kikuyu cultivators. After harvest, ole Mikoki leases the land to fellow Maasai for grazing. Ole Lapiya takes cattle to graze across the Tanzanian border further up the mountain, paying KSh 800–1,000 per hectare, for two months, before the crop residue is burnt in October. Similar arrangements exist wherever former common property land has been individualized, and Loitokitok Maasai pay to graze livestock as far away as the individual ranches in the north of Kajiado.

Beyond the range of the market, customary institutions often influence who gains access, as do local and supra-local networks of patronage and clientelism. The politics of age, clan and ethnicity has resulted in a rising tide of factionalism, and patron–client formations and political alliances have come to play pivotal roles in shaping patterns of access to resources, as we illustrate next.

Age grades

The male age-grade system historically played an important role in the management of rangeland resources, but this most celebrated of Maasai institutions is under considerable pressure from the formal institutions of the group ranch. Local and national political leaders have actively sought to install young, educated Maasai into group ranch leadership positions, where the authority to allocate land to individuals rests. Such positions, therefore, convey considerable political and economic power, and Maasai youth are no longer prepared to defer to their elders. While customary leaders remain highly respected, their power is increasingly inferior to that of group ranch leaders.

Maasai youths (*ilmurran*) have little independent authority until they inherit power and influence with maturity. Despite this, under customary Maasai law, male offspring always have a claim to rights of access to rangeland resources. However, under the Land (Group Representatives) Act, group ranch members have no legal obligations to transfer rights to their children. At the time of group ranch subdivision (if and when it occurs), those excluded from membership lose their previous rights to rangeland. Where group ranch subdivision has occurred, there has been much concern over the rapid disposal of land and the potential for families to be left landless. While Land Control Boards should 'deal with unscrupulous fathers who sell land only to squander the proceeds … gulping inordinate amounts of beer and roast meat' (Sammy, 1993:1), they have proved ineffective. *Ilmurran* have therefore campaigned vehemently for registration as group ranch members. In Kiboko and Elangata Wuas Group Ranches, some youngsters have filed court cases in support of their claims, and group ranch meetings have been attended by security personnel clad in anti-riot gear (ole Katampoi, 1993). In Kimana/Tikondo Group Ranch (Map 3.3), a similar, though less violent, campaign has been fought by the *ilmurran*. In 1995, their efforts were rewarded, and each existing group ranch member was given the opportunity to register up to four other family members.

This has exacerbated long-standing competitive relationships between chronologically adjacent age sets. Relationships between *ilmurran* and their 'firestick patrons' establish a strong spiritual association between alternate age sets (Ndagala, 1992). Thus the original members of Kimana/Tikondo Group Ranch (the majority of whom were 'senior elders') opposed membership being awarded to the 'junior elders'. Instead, they called for the registration of the younger *ilmurran*, of whom they are spiritual patrons. Consequently, most members of Kimana/Tikondo Group Ranch are now *ilmurran*. This presents a political problem to the 'junior elders', as their seniors now draw considerable support from the *ilmurran*. 'Junior elders', whose claims are neither sanctioned by custom nor supported by the age sets on either side, are predictably reluctant to call elections. It is in the interests of local MPs and bureaucrats to maintain the young élite as clients in control of group ranches, through whom land can be acquired in return for promises of political promotion and a share of the fruits of group ranch subdivision. Little wonder that group ranch elections are rarely the annual

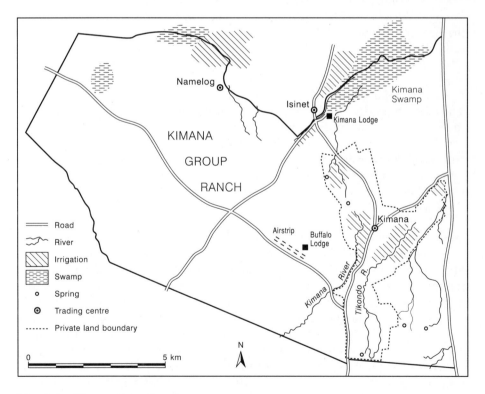

Map 3.3   Kimana Group Ranch

democratic events they are supposed to be. Kimana/Tikondo Group Ranch has only staged four elections in the past two decades.

As control of group ranch resources has become concentrated in the hands of younger educated clients of local and national leaders, relationships between neighbouring clan and section leaders, still conducted between senior elders, have become increasingly irrelevant. The support necessary to retain group ranch leadership positions emanates from above, with the promise of land the collateral used to secure it. The Maasai proverb proclaiming that 'the neck of a cow cannot overtake the head' – that one age set cannot gain a higher status than its predecessors – no longer holds, and so customary institutions, which retain some function (e.g. in tracking across the region for pasture and water), are under increasing strain.

Clans

Kinship has been generally regarded as the source, vehicle and essence of cooperation, reciprocity and resource distribution within Maasai society (Galaty, 1981). Yet the contest for control of Loitokitok's land is being fought between Maasai clans as vehemently as between age sets. Complex political alliances have developed, resulting in an escalation in inter- and intraclan dispute, and a perceptible deterioration of relations between and within Kisonko clans. Clans have become vehicles through which key political figures elicit support, in much the same way as through the age-group system. The escalation of clan rivalry is complex and is best approached through four ordinal levels within a simplified hierarchy of Kisonko kin relations, depicted in Figure 3.4.

Level 1: Kisonko and other *iloshon* (sections)
The relationship between Kisonko and other Maasai *iloshon* was not a focus of this study. However, a number of authors have commented on worsening relationships between *iloshon* in recent years. Galaty (1980), for example, reports that at least three armed clashes occurred between different *iloshon* during the decade after land adjudication (to determine the boundaries and rights to title on group ranches and individual plots) commenced, a trend also observed between *iloshon* in Narok District (Evangelou, 1984).

Level 2: *Orok-kiteng* and *Odo-mongi* (clans)
The two major clans of the Kisonko Maasai are *Orok-kiteng* and the *Odo-mongi*. Historically both were dispersed throughout the Kisonko territory, but today the former are concentrated in the west and north of Loitokitok Division, while the majority of the latter occupy Kuku and Rombo Group Ranches. With the expansion and commoditization of cultivation in Loitokitok, control over irrigation management has become highly contested by clans. The main channels down which irrigation water flows are locally known as 'furrows'. Furrow-group leaders with control over water allocation command considerable political power, given that all cultivators in the drylands are dependent upon their 'share' of water. In Kimana, despite the numerical dominance of the *Orok-kiteng*, irrigation

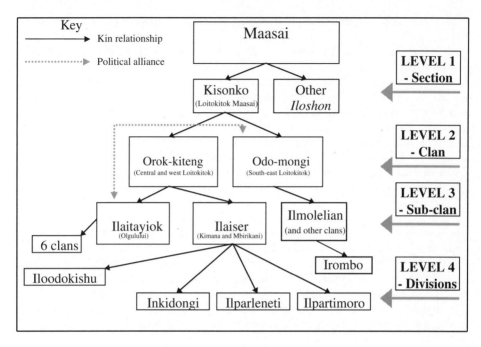

Figure 3.4 Simplified diagram of Kisonko clan relations

management is almost entirely under the control of the *Ilmolelian* subclan of *Odo-mongi* (Table 3.5).

The dominance of *Odo-mongi* in irrigation leadership is politically sensitive, exacerbated by party political divisions: the *Odo-mongi* are aligned with opponents of the government, while *Orok-kiteng* remain resolutely loyal to the ruling KANU party. Irrigators came under pressure to vote for *Orok-kiteng* candidates during recent furrow group elections. While *Odo-mongi* retained control, dispute continues and, according to several irrigators interviewed, many furrow groups were under pressure

Table 3.5 Furrow group leaders in the Kimana/Tikondo irrigation schemes (Map 3.3).

	Name	Major clan	Subclan (subclan division)
Kimana/Tikondo furrows	Jeremiah Ngerishoi	*Odo-mongi*	*Ilmolelian (Irombo)*
	Patrick Balozi	*Odo-mongi*	*Ilmolelian (Irombo)*
	Kaleyia Nailianga	*Odo-mongi*	*Ilmolelian (Irombo)*
	Ole Ngola	*Odo-mongi*	*Ilmolelian (Irombo)*
	Mungaya	*Odo-mongi*	*Ilmolelian (Irombo)*
	Kisilet	*Odo-mongi*	*Ilmolelian (Irombo)*
Isinet furrows	Kaleyia Kiyekiya	*Orok-kiteng*	*Ilaiser*
	Mokoi	*Orok-kiteng*	*Ilaiser*

Source: Southgate (1998).

from the local administration to repeat the elections and achieve a 'more acceptable' result.

Conflict between *Orok-kiteng* and *Odo-mongi* is most manifest in increasingly acrimonious battles for control of group ranches, of which Kimana/Tikondo Group Ranch is a case in point. In 1994, members voted in favour of subdividing the group ranch. According to the relevant legislation, from that moment on no elections should have been held, with land allocation proceeding under the direction of the incumbent committee members, led by the *Odo-mongi* chairman. However, the District Land Adjudication Officer (DLAO) called an election, pitching the chairman against the *Orok-kiteng* vice-chairman in an effort to have the subdivision process controlled by supporters of KANU. The chairman and incumbent treasurer of the group ranch took legal action (Civil Suit No. 5003 of 1994) against the DLAO and vice-chairman.

In support of the plaintiff's case, it was argued that *Orok-kiteng* and *Odo-mongi* are poised for war' and that there would ensue 'fighting, lawlessness and a breach of law and order unless [the election] is stopped by order of injunction' (High Court of Kenya, 1994). In July 1994, the plaintiffs lost their case, new elections were held and the former vice-chairman gained control of Kimana Group Ranch. This highlights the ability of KANU to suppress *de jure* governance in group ranches when it suits it to do so. Through such intervention, clients of national political and bureaucratic leaders are installed in positions through which resources (notably land) can be accessed.

Level 3: *Ilaitayiok* and *Ilaiser* (subclans)

Orok-kiteng, the victors in the struggle just described, comprises two subclans, *Ilaiser* and *Ilaitayiok*. With the prospect of subdivision of Kimana Group Ranch and given group ranch leaders' responsibility for land allocation, the two subclans have become embroiled in a contest for control. In anticipation of land ownership contestation among subclans, the initial Shamba Allocation Committee for Kimana was constituted in 1972 with nine *Ilaitayiok*, eight *Ilmolelian* and eight *Ilaiser*. The fact that the committee was chaired by an *Ilmolelian* (*Odo-mongi*) was, reputedly, a significant fact in land allocation at that time.

A political alliance between the *Ilaitayiok* and subclans of the *Odo-mongi* maintains control over *Ilaiser*. For several years, *Ilaitayiok* held key positions within Kimana; for example, the secretary of the group ranch has always been *Ilaitayiok*. However, when the *Ilaiser* MP for Kajiado South defeated his *Ilaitayiok* opponents for nomination as KANU representative in the 1992 general election and then his *Odo-mongi* Democratic Party (DP) opponent in the election itself, the *Ilaitayiok* lost control of Kimana Group Ranch. The most influential positions have been filled by *Ilaiser* at the expense of *Ilaitayiok* (Table 3.6). The only positions retained by *Ilaitayiok* are those of secretary, treasurer and vice-chairman of the group ranch, and the local councillor. Similar events occurred within Olgulului Group Ranch, where the actions of the MP and district commissioner led to the deposition of the *Ilaitayiok* committee.

Level 4: *Iloodokishu* and other *Ilaiser* subclan divisions

Analysis of infighting among the *Ilaiser* demonstrates the depth of clan factionalism in Loitokitok. Within the *Ilaiser* subclan, a vehement struggle is gaining momentum.

Table 3.6   Leaders of formal organizations in Kimana, 1996.

Position	Name	Clan
Member of Parliament	Philip Singaru	*Ilaiser*
Chief (government administration)	Joseph Naikoluyieu	*Ilaiser*
Assistant chief	Johnson Mpaayo	*Ilaiser*
Group ranch chairman	Paul Nangoro	*Ilaiser*
Locational KANU chairman	Paul Nangoro	*Ilaiser*
Group ranch vice-chairman	Saiko	*Ilmolelian*
Kimana ward councillor	Risie Parmuat	*Ilaitayiok*
Group ranch secretary	Kenyatta Oloitiptip	*Ilaitayiok*
Group ranch treasurer	Stephen Korinko	*Ilaitayiok*

Source: Southgate (1998).

The *Iloodikishu* division of *Ilaiser* has established control of Mbirikani Group Ranch to the north of Kimana. The current chairman and secretary, along with the previous two chairmen, are all *Iloodikishu*, as was the senior government chief of the location until 1994. *Iloodikishu* candidates have always been able to draw on the support of *Ilaitayiok* group ranch members, owing to a local political alliance between the two groups. However, the incumbent MP along with clan-mates in key positions, belongs to the *Inkidongi* division. The political alliance between *Ilaitayiok* and *Iloodikishu* thus poses a political threat to the MP, preventing him from establishing a clientele within Mbirikani as effectively as he has done elsewhere. During 1994 and 1995, a rift began to emerge at Kimana between the *Iloodikishu* and the other three *Ilaiser* divisions. A number of meetings were held, during which the MP and district officer sought to exploit this against *Iloodikishu*, who were publicly derided on account of their positive relationship with the *Ilaitayiok* subclan. At the time of writing, elections have not been staged and support for *Inkidongi* and the *Iloodikishu* alliance is closely matched. The main target of campaigns mounted by the opposing factions has been the minority *Odo-mongi* clan, whose members, potentially, hold the casting vote.

Clanship has thus become another medium through which national political parties compete to establish patron–client networks. By vesting the power to allocate land in the hands of young, educated and ambitious group ranch leaders, prominent national and regional figures seek to gain access to rangelands that will be privatized. For some Maasai, fostering these vertical relationships is more profitable than maintaining those with their neighbours, and further weakening of customary institutions of resource access seems likely to be an inevitable result.

Party competition and ethnicity

Loitokitok's population is today a mix of ethnic groups. The 1989 census indicated that more than 40 per cent of its inhabitants are non-Maasai. The dynamics of resource access are also affected by relations between Maasai and non-Maasai. While Maasai and non-Maasai cooperate in irrigation management, political party affiliations in

Loitokitok have exacerbated ethnic divisions leading, in some instances, to the collapse of joint Maasai and non-Maasai collective action and the increasing alienation of Loitokitok's non-Maasai population (Box 3.3).

In December 1992, the first multiparty elections were held in Kenya since the merger of KANU and KADU decades earlier. Voting behaviour closely reflected ethno-regional political allegiances. President Moi (KANU) attracted the votes of smaller ethnic groups, particularly in Rift Valley Province, home of the Maasai and the President's own Kalenjin. These groups had considered themselves marginalized under Kenya's first President, Kenyatta (a Kikuyu). The numerically dominant Kikuyu, in turn, voted in great numbers for opposition parties. Thus, while KANU polled 66.6 per cent of votes in the Rift Valley, it only received 2.1 per cent of votes cast in Central Province. In Rift Valley Province, FORD-A (part of a broad opposition alliance, which split into two parties) captured 22 per cent and Democratic Party Kenya (DPK) 6.1 per cent (NEMU, 1993). So, besides broad cultural differences between Maasai and incoming Kikuyu, there now exist fundamental party political divisions. In Kajiado South, KANU attracted 61 per cent of the vote, with DPK and FORD-A both capturing 19 per cent. While there were no great ideological differences between political parties, parliamentary elections fuelled long-standing ethnic animosities.

Given growing pressures on land and livelihoods in Loitokitok and the promotion of *majimbo*ism (regionalism) – a code word for ethnic political mobilization – by President Moi, competition for resources has assumed an overtly ethnic dimension, linked to manoeuvring and competition within and between political parties. For example, control over water allocation in Loitokitok is now entirely in the hands of Maasai leaders (as detailed above), although Maasai are only one-third of those culti-vating individually owned land in some furrow groups. The apparent democracy and accountability of furrow-group institutions conceals a more discriminative and exploitative institutional regime, based on unwritten and rarely discussed rules, such as that only Maasai should control water resources. A fear of losing their foothold in the area has prompted orders from local and national KANU leaders that pro-oppo-sition groups should not have a forum to canvas political support. Both KANU politicians and the KANU-controlled district administration (district commissioners, district officers and chiefs) coordinate this. As one senior elder and resident of Kimana

---

Box 3.3 The battle for control in Maasailand

An intense battle for control over Maasailand developed between Kenya's Vice-President and Minister for Planning and National Development, Professor George Saitoti, and the Minister for Home Affairs and National Heritage, Mr William ole Ntimama. The battle is not merely for control over Maasailand, but concerns the national presidential succession (*Economic Review*, 1997). The two factions are referred to as 'KANU A' and 'KANU B'. Where Ntimama campaigned on an anti-Kikuyu platform, vehemently opposing the migration of Kikuyu and other non-Maasai groups into Maasailand, Saitoti attracted the support of non-Maasai. Saitoti draws support from his political allies in Kajiado District, while Ntimama's camp is based in Narok. This factionalism within KANU has many local implications (see text).

explained, 'Maasai began to fear the political power of outsiders, so it was decided to remove them completely from all positions of authority, under instructions from the local MP, who instructed the Chief and local KANU Chairman.' Subsequently the 'outsiders' were 'threatened that if they started gaining political power in our stronghold, they would be kicked out, like in Narok'. Box 3.4 details the story of William Karanja, a victim of worsening ethnic relations in Kimana.

Conflict between the Maasai (who claim customary rights of access to key resources) and non-Maasai (whose claims are supported by legislation) has become particularly intense in Kuku Group Ranch. One Luo tenant irrigator in Olorika complained:

> We're just like horses here in Maasailand. We don't sleep, we don't water our *shambas* in peace, just because of the Maasai *murran*. All the time we are beaten like school pupils. I'm counting the days before I can leave this miserable place.

Other interviewees corroborated his experience. As ethnic relations in Loitokitok worsened during canvassing for the 1992 general election, many non-Maasai returned to their districts of origin: as many as 40 per cent of tenant farmers in Kisanjani, Elangata and Olorika were temporarily forced out. Subsequently, many returned, but they were openly concerned about the prospect of escalating ethnic conflict as the next general election, scheduled for 1997, approached. With this growing ethnic division, the MP found it increasingly necessary to appease the non-Maasai population (Box 3.5).

The 1997 general election

In Loitokitok, the 1997 general election was a contest between Southern Kajiado's two most prominent political figures, Philip Sing'aru (the incumbent MP) and Geoffrey Parpai. Five years earlier, Parpai, standing as the DP candidate, had challenged Sing'aru but narrowly lost. Parpai had attempted to win the KANU nomination prior to the 1997 general election, but defected back to DP when Sing'aru was declared the KANU

Box 3.4 The story of William Karanja

William Karanja, a Kikuyu, came to Loitokitok in 1968 while working for the police. At the time of land registration, he was allocated 12 hectares of medium-potential land on the mountain slopes, for which he was awarded individual title, and he was also the only non-Maasai to be granted membership of Kimana/Tikondo Group Ranch. In 1979 he left the police to spend time developing his farm. The drought of 1984 forced him to find another source of livelihood, and he was granted permission by the group-ranch chairman to produce charcoal, which he did until 1991. The group ranch committee allocated Karanja land by the Loitokitok to Machakos pipeline, which marks the eastern border of Kimana/Tikondo Group Ranch, and, taking advantage of a leak in the pipe, he began irrigated cultivation in 1993. He invited local Maasai to join him, but when his offer was declined he invited other Kikuyu from the area. He leased out plots of 'his' land for KSh 2,000 per hectare. But, after the first harvest, the group ranch committee confiscated the crops and demanded KSh 3,000 per hectare from each of the tenants. Karanja's grievance is that other registered group ranch members lease out the land allocated them by the group ranch without being subject to this punitive 'taxation'. His complaint has been taken to the chief, without success.

Box 3.5   The politics of resource access: cultivation in Kimana Swamp

As the number of non-Maasai cultivators has grown in Loitokitok, the MP has found it in his interest to accommodate their demands for access to irrigable land. In 1988, during a *baraza* convened in Kimana, the MP declared his intention to allow cultivation on the margins of Kimana Swamp. The Chiefs of Kimana and Mbirikani Locations opposed the decision on economic and environmental grounds. This pitched the local administration into conflict with the MP in a dispute that became complicated by clan allegiances. Such was the concern among the local administration that a leading official of the Permanent Presidential Commission on Soil and Water Conservation (PPCSWC) was summoned to Kimana. The PPCSWC declared its support for the local administration. Adding to the complexity of the dispute, the owner of a tourist lodge on the edge of Kimana Swamp also sided with the local administration as cultivation was deterring leopards, which many tourists visit Kimana specifically to see. However, the MP was victorious, the chief was replaced by a clan-mate and cultivation in the swamp was permitted and continues today. As Assistant Minister for Tourism and Wildlife, the MP declares the value of wildlife and tourism, and his ministry vehemently opposes the destruction of important habitats (Republic of Kenya, 1989), but his prime political concern is to secure his local support base by advocating a practice that has an adverse impact upon the environment and the wildlife his ministry supports.

---

candidate (despite reports that Parpai got the most votes!). Parpai, linked to the KANU A camp, belongs to the *Odo-mongi* clan, numerically dominant in the constituency. Sing'aru, a supporter of KANU B, is a member of *Orok-kiteng*. The *Odo-mongi* draw support from the Matapato Maasai section and the multiethnic electorate in the urban centre of Namanga. Perhaps most significantly, Parpai belongs to the *Ilkitop* age set, whereas Sing'aru belongs to the older *Iseuri*. While Sing'aru was always likely to win support from the non-Maasai community, because of KANU B's more tolerant attitudes toward non-Maasai, Parpai captured a large proportion of the Maasai vote by virtue of his age and clan. The 'block' *Ilkitop* vote secured victory for Parpai, wresting control in Loitokitok away from KANU, albeit only temporarily perhaps.

While an increasingly complex array of institutions – customary, market-based, ethnic and party political – influence access to natural resources in Loitokitok, the politicization of both customary and modern organizations, exploited to serve the political ambitions of local leaders and economic aspirations of a national élite, has marginalized some groups. The processes that seek to maintain domination of the Maasai over other ethnic groups, of *Orok-kiteng* over *Odo-mongi*, of *Ilaiser* over *Ilaitayiok,* and of *Inkidongi* over their political rivals, increase both land fragmentation and social factionalism.

Resource use in Loitokitok

The demise of pastoralism?

Before colonialism, resource use in the Loitokitok area was primarily pastoral, owing to the extreme variability and unpredictability of the environment. While many observers have warned that land tenure changes and the rapid expansion of cultivation threaten the viability of pastoralism (Rutten, 1992), our research reveals that the dynamics of resource use in Loitokitok are more complex than this static view suggests.

Cattle populations in Kajiado District have tended to fluctuate considerably during the past century, primarily as a result of periodic drought and disease (Fig. 3.5). The cattle population declined from an estimated 630,000 in 1960 (Fig. 3.6) to 208,000 in 1962 owing to drought, recovering to 430,000 by 1965 (White and Meadows, 1981). From a peak of 713,000 in 1982, total cattle numbers again fell following the onset of drought to a low of 311,409 in 1984 (KDDP, 1989), but had reached an estimated 846,600 by 1992 (KDDP, 1994). Drought in 1994 again affected livestock in many areas of southern Kajiado. No official figures are yet available, but the Maasai were thought to have lost up to 70 per cent of their herds in many areas (World Vision, personal communication).

1890–2	Major drought and rinderpest and bovine pneumonia epidemics, killing 90 per cent of Maasai livestock. Smallpox claims many human victims
1897–8	Outbreaks of contagious bovine pleuropneumonia in the Ngong area, and rinderpest among Naivasha Maasai
1909	Outbreak of East Coast fever in the southern Maasai reserve
1911–12	Large losses of livestock during the migration of Maasai from Laikipia towards the southern Maasai reserve
1918	Drought and disease, especially rinderpest
1925–7	Severe drought, famine and stock losses
1929	Severe drought and locust infestations, some 50,000 cattle lost
1933–5	Severe drought and the famine, *Olomeyu Looloyik*, 35 per cent of stock lost
1938–9	Serious drought
1943–6	Severe drought and famine, *Eboot Enkurma Nanyokie*
1948–50	Rinderpest epidemic and rain failure
1951	Flooding, *Olari Loonkariak*
1952	Foot-and-mouth epidemic, Kajiado put under quarantine
1953	East Coast fever in south-east Kajiado District, 75 per cent of stock lost
1953–6	Drought, East Coast fever in the north-west of Kajiado District
1959	Severe drought and contagious bovine pleuropneumonia outbreak
1960–61	Severe drought, up to 70 per cent of livestock lost, famine relief provided
1963	Flooding
1973–6	Severe drought, 150,000 cattle lost, famine relief to 60,000 people, outbreaks of rabies and anthrax
1979–80	Poor rains
1984	Severe drought and East Coast fever epidemic, resulting in 50 per cent livestock mortality
1986	Contagious bovine pleuropneumonia outbreak
1994	Drought, famine relief

Source: Rutten (1992).

Figure 3.5 A chronology of natural hazards in Maasailand

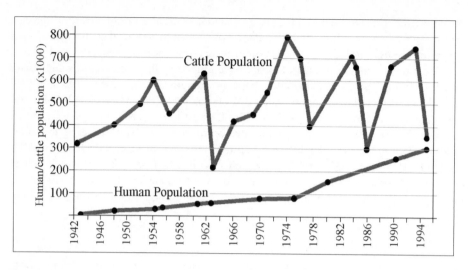

Figure 3.6   Cattle & human population in Kajiado District, 1942–94

Tracking for pasture and water

The Maasai have long had close relationships with their neighbours. Reciprocal trade between Maasai and Kikuyu, Chagga and Arusha cultivators, in particular, has been well documented (Kitching, 1980). Such relationships have become increasingly important as: (i) the Maasai's access to pastoral resources has diminished; (ii) they have pursued new economic opportunities; and (iii) they were pushed into the cash economy by both direct and indirect effects of colonial policy. The confinement of the Maasai to a single reserve and restrictions on livestock movements (see below) necessitated greater interaction with neighbouring cultivators, as transhumant pastoralism became increasingly difficult. The Maasai were also openly encouraged to purchase a wide range of consumer goods, as the colonial authorities attempted to 'create new appetites, for tea, and cigarettes, and gramophones, and spotted waistcoats, and ribbons, and hand mirrors, and umbrellas, and Worcester Sauce – all the innumerable objects with which modern civilisation has enriched the world' (Leys, 1973:138–9).

Hut and poll taxes, introduced in the 1920s, compelled the Maasai to enter the cash economy through the sale of livestock (Kitching, 1980). The Maasai were also subject to an array of penalties for the infringement of government rules and became the most heavily taxed ethnic group in Kenya, paying almost twice as much per capita as any other (Kituyi, 1990). While attempts to encourage marketing of dairy products met with little success, in 1933 Kajiado District exported 33 tonnes of hides and skins. The construction of a meat-canning plant at Athi River in 1949 encouraged a more market-orientated approach to livestock production. During the first year of operation, over 14,000 cattle were sold to the plant.

In common with pastoral systems across Africa (Scoones, 1994), indigenous herd management practices in Kajiado involved 'tracking' for pasture and water during the dry season and periods of drought. The move to a group ranching system did not consider this and, at least in theory, created fixed boundaries within which the herds of a group ranch's members would remain. While this was a simple and neat design for planners, it failed to reflect the constraints of rearing livestock in an arid area with unpredictable rainfall. The herders' response was to redesign the grazing system around a combination of 'customary' and 'modern' institutions. Interviews with Kimana/Tikondo Group Ranch members revealed that group ranch rules determine grazing patterns during the wet season, while customary rules and market processes replace them as local grazing resources are exhausted (Table 3.7 and Fig. 3.7). During the dry season of 1994, the only grazing areas available (Map 3.2) lay in the upland areas of the Chyulu Hills (to the east), Mount Kilimanjaro (to the south) or Amboseli National Park (to the west). Kimana/Tikondo Group Ranch members were able to maintain their herds until the rains returned by accessing pasture by various means: by using inter-section social relationships, by paying for access to individually held ranches and farms and by illegally grazing in Amboseli National Park.

Not all group ranch members have equal access to these modified tracking opportunities, however. In particular, leasing grazing rights requires readily available cash, while using the National Park entails ability to negotiate with park staff to avoid arrest and the seizure of livestock: this demands cash (for bribes) or social contacts. In all of these cases, wealthier group ranch members with more extensive socio-political networks are more likely to be able to track and access dry season grazing than poorer members.

Table 3.7 Grazing areas used by Kimana Maasai during the dry & wet seasons of 1994.

Dry season			Wet season	
Area	Map ref.*	Notes	Area	Notes
Near Loitokitok	1		Oltepesi	All wet-season grazing
Entatara		Individually	Oldepe	areas inside Kimana
Engama		owned land	Engaroni	Group Ranch
Iltilal			Ololi	
Rongena			Lemongo	
Nenjani (near Tsavo West)	2			
Kimana Swamp	3	Kimana/Mbirikani		
In Kuku Group Ranch				
Oldoinyo Emunyi	4	All in the lower		
Chyulu Hills		communal part of		
Isiruai Hills		Kuku Group Ranch		
Other areas				
Tanzania	5	With other Kisonko Maasai		
Amboseli National Park	6	Illegal grazing		
Konza ranches	7	Individual ranches in northern Kajiado		

*See Figure 3.7.

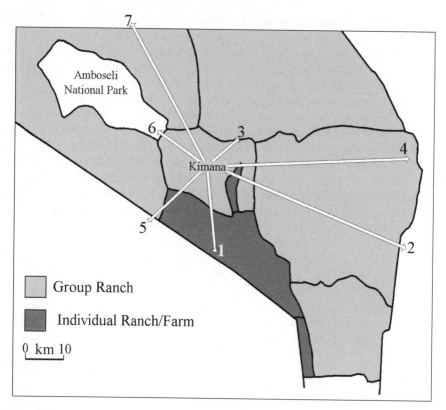

Figure 3.7 Grazing areas used by Kimana Maasai during the dry & wet seasons of 1994 (for key, see Table 3.7)

The economic transition engineered by rangeland planners has never materialized and, in Loitokitok Division, livestock production has become increasingly secondary to other forms of economic activity. Today, while pastoralism still engages over 75 per cent of the district's population (KDDP, 1994) to varying extents, cultivation is increasingly important. Between 1983 and 1987, the number of people engaged in cultivation is said to have increased from 22,260 to 42,516 (KDDP, 1989). Furthermore, livestock production is no longer the exclusive domain of the Maasai. Many Kikuyu residents of Loitokitok Division have adapted to favourable market opportunities and entered into zero-grazed cattle and small-stock production, while other non-Maasai are integrating cultivation with livestock production, using crop residue as cattle feed and profiting from the supply of manure.

In Loitokitok, the Maasai have entered into the wage economy in increasing numbers (Western, 1994), labour has acquired a market value (Kituyi, 1990) and market-based transactions have displaced earlier labour arrangements. For example, while livestock were customarily herded by young boys from within the domestic group, it has now become a significant source of paid employment. The rapid growth of Loitokitok town and other urban centres has created a variety of employment opportunities. The tourism industry now provides wage employment for many residents of Loitokitok, in positions as diverse as tour guides, waiters and mechanics, and in a host of other positions related to the wildlife 'safari' industry.

Monetization of the local economy has had an impact on indigenous institutions in other ways too. For example, while participation in elders' beer parties was once dependent upon age and status, today the availability of cash is a more important qualification, and Tusker Lager is widely preferred to locally brewed honey beer. In a similar fashion, customary 'fines' for cattle theft and other offences are now often settled in cash rather than cattle (Southgate, 1998). Commoditization has been accompanied by the growth of permanent market centres and trading centres for livestock and agricultural products, as well as consumer goods brought from Nairobi and Mombasa. Over forty small businesses, ranging from car mechanics to a variety of food and provision shops, now operate in Kimana Trading Centre in the south of Loitokitok Division, an increase from only twenty such businesses a decade ago (KDDP, 1989). Non-Maasai predominate in such business development, and some 85 per cent of businesses in Kimana are owned by incomers, mostly by individuals with interests in horticulture (Southgate, 1998). Both Maasai and non-Maasai also increasingly invest in formal education for their children. Many Maasai parents, faced with the dilemma of whether to send their children to school or utilize their labour in herding, now opt for the former.

Resource use dynamics in Loitokitok's 'wetlands in drylands'

Commoditization is nowhere more evident than around the few wetland environments in Loitokitok Division. Here the natural resource bases are relatively productive, and over several decades incoming ethnic groups have commingled to create considerable social and economic heterogeneity. Contemporary land tenure arrangements in Loitokitok (Fig. 3.8) reflect the diversity of agroecological conditions described earlier. Low-potential areas are predominantly under group ownership (group ranches), and account for approximately 80 per cent of Loitokitok's land area. High-potential land around the wetlands of Kimana and Rombo and on the slopes of Mount Kilimanjaro has been divided into individually titled farms, while individually titled ranches have been registered on the lower slopes of Kilimanjaro (Map 3.3).

The impetus for economic diversification in Loitokitok cannot simply be ascribed to the influences of 'incomers' or of government policies, as is sometimes portrayed. Such an analysis underestimates the central role played by Maasai 'pioneers' of change. While the state paid little attention to the development of small-scale irrigated cultivation in Loitokitok, particularly during the colonial era, a number of Maasai, through their own ingenuity, established rudimentary irrigation systems that have subsequently attracted the attention of both state and donor organizations. While Loitokitok is often cited in official publications as an example of the success of Kenya's small-scale irrigation sector (IDB, 1993, 1994; Republic of Kenya, 1994),

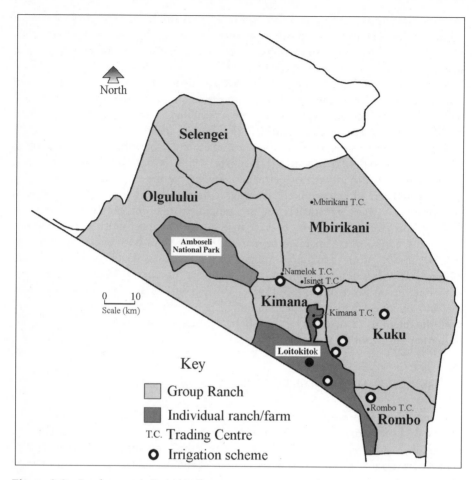

Figure 3.8   Land tenure in Loitokitok

the origins of irrigation in the area owe very little to official policy or government action or to incoming agriculturalists.

Indeed, the roots of irrigated cultivation in Loitokitok can be traced to long before non-Maasai cultivators arrived in significant numbers. Finkel and Darkoh (1990:13) observe that 'the process of diversification was initiated and led by the wealthiest and most influential Maasai of the region ... [although the] ... proximity of tribes with agricultural tradition was ... [a] ... major factor in establishing the process'. Lolkinyei ole Ntipilit, an elder resident of Isinet, recalls that, following the drought of 1931, a few Maasai in Kimana created simple irrigation systems, aided by a number of Chagga irrigators from Kilimanjaro. Although the rains returned and irrigation was abandoned soon after, 'the stories of how Maasai coped in 1931 remained'.

In the early 1950s, a prominent figure in the Namelok area, ole Musa, also returned from his travels equipped with the knowledge and resources to construct a system of irrigation furrows. He has been described by ole Marsharen (1989:1) as a 'typical Maasai father of the Green Revolution in Loitokitok'. Kimani (1988:6) remarks that he had 'sufficient social stature to demonstrate that irrigation was not the curse of the poor as the local Maasai believed … thus removing the stigma attached to cultivation'. Ole Musa is still a highly influential figure, and the immense popularity of irrigation among the Maasai in Namelok owes much to the wealth he has accumulated through irrigated cultivation. In Kimana the leading pioneer of irrigated cultivation was a man known locally as 'Singh' (Box 3.6), whose Indian father had come to Kenya to work on the construction of the Mombasa to Lake Victoria railway in 1906. The influence of Singh's father and his countrymen is reflected today in the range of horticultural crops of Indian origin grown in Loitokitok.

Immigrants are important in contemporary irrigation, however, and in Loitokitok Division 42 per cent of irrigators are Kikuyu and 19 per cent are Akamba. On the small-scale schemes within group ranches, many tenants or sharecroppers are non-Maasai incomers. A survey of Namelok in 1992 identified 480 Chagga cultivators (from Tanzania) engaged in informal sharecropping arrangements, although numbers have since decreased as ethnic tensions have risen.

While the roots of irrigated cultivation in Loitokitok lie in schemes developed by pioneering Maasai for local food production, today the sector is highly commercialized and orientated towards regional and national horticultural markets. Thirteen of Kajiado District's sixteen small-scale, farmer-managed irrigation schemes fall within Loitokitok Division. They cover 1,256 ha, are farmed by 3,219 families and are estimated to produce 70 per cent of the onions and tomatoes marketed in Mombasa and Nairobi. Both irrigable land and water have become valuable commodities. With increasing numbers of irrigators and decreasing per capita water supply, claims on rights to irrigation water have multiplied rapidly. Those leasing out land often demand separate payment for the lease of their water share. For example, Susan Wanjiru, a Kikuyu resident of Kimana for ten years, owns farmland in Kimana and leases irrigation water at an annual cost of KSh 6,000 for her annual share.

Box 3.6   Singh's story

When I was young, I went to Taveta for a job on a sisal plantation. I worked as a labourer for 6 years. I came back here in 1967 and found most parts of Kimana, particularly the good parts, had been taken when I was away. My prayers have always been to have land near a river and a good road, and I came to the place I am now and found that an old man called Munio ole Mbora had already started making a furrow into his *shamba*, but could not go far due to the hard rock on the way. We agreed that if I gave him a hand he would give me part of his land, and we made the furrow [today known as Kimana 'A' furrow]. I now have 11 hectares of land, which I was given after sending an application to the [*shamba* allocation] committee under the chairmanship of the late Norman Oloishorua Kapari. I went to Amboseli for a carpenter's job between 1969 and 1975, then worked in Buffalo Lodge until 1979, while developing my *shamba*. Horticultural crops have been very important to me. I have constructed a permanent house costing KSh 10,000, and I now have two wives and ten children, who are all in school.

Irrigation is managed through a hierarchy of irrigator organizations, in which the basic unit is the furrow group. The largest of the irrigation systems occupies the individually owned plots of the Kimana/Tikondo area. Here simple furrows convey water by gravity from the Kimana and Tikondo springs to individually owned landholdings. These water delivery systems have evolved along with locally formulated rules, which tend to vary from furrow to furrow. Among all furrow groups, however, water allocation is based on the provision of a timed 'share', when the furrow water becomes the exclusive property of each individual group member in turn. A share ranges from 24 hours per week in Isinet to three hours every 14–18 days in several of the Kimana and Tikondo furrow groups. Irrespective of plot size, in general each farmer is entitled to one share of water each cycle – thus water rather than land tends to be the limiting factor constraining the amount of irrigation cultivation possible.

To meet the costs of maintaining and developing each irrigation system (such as cement to line the furrows), furrow-group leaders collect monthly contributions from members. All furrow leaders impose fines on their members for failure to participate in furrow maintenance, typically KSh 50 per day. Fines are also levied as punishment for 'water theft', when individuals divert water on to their land out of turn. In Namelok, for example, water theft attracts a KSh 200 fine and, if it is repeated, the fine rises to KSh 500. Such penalties help to discourage water thieves. However, as water has become more scarce in Kimana/Tikondo, where the water share cycle has increased to 18 days, the incentive to steal is great and most farmers guard the water diversion structures while their crops are irrigated.

Furrow groups are headed by a committee comprising chairman, secretary and treasurer. Elections for each position are held annually, although the rules regarding the rights of tenant irrigators to participate vary from furrow to furrow. In Kimana and Tikondo, leaders of individual furrow groups form an association, which is meant to coordinate group use of the water resource. This umbrella organization, however, is ineffective in creating institutional incentives for cooperation between groups. Thus, in the case of Kimana 'D' and 'B' furrows, which have had to join forces owing to water restrictions, water theft is rife. Here, under orders of the local water bailiff (Ministry of Water Development), the two furrow groups can now only extract water from Kimana River on alternate weeks, but this arrangement is only partially effective.

Loitokitok's wetlands also sustain an important wildlife population, and wildlife tourism has become part of the local economy. This creates competition for resources in terms of the 'people versus animals' debate (Collett, 1987) and irrigators versus tour operators. With Amboseli National Park attracting over 200,000 visitors in 1990 and generating over KSh 30 million annually (Western, 1994), the service industry associated with wildlife tourism has become an important source of wage employment, but mostly for those from outside of the district. With as much as 70 per cent of Amboseli's wildlife regularly dispersing beyond the borders of the National Park in search of pasture and water, it competes with livestock for resources, damages crops and is a physical threat to local residents (especially in the form of elephants and lions). The springs, streams and swamp margins that have attracted so many cultivators to Loitokitok are also the focus for an emerging conservation lobby, keen to promote wildlife as an economic activity and to retain biodiversity.

Factionalism, fragmentation and resource degradation in Loitokitok

Several authors have warned of an impending environmental disaster in Kenya's Maasailand. Some predict escalating rates of desertification as populations exceed Maasailand's perceived carrying capacity (Bernard et al., 1989). Others are more concerned about the environmental effects of the Maasai's increasingly sedentary lifestyle since the introduction of group ranches (Ndagala, 1982). The trend towards individual land ownership, according to Asiema and Situma (1994:163–4), is resulting in a:

> total loss of forage regimes critical to the Maasai's own and their livestock's survival. The once sparsely populated areas have been converted to high-density human and animal regimes which are now more intensely used than before ... resulting in the destruction of land that is already environmentally fragile.

In these areas, soils are being exposed to often inappropriate land use practices, leading to rapid rates of erosion and soil degradation (Odundo, 1992). Land fragmentation and land use changes are also disrupting wildlife populations, increasing the pressure on the remaining accessible wetlands. Rangeland 'experts' continue to offer advice and policy recommendations, invariably calling for the Maasai to reduce their herds and to conform to government plans for their sedentarization. For example, a Ministry of Livestock Production report argues that Kimana/Tikondo Group Ranch is 'seriously overstocked' by some 306 per cent, which has caused areas of bare soil and the emergence of undesirable invading plant species (Range Planning Unit, 1990). Enforced destocking is called for to avert an impending environmental disaster – a recommendation range management 'experts' have been making for 60 years!

Our research has found that resource degradation is a complex issue, and such recommendations fail to address the most pressing socio-environmental problems facing the residents of Loitokitok. Rarely have the perceptions of the area's residents contributed to the formulation of policy. We conducted surveys among communities in the Kimana/Tikondo and Kuku areas of Loitokitok, whose members' views cast a new light on the issue of environmental change and degradation.

While the majority of non-Maasai identified overstocking as one of the main environmental problems of the area, few were able to identify manifestations of overstocking other than seasonal denudation of annual vegetation. With limited physical evidence of deteriorating rangeland conditions, there appears to be little to suggest any long-term environmental decline owing to excessive animal numbers. As several Maasai explained, what to outsiders appears as environmental degradation through overstocking is, in fact, a temporary reduction in productivity, caused ultimately by the seasonality of climate and historical patterns of environmental exploitation. Severe range degradation is avoided by the tracking strategies of Maasai pastoralists and, ultimately, by the high livestock mortality rates that occur during periods of drought.

The emotive desertification debate that preoccupies rangeland planners thus obscures the environmental concerns of the Maasai in Loitokitok. Interviews with Maasai heads of household identified bush clearance for cultivation (38 per cent), increasing frequency of drought (32 per cent) and charcoal production (16 per cent) as the perceived most serious environmental problems. Current pressures impinging on social institutions that promoted cooperation threaten to undermine the balance between environment and human activity sustained so far in Loitokitok, despite rapid rates of population growth. The consequences of this are most evident where cooperation gives way to commoditization and competition over Loitokitok's sparse water resources. For example, Kuku Group Ranch is dependent upon two principal sources of water. The Noolturesh River enters the group ranch in the south, close to the Noolturesh spring on the slopes of Mount Kilimanjaro (Fig. 3.9). The Kikarankot River flows out of Kimana Swamp, eastwards. Both rivers feed the once-extensive Olngarua Leinkati swampland in the north of Kuku Group Ranch, customarily available to all Kisonko pastoralists. However, the expansion of irrigation has greatly

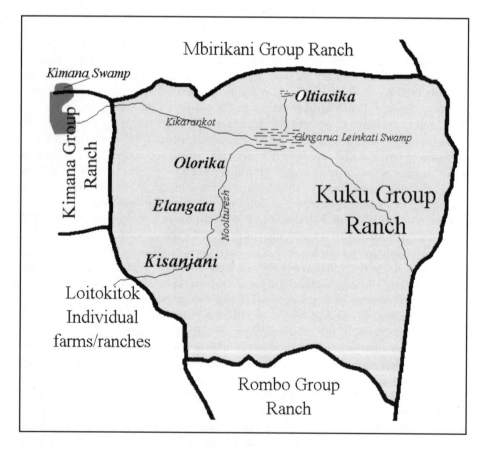

Figure 3.9 Streams flowing into and out of Kimana Swamp

reduced the yield of both rivers in their lower reaches. Another example is Isinet spring, which feeds Kimana Swamp and yields over 831,000 litres daily (District Water Development Officer, personal communication), theoretically enough to cater for the total water requirements within Kimana/Tikondo Group Ranch of around 510,000 litres per day (Range Planning Unit, 1990). But approximately 70 per cent of this is extracted for irrigation in Isinet and along the margins of Kimana Swamp within Mbirikani Group Ranch. Thus residents of Kuku Group Ranch, and other pastoralists dependent upon the remaining communally accessible wetlands, are affected by water management decisions taken in both Kimana and Mbirikani Group Ranches. Local residents reported that the once-perennial Kikarankot River now flows only after periods of rainfall, and Olngarua Leinkati Swamp is no longer anything more than an area of seasonal flooding.

The main issue reported by local residents is not land degradation but excessive water extraction reducing the extent of the 'wetlands' and causing problems. There now exists substantial qualitative evidence that excessive water extraction is resulting in the contraction of Kimana Swamp, to the long-term detriment of all those dependent upon it. Similarly, water extraction by irrigators on the foothills of Kilimanjaro is further diminishing water availability in the lowlands of Kuku Group Ranch (so much so, in fact, that the once-thriving irrigation settlement of Olorika is now virtually uninhabited). For pastoralists dependent upon the outflow of Kuku's irrigation systems, maintenance of their water supply has become increasingly dependent upon their ability to coerce irrigators into relinquishing their rights to water so that the lowland swamps are recharged, at least periodically.

Resource access and socio-economic differentiation in Loitokitok

To many observers, increasing social and economic differentiation in Maasailand is directly attributable to the policies pursued by central government, particularly the creation of group ranches (White and Meadows, 1981). While some have prospered from the opportunities provided by commoditization (Box 3.7), others have not and 'have either been forced into Nairobi for unskilled employment … or have been caught in the poverty trap on lands too arid to support them' (Asiema and Situma, 1994:165). Following the onset of drought in 1994, some 75,000 people in Kajiado District (29 per cent of the district population) were said to be 'in dire need of emergency relief supplies' (Daily Nation, 1994:8). The Chief of Kimana, early in that year, estimated that, of the Location's 18,000 population, half urgently required emergency food relief. Indeed, by the end of 1994, some 9,800 bags of maize had been distributed by the divisional administration. World Vision, one of the few active non-governmental organizations (NGOs) in Loitokitok, extended its famine relief programme to some 25,000 people in the division between 1993 and 1995.

Field research revealed that the losers in the contest to access resources are often caught within a poverty trap. For example, Ene Aramato lost her husband through illness some years ago. Today she relies on her children to herd and tend her cattle. As access to local pasture and fodder has become increasingly commoditized and beyond

---

Box 3.7   Economic accumulation: case-studies from Kimana/Tikondo

Joseph Lelei lost sixty head of cattle during the droughts of the early 1970s, leaving him with only four. 'I was a pastoralist all my life, and didn't know anything about crop farming … But I had to accept the bitter pill.' Lelei moved to Namelok in 1977 and sold his cattle to buy onion seeds and food for his family. He began irrigating a 2-acre plot, allocated to him by Olgolului Group Ranch, adjacent to Egumi spring. With the income from his first onion crop of KSh 32,000, he purchased twenty head of cattle. Since then he has subdivided the land he was allocated, now has almost 300 cattle, has invested in a shop and a vehicle and can afford to send his children to school.

Chief ole Musa was given a loan by the County Council in 1975, which he took to Tanzania to purchase cattle, which he sold in Nairobi. Within 33 days, he had made over 1,000 per cent profit, which he has since invested in cultivation and livestock. He now has a herd of 500 cattle, his own lorry to transport crops and a large brick-built house. He continues to invest profit from cultivation in cattle.

Lolkinyei ole Ntipilit earned money during army service, with which he purchased twenty cows and ten goats in 1949. Having lost many animals during the droughts in the subsequent 2 years, he began cultivating in Kimana, using knowledge acquired while in the army. By 1958, he had made enough to purchase a motor vehicle. Today he lists a lorry, a four-wheel drive car, three wives and 300 cattle as 'proceeds from cultivation'. A similar story is told by 'Singh', as detailed above (see Box 3.6). Through investment in irrigation development, he has been able to send his ten children to school.

---

her means during the long dry season, her children have to take the herd to the distant Chyulu Hills. In 1994, drought and disease decimated her cattle and she was left with only two head. At the time of the research, her family was dependent on government and NGO relief handouts and the support of neighbours, and she could see no way of rebuilding the family's asset base.

Many others in Ene Aramato's position are losing direct access to resources and becoming increasingly dependent upon 'off-farm' means of support. As Zaal and Dietz (1997:7) comment, 'At the bottom of the economic scale, those losing control of adequate pastoral resources will seek wage-paying employment, and some may become paid herders.' The authors, somewhat optimistically, argue that this allows the less well-off to rebuild their herds after drought or disease, particularly if they are allowed to share herd management with their employer. Consequently, so they argue, among all brackets of the Loitokitok population, 'livestock-related activities are only part of a broader survival package' (Zaal and Dietz, 1997:24).

To ascribe inequality solely to commoditization, entailing the integration of the area in the national economy and changing agrarian structures in Loitokitok, overlooks an important point. Opportunities made available by commoditization very much depend on the distribution and allocation of (*de facto* and *de jure*) rights of access to resources (and particularly land) in Loitokitok, and rights are much influenced by the politics of age, kinship and ethnicity. Thus, while commoditization is likely to generate a degree of economic differentiation, economically and politically powerful actors typically determine who the winners and losers are likely to be.

Wealth is now significantly related to land ownership, which is, in turn, affected by position within local (and wider) patronage networks. Vast areas of land in Loitokitok have fallen under the control of Kenya's political élite, as clan politics has become an element of party politics (see above). The national vice-president owns a large tract of land on the slopes of Kilimanjaro. More significantly, large areas of group ranch land are being given to local and national leaders, irrespective of group ranch members' views. As long as productive land remains under group ranch tenure, it will continue to be privatized on a *de facto* basis to the benefit of patrons of group ranch leaders.

Ethnicity, as discussed above, is also an important determinant of ability to access resources. The question of Maasai sovereignty in Kajiado and Narok Districts is highly sensitive, attracts international attention and is periodically intensified by inflammatory public declarations by senior Maasai political figures. The legitimacy of property and usufruct rights varies according to ethnic identity, as William Karanja's story testifies (Box 3.4). Tenant irrigators have been forced off their rented land, denied access to water for irrigation and, in many cases, driven away from Loitokitok altogether. The local Maasai élite and their regional and national patrons then seize these economic opportunities.

Among the Maasai, inequality is also closely associated with age-group politics. To many contemporary *ilmurran,* the opportunities of commoditization are linked to group ranch registration, and the individual ownership of land, which many expect this will offer. Thus a new cohort of *ilmurran,* numbering an estimated 10,000, are clamouring for group ranch membership and access to the land market in Loitokitok. Inequality threatens to become established in a more permanent form if a large proportion of the Maasai community are denied group ranch membership and, with it, the opportunity to acquire property rights in land. As long as the present group ranch arrangements exist, issues of age and inequality will not go away. Registration of the present cohort of *ilmurran* will merely herald the start of a new wave of protest by the next.

There are, of course, more than just political dimensions to inequality in Loitokitok. Many Maasai resident in areas of Kuku and Mbirikani Group Ranches are disadvantaged by a poor resource base and their geographical location. The shortage of income-generating opportunities in such remote areas and the poor infrastructure preclude many from diversifying their livelihoods, and consequently the nutritional status of the population in these areas is poor (KDDP, 1994). De Leeuw and Grandin (1990) report that large livestock losses in Mbirikani have required livestock slaughter and sales to make up household food deficits. These same areas are predominantly inhabited by the most marginalized Maasai, whose ability to secure access to resources has been systematically undermined. With a growing population, poor infrastructure and the capture of new economic opportunities by an increasingly ruthless national and local élite, rising inequality and poverty are the unsurprising result.

The future of uncommon property

A complex set of forces have reshaped the access, use and management of land and water in Loitokitok Division. These have involved both deliberate public policy interventions (and their mode of implementation or non-implementation) and more diffuse responses to changing economic, social and political conditions at local, national and international levels.

Policy efforts are often contradictory. While rangeland policy has attempted to formalize and modernize the common property institutions of Maasai pastoralists, other land reform policies have allowed the individualization of ownership and the formation of active markets for land and water. A set of institutional frameworks now overlie each other – the 'customary', the formalized common-property regime and the market. On the edges of the division, further complications are added: two large areas that were important to the pastoral resource – the Amboseli basin and the slopes of Kilimanjaro – are state-owned and controlled for conservation purposes. The neat plans and maps of ownership type and resource use drawn up by land-use planners in the late colonial period bear only a slight resemblance to the messy patchwork of ownership and uses that has developed since, but which they have partially shaped in unintended and contradictory ways.

Also significant is the trajectory of state formation in Kenya, which has created a dense web of competing patron–client chains as a rapacious national élite seeks to benefit from the country's natural resources by 'doing deals' with local élites. In particular, ministers, local MPs, functionaries of KANU and the district adminis-tration (controlled by the Office of the President) have sought to gain preferential access to resources and to ensure that the institutions that control access and manage land and water are headed by pro-KANU individuals. The means of achieving this range from the legal (e.g. canvassing for votes in general elections and group ranch elections; private purchases of freeholds in an open market) to the doubtful (e.g. recording non-local civil servants as members of group ranches) to the illegal (e.g. rigging elections, abrogating the requirements of Land Acts and physically threat-ening certain ethnic groups).

While this means that predicting the outcomes of policy interventions is difficult – given that the practice is quite different from policy as formulated – there is a clear social dynamic that underpins outcomes. This is the capacity of the patron–client chains that link the national élite to the local level to gain control over resources that offer opportunities for accumulation. As southern Kajiado's wetlands have been opened up to new forms of commoditization – particularly irrigated agriculture and wildlife tourism – powerful national groups have increasingly promoted local alliances to gain from these activities.

The overall results of this scramble for the wetlands are complex, but our research permits a number of conclusions to be drawn:

1. Sustainability. Concepts of sustainability range from biodiversity fundamentalism (the retention of all species and their genetic base at present levels) to more instrumentalist interpretations (the maintenance of fundamental hydrological and biological processes and not exceeding the 'sink' capacities of the envi-ronment). Recent environmental changes in the Loitokitok area certainly fail to meet a strict biodiversity criterion; the 'wetlands in drylands' have been 'simplified' and the area's capacity to meet the needs of large numbers of mobile

ungulate and predator populations has been reduced. However, biodiversity has not been greatly reduced (to date) and basic hydrological and biological processes continue to function. While the environmental crisis and desertification long predicted have not occurred, there are grounds for concern about water quality and quantity in the wetlands.

2. Productivity. In terms of economic productivity recent change in Loitokitok Division must be judged a success. Its economy has diversified from a pastoralist base into dryland cultivation, irrigated horticulture, wildlife tourism and rural service provision. Vegetable production makes a significant contribution to meeting demand in Nairobi and Mombasa, while the tourist activities generate earnings that run into several million dollars. 'Product development' in the tourist industry – such as walking safaris and the recently established Kimana Wildlife Sanctuary on the group ranch, 'village-based' holidays and wildfowl hunting – offer opportunities for further value-added activities and, perhaps, for channelling the wealth created by tourism into the local economy to a greater degree.

3. Inequality and poverty. It is most likely that inequality has increased greatly in recent times. Assets and income are concentrated in the hands of relatively few accumulators, alongside significant numbers of people who have persistent problems in meeting basic food needs, who cannot pay primary school fees and who have very limited access to primary health care facilities. This marks a fundamental change in terms of the distribution of wealth and well-being. As the National Poverty Eradication Plan (Government of Kenya, 1999) indicates, in ASAL areas, such as Loitokitok, more than 50 per cent of the population fails to meet the income levels of the national poverty line. The processes of change examined in this study suggest that the poor in Loitokitok have diminishing access to resources. Some would argue that such losses will be more than compensated by the generation of new employment opportunities as ownership of land and water is concentrated in the hands of those who can use them most efficiently. Evidence of such a positive labour market response in the Loitokitok area, or more widely in the region, was not found by this study.

The study reveals weaknesses in the theoretical frameworks that underpin analysis of governance of Kenya's wetlands in drylands, and which often underpin policy. At their heart is a quest for the optimal tenure and management regime for a particular use of a bounded natural resource. Neoclassical economic theory points to the advantage of private property and markets under certain conditions. The new institutional economics argues the optimality of collective ownership under a different set of conditions. Approaches that highlight the role of democratic or representative bodies in allocating rights and/or taking management decisions have foundered in the complexity of Kenyan politics.

Our study shows that resource use is dynamic, not fixed, and hence the effectiveness of institutions cannot simply be assessed in terms of their impact on any single use of a given resource. Rather, this judgement must be based on their capacity to change, combine and regulate multiple uses. Secondly, in wetlands in drylands, the relationships between different forms of institution – state, collective and private – are as important as the internal processes of each institution (see Robinson and White (1997) and Robinson et al. (2000) for discussions on the centrality of how sets of institutions relate to each other for the understanding of how development goals can be achieved). All three converge in (if not originate from) the same physical space, so an exclusive focus on any one institutional arena distorts analysis. Finally, such models have limited analytical use because of their failure to consider the political economies within which resource access and use occur. Entrepreneurs in Loitokitok are not individual firms seeking to maximize profits: they are also members of common property regimes and political actors with relations to bureaucrats and politicians. Local bureaucrats are not simply technically competent policy imple-menters (or rent seekers maximizing income): they are parts of the local and national political structure, probably businessmen/women in their own right and with perhaps an interest in common property forms as well. All of the actors have multiple identities and play multiple roles.

The competing normative theoretical models that have informed understanding and policy in Kenya's drylands fail to appreciate that change is not a design but is constituted by ongoing social and political struggles (Long and van der Ploeg, 1989, 1994). Such one-dimensional analyses may appear attractive, because of their simplicity, but may actively reduce our understanding of the overlapping institutional frameworks that shape access, management and use and of the struggles for change. Policy interventions to 'improve' the outcomes of land and water use in Kenya's drylands are merely an influence on what happens on the ground. The assumption that new institutions for access and management can be designed and imposed on the people who utilize such resources is a fiction in contemporary Kenya.

References

Adams, J.S. & McShane, T.O. (1992) *The Myth of Wild Africa: Conservation Without Illusion*. Norton, New York.

Asiema, J.K. & Situma, F.D.P. (1994) 'Indigenous peoples and the environment: the case of the pastoral Maasai of Kenya'. *Colorado Journal of International Environmental Law and Policy* 5, 149–71.

Bekure, S., de Leeuw, P.N., Grandin, B.E. & Neate, P.J.H. (1991) *Maasai Herding: An Analysis of the Livestock Production System of Maasai Pastoralists in Eastern Kajiado, Kenya*. International Livestock Centre for Africa, Addis Ababa.

Bernard, F.E., Campbell, D.J. & Thom, D.J. (1989) 'Carrying capacity of the eastern ecological gradient of Kenya'. *National Geographic Research* 5, 399–421.

Campbell, D.J. (1978) *Coping with Drought in Kenya Maasailand: Pastoralists and Farmers of the Loitokitok Area, Kajiado District*. IDS Working Paper 337, Institute for Development Studies, Nairobi.

Campbell, D.J. (1986) 'The prospect for desertification in Kajiado District, Kenya'. *Geographical Journal* 152, 44–55.

Collett, D. (1987) 'Pastoralists and wildlife: image and reality in Kenya Maasailand'. In: Anderson, D. and Grove, R. (eds) *Conservation in Africa: People, Policies and Practice*. Cambridge University Press, Cambridge, 129–47.

Daily Nation (1994) 'Hunger in Kajiado'. *Daily Nation* 30 January, 8–9.

Darkoh, M.B.K. (1990) 'Kenya's environment and environmental management'. *Journal of Eastern African Research and Development* 20, 1–40.

de Leeuw, P.N. & Grandin, B.E. (1990) 'Some aspects of pastoral livestock production in Kajiado District'. In van Klinken, M.K. and ole Seitah, J. (eds) *The Future of Maasai Pastoralists in Kajiado District. Proceedings of a Conference held in Brackenhurst Baptist International Conference Centre, Limuru, Kenya, 28–31 May 1989*. ASAL, Kajiado, 69–78.

Economic Review (1997) 'Maasailand: war by proxy'. *Economic Review* 8–14 September, 22.

Ecosystems (1992) *Amboseli/Lower Rift Regional Study Report for Wildlife Planning Unit, Ministry of Tourism & Wildlife*. Nairobi, Government Printer.

Evangelou, P. (1984) *Livestock Development in Kenya's Maasailand*. Westview Press, Boulder.

Finkel, M. & Darkoh, M.B.K. (1990) 'Sustaining the arid and semi-arid (ASAL) environment in Kenya through improved pastoralism and agriculture'. *Journal of Eastern African Research and Development* 21, 1–20.

Fosbrooke, H.A. (1948) 'An administrative survey of the Masai social system'. *Tanganyika Notes and Records* 26, 1–50.

Galaty, J.G. (1980) 'The Maasai group ranch: politics and development in an African pastoral society'. In: Salzman, P.C. (ed.) *When Nomads Settle: Processes of Sedentarization as an Adaptation and Response*. Praeger, New York, 157–72.

Galaty, J.G. (1981) 'Land and livestock among Kenyan Maasai'. In: Galaty, J.G. and Salzman, P.C. (eds) *Change and Development in Nomadic and Pastoral Societies*. Brill, Leiden, 66–88.

Galaty, J.G. (1992) '"The land is yours": social and economic factors in the privatization, sub-division and sale of Maasai ranches'. *Nomadic Peoples* 30, 26–40.

Ghai, Y.P. & McAuslan, J.P.W.B. (1970) *Public Law and Political Change in Kenya: A Study of the Legal Framework of Government from Colonial Times to the Present*. Oxford University Press, Nairobi.

Glover, P.E. & Gwynne, M.D. (1961) 'The destruction of Masailand'. *New Scientist* 11 (249), 450–3.

Government of Kenya (1994) *National Environmental Action Plan*. Government Printer, Nairobi.

Government of Kenya (1999) *National Poverty Eradication Plan*. Government Printer, Nairobi.

Grandin, B.E., de Leeuw, P.N. & Lembuya, P. (1989) 'Drought, resource distribution and mobility in two Maasai group ranches, southeastern Kajiado District'. In Downing, T.E., Gitu, W. and Kamau, C.M. (eds) *Coping With Drought in Kenya: National and Local Strategies*. Lynne Rienner, Boulder/London, 245–63.

High Court of Kenya (1994) *Transcription of Civil Suit No. 5003, Kimana/Tikondo Group Ranch versus District Land Adjudication Officer, Kajiado*. High Court of Kenya, Nairobi.

IDB (1993) *District Profile; Kajiado District, Rift Valley Province*. Irrigation and Drainage Branch, District Irrigation Unit, Kajiado.

IDB (1994) *District Profile; Kajiado District, Rift Valley Province*. Irrigation and Drainage Branch, District Irrigation Unit, Kajiado.

Jacobs, A.H. (1963) *The Pastoral Maasai of Kenya: A Report of Anthropological Field Research*. Department of Anthropology, University of Illinois, Illinois.

Jacobs, A.H. (1975) 'Maasai pastoralism in historical perspective'. In: Monod, T. (ed.) *Pastoralism in Tropical Africa*. Oxford University Press, London, 406–25.

KDAR (1957) *Kajiado District Annual Report 1957*. Government of Kenya, Nairobi.

KDDP (1989) *Kajiado District Development Plan 1989–1993*. Ministry of Planning and National Development, Nairobi.

KDDP (1994) *Kajiado District Development Plan 1994–1996*. Office of the Vice-President and Ministry of Planning and National Development, Nairobi.

Kimani, J.K. (1988) *Evaluation of Irrigation Developments in Loitokitok Division: Report of a Multidisciplinary Task Force*. Rural Development Services, Nairobi.

Kitching, G. (1980) *Class and Economic Change in Kenya: The Making of an African Petite Bourgeoisie 1905–1970*. Yale University Press, New Haven.

Kituyi, M. (1990) *Becoming Kenyans: Socio-Economic Transformation of the Pastoral Maasai*. ACTS Press, Nairobi.

Leach, M. & Mearns, R. (1996) *The Lie of the Land: Challenging Received Wisdom on the African Environment*. James Currey, Oxford.

Lema, A.J. (1990) 'East African climate: 1880–1990'. *Water Resources Development* 6, 270–7.

Lewis, E.A. (1934) 'Tsetse-flies in the Masai Reserve, Kenya Colony'. *Bulletin of Entomological Research* 25, 439–55.

Leys, N. (1973) *Kenya*, 4th edn. Frank Cass, London.

Long, N. & van der Ploeg, J.D. (1989) 'Demythologizing planned intervention: an actor perspective'. *Sociologia Ruralis* 29, 226–49.

Long, N. & van der Ploeg, J.D. (1994) 'Heterogeneity, actor and structure: towards a reconstitution of the concept of structure'. In: Booth, D. (ed.) *Rethinking Social Development: Theory, Research and Practice*. Longman Scientific and Technical, Harlow, 62–89.

MALDM (1993) *Asian Vegetable Production and Recipe Handbook 1993*. Ministry of Agriculture, Livestock Development and Marketing, Horticultural Division, Home Economics Branch, Nairobi.

Munei, K. (1991) *Study of Effect of Subdivision of Group Ranches in Kajiado District*. Department of Livestock Production/ASAL Programme, Kajiado.

Ndagala, D.N. (1982) '"Operation Imparnati": the sedentarization of the pastoral Maasai in Tanzania'. *Nomadic Peoples* 10, 28–38.

Ndagala, D.N. (1992) *Territory, Pastoralists, and Livestock: Resource Control Among the Kisongo Maasai.* Uppsala Studies in Cultural Anthropology 18, Acta Universitatis Upsaliensis, Uppsala.

NEMU (1993) *The Multi-Party General Elections in Kenya: The Report of the National Election Monitoring Unit.* NEMU, Nairobi.

Odundo, P. (1992) 'The environmental effects of sub-division of group ranches in Kajiado District'. In van Klinken, M.K. (ed.) *The Future of Maasai Pastoralists in Kajiado District: Proceedings of a Conference Held at Olkejuado High School, Kajiado, Kenya, 18–21 August 1991.* ASAL Programme, Kajiado, 19–23.

Okoth-Ogendo, H. (1991) *Tenants of the Crown: Evolution of Agrarian Law Institutions in Kenya.* ACTS Press, Nairobi.

ole Katampoi, A.K. (1993) 'Should the youth sit on the fence in matters of land?' *Kajiado Focus* 5, 2–3.

ole Marsharen, S. (1989) *The Green Revolution in Maasailand.* ASAL Programme, Kajiado.

Ottichelo, W.K., Kinuthia, J.H., Ratego, P.O. & Nasubo, G. (1991) *Weathering the Storm: Climatic Change and Investment in Kenya.* ACTS Press, Nairobi.

Oyugi, W.O. (1983) 'Local government in Kenya: a case of institutional decline'. In: Mawhood, P. (ed.) *Local Government in the Third World.* Wiley, Chichester, 109–43.

Range Planning Unit (1990) *Development Plan for Kimana Group Ranch.* Range Planning Unit, Department of Livestock Production, Kajiado.

Republic of Kenya (1989) *Republic of Kenya Development Plan 1989–1994.* Government Printer, Nairobi.

Republic of Kenya (1994) *Republic of Kenya Development Plan 1994–1996.* Government Printer, Nairobi.

Republic of Kenya (1996) *Kenya Population Census 1989, Analytical Report* Vol. VII: *Population Projections.* Central Bureau of Statistics, Office of the Vice-President, Ministry of Planning and National Development, Nairobi.

Rigby, P. (1985) *Persistent Pastoralists: Nomadic Societies in Transition.* Zed Books, London.

Robinson, M. & White, E. (1997) *The Role of Civic Organisations in the Provision of Social Services: Towards Synergy.* Research for Action Paper 37, UNU/WIDER, Helsinki.

Robinson, D., Hewitt, T. & Harriss, J. (2000) *Managing Development. Understanding Inter-Organizational Relationships.* Sage, London.

Roe, E. (1995) 'Except Africa: postscript to a special section on development narratives'. *World Development* 23, 1065–9.

Rutten, M.M.E.M. (1992) *Selling Wealth to Buy Poverty: The Process of the Individualization of Landownership Among the Maasai Pastoralists of Kajiado District, Kenya, 1890–1990.* Verlag Breitenbach, Saarbrücken.

Sammy, W. (1993) 'Kajiado youth speak out'. *Kajiado Focus* 5, 1.

Sandford, G.R. (1919) *An Administrative and Political History of the Masai Reserve.* Waterloo and Sons, London.

Scoones, I. (1994) 'New directions in pastoral development in Africa'. In: Scoones, I. (ed.) *Living with Uncertainty: New Directions in Pastoral Development in Africa.* Intermediate Technology Publications, London, 1–36.

Sindiga, I. (1984) 'Land and population problems in Kajiado and Narok, Kenya'. *African Studies Review* 27, 1–22.

Southgate, C. & Hulme, D. (1996a) *Environmental Management in Kenya's Arid and Semi-Arid Lands: An Overview.* IDPM GEC/ESRC Working Paper No. 2, IDPM, Manchester.

Southgate, C. & Hulme, D. (1996b) *Land, Water and Local Governance in Kajiado: A District Overview.* IDPM GEC/ESRC Working Paper No. 3, IDPM, Manchester.

Southgate, C. & Hulme, D. (1996c) *Land, Water and Local Governance in a Kenyan Wetland in Dryland: The Kimana Group Ranch and its Environs.* IDPM GEC/ESRC Working Paper No. 4, IDPM, Manchester.

Southgate, C.R.J. (1998) 'Understanding the decline of the Maasai commons: a case study from southern Kajiado, Kenya'. A thesis submitted to the University of Manchester for the degree of Doctor of Philosophy in the Faculty of Economic and Social Studies.

Spencer, P. (1990) 'Time and the boundaries of the economy in Maasai'. In: Baxter, P.T.W. and Hogg, R. (eds) *Property, Poverty and People: Changing Rights in Property and Problems of Pastoral Development.* Department of Social Anthropology and the International Development Centre, University of Manchester, Manchester, 121–8.

Sutton, J.E.G. (1993) 'Becoming Maasai'. In Spear, T. and Waller, R. (eds) *Being Maasai: Ethnicity and Identity in East Africa.* James Currey, London, 38–60.

Swynnerton, R.J.M. (1954) *A Plan to Intensify the Development of African Agriculture in Kenya.* Government Printer, Nairobi.

Thomson, J. (1886) 'East Central Africa, and its commercial outlook'. *Scottish Geographical Magazine* 2, 65–78.

van Klinken, M.K. & ole Seitah, S.T. (eds) (1990) *The Future of Maasai Pastoralists in Kajiado District (Kenya). Proceedings of a Conference Held at Brackenhurst Baptist International Conference Centre, Limuru, Kenya, 28–31 May 1989.* ASAL Programme, Kajiado.

Western, D. (1994) 'Ecosystem conservation and rural development: the case of Amboseli'. In Western, D., Wright, R.M. and Strum, S.C. (eds) *Natural Connections: Perspectives in Community-Based Conservation*. Island Press, Washington, DC, 15–51.

Western, D. (1998) *In the Dust of Kilimanjaro*. Island Press, Washington, DC.

White, J.M. & Meadows, S.J. (1981) *Evaluation of the Contribution of Group and Individual Ranches in Kajiado District, Kenya, to Economic Development and Pastoral Production Strategies*. Ministry of Livestock Development, Nairobi.

Zaal, F. & Dietz, T. (1997) 'Of markets, meat, maize and milk: pastoral commoditization in Kenya'. Mimeo, University of Amsterdam, Amsterdam.

4

Modernizing Communal Lands
Evolving Resource Use
in the Shoshong Hills, Botswana

ANDREW CLAYTON & PHILIP WOODHOUSE

Introduction

This case-study explores the management of land and water resources in Mmutlane village, in the Shoshong Hills, eastern Botswana. Historically dependent upon cash remittances from labour migrants to South Africa, Botswana has benefited from rapid economic growth since the development of diamond mining in the 1970s. High levels of state revenue, coupled with political stability since independence, have enabled the government to maintain a well-resourced state apparatus compared with many African countries. State policy towards rural areas has been characterized by support to large-scale livestock production and a series of welfare programmes delivered by 'deconcentrated' local agencies of government departments.

This study explores how government and village-level organizations control and manage resources, and the implications of current policies, which foster trends towards fencing of grazing and water resources. It is based on fieldwork and secondary research undertaken by Andrew Clayton in the village of Mmutlane, for three months between November 1994 and February 1995 (Clayton, 1995).

The context

The modern state of Botswana (Map 4.1) is dominated by the Kalahari desert, which extends from the south and west to cover some 84 per cent of the territory. Rainfall increases from an annual minimum of 250 mm in the Kalahari to around 650 mm in the north-east. The principal surface water resources are located at the country's northern and eastern margins: the Chobe River and the Okavango swamps at the Namibian frontier to the north-west, and the Limpopo River forming the border with South Africa to the east. Rain-fed agriculture is viable only on the 'hardveld' down the eastern side of the country, where higher rainfall and more fertile soils

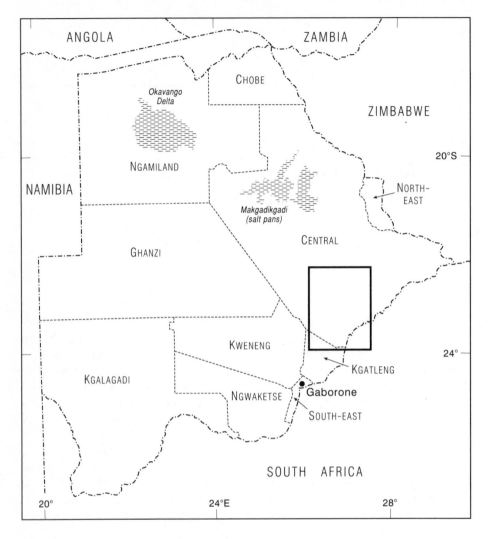

Map 4.1 Botswana: location of case-study

contrast with the arid 'sandveld' of the Kalahari.

Until the past half century, the sparse population of the Kalahari was made up almost exclusively of Kgalagadi and Sarwa (San) hunting people. The Tswana, moving across the Transvaal highveld are believed to have first settled the eastern fringes of the Kalahari in AD 500. However, the area remained peripheral to the Tswana states centred on the Transvaal until the early nineteenth century, when it received an influx of people and cattle fleeing the instability of the *mfecane* that accompanied the breakup of the Zulu kingdom and the impact of European incursion from the south. During the mid-nineteenth century, the western Tswana states, particularly the Kwena and Ngwato, were further enriched by the growing trade through their territory between the Cape colonies to the south and the Rhodesias to the north. Under increasing pressure from Afrikaner settlers, in 1885 the Tswana states (*morafe*) of 'Bechuanaland' agreed to protectorate status under the British, who thereby secured communications between the Cape and their central African colonies. Until the 1930s, the protectorate, administered from Mafeking, operated as a form of indirect rule *par excellence*. The *morafe* were translated into colonial districts administered by Tswana chiefs, the strength of whom was critical to, and enhanced by, the colonial authority (Peters, 1994:37). Despite the low profile of early colonial rule, the economy of the territory underwent profound change as a result of the growth in labour migration to the South African mines and of education and changing aspirations among the Tswana élite.

Labour migration to South Africa first began on a large scale at the end of the nineteenth century (Picard, 1987:110). The rinderpest epidemic of 1896–7 wiped out an estimated 90 per cent of cattle and the colonial administration introduced a hut tax in Bechuanaland in 1899 (Massey, 1980:7–15; Parson, 1985:21). This required cash income and, for many households, especially those without cattle, the only source of cash was waged employment in South Africa. The number of labour migrants gradually increased until, by 1935, an estimated 10,000 Batswana were working in South Africa (Schapera, 1947:32). During the period 1938–40, Schapera (1947:161) estimated that labour migration was the largest single contributor to household income: 42 per cent of the total.

The growth of labour migration was paralleled by the incorporation of the Tswana cattle economy into the wider livestock market of South Africa, and Tswana chiefs' attempts to improve and safeguard their access to this market through adopting white South African ranchers' production methods, notably breeding stock and boreholes. The first programme of drilling boreholes in the territory's African 'reserves' was undertaken in 1927 by the Kgatla leader Isang, using funds raised from a levy on taxpayers in Kgatleng district (Peters, 1994:58). It was followed in the 1930s by a British-funded drilling programme, which resulted in about 120 boreholes throughout the territory by 1940.

The focus of the economy on labour migration and commercial development of cattle-keeping continued in the postwar period, beyond independence in 1966, to the 1970s. By the mid-1960s, there were an estimated 50,000 labour migrants from Botswana working in South Africa, and by the 1970s approximately 70,000 (Colclough and McCarthy, 1980:171). The borehole drilling programme was expanded, allowing the extension of cattle grazing westwards into the sandveld, and an abattoir was opened at Lobatse in 1954, where cattle were processed for export. Between 1939 and 1957, it is estimated that cattle numbers doubled, reaching 1.3 million (Campbell, 1978). The growth in cattle numbers was accompanied by concerns about overgrazing and conservation of the range, and the onset of prolonged drought in 1960–5 resulted in the loss of about a third of the cattle population.

At independence in 1966, Botswana was among the ten poorest countries in the world, and meat and meat products accounted for over 90 per cent of the country's exports (Colclough and McCarthy, 1980:70). Approximately 50,000 of its men, a third of its male labour force, were working in South Africa (Colclough and McCarthy, 1980:170; Parson, 1985:40). The development of mineral resources, particularly diamonds, in the 1970s transformed the economy, producing an average annual gross national product (GNP) growth of 8.5 per cent during the 1980s. By 1992, Botswana was the third largest diamond producer in the world, and diamonds accounted for 79 per cent of export earnings, compared with only 3.5 per cent from meat and meat products (Central Statistical Office, 1993). The government's 50 per cent share of ownership of diamond production gives it a strong revenue stream, enabling it to invest in rural infrastructure and health and education services. While commercial cattle production has continued as a priority in government policy, reinforced through preferential trade arrangements for beef exports to the European Union (the Beef Protocol Agreement of 1972, under the Lomé Convention), since the 1980s the government has invested heavily in support for arable agriculture and in drought relief measures. Consequently, despite the frequent incidence of drought, and the lack of investment in arable agriculture during the colonial period (Picard, 1987:113–15), which made the country dependent on imports of food (MFDP, 1991: vol. 2, p. 9), the rural population has largely escaped malnutrition (FSG, 1990; Harvey and Lewis, 1990:302).

High rates of economic growth have led to a huge increase in employment opportunities. Harvey (1992:16) estimated that in 1989 total modern sector employment was 250,300 of a total population of about 1.3 million. Labour remittances from urban centres continue to form an essential part of rural household income, but in the 1980s increasing employment opportunities in Botswana resulted in a shift away from labour migration to South Africa. By 1986, there were four to five times as many Batswana employed in Botswana as outside the country (Harvey and Lewis, 1990:37). Temporary international labour migration has consequently been replaced by more permanent labour migration within Botswana. This has been reflected in a rapid urbanization of the population from the 1970s to the 1990s (Table 4.1).

Botswana is widely acknowledged as an African success story, with rapid economic development in the context of stable government and multiparty elections. The government is widely regarded as having avoided many of the pitfalls of other African governments through careful attention to macroeconomic planning (Good, 1992; Harvey, 1992) undertaken by a competent and efficient bureaucracy (Charlton, 1991; Borhaug, 1993; Somolekae, 1993). Adult literacy increased from 44 per cent in 1970 to 70 per cent in 1995, and infant mortality fell between 1960

Table 4. 1   Distribution of population between rural and urban areas in Botswana.

Year	Urban	Rural	Total
1971	54,416	519,678	574,094
1981	150,021	791,006	941,027
1991	606,239	720,557	1,326,796

and 1996 from 116 to 40 per thousand live births (UNDP, 1998:148). Multiparty elections, at national and district level, have been held every five years since independence. The Botswana Democratic Party (BDP), which depends on rural areas for the majority of its support, has won each of these with an overwhelming majority. The main opposition party, the Botswana National Front (BNF), has considerable urban support but has had less impact in rural areas except for Southern District. The need to maintain rural support has influenced government policies and programmes on rural development. This is critical, because surveys of rural income conducted in 1973–4 and 1986 showed that increasing inequalities in income have accompanied rapid economic growth (Molutsi, 1986), and, despite 13 years of rapid economic growth, there had been little measurable impact on the cash income of poor rural households (Harvey and Lewis, 1990:282). Moreover, poverty disparities were more marked in rural areas, with Gini coefficients increasing from 0.71 in 1981 to 0.76 in 1990 (Fidziani, 1996:21), compared with values of 0.57 for the country as a whole between 1974 and 1994 (Hudson and Wright, 1996; Reynolds, 1998). The main improvement for rural households during this period was the provision of services, notably water supply, education and health (Harvey, 1992:11).

A wetland in dryland

The study centres on the village of Mmutlane, at an altitude of 1,150 m in the Shoshong Hills in the eastern 'hardveld' (Map 4.2). Rainfall records from the neighbouring settlements at Mahalapye, 30 km to the south-east, and Kalamare, 15 km to the north, indicate an average annual precipitation of 470 mm and 434 mm, respectively, concentrated in the months October to April (Fig. 4.1). In addition to large year-to-year variations in rainfall, the recorded data (Fig. 4.2) show periods of greater frequency of drought years in the late 1920s and early 1930s, in the 1960s and in the 1980s. The Shoshong Hills give rise to a number of seasonal streams, the principal of which is the Bonwapitse River, which flows eastwards to join the Limpopo River. In addition, the microclimate and geology of the Shoshong Hills offer a relatively accessible and reliable source of groundwater throughout the year.

This may have been a significant factor in the establishment of the Ngwato capital from 1838 to 1889 on the site of the present village of Shoshong. Possibly during that time, a series of wells were sunk in the hills behind the site of the present village of Mmutlane by the Batalaote, a Tswana people who had left Kalamare to settle in Shoshong as subordinates to the Bangwato. According to Fosbrooke (1971), travellers in the 1860s reported Shoshong as a prosperous town of about 30,000 people, but 20 years later its population had halved and the site of the Ngwato capital was moved in 1889 to Palapye, and then in 1902 to Serowe, which has since remained the seat of the Bangwato tribal authority. Despite the removal of much of the population, control of the grazing and water resources of the Shoshong Hills remained ultimately with the authorities in Serowe, through resettlement of Shoshong village by Bangwato at the turn of the twentieth century and the settlement of the present

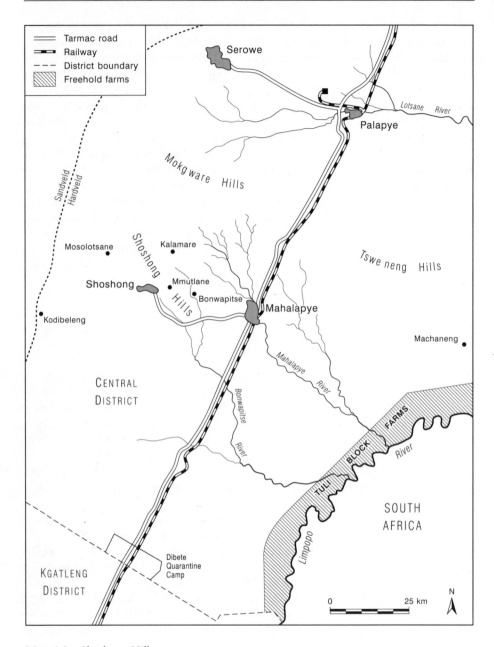

Map 4.2 Shoshong Hills

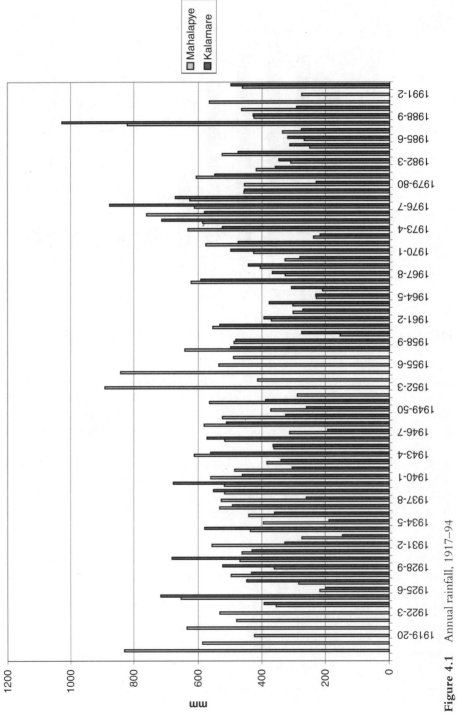

Figure 4.1   Annual rainfall, 1917–94

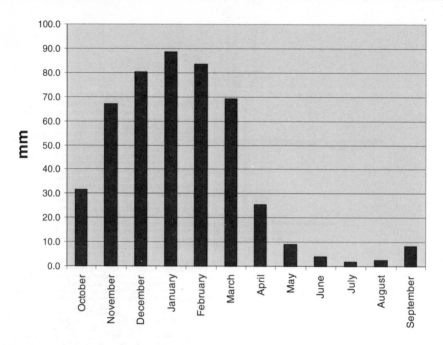

Figure 4.2 Rainfall distribution: Mahalapye (monthly average, 1917–94)

site of Mmutlane by seven Batalaote families in 1908. In addition, seasonally occupied herders' settlements or 'cattle posts' existed at Bonwapitse and Mahalapye. During the later colonial period, the latter's location on the railway line turned it into an administrative and transport centre, and its population growth eclipsed that of neighbouring villages (Table 4.2).

Although motivated primarily by the concerns of cattle production, settlements in the area were accompanied by rain-fed arable farming, most commonly of sorghum and cowpea. The combination of arable and livestock production was typically achieved by distributing activities between three sites: the residential village, the arable lands and the grazing areas around cattle posts. Historically,

Table 4.2 Population of villages in the vicinity of Shoshong Hills.

Village	1909	1936	1946	1964	1971	1981	1991
Shoshong	3,000	n/a	6,957	7,022	6,362	8,928	10,047
Kalamare	n/a	885	n/a	2,052	1,879	2,797	3,044
Mmutlane	n/a	302	n/a	540	764	962	1,004
Bonwapitse	n/a	n/a	n/a	n/a	n/a	409	465
Mahalapye	n/a	n/a	2,453	13,199	11,377	20,712	28,078

Source: Clayton (1995).
n/a, not available

resource use involved seasonal movement between cultivated and grazing areas, as well as movement between different seasonal grazing areas. Two trends in the cattle economy – towards permanent occupation of grazing areas around boreholes and towards fewer cattle-owning households (Peters, 1994:96, 117) – mean that there is less movement today than in the past, but interpretation of census data to specify this is tricky. For this reason, the data in Table 4.2 include population in both villages and their lands.

As a consequence of reduced movement, an estimated 75 per cent of human and livestock populations in Botswana depend on underground water supplies, through either boreholes or wells (Silitshena and McLeod, 1989:43). Given the lack of surface water, the production costs of irrigated agriculture are inflated by the costs of utilizing underground water, and imported produce from South Africa and Zimbabwe is cheaper.

Institutional frameworks

The village

The village of Mmutlane, on which this study centres, is ethnically homogeneous, populated by the Batalaote. According to the 1991 census, its resident population (as distinct from that in the village and its lands together, as given in Table 4.2) was 815, comprising 119 households organized in 15 wards. Each ward derives from different settler families (with one ward for each of the original seven families who founded the village in 1908) and has its own headman. Although membership of a ward is generally governed by kinship or marriage (daughters joining their husbands' wards), this is negotiable, and transfers may be authorized by ward headmen.

The village has a tribal court, local police station, primary school, agricultural office and health clinic. Institutionally, the village typifies the incorporation of Tswana customary forms into the modern state. The *kgotla* is the traditional Tswana village assembly. It remains respected as the primary forum for discussing village affairs, and all members of the village are allowed to attend and to speak at *kgotla* meetings. The *kgotla* also serves as the customary court where both civil and minor criminal cases are heard by the chief or headman. An estimated 80–85 per cent of all civil and criminal cases in Botswana are heard in the *kgotla* (Odell, 1982:9; Egner, 1986:17). The *kgotla* is also the primary means for the communication of government plans and policies. Officials and politicians address villagers at the *kgotla*, or the headman may call a *kgotla* meeting to inform villagers of government plans and proposals that will affect the village. The *kgotla* tradition of freedom of expression is seen as providing an opportunity for ordinary Batswana to discuss matters with civil servants, field officers, councillors and Members of Parliament. However, critics regard the *kgotla* as a means of legitimizing government policy and initiatives – informing villagers of policies already decided by central government or requesting their assistance in implementing programmes, rather than giving them an effective voice in decision-making (Odell, 1982:13; Lekorwe, 1989; Danevad, 1993:95).

The *kgotla* is presided over by the village headman, who is accountable, through the Shoshong subordinate tribal authority, to the Bangwato tribal authority in Serowe. Mmutlane also elects a district councillor to one of the 104 council seats in the Central District Council, also at Serowe. The District Council has departments responsible for education, health, works, roads, water supply and social and community development, each of which implements council programmes through staff based in five 'subordinate district councils'. Mmutlane comes under Mahalapye Subordinate District Council, whose Department of Social and Community Development supervises Mmutlane's Village Development Committee (VDC), responsible for promoting and coordinating village development. Although super-vised by district councils, the VDCs – established by a presidential directive in 1968 as non-statutory, non-political, voluntary committees of villagers – are legally separate from them. The VDC must communicate with the village, and seek approval of its plans and proposals at the *kgotla*. Most VDCs have between six and ten elected committee members, elected every 2 years at the *kgotla,* who then decide their chairman, deputy chairman, treasurer, secretary and assistant secretary. The headman and district councillor are ex-officio members, while government officials posted in the village are usually invited to attend as non-voting members. The extent to which other village leaders cooperate with and support the VDC varies from village to village. In some, the headman and VDC may work closely together. In others, there may be considerable tension between them, and the VDC may be used as a focus of opposition to the headman, whether from villagers or the councillor (Fortmann, 1986:39).

Government agencies

The key government ministries involved in natural resource management are Agriculture (MoA), Local Government, Lands and Housing (MLGLH) and Mineral Resources and Water Affairs (MMRWA), which has overall responsibility for the water sector in Botswana. However, the Ministry of Finance and Development Planning (MFDP) exerts an overriding influence on development planning.

The MoA is organized on sectoral lines, reflected in the major government agri-cultural programmes: the Tribal Grazing Lands Policy (TGLP), the Arable Lands Development Programme (ALDEP) and the Accelerated Rain-fed Arable Programme (ARAP), which concern either livestock or arable production but have not tried to integrate them. Sectoral divisions between livestock and arable production were further institutionalized in the restructuring of the MoA in 1990, and are reflected at the subnational level. There are six agricultural (i.e. arable) regions, divided into 25 agricultural districts in total, whose extension staff ('agricul-tural demonstrators') are concerned only with crop production. There are also 15 veterinary districts, whose staff cover animal health and production. The agricultural districts and veterinary districts maintain their own offices, and their boundaries do not coincide with each other or with the boundaries of administrative districts.

The MLGLH is responsible for four separate agencies of local government in Botswana. These are: the district administration, which represents the MLGLH at the district level; the district council made up of both elected and nominated councillors; the tribal administration, whose main responsibility now is to administer customary law through chiefs and village headmen; and the land boards, established in 1970 by the government to administer land, and comprising both elected and nominated members.

Local governance in Botswana depends on horizontal linkages between these agencies and on vertical linkages with central government ministries (Tordoff, 1988; Reilly and Tordoff, 1991). Decentralization in Botswana is characterized by decon- centration of power from central government to the district administration and field officers of central ministries, with limited decision-making powers devolved to elected local authorities (Egner, 1986:37; Reilly and Tordoff, 1991:152). District councils were established after independence in 1966 and took over many of the responsibilities of the district commissioners and the traditional authorities. However, within a few years, central government became disillusioned with the perceived inefficiency and ineffectiveness of the councils (Reilly and Tordoff, 1991:152). In addition, following the 1969 local elections, in which opposition parties made significant gains at the expense of BDP, the government was also concerned not to let district or town councils become centres of opposition (Gasper, 1990:234). The district administration was subsequently strengthened at the expense of the councils (Egner, 1986:38). For example, district development committees, established in 1971, were placed under the chairmanship of the district commis- sioner, not the council secretary. The district administration has continued to be strengthened *vis-à-vis* the councils.

Although the district councils' capacity to implement programmes has expanded greatly since they were established, they have little freedom to act independently of central government in financial management, revenue control and personnel management (Karlsson et al., 1993:19). Recruitment of council staff was taken over by central government in 1974 with the establishment of the Unified Local Government Service (ULGS) and the Unified Teaching Service. Consequent improvements in council staff career structures have been offset by concerns that councillors accountable to the electorate do not have sufficient authority over the actions of council staff. Proposals by the Local Government Structure Commission in 1979 to set up a statutory body with ultimate responsibility for all local authority staff, comprising representatives of MLGLH, local authorities and independent members, have not been implemented (Egner, 1986:56).

The most powerful form of control that central government exercises over councils is financial. Councils have a weak revenue base and are dependent on transfers from central government. Civil servants in MFDP and MLGLH make the key decisions about the funding that each council receives. Central government has discretionary powers to hold up or reduce disbursements of funds after each council's annual development budget has been agreed. Councils have not been able to decide how and when resources are used, but are subject to budgetary decisions made for them by central government (Egner, 1986:87–92; Danevad, 1993:122).

Land boards were established under the Tribal Land Act of 1968 to replace chiefs in the administration of 'tribal land', a designation applied by the newly independent government to 71 per cent of land in Botswana. Originally attached to each of the nine district councils, the land boards were subdivided in 1973 into twenty-three subordinate land boards (SLBs) in order to cope with their expanding workload in more populated districts. The number of SLBs has since been extended to thirty-six. Most land boards originally had six members: two from the district council, two from the tribal administration and two appointed by the MLGLH. Thus, although their role was to take over land allocation from chiefs, whose decisions were seen by government as inefficient and arbitrary, land boards retain a link with tribal administration.

In the mid-1980s, attempts were made to establish minimum educational require-ments for land board members and to ensure they received training in land board procedure. To improve the technical and organizational capacity of the land boards, responsibility for recruiting and training land board staff (the secretariat) was taken over by the ULGS. The autonomy of the land boards *vis-à-vis* district councils was strengthened, and the chief was removed as an ex-officio member of the land board. However, land boards were also encouraged to consult more carefully with tradi-tional authorities in reaching decisions. Peters (1994:130, 164) has observed that the continuing dependence of land boards on tribal authorities for advice is largely because the national government's designation of 'tribal' land as 'communal' (i.e. open to all Batswana) ignored the many claims of 'prior allocation' to which land in Botswana is subject. These claims stemmed, first, from chiefs' past delegation of rights to allocate land in specific areas to *badisa* ('overseers') or to particular families, and secondly, from the de facto control of grazing areas around boreholes by borehole owners, whether individuals or groups ('syndicates'). The issue of land tenure is explored further below.

The drought relief programme

During six consecutive seasons from 1981 to 1987, total rainfall in Botswana was between 16 per cent and 38 per cent below average (FSG, 1990: vol. 1, p. 4). Cattle losses amounted to 30 per cent of the national herd, and cereal imports were eleven times local production (MFDP, 1991:9, 14). Botswana avoided suffering a disaster of the kind that afflicted the Horn of Africa during this period, as a result of a government drought relief programme lasting from April 1982 until June 1988, at a cost of 258 million Pula. A drought recovery programme was then implemented for a further two years, at a cost of P182 million. In 1991, another drought began and government continued its drought relief and recovery programme. In addition to food provision to vulnerable groups, the 1991 drought relief programme had two main components: a public works programme – the labour-based relief programme (LBRP) – and support for agricultural activities. District councils and district agricul-tural offices are responsible for implementing these activities. District drought relief committees allocate LBRPs in their districts within overall funding limits fixed by the MFDP. The programme's size made it one of the main sources of rural investment funding managed by district councils. Evaluated as 'one of the most progressive responses to drought in Africa' (FSG, 1990: vol. 1, p. 14), it is believed to have prevented deaths from famine, contained rural malnutrition and limited the fall in rural incomes (FSG 1990: vol. 1, p. vii; Harvey and Lewis, 1990:305; see also Drèze and Sen, 1989).

The success of the programme derived from a number of factors. The government's revenue from mining allowed it to direct substantial expenditure to drought relief. Between 1984 and 1988, the four peak years of the programme, government expenditure on drought relief was approximately 15 per cent of the total development budget. Botswana also received substantial support from donors and non-governmental organizations (NGOs), mainly in the form of food aid rather than funding or operational support. Finally, and most significantly for this study, district councils had the main responsibility for implementing the drought relief programme at the local-level. Despite some constraints, district councils in Botswana display greater operational capacity than most local-level government elsewhere in Africa (FSG, 1990: vol. 1, pp. 4–14; vol. 6, pp. 2–5). The drought relief programme in Botswana exemplifies administrative deconcentration rather than devolution of decision-making. Key decisions about whether a drought is to be declared and the amount of funding to be made available are made by central government.

Through the LBRP, government provides cash-earning opportunities by providing materials and paying people for their labour. The district council appoints a drought coordinator to implement the LBRP, assisted by drought relief technical officers, who supervise LBRP projects. At village level, LBRP projects are managed by the VDC, who select both the labourers and supervisors for each project. The LBRP first started in 1980 and initially focused on rural road building and maintenance and construction of drift fences. Latterly, most LBRP projects undertake the construction of houses for teachers or other government employees posted to villages. LBRP projects initially followed the criteria that at least 70 per cent of total project costs must be for labour, later reduced to 60 per cent to enable a higher proportion to be spent on building materials in more sophisticated construction projects (Sorto, 1992).

The drought relief programme also provides subsidies for agriculture. This is handled by the MoA through the district agricultural offices. Until 1990, drought assistance was provided under ARAP. Since 1991, the subsidies are limited to a maximum of 5 hectares. In 1994–5, farmers received P120 per hectare for ploughing and P50 per hectare for row planting, and free seeds for planting up to 5 hectares. The considerable work required to measure farmers' fields and certify claims for payment has become the largest part of agricultural demonstrators' workload.

Access to land and water

The role of the land board

All the land in Mahalapye subdistrict is 'tribal' land, except for a strip of freehold land along the Limpopo, known as the Tuli Block, allocated to European settlers in the colonial period. Access to land and water in Mmutlane is governed by the Shoshong

SLB, one of 13 SLBs under the Bangwato Land Board in Serowe and one of three SLBs within Mahalapye Subordinate District. The boundary between the Shoshong SLB and the neighbouring Mahalapye SLB is marked by the Bonwapitse River in the vicinity of Mmutlane.

The Shoshong SLB has eight members, four selected from a list of 20 candidates elected by *kgotla* every five years in the villages covered by the SLB and four appointed by the MLGLH. The selection committee, chaired by the District Officer for Mahalapye Subordinate District, both selects elected candidates and also recommends members for the minister's nomination. In 1994, seven of the members of the Shoshong SLB came from the list of 20 originally elected by village *kgotla*, and five were re-elected members of the previous SLB.

The SLB is responsible for allocating rights to arable land and water points (including boreholes, wells and dams). While it is not responsible for allocating grazing rights, in the sense that grazing land is formally 'communal' and open to all Batswana, the SLB exerts control of access to grazing through permits for the development of water points or allocation of land for cultivation in designated grazing areas.

Arable land

Arable fields ('lands'), which in Mmutlane start about 2 kilometres away from the village, are allocated to individual families and can be inherited but not bought or sold. Formerly, allocations were made by the village headman, and some of the cultivated lands around Mmutlane were allocated before the establishment of the land board. Farmers in Mmutlane commonly assert that there is no shortage of arable land in the area. However, there is evidence, if not of current shortage, then of likely future scarcity of land. This is suggested by the increased use of fencing of allocated but 'undeveloped' land. Fencing is encouraged by the government's ALDEP and ARAP subsidies of 85 per cent of the cost. However, fencing of undeveloped land goes beyond the need to protect crops from livestock to a demarcation of boundaries for future cultivation, or even as a 'reserve' for the landholder's children. In general, land boards are supposed to reallocate land not developed within five years of allocation, and it may be that the absence of enforcement of this rule – or of demands for its enforcement – in Mmutlane implies the absence of competition for land. This is reinforced by the absence of land disputes in the minutes of the Shoshong SLB and in the casebook of the customary court since 1990.

However, the minutes of the Shoshong SLB for the period from March 1990 to September 1994 reflect a concern with formally demarcating land ownership through registration and fencing of land. Between 1990 and 1994, 36 villagers from Mmutlane applied for new allocations of arable lands and 27 applied to register land which they had used since before 1970. None of these applications was rejected, although three of the former and two of the latter were deferred, either because applicants were not present or because the land board wanted a letter of consent from the previous owner.

Land board minutes also indicate that it approves most applications for new fields in other villages within its area of jurisdiction. For example, between 1990 and 1994, there were 65 applications for new fields at Kalamare, of which 62 were accepted, two deferred and one rejected, and 39 applications for field registration, of which 35 were accepted, three deferred and one disapproved.

Grazing land

Historically, grazing areas centred on cattle posts distant from the village and lands. No formal permission is needed from the government to open a cattle post. In the past, the chief appointed *badisa,* or overseers, to control access to grazing land, but today this has been largely supplanted by control of grazing areas through borehole ownership. Cattle posts belonging to villagers from Mmutlane include some at Mmaphala, 30 kilometres east of Mahalapye on the Taupye River, a grazing area granted to the Batalaote by the Bangwato in the nineteenth century, and on the Mahalapye River, about 25 kilometres north of Mmutlane. These cattle posts include boreholes owned by individual Mmutlane villagers. No one in Mmutlane currently owns a borehole in the sandveld to the west, but villagers from Mmutlane who keep cattle posts in the west make arrangements with borehole owners for access to water.

In addition to cattle post areas, all land outside the village not allocated for arable use is referred to as 'communal grazing land'. Even in the lands area there are pockets that have not been allocated and are used for grazing cattle or small stock. The communal grazing land around Mmutlane is open to anyone, not just those from the village. The only measure the village has taken to control access has been to construct a 'drift fence' to keep cattle out of the lands area during the growing season. After harvest, livestock are allowed to feed on crop residues. The fence has become more important as an increasing number of owners keep cattle on the lands throughout the year (see below). The advantage of the drift fence is that, if herding labour is scarce, cattle can be kept on the far side of the drift fence and left unattended during the day with no danger to crops. One farmer described the drift fence as an extra herdboy.

Water (Map 4.3 and Table 4.3)

Since before the foundation of the village, the only dependable water for domestic and livestock use was from the Sepolwane wells in the hills behind Mmutlane. However, since 1967 a plentiful supply of good-quality domestic water in Mmutlane has been provided by a borehole, drilled by the government and maintained by the water unit of the district council, which employs a man from Mmutlane as the borehole operator. There are several standpipes around the village, and some households have paid to have their own standpipes. There are no boreholes or taps on the lands area, where people must rely on small dams or open wells for water for domestic use during the rainy season. During the dry season these sources dry up but by then most of the population have returned to the village. An alternative supply of water at the lands is to fill containers in the village and transport them back to the lands on donkey carts.

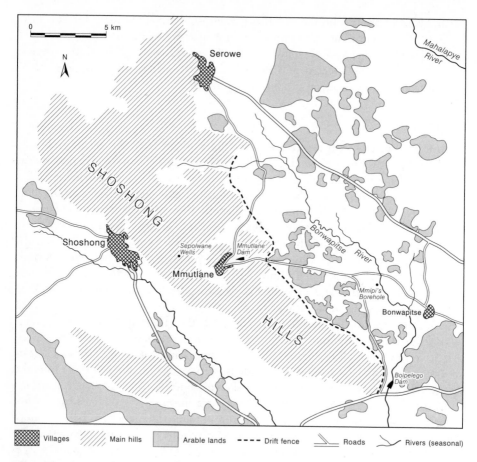

Map 4.3 Dams & boreholes in the case-study area

Villagers from Mmutlane who keep their cattle at cattle posts either own or have access to a permanent water supply. This is usually a borehole, but some use hand-dug wells in the river bed of the Mahalapye River. In the village and lands, the main source of water for livestock is the village dam, about half a kilometre from the village. The dam, constructed in 1952 by the colonial government, is shallow, with an earth embankment. It fills up during the rainy season, but in most years it dries up by September or October, when alternative sources of water for livestock are the old wells in the hills or a privately owned borehole near the Bonwapitse River. There is no charge for using the wells, about 2 kilometres from the village along a steep, boulder-strewn path, which is difficult for cattle. As a result, livestock owners usually prefer to pay to use the private borehole, because of ease of access.

There has always been open access to the Mmutlane dam. Cattle owners from neighbouring villages, notably Shoshong and Kalamare, drive their cattle there, where they can drink free of charge. A very different situation exists at the Boipelego

Table 4.3 Summary of water points used by Mmutlane villagers.

Water point and location	Access	Used for	Used by	Owner	Availability of water (months)	Distance (km)
Mmutlane borehole	Free	D	Any	District council	12	–
Mmutlane dam	Free	L	Any	Communal	9–11	0.5
Sepolwane communal well	Free	L	Any	Communal	12	3
Sepolwane private wells*	Free	L	Permission	Families	12	3
Mmipi's borehole – Bonwapitse River	Charge	L H D	Permission	Mmipi	12	12
Maologane dam	Free	D	Any	Communal	6	3
Wells at the lands†	Free	D	Permission	Families	6	4–8
Wells on Bonwapitse River	Free	L D	Permission	Families in Bonwapitse	9–12	12
Wells on Mahalapye River	Free	L	Permission	Families	12	25
Boreholes at cattle posts	Charge	L	Permission	Individuals or syndicates	12	25–100
Boipelego dam	Charge	L	Members	Dam group	12	15

D, domestic use; L, livestock; H, horticulture.
* These are the other wells at Sepolwane, which are owned by individual families.
† These are the various small, shallow wells found around the lands area, which collect rainwater.

dam near Bonwapitse, constructed after the formation of a dam group to whose members access has always been restricted. The Boipelego Dam Group was formed in 1982. A former policeman from Mahalapye took the initiative to find out about assistance with building the dam, and contacted the land board and the district agricultural office.

The site of the dam was selected because, at that time, the Mahalapye–Shoshong road was under construction and water collected where the Bonwapitse River was blocked while the contractors were building a bridge. People taking advantage of this to water their cattle realized that it would be a good site for a dam. In January 1985, they were formally allocated land by the Mahalapye Subordinate Land Board for building a dam. The dam was constructed in 1988–9 by the district council but paid for by the MoA. The dam group contributed P1,800 towards the cost of fencing wire and P600 for fencing poles.

There are now 112 members of the dam group, mostly from Mahalapye and Shoshong, with a few members from Mmutlane and Bonwapitse. Initially, it cost P10.25 to join the dam group, subsequently raised to P15.25, with an annual membership fee of P3. As more and more people continued to join the group, the fee was raised to P20.25 in 1990.

The land board's role in issuing permits for development of water points gives it significant control over access to land for both grazing and cultivation. The Shoshong SLB can recommend a borehole application, which must then be approved by the main land board in Serowe, which may reject the recommendation. Certificates for boreholes are issued by the SLB. All new water points must be at least 8 kilometres from existing water points (except for the registration of old water points allocated before the 8 kilometre ruling). After a borehole site is allocated by the land board, the owner can drill for water. If he strikes water, he must then apply to the Water Apportionment Board (WAB) at the Department of Water Affairs (DWA) in Gaborone for the right to use it. All borehole owners, both government and private, must obtain water rights from the WAB. The WAB usually agrees to issue these rights if an allocation has been made by the land board. In granting someone a water right, they specify how much water can be extracted from the borehole. The main purpose of the WAB is to ensure that the DWA knows how many boreholes there are in the country, and how much groundwater is being extracted.

Similarly, while the land board continues to allocate new arable fields for dryland farming, it is far more restrictive in approving applications for new water points or for land uses other than dryland farming. Any projects such as horticultural gardens, orchards and poultry farms must also be approved by the land board. Between 1990 and 1994, there were 34 applications for new agricultural projects or water sources for such projects in Shoshong SLB, most of them from individuals, of which only 11 were approved.

These 34 applications included 17 applications for field boreholes to provide water for irrigated cultivation, of which only four were approved. Most of the others were deferred until the applicant obtained a letter of support from the district agricultural office or had finished clearing and fencing the field. Four applications were rejected outright – two because the applicants had no experience of horticulture, one because the field borehole was explicitly for watering cattle and one because the proposed site of the borehole was on unregistered land. Four applications for open wells at the lands for vegetable growing were deferred, one pending a site visit and three pending letters of support from the district agricultural office.

There were nine applications for vegetable gardens or orchards, of which five were approved and four rejected or deferred. There was one application for an ostrich ranch, which was referred to (and approved by) the Sub-District Land Use Planning Unit (DLUPU), two applications for dairy farms, one of which was approved and one of which was also referred to DLUPU, and one application for a poultry farm, which was approved

Land and water use

Mmutlane's population has not increased significantly since 1971, in line with the national trend over the last 20 years of a massive increase in urban population with little change in the rural population (derived from census data for 1971, 1981 and 1991).

Cultivation

Arable farming is extensive rather than intensive, with large fields, ranging from 3 to 10 hectares. Ploughing begins following the onset of the rains, in November or December. Most farmers broadcast seeds as they plough, rather than using a seed planter after ploughing, and few use harrows or cultivators. Despite the subsidies offered through ALDEP, there has been little interest in investing in additional farming implements. Most farmers practise some form of crop rotation but rarely leave areas fallow. Fertilizer is never used. The main crops grown are sorghum and cowpeas, and most farmers also grow some maize, although yields are very low unless the rains are good. Other popular crops are groundnuts, soya beans and water melons.

A major factor affecting agricultural practice is the drought relief assistance for ploughing and planting. The scheme was devised to help those who lost draught animals through drought. The MoA pays each farmer P120 per hectare ploughed, up to a maximum of 5 hectares. Alternatively, a farmer with no draught animals or insufficient time to plough can ask a tractor owner to plough his land, for which the tractor owner is paid P120 per hectare. The government also pays P50 per hectare for row planting, again up to 5 hectares, and provides free seeds for planting up to 5 hectares. The work of measuring and recording every field is undertaken by agricultural extension staff, who consequently have little time for extension work during the ploughing season.

Agricultural officers interviewed observed that the scheme may have led to an increase in area under cultivation, but without any significant impact on crop production. They also noted that the introduction of ploughing subsidies led to a great increase in tractor ploughing. This may have amplified the year-to-year fluctuations in yield, with consequent increases in risk exposure, particularly for the poor. One of the problems of tractor ploughing combined with broadcasting seed is that the whole field is ploughed at once. When donkeys or oxen are used, it is impossible to plough a whole field at once and therefore planting is staggered, spreading the risk of crop failure from fluctuations in rainfall. If a whole field is ploughed and planted at the same time, followed by a dry period, the whole crop may be damaged. This is more likely for poorer farmers, who, dependent on others to plough for them, cannot guarantee that their fields are ploughed at the most opportune time. Often they have to wait until late in the season before a tractor owner finds time to plough their fields. They are thus unlikely to benefit from early rains and, given the annual variability of rainfall, such delays in ploughing and planting can have a strong negative impact on yields. Panin (1995) also found that more labour was needed for post-ploughing activities on fields ploughed by tractors than on those ploughed by animals. The former are weeded and harvested manually, while on the latter draught-animal technology is used, which is much more timely.

Livestock (Fig. 4.3)

Cattle are still considered the most important valuable asset by Mmutlane villagers. They are kept as a store of wealth, which can be drawn on when cash is needed. Some Mmutlane farmers with herds of forty cattle or more sell cattle regularly to the Botswana Meat Commission (BMC). Most cattle owners, however, only have small herds which they keep at the lands and sell only if they have a special need for money. According to the 1991 census, only 55 per cent of Mmutlane households owned cattle, a similar figure to the 60 per cent given by Peters (1994:96) for cattle ownership in other parts of the hardveld in Botswana.

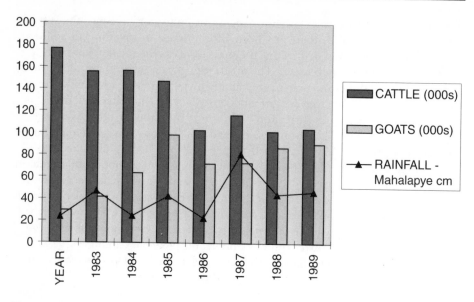

Figure 4.3   Livestock population, 1983–90

Villagers also claimed that fewer households own cattle now. Many farmers reported that they lost all their cattle in the 1980s or early 1990s, through starvation during drought and/or through disease. Unfortunately, there are no data to test this, since the 1991 census gives only the total number of households owning cattle, with no indication of numbers of cattle owned. However, of twenty-five households interviewed, only four had more than thirty head of cattle – the herd size commonly regarded as the minimum necessary to supply four draught oxen (Peters, 1994:96) – and nine had no cattle at all.

Another major change in cattle ownership is the decline of the *mafisa* system, which allowed farmers without cattle to borrow cattle from wealthier farmers. The borrower of *mafisa* cattle uses them for ploughing and milk in return for tending them (Schapera, 1947). Syson (1972) reports that, of sample households she interviewed in the Shoshong hills area, 24.5 per cent had loaned and 37.8 per cent had borrowed *mafisa* cattle. However, 25 years later, none of the Mmutlane farmers interviewed were borrowing or lending cattle, although many said they had done so in the past. This decline in the *mafisa* system has been noted elsewhere in Botswana, and this is attributed to two main causes. First, there are alternative sources of draught power in the form of either donkeys or tractors. Ploughing subsidies (see above) further reduce the need for poor households to borrow *mafisa* cattle. Secondly, prices offered by the BMC favour high-grade cattle. Rather than lending cattle for ploughing, which wears them out and decreases their value, it is more profitable for owners to sell surplus cattle (Molutsi, 1986:32; Harvey and Lewis, 1990:77).

More households in Mmutlane own goats than cattle – 77 per cent according to the 1991 census. Many farmers who lack cattle keep a few goats in the village or at the lands. Goats are more able to take advantage of grazing on the steeper slopes of the surrounding hills. Agricultural statistics for Mahalapye West Agricultural District (Fig 4.3) shows a more or less steady increase in goat numbers since 1983, as cattle numbers have steadily declined. The greater resilience of goats to drought and the relative improvement of goat prices over cattle prices offered by the BMC have also been important factors (Love, 1994).

As noted above, Tswana traditionally kept cattle at 'cattle posts' far away from their arable lands, ensuring that cattle did not destroy crops and had access to wider areas of grazing. Cattle were only brought to the lands for ploughing or milking. Mmutlane villagers with large herds still keep cattle at cattle posts, but owners of smaller herds (under 40 head) tend now to keep cattle permanently on the lands. It is impractical to keep a large herd of cattle on the lands, given the high degree of supervision they require to avoid damage to crops. The main reason for keeping cattle at a cattle post, particularly one with a borehole, rather than at the lands has long been recognized as a question of saving labour rather than the quality of grazing (Peters, 1994:67). However, cattle are also more vulnerable there as they are not supervised carefully. If there is a high death rate at the cattle post, the herd may be moved to the lands where management costs are higher but cattle are looked after more carefully.

The building of the village dam provided a major water source for livestock, making it much easier to keep cattle permanently near the village. Many of those who keep small herds of cattle on the lands at Mmutlane used to keep much larger herds at cattle posts. A common experience is that many of their cattle were dying at the cattle post, through disease or drought, so they brought the remainder of their herds to Mmutlane, where they can be tended more effectively.

Differentiation and diversification

Patterns of resource use in Mmutlane are linked to socio-economic differentiation and how that both reflects and generates opportunities for diversification of income sources in farming and agriculturally linked activities. The people of Mmutlane can be divided, albeit approximately, into wealthy, middle and poor households, which we illustrate with some examples. These show, among other things, that, while cattle remain important to wealth ranking, they no longer have the centrality they once did.

Two wealthy farmers, BM and G, each have three main sources of income. Both are tractor owners, which means they can earn a considerable income from government ploughing subsidies. BM cultivates and sells vegetables and G cereals and beans. BM's main source of income is selling water from his borehole, which has led to overgrazing around the borehole to the detriment of his own cattle, and he has moved away from investing in cattle since selling water is a more secure form of income. G's third source of income is cattle, but he plans to reduce his herd size, because of the poor grazing at his cattle post, and to invest in developing a small vegetable garden.

Middle farmers all have at least two main sources of income, though none comparable to that generated from owning a tractor or a borehole. Four of five middle farmers considered here own cattle, but their herds are relatively small and cattle sales low. Two receive remittances from children and one works as a roof thatcher. Three of them sometimes work on the drought relief works (LBRP) programme. One also collects grass and brews beer.

Three poor households have no regular source of income except for the remittances from employed children that two of them receive. None has managed to produce enough food for their needs in recent years. All claim to have owned cattle in the past but lost them through drought. One man earns small amounts from brewing beer and collecting firewood and grass for thatching, and his wife works in LBRP projects.

Evidently, the two wealthy farmers have gained most from the government's agricultural policies. As tractor owners, they have been able to generate considerable income through the ploughing subsidies of the drought relief programme. Most middle farmers own draught power and have been able to earn the ploughing subsidy for their own fields and to benefit from buying agricultural equipment at subsidized prices through ALDEP. The three poor farmers cannot generate income from ploughing because they lack draught animals and/or household labour for ploughing. Nor have they had the capital to benefit much from ALDEP, although one obtained donkeys and fencing materials through ALDEP.

Historically, rural households came to depend increasingly on remittances from labour migration during the colonial period. In contemporary Botswana, the trend is more towards permanent migration to urban centres within the country, rather than temporary migration abroad. Urban–rural linkages play a crucial role in sustaining the rural economy, both through direct transfers of cash and goods and through investment in cattle and commercial enterprises by the urban salariat. The drought relief programme has also made a significant contribution to rural incomes through transfers of food to the most vulnerable groups, ploughing subsidies and income-earning opportunities through the LBRP.

If urban–rural links and the drought relief programme both contribute to rural incomes, they do so in ways that provide little incentive to cultivation. The frequency of drought in Botswana makes arable production a high-risk investment of labour. LBRP is a more secure source of income, but farmers who work for the LBRP have less time for their own farming, both pre-planting activities, such as clearing the bush and fencing, and post-planting activities, such as weeding, bird scaring and protection against damage by cattle, which are important for improving yields.

On the other hand, those who own draught animals stand to gain more from ploughing subsidies than from work for the LBRP. Recent research in Botswana suggests a farmer takes on average about 37 hours to plough 1 hectare using draught animals (Panin, 1995). Ploughing is done in teams of two, one to hold the plough and the other the whip, to control the animals. If a farmer ploughs 6 hours a day (the number of hours worked daily by labourers on the LBRP), it will take about 6 days to plough 1 hectare. Five hectares require about 30 days in total, for which the farmer will receive P600 – P20 per day or P10 per person. This compares with a daily rate on LBRP work of P4.5. Many women from draught animal-owning households still work on the LBRP in order to supplement income from the ploughing subsidies. If the rains are particularly bad, the soil may be too hard to do much ploughing, and farmers may be unable to earn the full ploughing subsidy. Working on the LBRP is not as well paid but is at least secure and independent of rainfall.

No household in rural Botswana can risk investing all or most of its resources in arable production. Risks need to be spread, and alternative sources of income that are not rainfall dependent need to be exploited. The LBRP provides an important element of security for poorer households, even if their arable production suffers as a consequence. Only wealthy farmers with other sources of income can afford to invest substantially in cultivation. They can achieve good returns on arable production, as the examples of BM and G in Mmutlane show, but are only able to do so because they can rely on other sources of income if there is drought. The model for successful arable production these farmers have established is that wealth must first be accumulated from non-arable activities, and is better invested in irrigated rather than dryland cultivation.

All households in the middle and poor categories return from the lands to their houses in the village after harvest, and remain there until ploughing resumes again with the onset of the rains. The two wealthy farmers remain at the lands throughout the year, although both maintain houses in the village, which they use occasionally. Both are able readily to obtain water for domestic consumption on the lands during the dry season, BM from his borehole and G by transporting drums of water from the village to his farm with his tractor. This allows them to continue agricultural activities throughout the year: BM's vegetable garden needs daily attention, and G uses the dry season to continue to fence and clear his large allocation of land.

BM was granted permission by the headman of Mmutlane in 1970 to sink a borehole to water his cattle. He raised the money for the borehole by using a mule and cart to run a transport service between Mmutlane and Mahalapye. One reason BM is the only person from Mmutlane to farm at the river is that most people thought the Bonwapitse flooded every year, but BM has only experienced two bad floods since he started farming at the river in 1975, both of which washed his fences and crops away. Given the infrequency of floods, in his view the benefits of farming at the river more than compensated for the occasional years in which his crops were completely destroyed. Initially, he only used the area as a cattle post, but later realized that the alluvial soils there would be good for cultivation. In 1975, he started dryland farming there but only formally registered the land with the land board much later. He started the irrigated vegetable garden in 1991 at the suggestion of his daughter. She had no training in vegetable production but got the idea from school, and realized the potential of the good soils and abundant water from his borehole. BM has two vegetable gardens, both adjacent to his borehole. He grows onions, spinach, cabbages, tomatoes, green maize and potatoes, which are sold in Mmutlane, Bonwapitse, Kalamare and Mahalapye.

Few are likely to have the means to emulate BM's successful diversification into commercial horticulture. In fact, according to the horticultural officer for Mahalapye and Macheneng Agricultural Districts, there are only 14 irrigated gardens in total in the two districts. Most are located on the Mahalapye River, east of Mahalapye, where shallow boreholes are used on the river banks. There are no farmers growing vegetables in the neighbouring villages of Kalamare or Bonwapitse, but two in Shoshong. The most successful horticultural venture is a project run by the Shoshong Brigades Development Trust (SBDT). The manager is a Zimbabwean, with extensive experience of vegetable production and the Trust has its own borehole, which it uses for irrigation. Physical constraints are not the only problems with developing horticulture: there is no experience of vegetable growing in the area; the market for vegetables is dominated by cheaper South African and Zimbabwean produce; and fertilizers are not readily available locally (the SBDT manager says he has to order fertilizer from Zimbabwe).

A further obstacle to diversification into irrigated cultivation is the land board's policy not to allocate boreholes on the lands for watering cattle. Its stated reason is that these would attract cattle and lead to increased crop damage on neighbouring fields. Cattle owners who have moved their cattle to the lands, on the other hand, may regard a field borehole as the best means of meeting their need for water. In order to test if an applicant is serious about drilling a borehole for horticulture, the land board demands not only that the applicant has a field cleared and registered and a letter from the district agricultural office confirming it is suitable for vegetables, but also that the applicant has experience of growing vegetables. The administrative officer for the Shoshong SLB felt that many who apply for field boreholes claim they wish to grow vegetables but really want water for cattle. If the land board permits a field borehole and then finds it is used for cattle, it can charge the owner under the Tribal Land Amendment Act. In 1994, there were two cases of people found watering cattle from field boreholes in Shoshong SLB. They were warned and stopped. However, it is almost impossible for the land board to keep a continuous check on such abuses, given the huge area it covers.

Another restriction on the development of horticulture is the land board rule that no allocations can be made within 100 metres of a river and 50 metres of a stream. This came into effect in 1994 as national policy, following flood damage in 1989, when many people blamed the land board for allocating them land near rivers. The new policy aims to prevent claims for compensation from land boards.

Land and water management

Managing water

Fears of environmental degradation, widely publicized in Botswana, have not had much impact in Mmutlane. Low agricultural production is blamed on poor rains, rather than poor natural resource management. Unallocated land for cultivation is still widely available and grazing land is considered sufficient. Overgrazing is only perceived as a problem around water points. Pasture in the remoter cattle-post areas, where villagers once kept most of their (then larger herds of) cattle, is considered to have deteriorated owing to poor rainfall, but grazing adjacent to arable fields and in the surrounding hills is thought to be better. As a result, there has been a tendency recently to move cattle to the lands and adopt a mixed farming type of land use in and around Mmutlane. Currently, water for livestock, rather than pasture, is seen as under most pressure and the most constrained resource, leading to attempts to control access to the dam. Since the dam was constructed at Mmutlane, there has been no management or control: it has never been fenced and there have been no restrictions on access. This lack of control is now recognized by villagers as a problem. Cattle owners from neighbouring villages, notably Shoshong and Kalamare, drive their cattle to the Mmutlane dam, where their cattle can drink free of charge. As a result, the water in the dam is used up more quickly and in most years the dam dries up by September; the land surrounding the dam is also severely over-grazed. Another problem is that large herds from Shoshong are driven through the village on their way to the dam.

In response, a dam committee was formed in 1993 to manage and develop the dam. It plans to fence, dig out and extend the dam and to introduce membership as a condition of using the dam. However, no progress was made in its first year of exis-tence. One reason for the delay concerns the location of the dam. Officials from the Veterinary Department judge the current site to be too close to the road, the village borehole and houses, and government assistance with renovating the dam is unlikely unless it is resited further from the village. However, while this had the support of the councillor and the headman, most villagers were very reluctant to move the dam, and decided at the *kgotla* that the dam stay where it is, despite the objections of the coun-cillor and headman. In taking this stance, they are unlikely to get any help from the Veterinary Department. The VDC has suggested fencing the dam as a project under the drought relief programme, but this had not been approved by the district council at the time of fieldwork.

Issues confronting the longer-established Boipelego dam group should be instructive for progress towards resolution of the Mmutlane dam problem. According to the government, the number of cattle using Boipelego should not exceed 400. However, the chairman said that more cattle than this currently use the dam and more members would be allowed to join. They have never discussed limiting the number of cattle any one group member may bring to the dam. Although access is restricted by membership, there is still a problem of overgrazing around the dam. Dam group members themselves own more than 400 cattle between them, and other cattle left to roam in the grazing land to the south of the dam frequently break through its fence to drink. To try to reduce pressure, the dam group asked all members to contribute P10 for fence poles and P50 for an engine to pump water to troughs outside the dam. However, not all have contributed and the group has not yet raised sufficient money to buy an engine. The dam group used to meet every month when they started, but now meets about every two to three months. Caretakers for the dam have been selected but do not visit the dam very often.

Most cattle-owners in Mmutlane were prepared to pay a contribution to improve and fence the dam in the village, but did not see this as a membership fee for using it. Unlike the Boipelego dam, that in Mmutlane is regarded as a communal resource for all villagers. Further, given the close kinship and affinal ties among villagers, it is unlikely that the dam group would be able to restrict access to dam group members only. The prevailing view of Mmutlane villagers is that they should be able to water their livestock at the dam without charge, but that livestock owners from other villages should pay. They are blamed for overgrazing around the dam and the fact that it dries up most years. Excluding them or regulating their access to the dam is seen as the solution to these problems.

Managing cultivation

Government programmes have encouraged extensive farming practices, in which large areas are ploughed, but little labour is invested in farm management. Yields are very low but could be improved with increased investment of labour in arable production. Yet poorer households invest their labour in more secure forms of income generation. Urban employment and the LBRP offer attractive alternative sources of income to cultivation. Ploughing subsidies and the trend of moving cattle from cattle-post areas to the lands both put increased pressure on available land. Disputes over land are still uncommon in Mmutlane, but the combination of low-input, extensive arable production and keeping cattle on the lands may become increasingly problematic over time.

The case-study shows a clear link between successful arable production and other sources of income, in a sequence from labour migration to investment in cattle, to investment in boreholes or tractors and arable production. Government programmes, such as ALDEP, ARAP and the drought relief programme, have not recognized this. Subsidies have not helped poor farmers to farm more successfully, but increase their dependence on government transfers, which reproduce inequalities, rather than reducing them. Wealthy farmers with cattle gain most from government programmes, followed by middle farmers, who own draught animals and are able to buy implements through ALDEP. Poor farmers, without draught animals, do not receive any direct cash transfers and have gained least.

Can BM's (exceptional) mixed farm at the Bonwapitse River, incorporating dryland farming, horticulture and livestock, provide a model for other farmers? Although BM is the most successful farmer in Mmutlane, his farming activities conflict with current land board policy. He has a field borehole which he uses for cattle as well as irrigation, and his field is less than 100 metres from the Bonwapitse River. He has escaped current restrictions because he was allocated the borehole in 1970 and started farming there in 1975. Current land board rules prevent other farmers from following his example.

Managing grazing

Investing in cattle is the only way poor families without access to urban employment can generate income to reinvest in and improve arable production. Yet the government views overstocking of communal grazing land as the main reason for dryland degradation and does not encourage poor farmers to (re-)enter livestock production. Rather, its policies favour large cattle owners and give them opportunities to privatize the range. The government's 1991 National Policy for Agricultural Development (NPAD) is likely to increase pressure further on the Mmutlane lands and surrounding hills. The NPAD allows fencing of communal grazing land, paving the way for an increased commoditization of communal land in Botswana. It was yet to be implemented nationally in 1995, but pilot programmes on fencing communal grazing land were under way in remote cattle-post areas of Central District, Kgalagadi and Ngamiland. If the fencing policy is applied more widely, it will have major implications for Mmutlane.

The policy was to be implemented first in cattle-post areas, where borehole owners would be allowed to fence an area of land around their boreholes. This will have adverse effects on others with cattle posts in the area who have arrangements to use the borehole water. If the borehole owner fences his land, cattle belonging to others will be denied access to water. Furthermore, if there is a high concentration of borehole owners in an area who all decide to fence around their boreholes, remaining communal grazing land will be severely restricted, further stimulating transfer of cattle to the lands. The net effect of the fencing policy of NPAD in cattle-post areas, therefore, will be to increase the number of cattle at the lands and pressures on available pasture and water there, in the context of a national trend of increasing areas of the lands under the plough. At the same time, land boards refuse to allocate borehole permits for watering livestock on the lands, despite increased demand for water there.

Currently, fencing in the lands is defensive: to protect crops from cattle, rather than to enclose pasture. The NPAD also encourages group fencing of communal land to enclose pasture. This implies the ability of the community to manage enclosed pasture and to agree boundaries with neighbouring communities. Demarcating boundaries is likely to be a major source of conflict between communities. The NPAD states that community boundaries will be established by the land boards, and yet it is difficult to see how they could do this. The area between Kalamare and Mmutlane is one of open access, with no fixed division of Kalamare and Mmutlane grazing land. Also, a new institution would have to be created to manage the fenced communal grazing area, with authority to restrict cattle numbers on it. There is no precedent for an institution with such powers, and enforcement of any maximum limit is likely to be difficult. Traditional overseers or *badisa*, for example, controlled access to grazing land but did not impose restrictions on herd size for those granted access (a common feature of traditional institutions of range management in Africa (Knudsen, 1995:71)). In other words, there is a history of qualitative regulation/restriction, based on social relationships, not quantitative restriction based on numbers of livestock.

Increasing pressure on land and water will make it even more difficult for poor farmers to keep cattle. If plans for the dam at Mmutlane go ahead, water charges will be levied. Communal grazing land is still available, but for how long? The NPAD is likely to reinforce existing inequalities, underpin commoditization of land and further marginalize poor farmers. Grazing at the lands will be under more pressure, owing to an influx of cattle from cattle-post areas. If communal fencing is established, some form of fee will be necessary to cover management costs, a further hurdle for those seeking to (re-)establish herds and (re-)enter livestock farming.

Politics and the governance of land and water

Cattle, commercialization and conservation: politics and policies

The evolution of perceptions of natural resource use in Tswana society has been charted in detail by Peters (1994) in her study of Kgatleng district, a little way to the south of the Mmutlane study area. She emphasizes that the economic imperative for technological change in the form of boreholes to supply water in grazing areas brought with it new institutions and forms of organization. The benefits of boreholes in terms of reduced labour for herding and more certain water supply for cattle were secured by giving responsibility for maintaining boreholes to named individuals. In keeping with Tswana custom, individual improvements to land confer superior rights to its use, and the financial costs of borehole maintenance translated into ownership rights. Peters identifies the 'borehole syndicate' as the key institutional innovation through which Tswana leaders sought legitimacy for more restricted access to boreholes through an 'inclusive' or collective *kgotla* form of group ownership. Membership of borehole syndicates was a powerful factor expressing and generating differentiation in Botswana from the 1930s and greater permanence of grazing around boreholes extended notions of exclusive ownership and use from boreholes to their surrounding rangeland.

This historical process contrasts with the national government's reconceptualization (at independence) of grazing areas as a single 'tribal land' open to any citizen of Botswana and administered by land boards. This ignored prior local control of grazing areas by *badisa*, and also ran counter to widespread *de facto* private ownership instituted by borehole syndicates and individuals. This tension between social goals and accumulation by the class of large cattle owners underlies policies of natural resource management and their interpretation:

> Any attempt to explain agricultural policies in Botswana should take into account the political importance of the rural agriculturally dominated areas. The Botswana Democratic Party (BDP), which has won every election since 1965, has the rural population as the core of its electorate. It is important for the regime to demonstrate that it has the welfare of the rural poor in mind.
>
> (Borhaug, 1993:3)

> The strong association between government policy and large-scale ranching in post-colonial Botswana is quite conspicuous: large-scale ranchers in the post-colonial era have depended upon the state for their business and the state has subsidised the cattle industry.
>
> (Mazonde, 1994:19)

Government expenditure for livestock development was substantially greater than for arable farming in the first five National Development Plans (down to 1985) The Presidential Commission on Economic Opportunities, conducted in the late 1970s, concluded that public finance of the cattle sector averaged P12.1 million per year while flows from this sector to the government in the form of taxes and payments for services averaged P7.5 million, but the commission's recommendation of an additional slaughter tax to close the gap was rejected by the government (Harvey and Lewis, 1990: 89).

Government support for commercial livestock production, dominated by some of the wealthiest people in Botswana, is well documented (Parson 1981; Harvey and Lewis, 1990:89; Roe, 1993). It was explicit in the objectives of the TGLP of 1975 to commercialize livestock production and conserve the range, by allocating blocks of land in the communal areas to commercial ranching on 50-year leases. Measures were also planned to improve livestock production in communal areas, including improvement in extension services, strengthening of cooperatives and the promotion of group ranching (White, 1993).

An expression of reconciling commercial and conservation goals is the justification for increasing exclusive control of resources on environmental grounds. The TGLP offers a prime example: first, the creation of TGLP ranches would remove a large number of cattle from the communal grazing lands, thus reducing the pressure on them; secondly, the granting of long-term leases for TGLP ranches would encourage improved ranching methods, leading to better rangeland conservation and increased production; and, thirdly, this would encourage utilization of large areas of unexploited grazing land (Harvey and Lewis, 1990:86).

All these assumptions proved to be mistaken. A major problem with TGLP ranches is dual grazing rights. Ranchers move cattle between their ranches and surrounding communal grazing land to maximize available grazing, putting even more pressure on the communal grazing areas. There is no evidence that either range conservation or livestock productivity are significantly better on TGLP ranches than on communal areas, and in some cases they have been found to be worse (de Ridder and Wagenaar, 1984). Furthermore, many of the initiatives taken by the government to improve commercial production in communal areas fail to gain acceptance by farmers. Finally, much of the land allocated for leasehold ranches was already in use, either for livestock or for hunting and gathering. Former users were excluded from TGLP land (Harvey and Lewis, 1990:86; White, 1993:22).

Despite large government investments in the TGLP, a widespread view in Botswana is that it has failed and should be abandoned (Mazonde, 1994). The main beneficiaries of the TGLP are those who have obtained exclusive rights to rangeland and built up large herds. However, as yet the government shows no indication of abandoning the objectives of TGLP. In 1991, the National Assembly approved the NPAD as the basis for proposed agricultural developments under the Seventh National Development Plan (1991–7), including its controversial plan to extend the TGLP to all 'tribal' land:

> The TGLP will therefore be modified and expanded to cover all production systems. Farmers will be allowed, where feasible, to fence livestock farming land either as individuals, groups or communities to improve productivity of the livestock subsector and ensure sustainable use of range resources.
>
> (Government of Botswana, 1991:11)

The stated rationale is the same as that of the TGLP: that communal rangelands are unproductive and severely degraded. The NPAD recognizes that many problems were encountered in implementing the TGLP, including that of dual grazing rights, but supports its strategic commitment to strengthening individual tenure of rangeland.

Subsidy, security and settlement: policies and politics of cultivation

In relation to arable farming, the NPAD abandons the objective of food self-sufficiency for Botswana in favour of food security:

> To improve the contribution of agriculture to national development objectives, there has been a fundamental shift in strategy from NDP 6. This is a change from an objective of national food self sufficiency to one of food security at both the national and the household level.
>
> (MFDP, 1991: vol. 2, p. 21)

The new food security strategy relies on the continuing ability of diamond exports to generate sufficient foreign exchange to import food. This reverses the government-funded modernization of arable agriculture in the 1970s and 1980s, which was driven by the political imperative of providing for the rural majority who did not benefit from the growth of commercial ranching – under the banner of promoting self-sufficiency in food production.

The first major government programme for arable farming was ALDEP, introduced in the late 1970s and targeted on farmers who ploughed less than 10 hectares and had less than 40 head of cattle. Its main objective was to introduce improved farming methods and techniques and, unlike earlier extension efforts, ALDEP provided substantial financial assistance. In 1983, following various trials, the government decided that it would pay 85 per cent of the cost of any improvements made by farmers.

ALDEP was directed at relatively smaller farmers, while the TGLP was directed at large cattle owners. A substantial stratum of farmers, with over forty head of cattle and engaged in crop production for subsistence, did not benefit from these programmes. The MoA originally planned ARAP as a modernization programme targeted on this stratum, with the objective of commercializing their arable production. They were to be provided with grants for ploughing fields up to 10 hectares, and with seeds and fertilizers for up to 3 hectares.

However, the Minister of Agriculture insisted that ARAP must be available to all farmers, and it consequently became a massive programme, which paid grants to all farmers in Botswana to plough up to 10 hectares. The original plan was that ploughing grants would be a one-off payment in the first year of the programme, but the government decided to give grants for ploughing every year. ARAP was implemented in 1985, and effectively became a large-scale drought relief programme to try to reduce further urban migration, rather than a targeted modernization programme as originally intended. Under ARAP, the government paid farmers for destumping, ploughing, row planting and weeding, up to the maximum of 10 hectares. Seeds were distributed free and 85 per cent of fencing costs provided by the government. ARAP was terminated in 1990. However, since 1991, ploughing subsidies have continued under the drought relief programme (see above), in which farmers receive grants for ploughing and row planting up to 5 hectares, and seeds are provided free of charge.

ARAP was very popular and had major political benefits for the BDP, which maintained its support in rural areas and increased its support among the Ngwaketse in Southern District, a former opposition BNF stronghold, to some extent countering the growing support for the BNF in urban areas (Molutsi, 1989:128; Tsie,

1995; Borhaug, 1993:111–12). However, while ARAP fulfilled the political objectives of the BDP, it failed to fulfil the agricultural development objectives of the MoA. Government transfers to farmers under ARAP were not invested in modern or more commercialized farming methods, but were used by most farmers to subsidize their existing systems of cultivation. The area ploughed increased under ARAP, but aggregate output did not increase significantly and, as illustrated in the study of Mmutlane, the subsidies widen wealth differentiation in the countryside.

Neither ARAP nor ALDEP addressed the crucial constraint on arable production in Botswana: that returns on investment in cultivation are much lower than in livestock or wage employment. For example, Lipton (1978: vol. II, pp. 188–9) estimated that, even with above-average yields, a farmer would need over 33 hectares to earn as much as the minimum unskilled wage in the public sector. Most farmers who produced surplus crops with ARAP subsidies invested their gains in livestock. Only wealthy farmers with diverse sources of income could take the risk of investing in arable production (Borhaug, 1993:67). The low returns to cultivation are further highlighted by the diamond 'boom' economy of Botswana. Love (1994) argues that exchange rate movements, combined with the exceptional growth of the mineral sector, created relative price disadvantages for crop production. Botswana imports 90 per cent of its cereals, mostly from South Africa (MoA, 1991:3), and between 1981 and 1989 the Botswana pula rose by 24.1 percent against the South African rand. The Botswana Agricultural Marketing Board (BAMB) bases its buying price for domestically produced sorghum and maize on the import parity price of South African grains. Exchange rate changes cheapened South African imports further and BAMB lowered its prices to Batswana farmers. Love estimates that the real purchase price offered to farmers by BAMB fell by 22.5 per cent between 1985 and 1989.

Whereas increasing commercialization has been linked to increasing competion for land in other parts of Botswana, this case-study suggests that in the Shoshong Hills this is not yet the case. In Mmutlane, large cattle owners have not encroached on arable areas for grazing, as has happened in parts of Southern District (Gulbrandsen, 1986), no TGLP ranches have been demarcated, nor have commercial farmers attempted to acquire land, as has happened on the Baralong farms in southern Botswana (Comaroff, 1982). However, the case-study does indicate farmers in Mmutlane increasingly seeking long-term exclusive tenure through registration and fencing of arable areas, including 'uncleared' (i.e. rangeland) areas for arable. The experience of larger local farmers suggests that, with access to water, such holdings could form the basis of a mixed farming system, including livestock and irrigated cultivation. This route to increasing productivity on smaller landholdings – potentially supported through a retargeting of resources used for ploughing subsidies – is currently blocked by the Shoshong SLB's refusal to grant permits for water points in arable areas on conservation grounds: protection of watercourses from erosion; protection of cultivated areas from livestock; and maintenance of the 8-kilometre distance between water points to prevent overgrazing.

As a consequence, cultivation will remain dominated by high-risk and low-productivity rain-fed crops, and productive investment in land and water will continue to be dominated by enclosure of rangeland for large-scale ranching. While enclosure of communal grazing areas by 'communities' is envisaged under the

NPAD, this seems unlikely to produce benefits for the majority in the face of exclusive access to water points and highly skewed livestock ownership.

Governance of land and water: assessing the land board model

The conclusion suggested above raises the question of why the land board, an institution designed to bring the administration of customary tenure under democratic control, should preside over widening differentiation in benefits gained from using land and water. Two important limitations appear in the board's accountability to the rural majority: first, dependence on tribal authorities for arbitration on questions of access to land and water; and, secondly, subordination to conservation criteria centrally determined by the MoA's technical departments.

Evidence for the first is less apparent in the Mmutlane case-study, which focused mainly on the village and its cultivated lands, than in studies that have found greater competition for grazing. Peters's study of land boards' resolution of disputes over grazing rights in Kgatleng showed that, whereas many members of the board were concerned to weigh the need for continued access to seasonal grazing areas for non-borehole owners against the exclusive rights claimed by individuals and syndicates who had sunk boreholes there, the local chief's unequivocal advice to the board was to uphold borehole owners' claims (Peters, 1994:133–7). This highlights the point that land boards' administration of tribal or communal land is subject to different but parallel sets of rights, which may be explicit (as in the case of borehole owners' claims to the surrounding rangeland) or implicit (the reversion to devolved chiefly authority, rather than nationally determined citizenship rights to communal grazing). In practice, land boards' continued acceptance of local tribal authorities' interpretation of customary tenure, coupled with the fact that those authorities are often large cattle owners, makes it likely that intensifying competition will reduce access to grazing and water for smaller cattle owners.

The second limitation to land boards' accountability to the rural majority is illustrated by the Shoshong SLB's strict adherence to MoA technical criteria in issuing permits with implications for changing land use. There are grounds for questioning whether such criteria need review, however. The study in Mmutlane found not only a stark contrast between local MoA officials' concerns about overgrazing and local farmers' perception that this was not a problem, but also the absence of any mechanism through which this was being addressed. This is made more significant by the contentious nature of technical assessments of 'carrying capacity' of rangeland in Botswana (Odell and Odell, 1980; Odell, 1982; Abel and Blaikie, 1990; Abel, 1993; Biot, 1993; de Queroz, 1993), by the low level of resources available for making such assessments within the MoA – range ecology has the same departmental status as bee-keeping (Reynolds, 1998:313) – and by the absence of any MoA staff with such a role at local level (Clayton, 1995:58). That the MoA should by default take a strongly conservative technical stance on land use owes much to conservation policies established in the colonial period (Peters, 1994), but also to the importance of environmental conservation in Botswana's international relationships. By 1989, Botswana had the highest receipts of external aid among all World Bank member countries

(World Bank, 1993), a position achieved not only through the country's reputation for stable democracy, but also through its wholehearted integration of environmental sustainability into its development policy. Botswana was a pioneer in the development of a National Conservation Strategy in 1990, and the identification of wildlife tourism as an 'engine of growth' involving community-based natural resource management has been an important channel for external aid (Government of Botswana, 1994:4; Reynolds, 1998:29–32). The focus for much of this conservation-linked development is in the sandveld, rather than the hardveld, with which we are concerned here, but emphasis on livelihoods based on wild plants and animals clearly takes precedence over livelihoods based on agriculture, and this does little to generate interest within MoA to search for alternatives to rain-fed cultivation as a basis for farming livelihoods for the rural majority, who must seek wage employment or further impoverishment.

While the rich literature on socio-economic and political change in Botswana cautions against deriving general conclusions from single case-studies, the analysis developed above suggests that land boards may be failing to match the accumulation goals of large cattle owners with the livelihood requirements of the rural majority, because they are dependent on rules of access governed by local hierarchy and rules of land and water use governed by conservative technical norms defined at national level. The implication is that a more equitable outcome might be possible if these centres of control were reversed, with technical criteria based more on dialogue between resource users at local level, and rules of access negotiated from a set of nationally enunciated citizenship principles, which make explicit the realities of the 'commons'.

Politically, however, the fiction of the national 'common grazing land' has been a powerful unifying image of *kagisano*, or social harmony (Government of Botswana, 1991:82; Reynolds, 1998:49), masking rapidly differentiating access to land and water in rural society, and for this reason the government will be reluctant to abandon it.

References

Abel, N. (1993) *Carrying Capacity, Rangeland Degradation and Livestock Development Policy for the Communal Rangelands of Botswana.* Pastoral Development Network 35c, ODI, London.

Abel, N. & Blaikie P. (1990) *Land Degradation, Stocking Rates, and Conservation Policies in the Communal Rangelands of Botswana and Zimbabwe.* Pastoral Network Paper 29a ODI, London.

Biot, Y. (1993) 'How long can high stocking densities be sustained?' In: Behnke, R. and Scoones, I. (eds) *Range Ecology at Disequilibrium: New Models of Natural Variability and Pastoral Adaptation in African Savannas.* ODI, London, 153–72.

Borhaug, K. (1993) *Politics, Administration and Agricultural Development: The Case of Botswana's Accelerated Rainfed Arable Programme.* Chr. Michelsen Institute, Bergen.

Campbell, A. (1978) 'The 1960s drought in Botswana'. In: Hinchey, M. (ed) *Proceedings of the Symposium on Drought in Botswana.* Botswana Society and Clark University Press, Gaborone, 98–109

Central Statistics Office (1993) *Statistical Bulletin.* Government Printer, Gaborone.

Charlton, R. (1991) 'Bureaucrats and politicians in Botswana's policy making process: a reinterpretation'. *Journal of Commonwealth and Comparative Politics* 29 (3), 265–82.

Clayton, A. (1995) *Land, Water and Local Governance: Botswana Case Study.* Rural Resources; Rural Livelihoods Working Paper 1, Institute for Development Policy and Management, University of Manchester, Manchester.

Colclough, C. & McCarthy, S. (1980) *The Political Economy of Botswana*. Oxford University Press, Oxford.

Comaroff, J. (1982) 'Class and culture in a peasant economy: the transformation of land tenure in Barolong'. In: Werbner, R. (ed.) *Land Reform in the Making*. Rex Collings, London, 85–113.

Danevad, A. (1993) *Development Planning and the Importance of Democratic Institutions in Botswana*. Chr. Michelsen Institute, Bergen.

de Queroz, J. (1993) *Range Degradation in Botswana: Myth or Reality?* Pastoral Development Network 35b. ODI, London.

de Ridder, N. & Wagenaar, K. (1984) *A Comparison Between the Productivity of Traditional Livestock Systems and Ranching in Eastern Botswana*. International Livestock Centre for Africa Newsletter 3, Addis Ababa.

Drèze, J. & Sen, A. (1989) *Hunger and Public Action*. Clarendon Press, Oxford.

Egner, B. (1986) *District Councils and Decentralisation 1976–1986*. Report to SIDA, Gaborone.

Fidziani, N. (1996) 'Wealth accumulation and distribution in Botswana'. Paper presented to the Botswana Society Symposium on Quality of Life in Botswana, 15–18 October 1996, Gaborone.

Food Studies Group (FSG) (1990) *Report on the Evaluation of the Drought Relief and Recovery Programme, 1982–90*, 6 vols. Government Printer, Gaborone.

Fortmann, L. (1986) *The Role of Local Institutions in Communal Area Development in Botswana*. Land Tenure Center, University of Wisconsin, Madison.

Fosbrooke, H. (1971) 'Land and Population'. *Botswana Notes and Records* 3, 172–87.

Gasper, D.R. (1990) 'Development planning and decentralisation in Botswana'. In: de Valk, P. and Wekwete, K.H. (eds) *Decentralising for Development Planning*. Avebury, Aldershot, 224–54

Good, K. (1992) 'Interpreting the exceptionality of Botswana'. *Journal of Modern African Studies* 30 (1), 69–95.

Government of Botswana (1991) *Government Paper No. 1 1991: National Policy on Agricultural Development*. Government Printer, Gaborone.

Government of Botswana (1994) *Mid-term Review of NDP VII*. Ministry of Finance and Development Planning, Gaborone.

Gulbrandsen, O. (1986) *When Land Becomes Scarce*. Bergen Studies in Social Anthropology No. 33, University Printer, Bergen.

Harvey, C. (1992) *Botswana: Is the Economic Miracle Over?* Discussion Paper 298, Institute of Development Studies, Brighton.

Harvey, C. & Lewis, S. (1990) *Policy Choice and Development Performance in Botswana*. Macmillan/OECD, London.

Hudson, D. & Wright, M. (1996) 'Income distribution in Botswana: trends in inequality since independence'. Paper presented to the Botswana Society Symposium on Quality of Life in Botswana, 15–18 October 1996, Gaborone.

Karlsson, A., Heilemann, A. & Alexander, E. (1993) *Shifting the Balance? Towards Sustainable Local Government, Decentralisation and District Development in Botswana*. SIDA Evaluation Report, Stockholm.

Knudsen, A.J. (1995) *Living with the Commons: Local Institutions and Natural Resource Management*. Chr. Michelsen Institute, Bergen.

Lekorwe, M. (1989) 'The Kgotla and Freedom Square'. In: Holm, J. and Molutsi, P. (eds) *Democracy in Botswana*. Macmillan Botswana, Gaborone, 216–30.

Lipton, M. (1978) *Employment and Labour Use in Botswana*. Government Printer, Gaborone.

Love, R. (1994) 'Drought, Dutch disease and controlled transition in Botswana agriculture'. *Journal of Southern African Studies* 20 (1), 71–83.

Massey, D. (1980) *The Development of a Labour Reserve: The Impact of Colonial Rule on Botswana*. Working Paper 34, Boston University African Studies Centre, Boston.

Mazonde, I. (1994) *Ranching and Enterprise in Eastern Botswana*. International African Institute, Edinburgh.

MoA (1991) *Bostwana's Agricultural Policy: Critical Sectoral Issues and Future Strategy for Development*. Ministry of Agriculture. Government Printer, Gaborone.

Ministry of Finance & Development Planning (MFDP) (1991) *National Development Plan VII*, 2 vols. Government Printer, Gaborone.

Molutsi, P. (1986) 'Social stratification and inequality in Botswana: issues in development 1950–1985'. Unpublished D Phil. thesis, Oxford.

Molutsi, P. (1989) 'Whose interests do Botswana's politicians represent?' In: Holm, J. and Molutsi, P. (eds) *Democracy in Botswana*. Macmillan Botswana, Gaborone.

Odell, M. (1982) *Local Institutions and Management of Communal Resources: Lessons from Africa and Asia*. Pastoral Network Paper 14e, ODI, London.

Odell, M. J. & Odell, M. L. (1980) *The Evolution of a Strategy for Livestock Development in the Communal Areas of Botswana*. Pastoral Network Paper 106, ODI, London.

Panin, A. (1995) 'Empirical evidence of mechanisation effects on smallholder crop production systems in Botswana'. *Agricultural Systems* 47, 199–210.

Parson, J. (1981) 'Cattle, class and the state in rural Botswana'. *Journal of Southern African Studies* 7 (2), 236–55.

Parson, J. (1985) 'The labour reserve' in historical perspective: toward a political economy of Bechuanaland Protectorate'. In: Picard, L. (ed.) *The Evolution of Modern Botswana*. University of Nebraska Press, Lincoln, 40–60.

Peters, P. (1994) *Dividing the Commons: Politics, Policy and Culture in Botswana*. University Press of Virginia, Charlottesville.

Picard, L. (1987) *The Politics of Development in Botswana*. Lynne Rienner, Boulder.

Reilly, W. & Tordoff, W. (1993) 'Decentralisation in Botswana: myth or reality?' In: Mawhood, P. (ed) *Local Government in the Third World*, 2nd edn. Africa Institute of South Africa, Pretoria, 144–86.

Reynolds, M. (1998) 'Natural resource-use appraisal for a national conservation strategy: Botswana case study'. PhD thesis, University of Manchester.

Roe, E. (1993) 'Public service, rural development and careers in public management: a case study of expatriate advice and African Land reform'. *World Development* 21 (3), 349–66.

Schapera, I. (1947) *Migrant Labour and Tribal Life*. Oxford University Press, Oxford.

Silitshena, R.M.K. & McLeod, G. (1989) *Botswana: A Physical, Social and Economic Geography*. Longman Botswana, Gaborone.

Somolekae, G. (1993) 'Bureaucracy and democracy in Botswana: what type of relationship?' In: Stedman, S. (ed.) *Botswana: The Political Economy of Democratic Development*. Lynne Rienner Publishers, London.

Sorto, E. (1992) *Labour Based Relief Programme Technical Manual*. MLGLH, Gaborone.

Syson, L. (1972) *Income, Expenditure and Wealth in the Shoshong Area*. UNDP/FAO Technical Note 31, Rome.

Tordoff, W. (1988) 'Local adminstration in Botswana'. *Public Administration and Development* 8, 183–202.

Tsie, B. (1995) *The Political Economy of Botswana in SADCC*. Harare: Sapes Books.

UNDP (1998) *Human Development Report*. Oxford University Press, Oxford.

White, R. (1993) *Livestock Development and Pastoral Production on Communal Rangeland in Botswana*. The Botswana Society, Gaborone.

World Bank (1993) *World Development Report 1993*. World Bank, Washington, DC.

5

The Mutale River Valley
An Apartheid Oasis

EDWARD LAHIFF

Introduction

This study examines the use and management of natural resources in an area of South Africa at a time of profound political and social change. It is based on documentary research and fieldwork conducted in the Mutale River valley, in the former 'homeland' of Venda (now part of Northern Province), during 1995 and 1996. Research included interviews with a wide range of informants, including government officials, tribal leaders, local councillors and farmers, as well as a detailed survey of plot-holders on the Tshiombo irrigation scheme. Further details of the study are given in Lahiff (1997a, b).

Despite the formal ending of apartheid and the election of the country's first democratic government, South Africa remains a deeply divided society. Extreme inequalities exist in virtually every area of life, particularly between the 'white' (European) and 'black' (African) sections of the population. Much of the worst poverty is concentrated in the former homelands, or Bantustans, the 13 per cent of the country reserved for occupation by black people and an enduring legacy of apartheid's policy of divide and rule (Map 5.1). These homelands had their origins in the areas of land left in the hands of African peoples following colonial and settler conquests, with a special significance in South Africa's political economy following the discovery of major diamond and gold deposits. In the twentieth century, these 'native reserves' were preserved and even expanded by the state as reservoirs of cheap labour for the mines, factories and farms of 'white' South Africa. Denied political and other rights in the white areas, black workers and their families were left to supplement their meagre wage-earnings with whatever they could produce for themselves in the poorly developed and increasingly overcrowded rural reservations.

Under the apartheid regime, from 1948 to 1994, millions of black people were forcibly removed from cities and farms and dumped in the ten homelands designated for the country's various linguistic groups. These territories all acquired the trappings of self-rule, including their own authoritarian regimes, and four – Transkei, Ciskei,

155

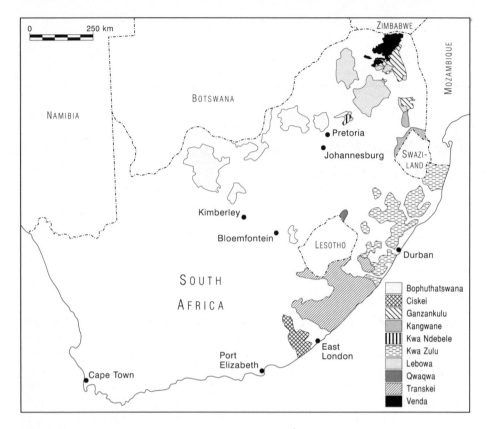

Map 5.1   Ex-Bantustan areas in South Africa

Bophuthatswana and Venda – were granted the unlikely status of 'independent' republics. While strongly opposed by most of the black population, the homelands policy was supported by an emerging stratum of compliant, and generally corrupt, tribal chiefs, local officials and petty capitalists. Economically, the homelands remained extremely poor and underdeveloped, and heavily dependent on remittances from migrant workers in industrial South Africa. The prevalence of male migrancy meant that demographic structures were heavily biased towards women, children and the aged. Industrial development, other than mining, was virtually non-existent and few formal employment opportunities existed outside the public service.

Land in the former homelands is almost entirely held under so-called communal tenure (see below), nominally controlled by tribal chiefs and village headmen. These 'traditional' leaders dominate the Tribal Authorities, introduced first under colonial administration and remodelled and refined by the apartheid regime as the principal form of local government in the homelands (Mamdani, 1996:62–72, 90–102). Communal tenure ensured that, at least until the 1970s, most households in the homelands had some access to arable or grazing land, but the small size of plots and herds meant that agriculture provided a relatively minor proportion of household subsistence requirements in most cases (Simkins, 1981:262).

Agriculture in the homelands today is commonly perceived as 'subsistence' (or even 'sub-subsistence') and extremely marginal in terms of the white-dominated agricultural sector (Bembridge, 1990:22). Local studies over many years, however, have shown that agriculture continues to play a part in the livelihoods of large numbers of households (Cooper, 1988:94). Far from being homogeneous, agriculture is differentiated along lines of class, gender and age, with substantial numbers of farmers engaged in commodity production.

By the final years of apartheid, the homelands were home to over half the black population of South Africa (or over 40 per cent of the entire South African population) and were characterized by extremely low incomes and high rates of infant mortality, malnutrition and illiteracy relative to the rest of the country (Wilson and Ramphele, 1989:25). Whiteford and McGrath (1994:59) estimate that two-thirds of black households are living below the official poverty datum line, and those headed by women are substantially worse off than those headed by men. The problems associated with poverty and underdevelopment were greatly compounded by the inefficiency of homeland governments and the collapse of many state services during the political turmoil of the late 1980s and early 1990s (Murray, 1994:66).

The political isolation of the homelands under apartheid meant that many institutions, including those associated with environmental management, were very different from those found in the rest of South Africa or did not exist at all. A system of democratic local government was instituted, with elections in November 1995, but was not yet operational by mid-1996. This has left the 'traditional' leaders, who have survived the transition to democracy with their powers virtually intact, as the most important institution of local governance within the black rural areas. In the new Northern Province, composed of three former homelands (Lebowa, Gazankulu and Venda) and one former 'white' area (Northern Transvaal), the tasks of integrating a multiplicity of institutions to tackle the enormous social and economic problems inherited from apartheid are proving particularly difficult.

Overcoming the legacy of inequality and oppression within the rural areas is one of the most pressing challenges facing the new government, led by the African National Congress (ANC). Indeed, demands for a radical redistribution of land and other resources to dispossessed groups were central to the struggle against apartheid (Levin and Weiner, 1997:14). Since coming to power, however, the government has adopted a broadly neoliberal approach to economic policy and eschewed many of the demands of its more radical supporters for nationalization or expropriation of white-owned lands.

The Mutale River: physical characteristics

Under apartheid, Venda, situated in the north-eastern corner of the Transvaal, was declared to be the 'homeland' of all speakers of the Venda language (Luvenda) (see Map 5.1). It became an 'independent' republic in 1979, a status not recognized by the international community, and on 27 April 1994 was reincorporated into the

Republic of South Africa (RSA). Today it forms part of the new Northern Province and, although the territory has no formal administrative significance, it retains a strong cultural identity, and many of its former institutions, including the Tribal Authorities and the homeland bureaucracy, remain more or less intact.

The 'Republic' of Venda consisted of two separate territories, between latitudes 22.15 and 25.24 south and longitudes 29.50 and 20.31 east, completely surrounded by the RSA (Map 5.2). The main block of Venda territory was separated from the Limpopo River (the border with Zimbabwe) by the Madimbo corridor, a narrow strip of territory excised from the homeland and occupied by the South African military in the mid-1970s. To the north-east, Venda was separated from the border with Mozambique by the Kruger National Park; to the south and south-east, it was bordered by the former homeland of Gazankulu; and to the west and south-west it was bordered by the Soutpansberg and Messina districts of the RSA. The main town and homeland 'capital' was Thohoyandou, which embraces the older administrative centre of Sibasa, but the area depends for much of its services on the former 'white' towns of Louis Trichardt and Messina and, to a lesser extent, the provincial capital of Pietersburg. The total area of Venda in 1991 was approximately 680,700 hectares (6,807 square kilometres), with a resident population of 558,797 people (DBSA, 1993).

Climatic conditions in Venda are generally subtropical, but show considerable local variation. Rainfall declines and air temperatures rise as one moves northwards and towards lower-lying areas (Fig. 5.1), giving rise to relatively cool, wet highlands, and warmer, drier lowlands. More than 90 per cent of annual precipitation occurs during the six months from October to March (Fig. 5.2), mainly in the form of thunderstorms. Frost, snow and hail are all rare. The region is prone to periodic droughts, with particularly severe droughts occurring in 1963–4, 1972–3, 1982–3 and especially 1991–2, the driest year on record.

The Mutale River, the geographical focus of this study, lies almost entirely within the former Venda. It rises in the Soutpansberg range, an area of relatively high rainfall, and passes through progressively drier areas as it enters the low-lying country to the north-east. It flows for a total of approximately 120 kilometres from source to join with the Luvuvhu River just inside the Kruger National Park (see Map 5.2). From there, the Luvuvhu flows eastward for another 20 kilometres before it empties into the Limpopo at Crook's Corner, on the international frontier of South Africa and Mozambique.

Considerable variation in physical and social conditions are found along the course of the Mutale. For the first 15 kilometres from its source, the river descends rapidly through mountainous forested terrain, formed by a succession of volcanic and sedimentary rocks overlying the archaic bedrock. Peaks rise to more than 1,300 metres and valley floors lie at over 700 metres above sea level. The terrain contains a few patches of deep red clay soils but offers little scope for cultivation (Institute for Soil, Climate and Water (ISCW) Land Type Ib441). In the higher, wetter parts of the Soutpansberg, the climax vegetation is forest but has been largely replaced by grassveld on the mountain tops and by scrubby thornveld on escarpments and slopes (Acocks, 1988:43). This area is sparsely populated.

Ten kilometres north-east of Lake Fundudzi, the Mutale emerges into the Tshiombo valley, a broad, almost flat area approximately 33 kilometres long and 4 to

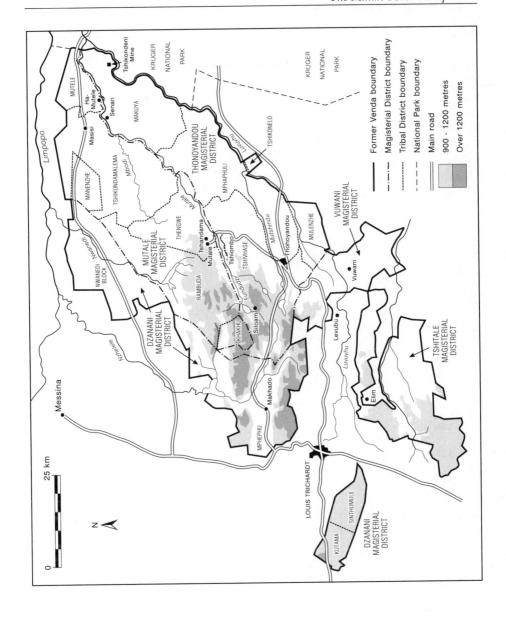

Map 5.2
Venda &
the Mutale valley

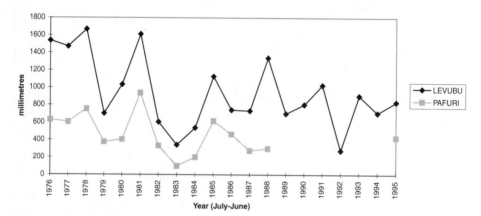

Figure 5.1   Annual rainfall in the upper & lower Mutale River valley
Source: South African Weather Bureau, Station Reports.

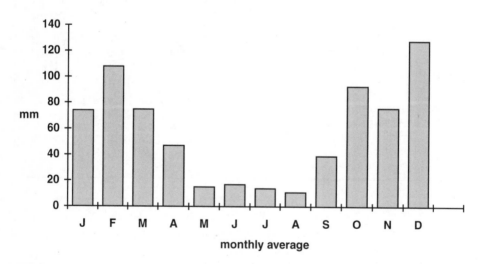

Figure 5.2   Average monthly rainfall, Thohoyandou
Source: South African Weather Bureau, Station Report.

7 kilometres wide, at an altitude of about 600 metres above sea level. The valley covers some 18,800 hectares, 80 per cent of which is estimated to be cultivable (ISCW Land Type Ba60). About half of this area consists of red, well-drained sandy loam soils, with the remainder made up of grey, poorly drained soils of a higher clay content. Annual (calendar year) rainfall in the Tshiombo valley for the period 1982–93 averaged 688 millimetres, but the totals for the agricultural year (July to June) varied from a low of 240 millimetres in 1991–2 to a high of 1,120 millimetres in 1987–8 (South African Weather Bureau, Tshandama Station, Table WB42).

The Tshiombo valley is relatively densely populated and well integrated into the economy of greater Thohoyandou, less than 20 kilometres away (see Map 5.2). Plentiful water and rich soils make it suitable for intensive agriculture, and the area has been the subject of a range of development initiatives over the past 40 years. Two smallholder irrigation schemes, Tshiombo and Rambuda, were developed at the head of the valley in the early 1960s (Map 5.3), based on gravity-fed furrow irrigation systems drawing water from the Mutale and Tshala Rivers, respectively. Tshiombo is much the larger of the two, with a total of 1,150 hectares under irrigation, divided into 930 plots, making it one of the largest of its kind in southern Africa. Immediately downstream from Tshiombo lies the 540-hectare Tshandama/Makonde scheme, developed by the Venda government in the 1980s, utilizing sprinkler irrigation on plots of 10 hectares and upwards. Elsewhere in the valley, stock farming, of both cattle and goats, is widespread but on a relatively small scale. Dryland (rain-fed) agriculture is also carried out in many parts of the valley, particularly in the eastern end, while areas of informal (non-scheme) irrigation are located along both banks of the Mutale and its tributaries.

Moving downstream, the Mutale exits from the Tshiombo valley through a narrow gorge, flowing for approximately 20 kilometres through the hilly terrain of the north-eastern Soutpansberg, dominated by rocky slopes with shallow soils. Peaks rise to about 800 metres, separating the Tshiombo valley from the drylands to the north. The area is sparsely populated and cultivable soils are estimated to cover only 8 per cent of the land area (ISCW Land Type Fb498). Moving northwards, the landscape through which the river flows becomes progressively flatter and the hills more dispersed. North of Mutale Bridge (Map 5.4), the river turns to the east to skirt the southern edge of a rocky quartzite and sandstone ridge around Ha–Mutele, before turning north-eastwards once again. At this point, extensive areas of alluvial and deep clay soils make up 70–80 per cent of the gently sloping riverine land on both banks (ISCW Land Type Fb499).

For its last 15 kilometres, the Mutale turns to the east once more, flowing through terraced valleys to its confluence with the Luvuvhu. Away from the immediate flood-plain, soils are sandy and shallow, giving way in the north to extensive areas of deep sandy soils bordering the Malonga Flats. Vegetation is largely short, shrubby mopane trees (*Colophospermum mopane*), with scattered baobab trees (*Adansonia digitata*) and some mixed bushveld and sourveld (Acocks, 1988:43). Annual rainfall in these lower reaches falls below 500 millimetres in parts. Vegetation consists of mixed bushveld of the tropical savanna types, merging with mopane-veld of the tropical bush and savanna types towards the north-east (Rand Afrikaans University, 1979:14).

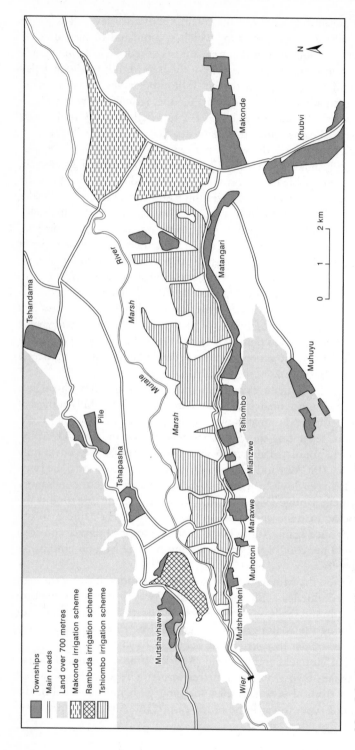

Map 5.3   Irrigation in Tshiombo, upper Mutale valley

Map 5.4   Irrigation in the lower Mutale valley (opposite page)

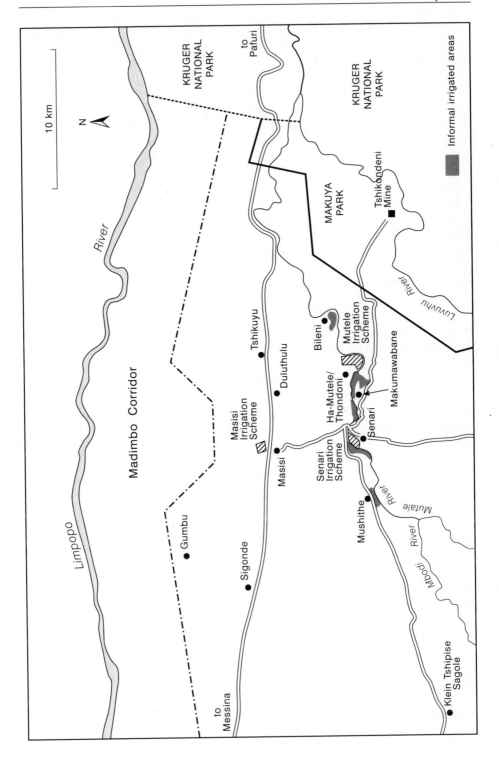

Informal irrigated areas

In socio-economic terms, the lower reaches of the Mutale are poor, sparsely populated and underdeveloped relative to the rest of Venda. The population is scattered in
small villages, living largely in mud and thatch huts, generally without electricity,
telephones, tarred roads or public transport and with only the most rudimentary
water supply, health services, schools and shops. The physical conditions are harsh
and unforgiving, with much marginal land suitable only for extensive grazing of livestock or cultivation of hardy grains, such as sorghum and millet. Two agricultural
projects, using sprinkler irrigation, have been developed, at Senari and Mutele, and
sizeable areas along both banks of the river have been brought under irrigation by
private individuals (see Map 5.4).

Figures for the monthly volume of water flowing in the Mutale River, measured at
Thengwe (Stream-flow Gauge A9M04), available, with some gaps, for the period
August 1932 to July 1995, show a dramatic decline in water volumes in recent years
(Fig. 5.3). With the exception of two years (1937–8 and 1941–2), the entire period
from 1932–3 to 1962–3 shows volumes of above 50 million cubic metres per annum.
After 1962, the record shows a substantial decline, and it would appear that, from
1982–3 to 1994–5, no year has experienced more than 50 million cubic metres (i.e.
well below the previous norm). The lowest confirmed figure is 1.28 million for
1991–2, with less than 50,000 cubic metres (i.e. virtually no flow) for each month
from February to October 1992. Informants in the lower Mutale area reported that
the Mutale dried up completely in the 1992–3 season, the only time that they could
recall this happening

There is no single explanation for the severe decline in water volumes in the
Mutale River, but the most obvious is the changing rainfall pattern in the region,
which seems to be in long-term decline. To this must be added, however, the
increasing extraction of river water for irrigation schemes and by private irrigators

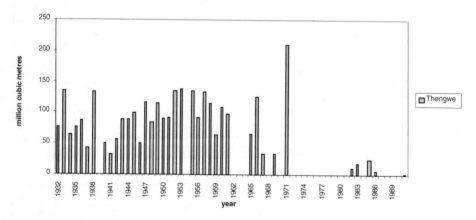

Figure 5.3 Flow records for the Mutale River
Source: Stream-flow Station, Thengwe. Department of Water Affairs and Forestry.

all along the valley. In addition to the 8.14 million cubic metres required every year by the Tshiombo scheme, an estimated 4 million is extracted for the Makonde irrigation scheme and another 1.8 million between Tshiombo and Thengwe for animal and human consumption (Murray Bisenbach and Badenhorst, 1989:32). Another contributory factor is the damming of the Tshirovha River, a tributary of the upper Mutale, in order to provide irrigation water for the tea plantations at Makumbane, on the south side of the mountains. Whatever the reason, or combination of reasons, the general pattern of decline fits that described by O'Keeffe et al. (1992:288) for the rivers draining through the Kruger National Park (the Luvuvhu, Great Letaba, Olifants, Sabie and Crocodile), all of which were formerly perennial:

> In recent years the flow in the Letaba River has been so reduced that it flows for only a few months each year. The Luvuvhu River first stopped flowing in 1948, and again in 1964–65, but it now stops flowing in most years.

Access to land and water: institutional framework

Most of the land in the Mutale valley, in common with the rest of the former homelands, is officially classified as communal (or 'Tribal') tenure. Over the years, this system has undergone considerable modification, with the result that a variety of property forms now coexist in the area, none of which could be described as private property, strictly speaking.

Communal land tenure in South Africa is a hybrid form, specific to the homelands, which combines elements of individual and collective property rights. The system is communal in the sense that an individual's entitlement to land flows from membership of a socio-political community (a village or tribal unit), rather than from private ownership, but, with some exceptions, it does not imply collective forms of production (Bennett, 1995:168). Although having some basis in African customary law, communal tenure has been greatly modified by successive governments over the course of the twentieth century, while alternative forms of landholding were effectively denied to black people. Authors such as Lacey (1981), Haines and Cross (1988) and Hendricks (1990) argue that communal tenure was an essential component of the migrant labour system, facilitating the concentration of the maximum possible number of Africans in the reserves/homelands, preventing the emergence of a stratum of rich peasants or capitalist farmers and providing the basis for a high degree of social control through the tribal leaders, who controlled access to land.

Communal land is nominally owned by the state, but is held 'in trust' by tribal chiefs, and allocated to people living under their jurisdiction on a usufructuary basis (Budlender and Latsky, 1991:121). It largely comprises land 'scheduled' for occupation by named tribal groups under the 1913 Natives Land Act, and 'released' land acquired by the South African Native Trust under the terms of the 1936 Native Trust and Land Act. Various Proclamations (R5 of 1963, R191 of 1967, R188 of 1969) attempted to regulate access to scheduled and released land, as well as land on irrigation schemes, but since the abolition of all 'racially based' land laws in 1991 the legal situation is far from clear (Vink, 1986; Cross and Rutsch, 1995:23).

Every household within a communal area has, in principle, a right to a residential site, an arable plot for subsistence purposes and access to common property resources, such as grazing. In practice, however, a substantial proportion of people in communal areas have little or no access to land. The right to land usually applies only to male 'household heads' but is sometimes extended to women (Bennett, 1995:170). Those who obtain land receive a right to its permanent use, but not to sell it, and can only transfer it to another family member with the permission of the tribal leaders. Unallocated lands are generally available to community members as a common pool resource (commonage), providing pasture for livestock and other natural resources such as timber, thatching grass, edible fruits and plants and materials for use in traditional medicine (Cousins, 1996:168). Tribal leaders have, in principle, the power to repossess land if it is abandoned, if it is needed for another purpose such as a road or a public building, if it is deemed surplus to the needs of the holders or in order to punish a landholder for some offence, but examples of such repossession are rare and the communal system is generally seen as a reasonably secure form of tenure (Bromberger, 1988:208).

Like most of the rest of the homelands, the Mutale valley was subjected to 'betterment' planning during the 1960s, whereby lands were surveyed by government officials and demarcated into residential, grazing and cropping areas. Local informants reported that not every household obtained land under betterment, especially in more densely populated areas, and that subsequent population growth in most areas has led to a growing incidence of landlessness. Today, access to arable plots varies considerably from village to village. In the fertile and well-populated areas of the upper Mutale valley, no more than half the households have access to arable land, whereas in the sparsely populated lower valley, upwards of 90 per cent of households in many villages have plots. Typical allocations are in the range of 1 to 3 hectares, although a small number of significantly larger holdings were encountered in the area. No evidence could be found to suggest any significant redistribution of arable plots since betterment, and extension of the total area under cultivation has been resisted (at least until very recently) by the tribal and government authorities.

The most significant development in the use and allocation of communal land in the Mutale in recent years has been the introduction of irrigation, both 'formal' and 'informal'. On the smallholder projects run by the Department of Agriculture (Tshiombo and Rambuda), irrigable plots are allocated jointly by the village headman and the agricultural extension officer, and plot-holders must pay an annual fee of 12 rand (R12) per plot to the state. Occupants are given permission to use the land, but no title deed, and are free to pass their plots to other family members on their death or retirement. There would appear to be no effective means of repossessing land, however, even when it is unused, unless the occupant surrenders it. The bulk of plots appear to have been allocated to the original occupants of the land incorporated into the schemes but, over the years, especially at Tshiombo, there has been considerable in-migration from other parts of Venda and beyond.

The official irrigation schemes on the lower Mutale (Senari and Mutele) present a different model of 'development' and of landholding. Both were constructed by the Venda Department of Agriculture in the late 1970s, on pockets of rich, alluvial soil within bends of the Mutale River (see Map 5.4). Unlike the older schemes at Tshiombo and Rambuda, they were not introduced for the benefit of the local inhabitants but as prestige projects for the Tribal Areas concerned (Makuya and Mutele, respectively). Plots were allocated by the Venda Department of Agriculture and the Tribal Authorities, and went to well-connected (and relatively prosperous) individuals from outside the immediate locality. The scale of the plots – at 3 to 6 hectares each – and the method of irrigation – sprinklers and diesel pumps – would suggest a more 'commercial' orientation than the schemes on the upper Mutale. Plot-holders must pay an annual rent of R60 each per plot, which entitles them to fuel for the pump and maintenance of the irrigation equipment. No plots have been reallocated since the inception of these schemes.

Projects run by the parastatal Venda Agricultural Corporation (Agriven) offer yet another example of landholding within what is nominally a communal system. At Makonde, adjacent to the Tshiombo scheme, an area of approximately 540 hectares has been developed by the Venda authorities for sprinkler irrigation. This project is managed by the parastatal Agriven, which leases plots ranging from 8 to 25 hectares to individual farmers. Plot-holders are granted their land for a fixed period under a renewable, written contract, and are liable to forfeiture of their tenancy if they do not meet their rental and other financial obligations. Officially, Tribal Authorities have no influence over state land and large-scale Agriven projects, but the allocation of land by government agencies was (at least until 1994) highly politicized, which often meant preferment for tribal leaders, politicians or business figures close to the homeland regime.

Substantial pockets of informally irrigated land were identified along the north bank of the Mutale in Rambuda and Thengwe Tribal Areas, along tributaries, such as the Tshiombedi and the Sambandou, on so-called 'wasteland' around the margins of the Tshiombo scheme and on the lower Mutale north bank, around the villages of Mushithe and Makumawabane. All those interviewed reported that they had obtained their plots by the 'traditional' route, that is, by applying to the chief or headman. In Makuya district in particular, respondents said they had received strong encouragement from the chief, who invited them to clear as much riverine land as they could work. Approximately half of those interviewed had had their plots surveyed by the Department of Agriculture and had obtained a formal 'Permission to Occupy' from the District Magistrate's office. While this process does not confer rights of private ownership, it is seen as a safeguard in the event of any other party claiming the land or in a dispute over plot boundaries. Since 1990, one local businessman has acquired an exceptionally large holding, approximately 150 hectares, adjacent to the Mbwedi River, where he is growing tomatoes under drip irrigation. During 1996, he was reported to have approached the Tribal Authority with a view to acquiring (whether by grant or purchase) some form of permanent private title to the land, but, according to local officials, this was resisted by the tribal leaders. As with areas of private irrigation elsewhere, this riverine land in question was reported to have been cleared 'from bush' and to have been uncultivated previously. None the less, such developments point to a major challenge to the system of communal tenure, and suggest that individuals with influence and capital to invest may no longer be looking to the state to develop agricultural 'projects' on their behalf, but are able to avail themselves of 'traditional' rights to land to establish themselves on a much larger scale than previously possible.

As well as land, water in the 'tribal' areas is also considered a communal form of property, and all members of the community are entitled to access springs, streams and rivers for domestic or agricultural purposes. The right of access to rivers for live-stock is well established, and is facilitated by a tradition of not using river banks for cultivation. There does not appear to be any long-standing tradition of irrigated agri-culture in the Mutale valley and, as a consequence, there are no codes governing the use of water for this purpose. The extraction of water from the Mutale and other rivers in the area for irrigation or other purposes is, therefore, effectively unregulated.

In addition to varieties of landholding outlined here, there are four major examples of non-agricultural land use in or around the study area – the Madimbo corridor, Tshikondeni mine, Makuya Park and Kruger National Park. All involve an effective break with the communal system and, to varying degrees, a loss of 'traditional' rights of access to land, water and organic materials.

The Madimbo (or Mashakatini) corridor is a military zone 5 to 10 kilometres wide, running eastward from Messina along the south bank of the Limpopo River. It was cleared as a security measure in the late 1970s and is still occupied by the South African defence forces. A number of communities were removed from the corridor and relocated to villages in northern Venda. South of the corridor, cattle owners from villages such as Masisi and Gumbu, accustomed to grazing their cattle as far north as the Limpopo, were denied access to the river and cattle that strayed into the strip were impounded. With the transition to democracy in South Africa, it appears likely that the Madimbo corridor will shortly be vacated by the military, giving rise to considerable debate at the national level. Among the interested parties are mining companies, which wish to begin exploration for diamonds in the corridor, and wildlife interests, with schemes to make it the centre-piece of an international wildlife reserve stretching from Mozambique to Botswana.

Makuya Park, located in the north-eastern corner of Venda, consists of approxi-mately 16,000 hectares of land, leased from the tribal authorities of Makuya, Mutele and Mphaphuli by the provincial government. It was created as a 'national' wildlife park during Venda's independence period, but has never become fully operational. For all practical purposes, it is effectively an extension of the Kruger National Park, with which it shares a long, unfenced boundary. For reasons that are not entirely clear, the Makuya Park has never been properly promoted or able to attract more than a trickle of visitors. With the formation of the new provincial administration, however, there has been a fresh approach to the management of wildlife reserves, and attempts have been made by the government to promote debate on the future of Makuya Park. The newly created provincial Department of Environmental Affairs has adopted a policy of community participation in the management of nature reserves and other amenities under its control, and is attempting to create structures that will give local communities a direct involvement in the management of such resources. Thus, in late 1995, the department initiated the Makuya Park Forum, a consultancy body consisting of representatives of the department and Tribal Authorities in the vicinity of the Park, as a first step towards planning its future.

Tshikondeni mine, located just east of the study area, adjacent to Makuya Park and the Kruger National Park, is the only working mine in Venda and the only industrial enterprise of any note within an 80-kilometre radius. It is owned by ISCOR, the South African government-owned iron and steel corporation, and produces high-grade coking coal for use in ISCOR's steel plants. The mine concession area totals 22,000 hectares, much of which overlaps with the Makuya Park but, under terms negotiated with the former Venda government, the total surface area allowed for development is limited to 600 hectares at any one time.

The Kruger National Park, running along the eastern fringe of Venda, is the largest wildlife reserve in South Africa and a major tourist attraction. It has little positive impact on adjoining communities, however, being effectively closed to people and livestock. The last inhabitants of the Park, over 3,000 of the Maluleke people who lived around Pafuri, were forcibly removed to Gazankulu in 1969 (Harries, 1987:107). The only impact on the area under investigation is occasional escapes by lions, which have taken cattle along the Limpopo, and of elephants, which have trampled crops in the area. Some attempts have been made by the Park to involve local communities in planning future developments, in line with the prevailing political taste for 'participation', but it was not clear at the time of study what form this might take.

Access to land and water: demand, competition and conflict

Rising population and changing agricultural practices are creating considerable demand for land and other natural resources in the area of the Mutale River. Official estimates of population show a doubling over a 20-year period (1970–90), and anecdotal evidence suggests there has also been a substantial concentration of population from outlying areas into more dense settlements. However, low returns from agriculture, relative to wage employment or other forms of activity, make it unattractive to much of the population and serve to reduce the overall demand on resources. Furthermore, the prevailing system of land tenure has, to date, effectively inhibited the emergence of any market in land. While this means relative security of tenure for those with established land rights, it also means that those with excess land are unlikely to part with it, while a growing proportion of the rural population, both incomers and newly formed households, have little access to land for agriculture or other purposes.

The most obvious demand for land is coming from so-called 'progressive' farmers, those who are seen as capable of developing their agricultural enterprises beyond that of the typical smallholding in terms of scale of production, technical inputs and market orientation. Such candidates tend to be older men, typically in their fifties, with a history of migrant employment and who wish to move into full-time farming, or urban-based officials or businessmen who want to expand their activities. Both are likely to exploit their links to the Tribal Authorities to obtain above-average plots, often in prime riverine sites, and usually have the capital required to clear the land with tractors, install irrigation equipment and employ agricultural labour.

On the Tshiombo scheme, nearly three-quarters of the plot-holders interviewed stated that they were satisfied with the amount of land they had at present. Some said they would like to have more land but, with constrained resources – particularly labour, cash and water – would not be in a position to use it. Of the remaining one quarter, most said that they would be satisfied with a total holding of 2 to 3 hectares under irrigation, which was commonly thought to be as much as a single household could manage. A small minority, however, said that they required larger holdings, in the order of 10 to 25 hectares, and believed that the government should be making more land available to 'progressive' black farmers. On the newer schemes, such as Makonde and Mutele, there has undoubtedly been some exclusion of previous users, as relatively large plots were allocated to relatively well-off farmers drawn from a wide area. While such land has effectively been lost to the local community, there is no evidence that this has led to the creation of a distinct landless group. Only at Senari could evidence be found of direct conflict between social groups, as the perceived underutilization of plots and the fact that the two active plot-holders were from outside the immediate area were creating resentment among sections of the local community. The Senari civic (see below), with the backing of the ward councillor, was campaigning to have the unused plots reallocated to people from Senari village, and appears to have the support of the provincial Department of Agriculture. If this were to occur, it would signal a significant shift in power over land in favour of local democratic structures and away from the tribal authorities.

The 'colonization' of riverine land for informal (private) irrigation is well advanced throughout the Mutale area, and may be reaching its limits. Most 'wasteland' around the Tshiombo scheme that is cultivable would appear to be occupied, while, in the lower Mutale area, observations suggest that most of the cultivable land along both sides of the river in the study area has now been claimed. Indeed, it is not just land immediately adjoining the river that is being cleared and irrigated. In places where all the riverine land has already been occupied, farmers were using lengthy pipes to irrigate land further away from the river. Despite this, it was generally reported that competition for land was not particularly intense, as demand was limited by people's ability to raise the capital necessary for clearing plots and purchasing irrigation equipment.

Differential access to land and water

Ethnically and linguistically, Venda has been a relatively homogeneous area for the period of recorded history. The only significant linguistic minorities, Shangaan-speakers and, to a lesser extent, Northern Sotho-speakers, were, with few exceptions, forcibly removed elsewhere as part of the process of homeland consolidation during the 1960s and 1970s (Surplus People Project, 1983:164). The only other subgroup in rural Venda, the BaLemba, is a caste of craft-workers and traders, who tend to be well integrated into Venda-speaking communities and do not constitute a distinct social group. No evidence was found of any discrimination against such minorities – indeed, a Shangaan-speaker and a Lemba were among the larger landholders on the Tshiombo scheme.

Differentiation along lines of gender is more clearly evident throughout Venda. The widespread attitude among state officials and 'traditional leaders' interviewed and among male farmers was that women in need were entitled to small allocations of land for 'subsistence' purposes, but that priority should be given to men with families or with proven agricultural ability. Plots held by women tended to be considerably smaller than those held by men, and women were far less likely to expand their holdings beyond the initial allocation. On the Tshiombo scheme, for example, the average size of female holdings was only 70 per cent of average male holdings. On the informal irrigation plots on the lower Mutale, none of the women encountered held more than 1 hectare, compared with plots of 1 to 25 hectares for the men. No women held plots on the state-run schemes at Makonde, Senari or Mutele. Women who had acquired land – mainly women with young children and some elderly women living alone – generally did so on the death of a husband, father or son, rather than through direct application to the Tribal Authority. Inheritance of a late husband's holding is by no means assured, however, as land (along with other property, such as cattle and vehicles) commonly passed to another male relative rather than to a widow.

Differential access to land forms only one aspect of a growing social, economic and political cleavage between the generations in Venda (and in other homelands), which is being expressed in growing tensions between local 'civics' and tribal leaders (see below). Landholding tends to be dominated by tribal leaders, local businessmen and retired migrant workers, typically in their fifties, sixties or even seventies. Younger men have tended to receive their first plot once they have established a household of their own, but, since 'betterment' in the 1960s and the rapid increase in population since then, this is now far from assured. Furthermore, widespread unemployment in the homelands means that many men in their twenties are unable to establish households of their own and continue to live with their parents. Potential conflict over land is tempered, however, by a widespread lack of interest in farming among many younger men, although they tend to view it as an option for when they are older.

A rising population, a history of forced removals and an inflexible land tenure system have led to a growing distinction between those households with and those without land. At the same time, however, there is evidence of differentiation between existing landholders – not in itself a new development, but one that appears to have gathered pace in the last decade. On the Tshiombo scheme, despite an official policy of 'one man, one plot', over a third (36 per cent) of plot-holders surveyed had multiple plots (Table 5.1), and the accumulation of land would appear to have accelerated in recent years. In 1980, only fourteen households in the sample (17 per cent) had more than one plot on the formal scheme and the highest number of plots held by one household was three. By 1995, there were thirty households with multiple

Table 5.1 Combined landholding at Tshiombo, per household.

No. plots per household	1 Plot	2 Plots	3–6 Plots
No. of households	53	21	9
Total wasteland (ha)	7.0	22.75	21.0
Average wasteland/household (ha)	0.1	1.1	2.3
Average land/household (ha)	1.3	3.5	6.6

plots and the highest number of plots had risen to six. A similar pattern was found with regard to the acquisition of wasteland in the vicinity of the scheme and on the lower Mutale, where the small minority of households with irrigable holdings of 3 hectares or more had all acquired them in the past ten years.

While it was not possible to ascertain the precise reasons why certain individuals were able to increase their holdings above the norm, it would appear that, in most cases, this was related to a proven record in agriculture and a desire for expansion, coupled with good standing in the eyes of the Tribal Authorities. Analysis of household income data suggested that these households were not particularly well-off, but generally obtained income from at least one non-farm source (e.g. a wage-earner or pensioner, or both) (Lahiff, 1997b:266).

The growth of larger holdings and of the numbers of landless households has created conditions for growing differentiation between employers and providers of agricultural labour. Agricultural wage labour is overwhelmingly seasonal and casual (or informal), and wages (typically R100–200 per month in 1995) were less than half the minimum rates in the non-agricultural formal sector. Just over a third of plot-holders on the scheme had hired labour in the previous year, generally for set tasks, such as planting, weeding or harvesting. Most hired one worker at a time, but a small minority (4 per cent) said they occasionally hired between three and five workers at once. Use of hired labour was universal among plot-holders on the other formal schemes and among the larger informal irrigators on the lower Mutale. Workers at Tshiombo and elsewhere, both men and women, were drawn from the ranks of the landless or near-landless.

The politics of access

Control of communal resources is central to the material and symbolic position of the tribal chiefs, who, despite the transition to democracy, remain the most powerful political force in rural Venda. It is not altogether surprising, therefore, that land lies at the heart of much of the emerging political struggle between 'traditional' and 'democratic' forces here and elsewhere in the homelands. The main function of tribal leaders in this respect is to decide how resources, particularly land, are divided between members of the community. Chiefs have an implicit duty to cater for all of their followers, although not necessarily equally, and have the right to retain the biggest share of resources for themselves.

Against this background, the new, democratically elected, local councils in Venda are struggling to establish themselves and define their role, and find themselves in direct competition with tribal leaders for local power. Interviews with councillors revealed a cohort of political activists who were eager to engage with the process of local government, but who were receiving little support from other tiers of government in establishing the new councils or identifying their powers and responsibilities. Councillors were vociferous in their criticisms of both the local chiefs, whom they accuse of resisting the transition to democracy, and the provincial government, which they accused of failing to support them in their struggles with the chiefs or to provide for a timely transfer of powers to the new authorities.

One of the main forces behind the newly elected local councillors are the 'civics' (civil associations), which in some areas, have assumed the role of an additional, unofficial, tier of local governance. Civics are open to all members of the community, but draw their membership mainly from the ranks of young men and from families that are not related to or supportive of the village headmen. The civics in the rural areas combine elements of a village council with party politics, acting as branches of the 'mass democratic movement' (effectively the ANC) at the local level. Civics in some areas are involved in resolving disputes between villagers and in the administration of justice. Since 1995, civics at Tshiombo have been making representations to the agricultural officers on behalf of plot-holders experiencing problems with the supply of irrigation water and of people waiting to acquire plots on the scheme. At Senari, the civic had recently begun allocating house stands to people in the village, without reference to the headman or chief, and was in dispute with the tribal leaders over the allocation of plots on the Senari irrigation scheme.

The political priorities expressed by new councillors and civics in the Mutale area were largely to do with service provision – housing, health care, drinking water, electricity supply – rather than land. This can be attributed to the fact that the new councils have been given no legal powers over communal land, or natural resources more generally, and all physical planning powers rest with the higher (indirectly elected) district councils. However, it also reflects the division between younger political activists, eager for change, and older, more conservative people, who wish to retain elements of the old order. Members of the mass democratic movement in the area, including ANC councillors, were drawn mainly from the ranks of landless youth, workers in the industrial or service sectors, the unemployed and teachers. These are the people who benefited least from the tribal system in areas such as land allocation and are most eager for change. Tribal Authorities, on the other hand, draw their support largely from the older generation and those who have benefited from the patronage of tribal leaders.

In general, councillors appeared willing to work with other local structures, including the chiefs, in order to promote the development of their area, but they were adamant that they would not allow the traditional leaders to stand in the way of change. Part of their strategy was to promote the civics as the principal democratic structures at village level, as a counterweight to the power of village headmen, and to ensure that they have a say in issues such as the allocation of residential plots.

Council leaders stressed that they were not advocating the abolition of the chief-taincy, but believed that chiefs should be restricted to 'ceremonial' duties, such as holding initiation schools, rather than 'political' issues, such as land allocation and local administration.

Two examples of the emerging tension between the generations and between the new and the old political orders emerged during the study. At Tshiombo, attempts to form a plot-holders' organization led to disputes between younger farmers and older, more established farmers, whom they accused of dominating the scheme. Many of the younger generation, particularly those associated with the civics and the culture of democratic transformation, were clearly intolerant of the continued domination of local life by the 'traditional' élite and impatient with the slow rate of change following the elections of 1994 and 1995, challenging representatives of the old order as the opportunity arose. A similar tension was apparent in the Makuya Park forum, established by the Northern Province's Department of Environmental Affairs in 1995, prior to the first council elections. As a result (possibly deliberate), the forum did not include representatives of the democratic movement, which led to confrontation between tribal representatives on the forum and newly elected councillors. By late May 1996, it was clear that the council members had little intention of cooperating with tribal leaders and were questioning the composition and legitimacy of the forum. Councillors argued that there was no need for such a forum now that there were legitimate elected representatives, who could speak and act on behalf of the community.

Land and water use: production systems

Apart from mining, productive land use in the Mutale valley is limited to three main activities – dryland cropping, irrigated cropping and extensive livestock grazing.

Dryland (rain-fed) cropping is carried out in most parts of the valley, particularly in the eastern end of the Tshiombo valley and in the lower Mutale area. The main exception is around the Tshiombo scheme, where virtually all arable land between the river and the mountains is given over to the irrigation scheme. Although once an essential part of livelihoods, dryland cropping is now probably the least important type of farming in the area, and would appear to be set for even further decline as alternative sources of income – agricultural and otherwise – become the norm. Generally speaking, dryland cropping tends to be less developed than irrigated production, particularly in drier areas of the lower Mutale. Some dryland ploughing is done with privately hired tractors in the upper Mutale, but in other areas ploughing with donkeys is still the norm. Use of purchased inputs – improved seed, fertilizer and pesticides – is well below the levels found on the irrigation schemes and, in many cases, is absent altogether. The proportion of produce sold also appears to be very low, with most dryland crops being consumed directly by producing households.

Dryland plots typically range from less than half a hectare to approximately 3 hectares, but most are in the order of 1 hectare. The dominant dryland crop in the Tshiombo valley is maize, usually intercropped with varieties of pumpkins and squash, along with smaller areas of groundnuts and sorghum. In the lower Mutale, sorghum is the most common crop, closely followed by maize. Maize is less resistant than sorghum to the dry conditions of the lower Mutale and, according to local farmers and agricultural officers, has completely failed roughly one year in three over the past two decades. None the less, it appears to be growing in popularity and is probably set to replace sorghum as the main dryland crop in all areas in the near future. The area of millet grown is small relative to both maize and sorghum. The bulk of sorghum and millet is used for domestic production of beer, and no evidence could be found of a market for either crop anywhere in Venda. Furthermore, it was widely reported that sorghum porridge, the one-time staple food of the far northern districts, has been almost entirely replaced by maize meal porridge in the course of little more than a generation, indicating a shift not just in taste but from a largely self-provisioning to a more market-dependent local economy. The other dryland crops suited to the area, water melons and pumpkins, are usually intercropped with either maize or sorghum. From what information could be obtained, it appears that these crops are also intended mainly for domestic consumption, although a proportion is sold informally within the local area.

Irrigated cropping, both on and off the formal schemes, tends to be considerably more developed than dryland agriculture in terms of the range of crops grown, the use of purchased inputs and marketing. Cropping on the Tshiombo and Rambuda schemes is based on relatively simple technology, using furrow irrigation fed from purpose-built canals supplied via a barrage and canal from the Mutale and Tshala Rivers, respectively. Holdings at Tshiombo ranged from 1.2 hectares (a standard plot) to 7.2 hectares (or 17 hectares if so-called wasteland is included). The main crop grown, in terms of area, is maize, with many households producing two crops a year. A group of seven crops – groundnuts, China spinach, *muxe* (a local variety of spinach), tomatoes, sweet potatoes, dry beans and cabbage – make up most other cultivation, along with relatively small areas of chilli peppers, pumpkins, onions, *jugo* beans, tobacco, sugar cane, sweet melons, millet, carrots, lettuce and okra. Output peaks in the summer rainy season, but in most years there is some year-round production.

The great majority of plot-holders at Tshiombo sell some portion of their produce every year, and most sell well over half their total output (by value). Households with relatively small holdings and low output generally consume some or all of every crop grown but larger producers grow particular crops (such as green maize, cabbage and chillies) specifically for sale. The most common crop, summer maize, is grown almost entirely for household consumption (in the form of maize meal). Crop sales are mainly through informal (i.e. unrecorded) channels, in the form of direct sales to the public in and around Tshiombo or to traders, who call at plot-holders' fields or homes. Formal marketing channels (used by only 12 per cent of plot-holders surveyed) include the sale of tomatoes to a canning factory at Makhado (80 kilometres away), of mangoes to *achar* (pickle) factories at Shayandima or Levubu and, in a small number of cases, trucking chilli peppers or cabbage to the Johannesburg morning market.

The irrigation schemes at Senari and Mutele appear to have deteriorated in recent years for a variety of reasons, and now operate well below their potential. At Senari, only two farmers were actually using their land, one cultivating less than half his plot, and the other cultivating both his own plot and another, which he is subleasing, unofficially, from its official occupant. The larger of these two farmers operates a highly commercialized operation, employing ten people full-time and producing tomatoes, maize, cabbage and spinach for sale. He owns his own tractor and ploughing implements, as well as a van, with which he transports produce to Thohoyandou market and to the tomato canning factory at Makhado. The other active farmer on the scheme was producing only maize and sorghum for his own household use. The remaining, inactive, plot-holders were reported to have abandoned their lands at various times over the last ten years, owing to a combination of poor harvests and severe debts. The Mutele scheme was found to be in an even poorer state, as the main pump had been out of order for five months following flood damage. As at Senari, the majority of plot-holders had ceased using their lands in recent years, and the two farmers who remained were struggling to produce crops of maize and sorghum under what were effectively dryland conditions.

Away from the formal schemes, informal or private irrigators produce a wide range of crops, with the main emphasis on tomatoes. While they varied considerably in approach and scale of operation, these informal irrigators all had a strong commercial orientation, by Venda standards, and the majority of those interviewed stated that farming was their only occupation or principal source of household income. On the lower Mutale, most informal irrigators sold tomatoes to the factories at Messina and Makhado, and one had a fixed-price contract to grow 5 hectares of tomatoes for the Makhado factory. Other crops included maize, cabbage, spinach, beans, butternut squash, gem squash, pumpkins and water melons. The bulk of these are sold directly by the farmers or members of their households in neighbouring villages, in the Thohoyandou market or to hawkers who come to their plots. Only one farmer regularly sent produce to markets outside the region – mainly Johannesburg – using a commercial transport company.

Maize is grown by all these farmers, mainly for domestic consumption, although some fresh cobs (green mealies) are sold within the local area. The bulk of the maize harvest is brought for milling either to the Northern Transvaal Cooperative (NTK) roller mills at Shayandima or to one of the small tractor-powered mills operating in nearby villages. The stamping of maize by hand seems to have died out almost entirely among this group of farmers, although it is still practised among other households in the area with relatively small quantities of grain.

Livestock farming is carried out on communal land throughout the study area (Fig. 5.4). Herds tend to be small – in the order of five to ten head for both cattle and goats – but a few exceptionally large herds were encountered in the dry areas of the lower Mutale (see below). At Tshiombo, virtually all households reported keeping cattle at some time in the past, but only a quarter kept cattle at the time of the survey, mostly indigenous Nguni and Afrikander breeds with some admixture of Brahman. Among households keeping cattle, the number of head ranged between 2 and 45, with an average of 14.6 per cattle-owning household (Table 5.2).

Various reasons were given for the reported decline in cattle-owning at Tshiombo. A number of households stated that they had sold off their cattle when they first came

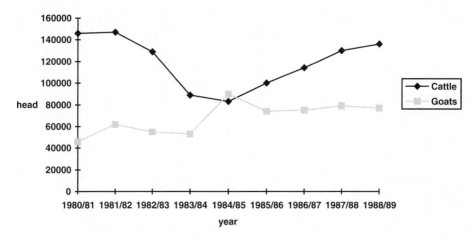

Figure 5.4 Livestock numbers in Venda, 1982–9
Source: Development Bank of South Africa (DBSA, 1993: Table 6.30).

to join the scheme or over the years to pay debts, while others said they had sold off their cattle owing to a shortage of household labour, especially as children grew up. One woman plot-holder said that she had sold off all her late husband's cattle to send her sons to university. The recurring drought of the 1980s and early 1990s also took a heavy toll of cattle in the area, and one household reported losing 20 cattle over the previous five years. Farmers at Tshiombo, as in other parts of Venda, depend on natural replacement to rebuild their herds, and once herds are lost completely they tend not to be replaced. Official disapproval of livestock farming at Tshiombo, a feature of the early years of the scheme, would appear to have abated in recent years but there was still opposition from some non cattle-owners, who expressed strong feelings about cattle damaging their crops.

Underlying these contingent factors, however, there was evidence of changing attitudes towards cattle-owning at Tshiombo. As a form of bridewealth (*lobola*), as an indicator of wealth or social status, as a source of income or even as a form of savings, cattle have been effectively replaced by other more accessible, more flexible and more productive forms of property, obtained through participation in the market economy. Farming households at Tshiombo are today more likely to

Table 5.2 Distribution of cattle among households at Tshiombo.

No. of cattle	No. of households	% of households
Nil	53	63.9
1–10	10	12.0
11–20	7	8.4
21+	3	3.6

invest in capital and cultural goods, such as vehicles, agricultural inputs, clothing or education, which are more highly regarded or capable of generating a higher return than cattle. Bridewealth, if paid at all, is most likely to be paid in cash. With the growing importance of the cash economy over many decades and the multiple daily demands on households for cash, tying up household wealth in cattle is no longer seen by many people at Tshiombo as an appropriate use of available resources.

Livestock farming is much more important in the drier regions of the lower Mutale. Veterinary officials estimated that roughly 50 per cent of households in the area owned cattle, and that most cattle farmers had between ten and forty animals. In the very remote area north-east of Masisi, two farmers were found with exceptionally large herds – one with 215 cattle, and another who reported a herd size of 600 head. Official dipping records and the statements of veterinary officers in the area suggest that total cattle numbers in the area increased considerably during the 1960s and 1970s, but expansion was reversed by the drought of the early 1980s and numbers continued to fall into the 1990s.

Rainfall is the key limiting factor in livestock production in the lower Mutale area, determining the rate at which rivers, streams and groundwater reserves can be replenished and at which grazing can be restored. At times of severe drought – as occurred in 1982–3 and again in 1991–2 – the quality of grazing on the veld deteriorates rapidly, rivers and springs are in danger of drying up and even boreholes are liable to fail. Farmers interviewed for this study reported sizeable losses of livestock throughout the 1980s and early 1990s, but the ability to withstand unfavourable conditions varied widely. A number of smaller cattle owners – typically those with fewer than twenty head – reported that all of their animals were wiped out during the 1980s, while others were forced into distress sales. One larger herd owner at Makumawabane reported a reduction in herd size from 100 to 68 between 1991 and 1993, as calves and some mature cattle died from a combination of starvation and thirst. Grazing, which had deteriorated badly during the 1980s, was virtually eliminated in the 1991–2 season, and the river and many local boreholes dried up, causing severe shortages of drinking water for both animal and human populations.

An important feature of livestock farming in the lower Mutale area is the disease control barrier, or 'red line'. This line consists of a secure fence with supervised gates, running the entire length of South Africa's northern and eastern borders, and is intended to prevent the spread of infectious diseases, especially foot-and-mouth disease, to South African livestock from wild animals in the Kruger National Park or from livestock in neighbouring countries. The line runs approximately 10 kilometres south of the Limpopo and between 10 and 20 kilometres outside the perimeter of the Kruger Park. The red line does not appear to cause any major inconvenience for the inhabitants of the area, as gates are operated around the clock. Likewise, as it does not cut across any villages, it does not impose any additional restriction on grazing. Only when it comes to selling cattle across the line do difficulties arise, as cattle coming from the restricted zone must be inspected and quarantined for two weeks prior to being moved on.

No official records are kept regarding small stock – goats and sheep – but field esti-mates suggest that total numbers are greater than those of cattle, and ownership is certainly more widely spread. An informal survey of households in the lower Mutale suggested that at least 75 per cent kept goats. Herd sizes were generally in the range of 5 to 20 goats, and 45 was the largest herd encountered. Sheep are comparatively rare and flock sizes again tend to be small, in the range of 10 to 20 head. At Tshiombo, ownership of goats is even less widespread than cattle: just six respondents (7.2 per cent of the sample) reported keeping goats at the time of the household survey, all of them of the short-eared 'Boer' variety. Five of the six households with goats owned between 2 and 17 each, while the other kept a herd of 100. Grazing for goats is restricted to the rocky outcrops to the south-west of the irrigation scheme. Goats were extremely unpopular with scheme officials; most plot-holders and other informants told of goats damaging crops in their home gardens and irrigated plots.

Donkeys were reported to have been widely used for tillage and transport purposes throughout Venda up to the 1970s, but numbers now appear to be in severe decline. At Tshiombo, only three households (3.6 per cent of the sample) kept donkeys at the time of the survey, owning four, six and six animals, respectively. Just one household relied on donkeys for ploughing, but the other two used them for harrowing, following tractor ploughing. In the lower Mutale, many poorer households continue to plough with donkeys, but tractor ploughing is increasingly common. Donkey-drawn carts are also used for transport but are unsuited to the stony roads in much of this district, and transport by motor vehicle or bicycle and on foot is more common.

Chickens are widely kept, but in relatively small numbers. At Tshiombo, less than half the households surveyed had chickens, with numbers ranging from 2 to 50 per household. Chickens are generally kept for domestic consumption of meat, rather than for eggs or for sale. Only two plot-holders, both men, reported selling any chickens during the previous year. Chicken eggs are not widely exploited by the farmers of Tshiombo, either as food or for sale, and the local varieties of birds are not considered reliable layers. Pigs are not widely kept in Venda and there is a strong (cultural) antipathy to them in many areas. A small number of pigs were in evidence around Tshiombo, but just one respondent reported keeping a pig for own consumption.

Agricultural services

The range and quality of agricultural services – state, private commercial and cooper-ative – available to farmers in Venda vary widely between districts, but are generally extremely poor relative to those in 'white' farming districts. Most services are provided by the state, either directly through the line departments of the former homeland government (now absorbed into the provincial administration) or through the parastatal development corporation, Agriven. Most state services, particularly tractor ploughing, are tied to specific state-run projects, but a network of agricultural extension officers and veterinary technicians also provides limited services to farmers outside the formal schemes.

The Tshiombo irrigation scheme has probably the greatest concentration of agricultural services anywhere in Venda. Four tractors belonging to the Department of Works are permanently based on the scheme, and tractors from other (dryland) areas are available for hire in winter. A financial crisis in the government service during the transition from apartheid meant that state-run tractors were out of commission for much of the period of fieldwork, creating opportunities for a growing number of private owners offering tractors for hire. During the year 1994–5, over 90 per cent of plot-holders on the scheme hired tractors for ploughing, three-quarters of them from private operators. Of the remaining six households in the sample, two ploughed using animal traction (oxen and donkeys, respectively), one by hand-hoe and three did not cultivate at all. Plot-holders at Tshiombo also made relatively high use of purchased inputs – organic and inorganic fertilizer, certified seed and chemical sprays (insecticides and fungicides) – which they obtained mainly (for cash) from the Tshiombo Cooperative.

The Tshiombo Cooperative was founded in 1973 as a collective purchasing organization for farmers and provides a rare example of a (relatively) successful independent cooperative in a former homeland. It had 630 members in 1995, paying an annual fee of R10, and is run by a management committee, elected annually by the membership, and a full-time staff of six. The co-operative is essentially a retail operation, its main activities being the sale of agricultural inputs, petrol (it has the only filling station in Tshiombo), hardware and basic foodstuffs. The management of the cooperative reported problems of competing with the Agriven-run stores at Makonde and Malavule and the 'white' cooperatives in the region (NTK and Levubu Cooperative), owing to the poor terms it obtained from suppliers and its inability to offer credit facilities to its members.

The vast majority of farmers at Tshiombo, as elsewhere in the former homelands, do not have access to formal credit facilities through state or commercial sources. Agriven did provide short-term credit through the Tshiombo Cooperative in the 1980s and early 1990s, but this facility was withdrawn in 1991–2 in the face of widespread default following the severe drought of that year and amid reports of major financial problems within the parastatal. No evidence could be found of informal credit systems – moneylenders, communal savings schemes, goods on credit from local shops or the like – with any significant role in agriculture at Tshiombo or elsewhere in Venda. During 1994–5, limited funds were made available by the South African Agricultural Credit Board for seasonal loans to small farmers in the former homelands, but only four plot-holders at Tshiombo (4.8 per cent of the sample) received credit under the scheme, in amounts ranging from R5,000 to R14,000. Credit was used mainly to pay for tractor ploughing, fertilizers and irrigation equipment.

Plot-holders at Tshiombo were satisfied, by and large, with the agricultural extension service, but there was some criticism of a lack of specialist knowledge among extension officers and a degree of unwillingness to visit farmers in the field. Extension officers themselves spoke of a lack of adequate housing on the scheme, shortages of stationery and training aids and poor communications with head office. Overall, extension appeared to be based on relatively developed models of 'commercial' agriculture, with limited awareness of the resource constraints facing small farmers on the scheme and of their cultivation practices.

Elsewhere in the Mutale valley, the quality of state services to farmers is far below that available at Tshiombo. Despite their pioneering spirit and considerable agricultural success, private irrigation farmers in the lower Mutale receive virtually no official recognition and little or no direct assistance from the state in terms of credit, irrigation works or ploughing services. Agricultural extension officers based on the Senari and Mutele irrigation schemes, however, attempt to provide a basic service to those they can reach in the surrounding areas. The only other extension officer in the area is based at Masisi, along with a veterinary technician, who supervised the dipping of cattle. Ploughing services are also in short supply, and every farmer interviewed, even the few with their own tractors, stated that a lack of capacity prevented them from ploughing as much land as they wanted to. There are government tractors based on the Nwanedi block (west of Masisi), which occasionally come to plough on the Senari and Mutele schemes, but are rarely available to private farmers. Most farmers here relied on donkeys or privately hired tractors for ploughing.

Farmers in the lower Mutale area are further hampered by their remoteness from supplies of agricultural inputs and from markets. Inputs such as approved seed, fertilizer and pesticides are widely used on irrigated plots, but have to be purchased from the Agriven depot at Nwanedi (25 kilometres away) or from NTK branches at Shayandima (90 kilometres) or Messina (100 kilometres). The distances involved are clearly a problem for all farmers, but especially for those without their own transport and who have to hire or borrow a truck as required. Finally, there are no established market places for crops in the lower Mutale. Cattle auctions are held every two months at the state-run Sigonde agricultural station (8 kilometres west of Masisi), but farmers in the area complained of the low prices on offer, owing to a shortage of buyers. Larger herd-owners preferred to take their cattle to a more distant auction at Tshipise, which is used mainly by white farmers and attracts a wider range of buyers.

Commoditization and differentiation

There were wide differentials between households in the study area in terms of landholding, agricultural production and income. It was also apparent that the processes generating such differentiation were dynamic, reflecting substantial accumulation by a minority of households through agricultural and non-agricultural activities.

While it is not possible to be precise, the evidence of this study suggests that the great majority of households engaged in agriculture in the Mutale valley have little or no involvement in the market for agricultural produce and obtain a relatively small share of total household income (in cash and kind) from agriculture. A small minority, however, mainly with irrigated plots (on or off the formal schemes) or relatively large herds of livestock, is relatively well integrated into markets for both agricultural inputs and outputs, and obtains a substantial part of its income from agricultural commodity production.

The largest category of farming households in the Mutale area is very small producers, growing rain-fed crops on small arable plots (commonly less than 1 hectare) or keeping small numbers of either cattle or goats (typically fewer than ten head). They make little use of purchased inputs (with the possible exception of a hired tractor or donkey team for ploughing) and sell their produce only in times of extreme hardship. Few are entirely dependent on agriculture for their livelihoods, and those that are tend to be among the very poorest. As with the great majority of farmers in the area, the bulk of household income is likely to come from some combination of local wages, migrant remittances, state old-age pensions and petty trading.

Substantial numbers of households have expanded their agricultural activity beyond this very basic level, producing larger quantities of crops and livestock for consumption and sale. They include many of the smaller plot-holders on the Tshiombo scheme, the majority of 'informal' irrigators throughout the Mutale valley and medium-sized dryland farmers (on 1 to 3-hectare holdings). These medium-scale producers are loosely distinguishable from the first group by their larger scale (and range) of production, use of purchased inputs and regular sales of their produce (whether through formal or informal marketing channels). In common with the very smallest producers, however, they are unlikely to depend entirely on agriculture for their livelihoods.

Estimates of gross agricultural output at Tshiombo (Table 5.3) suggested that only 24 per cent of households produce more than R5,000 per annum (the equivalent of an unskilled wage in the formal non-agricultural economy). While this represented total income for a few households, for the majority it represented less than half of total household income (Lahiff, 1997b:266). The high proportion of produce sold by smallholders at Tshiombo (over 80 per cent, by value, in the majority of cases) suggests a much stronger 'commercial' orientation than might be suggested by the their scale of operation. While households in this category may not be 'full-time commercial farmers' (in the conventional South African sense), their integration in agricultural markets means they are certainly not 'subsistence farmers' either.

Among small livestock owners, commoditization appears to be much less advanced than among irrigation farmers. With one notable exception, cattle farmers in the study area reported that their aim was to maximize the size of their herds; while some cattle were sold from necessity, this was usually regretted and the numbers sold were kept to a minimum. A few reported selling cattle because their herds were

Table 5.3 Estimated crop value per household at Tshiombo, all lands.

Crop value	Households	Average plots (ha)	Average wasteland (ha)	% of sample
R0–1,999	31	1.2	0.1	37.4
R2,000–4,999	32	1.5	0.3	38.5
R5,000–10,999	15	1.7	0.6	18.1
R11,000–40,000	5	3.4	5.6	6.0

becoming 'too big', but these were once-in-a-lifetime events for the individuals concerned, occasioned by shortages of grazing during periods of drought or the lack of a herdboy, typically when the last child in a family went to school or left home. Even at Tshiombo, only half the cattle owners surveyed reported selling stock in the past year, each disposing of between one and six head (1.6 head per owner, or 11 per cent of the total cattle population). Sales were all confined to the Tshiombo area, mostly to private individuals and a few to local butchers. In two cases cattle were slaughtered on the occasion of a funeral and in another for a wedding, with the rest being killed for family gatherings at Christmas or Easter. The usual reasons given for the sale of cattle at Tshiombo and elsewhere were to meet pressing household needs, such as food, school fees or uniforms or the purchase or repair of a motor vehicle. The sale of milk from cows or goats does not make much contribution to household income in the Mutale area, although some milk is consumed within cattle-owning households. In most of the villages visited, one or two households had milk for sale. Thus, while it is not accurate to speak of livestock farming as 'subsistence orientated' or 'non-commercial', for the majority of farmers it is not primarily driven by market considerations.

A more comprehensive picture of the opportunities and constraints facing those trying to obtain a livelihood from agriculture can be gained by looking in greater detail at a third category: the very biggest producers identified during the study, starting with those on the Tshiombo scheme.

No single factor or set of factors explains the wide differentials in the value of crop output among households at Tshiombo, although size of landholding, choice (and area) of crops and the sex of the plot-holders would all appear to play a part. Not surprisingly, larger landholders tended to produce more than smaller ones, although there were exceptions to this pattern. Plot-holders with relatively high output also tended to concentrate on higher-value crops, such as tomatoes and green maize, and to plant larger areas of each crop, typically from half a hectare upwards. Smaller producers, especially those with a relatively good supply of water, tended to produce just as wide a range of crops as larger ones, but usually limited production to one or two beds of each crop. They also gave more emphasis to crops with relatively low production costs (and market value), such as *muxe* and sweet potatoes, mostly for own consumption.

Plot-holders with a relatively high value of crop output tended to be men, usually in their fifties or sixties, but the sex of plot-holders cannot be separated from other factors, particularly the size of landholdings. Women plot-holders had, on average, only 70 per cent as much land as men and produced roughly half the value of crops. Men are also able to draw on the labour of their wives and other women in their households, whereas most women plot-holders receive only minimal assistance from their husband (if they have one) or other men in their households.

For larger producers, many of whom had relatively low off-farm income, agriculture was effectively self-financing, with the income from one year's production invested in the next. Smaller producers tended to consume a higher proportion of their produce and, therefore, relied more on transfers from other income-generating activities to finance agricultural production. Larger producers (and larger landholders) were more likely to hire labour, although some near-average producers with relatively small holdings also hired labour. In the latter case, hired labour was not used as a means of expanding the area under cultivation, as it appeared to be for larger landholders, but as a way in which plot-holders (particularly women) with access to regular wage income could generate some additional earnings and a supply of food for their household.

Considerable variation in marketing strategies was also evident between plot-holders in the sample. Larger producers were more likely to own their own vehicle and make use of a range of formal and informal marketing opportunities over a wide geographical area. Smaller producers tended to have a single channel to exchange their produce, typically through selling to hawkers or to the passing trade at Tshiombo. Finally, relatively successful crop producers at Tshiombo were also found to be the biggest accumulators of livestock – chickens and goats, as well as cattle.

Larger crop producers in informally irrigated areas on the lower Mutale also stood out from the rest of the local population in a number of ways. A number of them, all men, came to the lower Mutale area from 'white' farming districts, bringing with them tractors or draught animals and considerable agricultural expertise, as well as cash earned through employment in the urban areas, with the specific intention of taking up irrigated agriculture. Most of the others encountered had a household member in full-time employment (two of them at Tshikondeni mine), which allowed them to invest in the pumps, pipes and other materials necessary to begin irrigating. Most private irrigators were using diesel pumps and sprinklers to irrigate their land, drawing water directly from the Mutale. Just one had any water storage capacity on his land, in the form of a large concrete tank.

The largest livestock owners in the lower Mutale were distinguished in particular by their access to water. When the Mutale and its tributaries dried up during the drought of 1991–2, livestock owners were forced to fall back on the village pumps intended for domestic supply, but many of these also ran dry during the height of the drought. For some stock owners with close family ties in other villages, moving their herds was an option, and examples were found of farmers moving their cattle up to 50 kilometres in search of alternative water supplies during this period. The largest cattle owner encountered (with a reported 600 head) invested in a borehole, pump and reservoir next to his kraal early in 1991, a timely decision as it allowed him to survive the drought without losing any cattle. The other large cattle owner (with 210 head) used his tractor and tanker to travel to other villages that still had borehole water to collect supplies for his cattle, and was able to see out the drought with losses of only six head. For the great majority of farmers, however, none of these options was available, and their herds suffered as a result.

The farmer with 210 head was the only one encountered in the entire study area with a well-developed marketing strategy. All bull calves, and the majority of heifers, amounting to eighty or ninety head per year, are sold at between 9 and 14 months. In addition to selling at auction, he slaughters some of his own cattle and sells the meat to local shops. He has a gas-powered refrigeration unit deep in the bush, and was planning to open his own abattoir at Masisi if he could find a reliable source of water. He hoped to build a cold-room big enough for 200 carcasses, from his own herd and whatever cattle he could purchase in the locality, and planned to transport them to

Johannesburg. This exceptional individual was also one of the few farmers in the area involved in commercial production of milk. At the time of fieldwork, he was obtaining only 50 litres per day, but said that this would rise to 300 litres once his calves were weaned. He had his own separator, for extracting the cream, which he kept in his refrigerator and sent to Johannesburg once a month for butter making. He also sold fresh milk from a roadside stall at Nwanedi.

Resource management and sustainability

Recent decades have seen substantial changes in the use of natural resources in the Mutale valley and in the ability of rural people to gain access to the resources they require to sustain livelihoods. Overall, the evidence of this study points to an intensification of resource use, particularly of water and irrigable land, over the last 30 to 40 years. While no examples could be found of social groups actually losing access to resources they previously used within the communal areas, the intensification of resource use, by both individuals and the state, coupled with a high rate of population increase, has meant that a growing section of the population can no longer obtain any part of their livelihood from farming.

The most striking change in resource use is the decreased flow of the Mutale River itself. The absence of any comprehensive hydrological study of the river makes it difficult to state with any certainty the extent or precise causes of this. However, the available evidence from stream flow records and from people living in the area certainly points to a major flow reduction in the last 10 to 15 years.

The intensification of water use begins in the upper catchment in the eastern Soutpansberg, where there has been extensive afforestation over the past 30 years, and the damming of the Tshirovha River to supply commercial tea estates at Makumbane. On the middle reaches of the river, water use has also increased dramatically, with the main irrigation projects and domestic water schemes abstracting over 14 million cubic metres per year, which may be unsustainable. The last 20 years have also seen the rapid expansion of informal (private) irrigation by individual farmers along the length of the Mutale from Tshiombo to Mutele. No information is available on the volume of water extracted by individual irrigators, or even on the numbers of farmers or areas of land involved. In the lower reaches of the Mutale, the formal irrigation schemes account for relatively little water usage, and the main pressure on river water is from private irrigators. There has also been a considerable increase in the pumping of groundwater, through the introduction of new drilling and pumping technology, both by the state and by private individuals.

Changes in land use in the area over the last 30 years have also been substantial, the most significant being the rise of irrigated agriculture, both on formal schemes and on individual holdings. Over 1,800 hectares of high-potential land in the Mutale valley have been put under irrigation by the state since 1960, and possibly half that amount again by private farmers, creating opportunities for more commercially orientated production. As yet, there is no evidence of major degradation of soil resources as a result of these developments. On the Tshiombo scheme, long-term use of irrigation has created substantial gullies in places and waterlogging in others, and there was evidence of a build-up of mineral salts in parts of the scheme, but this did not appear to be creating major problems for farmers. The cultivation of riverine land along the valley may be causing some erosion of river banks or changes in the flow of the river, but as this is a relatively recent development it is too early to assess.

Other types of farming, particularly dryland cropping and livestock, do not appear to have undergone the same degree of change in recent years. The area under rain-fed crops, particularly maize, has expanded as the population has grown and as new forms of technology, such as tractors and fertilizer, have become available, but this process is subject to severe climatic constraints, especially in the northern areas of the valley. Certainly, the Mutale area has seen nothing like the expansion of maize culti-vation that has occurred in the heavily populated, high-rainfall areas south of the Soutpansberg, where many hillsides are being severely eroded. As with irrigated land, however, the lack of any firm longitudinal data on questions such as soil quality or the extent of cultivation precludes any definitive conclusions, but there were no reports from farmers, extension officers or others that the intensification of agriculture has led to major degradation of soil resources.

The overstocking of homeland pastures is a well-worn point of debate in South African studies, but there is no evidence from the Mutale valley of major problems, such as large-scale soil erosion, caused by excessive grazing. While a number of farmers have managed to overcome some of the historic constraints by drilling wells, transporting and storing water and buying in supplementary feed, the relatively small numbers involved would not appear, as yet, to have much impact on the overall stocking pattern. The loss of livestock in the droughts of 1982 and 1992 clearly points to a major deterioration in environmental conditions, linked to a decline in rainfall, but farmers in the study area appeared to accept that herd sizes would fluctuate from year to year. High stocking rates in periods of above-average rainfall and abundant grazing do not necessarily point to unsustainable resource use over the longer term, and there is insufficient evidence to speak of either a long-term increase in stock numbers or a consequent degradation of pastoral resources.

Other forms of commercial or industrial development in the Mutale valley have been extremely limited. The area has not seen the development of any large-scale tea, coffee or subtropical fruit plantations, such as are found elsewhere in Venda. With the exception of Tshikondeni mine, there has been no significant industrial devel-opment either, and the mine itself, located in a remote and sparsely populated area, has had relatively little impact on overall land use. The establishment of a nature reserve at Makuya Park, in an extremely harsh and unpopulated area, has also had little direct impact on resource use, although it probably has made some contribution to the conservation of the ecosystem, particularly the protection of larger mammal species.

Clearly, the changes in resource use in the Mutale valley have not affected all the people of the area in the same way. Those best able to take advantage of develop-ments such as the rise of irrigated agriculture have been those with access to modest amounts of capital, usually obtained through migrant labour or employment in the Venda government service. Such people have been able to exploit what is effectively free land, cheap household or hired labour and subsidized government services, to boost household food supply and engage in varying degrees of commodity production. Those best positioned to obtain good-quality land have been older males, usually over forty, with experience of agriculture and/or with capital to invest, and who are on good terms with the tribal leaders and the homeland authorities. They have managed to accumulate multiple plots on the Tshiombo scheme and substantial plots on the Makonde, Senari and Mutele schemes, and are also the pioneering private irrigators along the banks of the Mutale.

The system of land allocation does little to advance the interests of the poor and disadvantaged sections of rural society. Unless they came with some assets, households forcibly removed from other parts of the country continue to be seen as 'outsiders' in their new homes, and are less likely than long-standing inhabitants to gain access to agricultural land. Women, too, are unlikely to obtain more than a minimum amount of land, such as a single plot at Tshiombo or Rambuda, or small areas of dryland. While this is obviously based on the historically subordinate position of women in Venda society, it is heavily reinforced by men's control of newer forms of non-farm income, which can be invested in agriculture. Furthermore, given their heavy commitment to domestic work, women tend to have little or no access to either tribal or senior government officials, the other essential factor in obtaining prime land.

In practice, the power that tribal leaders exercise over land is limited by a number of factors. First, decisions regarding land use – in terms of its division into arable, grazing and residential areas – are made not by chiefs, but by state officials. Secondly, tribal authorities have little or no control over arable or residential land once allocated, unless it is abandoned or used in a way that interferes with other users, and there appears to be no duty on landholders to conserve soil quality. The situation with regard to grazing land is quite similar. Villagers decide whether or not a person is a genuine resident and hence entitled to use the communal grazing, but they do not have any formal role in restricting the number of livestock or the manner in which grazing is utilized. There is also evidence that some, especially younger people and members of the civics, reject the authority of tribal leaders. Two of the headmen at Tshiombo, for example, complained that 'comrades' (i.e. young political activists) had allocated themselves house-sites on the outskirts of the villages, and there was little tribal authorities could do to prevent this. There were not, however, any reports of people occupying agricultural land without approval.

With regard to water, the power of the 'traditional' leaders is even more loosely defined. The chiefs are generally seen as the guarantors of communal access to rivers and springs, but this is largely a symbolic notion without practical power to regulate water use. The power to allocate riverine lands could be seen as a form of control in this area, but again chiefs and headmen have no direct control over the extraction of water from rivers, either on formal irrigation schemes or among private irrigators. Overall, there would appear to be no 'traditional' practices or institutions concerned with the regulation or conservation of water resources, and no institutionalized forms of cooperation between different tribal areas sharing the same resource. At Tshiombo, for example, where six villages, all under one chief, share the irrigation scheme, there are no structures that allow headmen from the different villages to meet or to act collectively to resolve common problems.

There appears to be little prospect that tribal leaders will cooperate with other bodies in the area to address common concerns. Chiefs and headmen interviewed for this study expressed support for the new national government, but were extremely resentful of the 'youngsters' in the elected councils, who were challenging their authority at the local level, and showed no willingness to work with the new democratic institutions. The lack of an effective conservation function within the 'tribal' system of governance and the growing antagonism of chiefs towards the newly elected local councils would appear to make chiefs unlikely candidates for roles in regulation or conservation. By the same token, none of the councillors interviewed expected to have any direct involvement in farming issues or in the management of natural resources. When it comes to development of the local economy, councillors were more likely to speak of new industries rather than agricultural development; there was a consistent lack of interest in farming issues among councillors and political activists.

Implications for the future governance of land and water

The main finding of this study is that a dramatic increase in population, accompanied by a limited degree of economic development, has intensified pressure on all aspects of the natural environment, but particularly on water resources, in the Mutale valley over the last 30 years. In social terms, this has not, as far as could be ascertained, caused the displacement of any one group of resource users by another, nor has it greatly increased competition between different groups, but it has given rise to an ongoing process of differentiation between rural households. At one end, there has emerged a small élite of commercially orientated farmers, backed by the state and tribal authorities, who have been able to acquire substantial areas of irrigated land both on and off official schemes, while, at the opposite extreme, a sizeable number of households have access to neither arable land nor livestock. Very few households in the study area obtain a living from farming alone, with the great majority dependent on a variety of income sources, including wages, pensions, petty trading and farming.

The relative poverty and underdevelopment in the Mutale River valley, and throughout the former homelands, obviously poses a severe and pressing challenge to the new government's reform policies. During this study, however, it became apparent that very little is actually known about conditions in the homelands, in terms of either documentary sources or general levels of awareness among public officials. One of the more surprising discoveries of the study was the existence of virtually an open frontier along the banks of the lower Mutale, possibly the last remaining pocket of irrigable land anywhere in the province. This land is in the process of being colonized by a small group of pioneer farmers but, as far as could be ascertained, is not referred to in any documentary sources and did not feature in discussions with any government officials other than local field officers. This lack of information on household livelihoods, farming practices, landholding and general resource use created considerable difficulties for this study, and will certainly impose serious limitations on any reform programme in the area. A major overhaul of data collection and reporting procedures among all public bodies and other organizations in the former homelands is a matter of priority, along with further local studies, to shed light on current economic and environmental conditions and the prospects for reform and development.

The lack of reliable baseline information at the local level tends, among other things, to obscure the wide range of social and environmental conditions existing in the former homelands, even within an area as limited as the Mutale valley. The upper Mutale, with a number of small- and medium-scale irrigation schemes, is well integrated into the economy of greater Thohoyandou and, by homeland standards, supplied with a good range of farm-related and other services. The Tshiombo scheme is well known within the provincial administration and has been the subject of a number of consultancy reports in recent years and visits by prominent officials and politicians. In contrast, the lower Mutale area, only 60 kilometres from Tshiombo, rarely features in documentary sources and lies beyond the horizon of most senior officials and politicians alike. With the exception of Tshikondeni mine, social and economic services in the area are extremely underdeveloped, and poor transport links compound its isolation. Formal agricultural projects in the lower Mutale suffer from severe neglect, and services to farmers are minimal. Such disparities demand considerable caution in generalizing about conditions in the black rural areas, and also raise many questions regarding the continued funding of a few show-piece development projects, such as Tshiombo, while other areas remain relatively neglected.

In the former homelands, where environmental issues have received relatively little attention and the need for economic development is most pressing, the promise of major reform following the ending of apartheid has yet to become a reality. Among the reasons for this are the severe lack of government capacity within the homeland areas, but also, as this study has shown, the absence or weakness of other institutions of local governance that could play a part in the reform process. Under apartheid, the state – whether in the form of the South African government or of the various homeland regimes – took a highly authoritarian approach to environmental matters and did little to promote effective local governance or popular participation in local affairs. Furthermore, the former Venda government did not possess anything that could be described as an environmental policy or an effective system of environmental monitoring or protection, and was able to allocate agricultural land and water to commercial estates, irrigation schemes and other users with no public debate or consideration of resource sustainability. At the local level, the 'tribal' system created by the apartheid regime acted as little more than a bureaucratic device for the allocation of scarce supplies of land, and so-called communal tenure in fact allowed little scope for collective management of shared resources. Since the end of apartheid, the chiefs have managed to hold on to much of their power and remain strongly antipathetic to any changes in the system of land allocation. The homeland administration has been absorbed into that of the new Northern Province, but this has yet to have any significant impact on natural resource use or protection. The newly elected local councils have no formal powers of environmental management and do not seem to view it as a priority, while the higher-level district councils are little more than the service delivery arm of the provincial government, and are most unlikely to become involved with environmental management (or any other areas of governance) at the local level.

The weakness of official institutions is compounded by the absence of civil or non-governmental bodies, particularly in relation to natural resource management. Civics are the most prominent non-governmental organizations to have emerged in recent years, but these are still struggling to establish themselves and to find their place within the new political order. The absence of formal organization among resource users (other than the Tshiombo Cooperative) is particularly striking in situations of shared resources, such as grazing and irrigation water. The difficulties of forming a plot-holders' association at Tshiombo (see above) illustrate how much remains to be done in this area. Much of the weakness of non-official institutions in Venda can be attributed to the active discouragement of independent organizations by the chiefs and the homeland regime during the apartheid era, and activities that do not have the support of the local chief are still viewed with grave suspicion by much of the rural population.

If local governance in Venda is to be reformed and strengthened, it is likely that the initiative will have to come from a higher level (i.e. from provincial or national government), and will need to be directed along three main lines: the reform of existing statutory institutions, the creation of (a very few) new specialized bodies and the empowerment (and, if necessary, the creation) of independent local organizations.

Reform of existing institutions is probably the most difficult of these tasks and has limited potential, but two critical issues need to be addressed for any progress towards improving local governance or promoting local development of any kind. First, the grounds for conflict between local councils and tribal authorities must be minimized, even if, as seems likely, they cannot be removed altogether. Current rivalry between councils and 'traditional' leaders stems in part from a failure at the national level to determine their respective powers, and has the potential to seriously divide rural communities and jeopardize local development initiatives. Secondly, the provincial government must delegate the maximum possible powers to rural local councils if they are to act as effective institutions of local governance and be able to engage with other local organizations in any productive fashion.

Where functions do not fall clearly within the ambit of any one local council or Tribal Authority, there may be a need for new institutional forms, while constrained by lack of institutional capacity. The Makuya Park Forum provides an example of a less than successful attempt by provincial authorities to create a new local institution without adequate planning or consultation. Such single-purpose bodies have a potentially important role in the development of local resources, but need to be approached with greater transparency by the authorities and to include all legitimate local representatives. The most urgently required new body suggested by this study, however, is a catchment authority for the Mutale River, which would have the power to regulate water use in the area at the most appropriate level. It is important that government (whether provincial or national) resists the temptation to assume this responsibility itself, and rather puts its weight behind a forum where all stakeholders (particularly water users and local representatives) can participate in producing and implementing a sustainable water policy.

The lack of capacity for effective local action within all branches of government operating in Venda makes it essential that appropriate non-governmental bodies be mobilized, even if, as appears likely, the initiative for this must come from government itself. A good start would appear to have been made with the Venda Farmers' Union, which has received active encouragement from the Department of Agriculture. Other, more locally based, organizations of resource users have yet to emerge, but may do so with sufficient encouragement and the commitment of chiefs and officials to allowing them a say in local affairs. Tentative steps have been made towards a farmers' committee on the Tshiombo scheme, but there have not been any similar moves in the lower Mutale area. Users of communal grazing lands would also appear to be likely candidates for collective action, but the open nature of the resource and the widely different scales of users seem to militate against this; again there was no evidence of such organizations emerging among livestock farmers in the study area.

Central to any substantial change in the former homelands is 'communal' tenure, identified by central government as a priority for reform. The evidence from this and other studies suggests that most people in the homelands are strongly in favour of communal tenure, mainly because, in principle, land is available only to community members, without the need to purchase, and cannot be permanently alienated by individuals. Criticisms of communal land tenure from within the homelands are most commonly aimed at practices of allocation (by chiefs and headmen), rather than at the tenurial principle itself. A first step would be for civics, councillors and tribal leaders to take joint responsibility for allocating residential land, which, if successful, could be extended to arable land. Such a move would undoubtedly be resisted by tribal leaders, and would require forceful intervention by government to make it succeed. By building on the more progressive aspects of communal land tenure, it may also be possible to develop new forms of collective land and water management, based on the principles of local democracy and user participation.

Overall, the prospects for development of the Mutale area and for more effective local control of resources, such as land and water, appear to be good. Farmers throughout the area, on and off the official schemes, have shown considerable enterprise in adopting new methods and increasing the area under cultivation. Livestock farming in the northern districts remains severely underdeveloped, but the experience of a few larger farmers suggests that it has considerable potential. The expansion of Tshikondeni mine and the likelihood of further mineral finds in the Madimbo corridor offers the hope of increasing much-needed off-farm employment, while the development of tourism is also possible in the longer term. Institutions of local governance in the area remain extremely weak, but there is widespread expectation of change and willingness to participate in activities aimed at local economic development. The critical challenge for future policy is to ensure that the benefits of development are more widely distributed than in the past, and that government spending is concentrated in areas that reach the maximum possible number of rural households. Among the priorities for government action identified by this study are the expansion of tractor ploughing services, the provision of transport services for farm produce, the supply of small-scale production credit to farmers and more effective means of reallocating unused plots on irrigation schemes. Specific measures are also required to target resources towards the very poorest sections of rural society, including women, young people and the unemployed, many of whom have been effectively excluded from access to land and from past development programmes.

References

Acocks, J.P.H. (1988) *Veld Types of South Africa*. Botanical Research Institute, Pretoria.

Bembridge, T.J. (1990) 'Agricultural development in the developing areas of Southern Africa'. *Africa Insight* 20 (1).

Bennett, T.W. (1995) *Human Rights and African Customary Law Under the South African Constitution*. Juta, Cape Town.

Bromberger, N. (1988) 'Cash-cropping, subsistence, and grazing: prospect for land tenure in KwaZulu'. In: Cross, C.R. and Haines, R. (eds). *Towards Freehold? Options for Land and Development in South Africa's Rural Areas*. Juta, Johannesburg, 207–13.

Budlender, G. & Latsky, J. (1991) 'Unravelling rights to land in rural race zones'. In: de Klerk, M. (ed.) *A Harvest of Discontent: The Land Question in South Africa*. Institute for a Democratic South Africa, Cape Town, 115–37.

Cooper, D. (1988) 'Ownership and control of agriculture in South Africa'. In: Suckling, J. and White, L. (eds) *After Apartheid: Renewal of the South African Economy*. James Currey, London, 45–65.

Cousins, B. (1996) 'Livestock production and common property struggles in South Africa's agrarian reform'. *Journal of Peasant Studies* 23 (2/3), 166–208.

Cross, C. & Rutsch, P. (1995) 'Losing the land: securing tenure in tribal areas'. *Indicator S.A.* 12 (2), 23–8.

Development Bank of Southern Africa (DBSA) (1993) *Statistics on Living Standards and Development. Regional Poverty Profile: Eastern and Northern Transvaal*. Development Bank of Southern Africa, Halfway House.

Haines, R. & Cross, C.R. (1988) 'An historical overview of land policy and tenure in South Africa's black areas'. In: Cross, C.R. and Haines, R. (eds) *Towards Freehold? Options for Land and Development in South Africa's Black Rural Areas*. Juta, Johannesburg, 73–92.

Harries, P. (1987) '"A forgotten corner of the Transvaal": reconstructing the history of a relocated community through oral testimony and song'. In: Bozzoli, B. (ed.) *Class, Community and Conflict*. Ravan, Johannesburg.

Hendricks, F.T. (1990) *The Pillars of Apartheid: Land Tenure, Rural Planning and the Chieftaincy*. University of Uppsala, Uppsala.

Lacey, M. (1981) *Working for Boroko: The Origins of a Coercive Labour System in South Africa*. Ravan Press, Johannesburg.

Lahiff, E. (1997a) *Land, Water and Local Governance in South Africa: A Case Study of the Mutale River Valley*. Institute for Development Policy and Management, Manchester.

Lahiff, E. (1997b) 'Agriculture and rural livelihoods in a South African "homeland": a case study from Venda'. PhD dissertation, School of Oriental and African Studies, University of London.

Levin, R. & Weiner, D. (1997) 'From apartheid to development'. In: Levin, R. and Weiner, D. (eds) *No More Tears: Struggles for Land in Mpumalanga, South Africa*. Africa World Press, Trenton, New Jersey, 3–25.

Mamdani, M. (1996) *Citizen & Subject. Contemporary Africa and the Legacy of Late Colonialism*. James Currey, Oxford.

Murray, M.J. (1994) *Revolution Deferred: The Painful Birth of Post-Apartheid South Africa*. Verso, London.

Murray Biesenbach & Badenhorst (1989) *Venda Farmer Support Programme: Tshiombo and Rambuda Farmer Support Projects*. Murray Biesenbach and Badenhorst Inc., Pretoria.

O'Keeffe, J.H., Uys, M. & Bruton, M.N. (1992) 'Freshwater systems'. In Fuggle, R.F. and Rabie, M.A. (eds) *Environmental Management in South Africa*. Juta, Cape Town, 277–315.

Rand Afrikaans University (RAU) (1979) *Planning Proposals for Venda*, Vol. 1. Institute of Development Studies, Rand Afrikaans University, Johannesburg.

Simkins, C. (1981) 'Agricultural production in the African reserves of South Africa, 1918–1969'. *Journal of Southern African Studies* 7 (2), 256–83.

South African Weather Bureau (various) Unpublished reports from meteorological stations in the Northern Transvaal. South African Weather Bureau, Pretoria.

Surplus People Project (1983) *Forced Removals in South Africa*: Vol. 5, *The Transvaal*. Surplus People Project, Cape Town.

Vink, N. (1986) *Survey of Land Tenure: Implications for Development in Southern Africa*. Development Bank of Southern Africa, Sandton.

Whiteford, A. & McGrath, M. (1994) *The Distribution of Income in South Africa*. Human Sciences Research Council, Pretoria.

Wilson, F. & Ramphele, M. (1989) *Uprooting Poverty: The South African Challenge. Report for the Second Carnegie Inquiry into Poverty and Development in Southern Africa*. David Philip, Cape Town.

6

Whose Environments?
Whose Livelihoods?

HENRY BERNSTEIN & PHILIP WOODHOUSE

> The driving force behind much environmental policy in Africa is a set of powerful, widely perceived images of environmental change. They include overgrazing and the 'desertification' of drylands, the widespread existence of a 'woodfuel crisis', the rapid and recent removal of once pristine forest, soil erosion, and the mining of natural resources caused by rapidly growing populations. So self-evident do these phenomena appear that their prevalence is generally regarded as common knowledge among development professionals in African governments, international donor agencies, and non-governmental organizations. They have acquired the status of conventional wisdom: an integral part of the lexicon of development.

This is the opening paragraph of a lucid and representative critical review of the sources and effects of 'received wisdom' on environmental change and policy in Africa, and of a programmatic challenge to it, by Leach and Mearns (1996:1). The challenge to the conventional wisdom they and their co-authors present (cited in Chapter 1) contests both the empirical validity of the trends thus summarized and the neo-Malthusianism at the core of their explanation. This challenge proceeds in two ways: by deconstructing this dominant narrative and explaining its potency and reproduction – both in general terms (the discourses of 'Enlightenment science') and more specifically (e.g. how 'crisis narratives' justify intervention) – and by detailed investigation of 'the rich diversity of people's historical interactions with particular environments', including the 'logic and rationality of "indigenous" knowledge and organization in natural resource management' (Leach and Mearns, 1996:20): telling environmental change like it is. The latter can yield useful results, as some of the contributions to Leach and Mearns's collection show.

At the same time, in the accounts of environmental and social change produced by this challenge/counternarrative to the prevailing conventional wisdom, there is a striking absence of any analysis of processes of commoditization of the conditions of social existence in African countrysides, and their effects for patterns of resource use and livelihoods. While Leach and Mearns (1996:5) claim history and social anthropology, together with ecology, as the 'three principal angles' or intellectual sources that inform the challenge to conventional wisdom on African environments, there is no reference in the extensive bibliography of their collection to creative research and analysis at the interface of history and social anthropology (and political economy) in the field of agrarian change in Africa, exemplified by scholars like Kitching (1980), Guyer (1981, 1984), Mackintosh (1989), Murray (1992), Moore and Vaughan (1994), and Peters (1994) – and Berry (1993), though see further below. What the scholars cited also have in common is their understanding of the centrality of commoditization to trajectories of agrarian change in modern African history. This chapter first considers the effects of its omission from the environmental 'counter-narrative' and then briefly reviews ideas about commoditization as a central theme in agrarian change in Africa. The main part of the chapter applies ideas about commodi-tization and social differentiation to relations and practices of resource access, use and management in our four case-studies.

Telling environmental change like it is?

Some effects (and possible explanations) of the definitive absence of any recognition of commoditization in the conceptual apparatus of the new environmental counter-narrative can be suggested. First, the dominant narratives of 'modernization' and 'development' that it seeks to challenge in relation to environmental change and policy are generated, above all, by models of capitalism that yield particular concepts of rationality, efficiency, productivity, and so on. In short, there is as strong – and connected – a case for counterposing to those dominant models and concepts a historical analysis of 'actually existing' forms of commoditization in sub-Saharan Africa, as there is for (re)constructing histories of environmental change to challenge the conventional wisdom. This can be illustrated by the emblematic debate of 'the tragedy of the commons' (Hardin, 1968; Leach and Mearns, 1996:12–13). While the trigger of environmental degradation in Hardin's model is population pressure on resources in 'common' (in fact, 'open access') property regimes, its central logic stems from a profoundly bourgeois belief in the superiority (and necessity) of private property right and the ('rational') economic behaviour it generates, the proper domain of *Homo economicus*.

Secondly, Leach and Mearns's riposte to (conventional) generalizing discourses of environmental 'crisis' in Africa is that environmental problems 'take different forms for different people in different places' (Leach and Mearns, 1996:3, see also p. 29). Indeed, but one has only to add that these problems typically take different forms for different (types of) people in the same place(s) to signal as (or more) instructive a field of analysis – the dynamics and effects of social differentiation, not least as generated (and reconfigured) by processes of commoditization. The attachment of difference primarily (or exclusively) to locale rather than to social inequality (of class, gender, other forms of social divisions of property, labour and income) resonates a familiar populism which finds 'resource poor farmers' only in 'resource poor environments' (Chambers et al., 1989).

Thirdly, there is the always vexed issue of boundaries: establishing the 'interior' and 'exterior' of any particular object of analysis, be it entity, structure or process.

This is a basic, and invariably difficult, methodological challenge, not least in relation to the spatial and social boundary demands of investigating environmental change. Typically, as we observed in Chapter 1, relevant spatial and social boundaries are likely to diverge in ways that subvert any simple identity, let alone harmony, of locale and 'community', which 'green' discourses of rural resource management and sustainability are apt to assume and commend.

Such boundary issues have a particular weight and edge in the current conjuncture of sub-Saharan Africa, where the currency of anti-statism is so strong across the ideological spectrum. Populist motifs and claims are now not only detached from the regimes that once sought to monopolize them in the name of 'national development' and 'nation-building' but are typically articulated in opposition to them. Thus 'community', 'civil society', the 'local' and, most broadly, 'the people' are located in opposition to the state or the centre as the encompassing shorthand for 'external' forces and the threats they pose (or impose). This may help explain the silence of the emergent environmental counternarrative about processes of commoditization for the following reason.

The negative pole of that discourse easily (mis)conceives the source and dynamic of commoditization in the project of state modernization/development that corrodes the bonds of rural community through social differentiation, and undermines prudent ecological management through its demands for 'surplus' and/or faulty technical designs for increasing crop and livestock production and 'conserving' resources. In short, the conflation of state and market, of political domination and commoditization, reinforces the essentially 'external' quality of both as alien disruptions of the 'pristine' social nature of rural community (and its harmony with its environments). The effects of such conflation – which avoids confronting issues of how commodity relations are internalized in the social dynamics of 'household' and 'community' – are compounded to the extent that the research programme of the 'green' counternarrative seeks out ('privileges' ?!) areas of 'resource poor' and/or high-risk environments peopled by 'resource poor' farmers (and 'communities') who appear untouched by commoditization and devote their energies (and sagacity) to 'subsistence' production. The latter, of course, resonates the positive pole of this discourse: the 'interior' demarcated by such boundaries within which African farmers can do what they do (and know) best – securing their material and cultural needs in ways that reproduce both their communities and the resource endowments of their habitats: in effect, approximating a pristine 'pre-contact' condition.

The case-studies in Chapters 2–5 suggest the need to investigate who 'the people' or 'rural people' are, what constitutes locale and 'community' in the light of ideas and issues of commoditization and social differentiation, and to incorporate questions of whose environments and whose livelihoods in seeking to tell (and explain) environmental change like it is.

Commoditization: some basic theory

Debates about the commoditization of agricultural production in Africa – its forms, dynamics and contradictions – are characterized (as one should expect) by a range of analytical approaches, substantive conclusions and, inevitably, ideological differences. Constraints of space allow only a brief summary of the theoretical approach to commoditization applied and illustrated below, and a likewise brief outline of the work of Sara Berry (1993). The latter is included for two reasons: first, because Berry's emphasis on social ambiguity and fluidity (but not her concern with commodity production and its dynamics) has become influential in recent attempts to theorize natural resource use and management (Leach et al., 1997; Carney, 1998; Scoones, 1998); and, secondly, because our own interpretation is in part an ongoing critical engagement with Berry's approach and its claims.

Commoditization: a historical materialist approach

The theoretical content of commoditization in historical materialism is the formation and functioning of systems of production and reproduction based in the essential social relation of capitalism between capital and (wage) labour. That relation is essential in the sense of theoretically definitive, but not exclusive: capitalist divisions of property (who owns what), labour (who does what), income (who gets what) and the social dynamics of the reproduction and accumulation of capital incorporate and generate other social differences/divisions – social relations of gender, generation, ethnicity, mental and manual labour, countryside and town, and so on.

Within this framework, 'petty commodity production' is a form of small-scale enterprise in capitalism constituted by the class relation of capital and wage labour in a specific way: petty commodity producers are capitalists and workers at the same time – capitalists because they own or have access to means of production, workers because they use their own labour. 'Peasants' or 'small farmers' become petty commodity producers in this sense when they are unable to reproduce themselves outside the relations and processes of capitalist commodity production, when the latter come to constitute conditions of their existence and are internalized in their organization and activity. That historical moment is satisfied when 'forcible commercialization' (Bharadwaj, 1985) gives way to commoditization under 'the dull compulsion of economic forces', as Marx put it. A similar, and related, contention is applicable to social formations, that is, they can be fully capitalist – characterized by generalized commodity production – even when this does not take the (often stereotyped) forms of 'advanced' capitalist formations and their phenomenal class correlates: ostensibly clearly demarcated classes of capital and labour, bourgeoisie and proletariat. In the global division of labour, peripheral formations (as in sub-Saharan Africa) may exhibit the prevalence of petty commodity production – peasant and artisanal 'household' forms of production – over large-scale capitalist production, which is mostly restricted to extractive sectors.

There are a number of important applications and implications of this theoretical approach, some of which it is useful to note briefly. First is its insistence on the internalization of commodity (class) relations within the circuits and practices of peasant economy (as already emphasized). This affects linkages between commodity and 'subsistence' production, with the specific conditions and patterns of the former shaping the economic spaces, social forms and divisions of labour of the latter. Secondly, commoditization generates inter- and intrahousehold differentiation in various ways – not least in (changing) gendered divisions of property, labour and income – without necessarily eventuating in phenomenally evident classes of agrarian capital and labour (and especially the former). Thirdly, processes of differentiation are expressed in competition between peasants as petty commodity producers: for land, labour, credit, and connections to access politically allocated resources. Fourthly, one possible outcome of such competition and differentiation is the consolidation of 'middle' peasants, together with the marginalization of poor peasants, unable to reproduce themselves as capital because of their diminishing command of the means of production. This deserves emphasis, because of the tendency of agrarian populism to 'naturalize' the middle peasant condition, of which Williams (1985) is a classic statement in the African context. Fifth is the multiple links between farming and other arenas and practices of economic activity constituted by commodity relations, such as wage employment and non-agricultural self-employment in other branches of petty commodity production (handicrafts, trade, etc.) – which are also distributed unevenly across different classes of the peasantry (Berry, 1980).

Last, and not least, is the particular instability of petty commodity production and its tendencies to dissolution. There are two general theoretical reasons that explain this (Gibbon and Neocosmos, 1985). One is its distinctive contradictory combination of the class places of capital and labour within 'household' enterprise (or, for that matter, within the person of an individual petty commodity producer), which discloses the tendency to differentiation: at one extreme, the failure of petty producers to reproduce themselves as capital (dispossession/proletarianization) and, at the other, accumulation of means of production beyond the capacity of 'household' labour to work them, and hence transition to capitalist (wage-labour-hiring) enterprise. The second reason is that changing social divisions of labour within the wider capitalist economy can both destroy the spaces of petty producers in particular branches of production and create new spaces for petty production.

The ideas sketched here are abstract but necessary to provide a theoretical point of entry and basis for more concrete investigation, suggesting 'very general themes', from which specific histories create 'complex variations', to adapt from another context the formulation of Gilsenan (1982:51). More concretely, then, and recognizably from the studies of the 'complex variations' and dialectics of commoditization in sub-Saharan Africa cited, in striving to reproduce themselves as both capital and labour small farmers/peasants confront various sources and types of risk and opportunity with respect to the following:

1. Conditions of access to key resources and markets, and relations with other class elements and social categories (merchants, agrarian and industrial capitals, state officials).
2. The appropriation of nature (climatic uncertainty, ecological pressure, on the one hand; intensification of resource use, availability of land and labour-enhancing technologies, on the other).

3. Markets: the relative prices, or terms of trade, of what they sell and need to buy as means of production and means of consumption.
4. Combining farming with other income-earning activities (diversification strategies for 'survival' or investment/accumulation).
5. How all the above are affected by government policies and practices (including access to public/merit goods, such as health care, clean water, education, which affect the reproduction of labour).

Commoditization: Berry's 'social networks'

The object of Berry (1993) is to analyse the effects of commercialization and state formation (what she calls 'state centralization') – the key processes of macro 'structural' change in modern African history – on the conditions of farmers' access to resources, above all land and labour, and how resource access influences patterns of resource use. Conditions of access centre on claims to land and the labour of others negotiated and exercised through social relations and cultural practices that are 'fluid, dynamic and ambiguous' (Berry, 1993:6) and that mediate (and can deflect) the allocative effects of market processes and state actions. Berry's investigation of 'different local configurations of power, production and culture' in agrarian economy (Berry, 1993:8) and how and why they change is explicitly counterposed to the inadequacies of both conventional economics and historical materialism (interpreted as, and limited to, the 'Lenin model' of concentration/dispossession of the means of production and formation of an agrarian bourgeoisie and proletariat), and pursued through case-studies of four areas from the inception of colonial rule to the general crisis of the 1980s: the cocoa-growing zones of south-central Ghana and south-western Nigeria, the Central Province of Kenya and north-eastern Zambia (all high-rainfall areas in former British colonies).

The central feature of Berry's interpretation is the imperative for African farmers to invest in social status and identity via membership(s) of various 'networks' that establish claims on resources. These networks are, above all, those of descent (sometimes designated more loosely by Berry as 'family' and 'community') and patron–client relations, but can include religious, political and other (e.g. self-help) association and affiliation. Because they are not corporate entities clearly demarcated by ascriptive criteria but are 'fluid, dynamic and ambiguous', such social networks allow scope for individual mobility through skill in negotiating their rules. Investment in them typically entails monetary payments to establish or boost status (Berry, 1993:160–2), with the return to investment the capacity to claim access to land and the services of clients and followers, and the incentive to so invest intensified in periods of rapid economic growth.

Berry's principal conclusions relevant to this discussion can be summarized in two contrasts or divergent outcomes she presents. The first is that, while accessing land through the social mechanisms outlined persists, commanding labour does not. On the former, 'most people in rural areas have access to land, and are therefore able to cultivate on their own account' (Berry, 1993:135). Moreover, the continuing salience of social and cultural claims to land obstructs tendencies to its commoditization and effective privatization, even when *de jure* property rights exist. On the other hand, 'the open-endedness and negotiability of labor arrangements based on social relationships helped to make them as risky as taking part in an impersonal labor market' (Berry, 1993:174); or what (still) works to access land no longer works to access labour. Another, complementary, reason seems to be that periods of both economic buoyancy and recession reduce farmers' social and cultural capacity to command kin and non-kin labour, because of more attractive opportunities to earn income in the former circumstance and the necessity to diversify income sources in the latter (which has prevailed since the 1980s).

The second contrast is between the two cocoa zones of West Africa (especially during the long period of their expansion to the 1960s) and the other two areas, with their very different historical trajectories: settler colonialism and land alienation in Kenya, and labour migration to the mines of the copper belt and beyond from north-eastern Zambia, with the growth of peasant commodity production in both areas after independence concentrated on food crops.

> In Ghana and Nigeria, the growth of cocoa production gave rise to widespread use of hired farm labor and to a high incidence of modest upward mobility among both farmers and farm workers. In the predominantly food-crop producing economies of central Kenya and northeastern Zambia, agricultural employment has been less commercialized and more differentiated along lines of gender and class ... In West Africa commercialization of farm labor occurred without agricultural class formation; in central Kenya and northeastern Zambia, where the commercialization of agricultural employment has been more limited, rural differentiation has been more pronounced.
>
> (Berry, 1993:180)

This is not the place to embark on a full critique of Berry, whose work contains as many ambiguities and lacunae as it does insights. The passage cited is sufficient to show her view of the development of (petty) commodity production (in West Africa) without class relations. For Berry, class relations are present only when a phenomenally evident agrarian bourgeoisie and proletariat (or peasant classes) are evident. Her principal empirical conclusion about social differentiation in contemporary rural Africa and its link to commoditization is that it primarily disadvantages women and 'strangers' (rural migrants) as social categories in relation to the functioning of networks, rather than generating class formation.

This also resonates her polemical stance regarding 'the Lenin model'. And yet, as Berry should be among the first to appreciate, materialist analysis of the commoditization of agrarian social relations in sub-Saharan Africa has developed more nuanced versions of the theoretical logic of Lenin's approach, expanding its explanatory apparatus and range of application, rather than seeking to 'verify' any stereotypical outcome of the formation of phenomenally evident (unambiguous!) agrarian classes. Indeed, the absence of, or limits to, such class formation has been the starting point of such materialist analysis: an issue to be explained, and investigation of which has identified and addressed other (or additional) forms of social differentiation intrinsic to processes of commoditization in sub-Saharan Africa, including those linked to the locations of farming within generalized commodity production, the 'entry'/reproduction costs of petty commodity production in farming (generating and/or consolidating 'middle' peasantries as one kind of outcome of class differentiation), competition between African farmers *qua* petty commodity producers, and so on.

Symptomatically, two of the authors Berry cites extensively in her account of Central Province were important innovators of such analysis – Cowen (1981a, b) in his work on the conditions of specialized commodity production by 'middle' peasants, and Kitching, whose major historical study (1980) was subtitled 'the making of an African petite-bourgeoisie' – but then she draws on their empirical findings and entirely disregards their theoretical arguments.

More generally, and despite all the specific instances Berry gives of how commodity relations and practices permeate the functioning of social networks, her understanding of 'commmercialization' sometimes seems much closer to that of conventional economics. Thus, 'African farmers gain access to productive resources through social relations *as well* as market transactions' (Berry, 1993:179, emphasis added), as if 'market transactions' in capitalism (or, for that matter, any other mode of production with commodity production and exchange) do not require specific social conditions of existence: particular types of social relations and social divisions of labour. Finally, is it also symptomatic, perhaps, that she translates her proposition of the continuing salience of social networks to access land into the generalization that 'most [sic] people in rural areas [still] have access to land, and are therefore able to cultivate on their own account' (Berry, 1993:135)? This is empirically dubious, disregards conditions other than access to land that are necessary to farm 'on their own account' and seems to contradict the divergent outcomes we would expect 'different local configurations of power, production and culture' – and different 'local' patterns of commoditization and of environmental and demographic change – to reveal.

The case-studies: contexts and trajectories

The four 'wetlands in drylands' studied occupy areas with very different historical trajectories of settlement and demographic change, communications and economic and political linkages, and patterns of commoditization, all of which shape their contemporary socio-economic dynamics.

For much of the twentieth century, all four areas described were relatively isolated and marginal to larger economies in terms of their agrarian production, that is, 'peripheral' in a relational, rather than residual, sense, which registers their specific forms of connection, rather than lack of connection, with the development of commodity production and its spatial configurations. The formation of the Southern Maasai Reserve and relocations of Maasai pastoralists and their herds there were prompted by the early aim of the colonial state in Kenya to 'clear' land for commercial ranching by (white) settler farmers. Land alienation was also key to the trajectory of colonial, union and republican South Africa, where the racial division of labour and political authority was further consolidated under apartheid from 1948 to 1994. This had similar effects in Venda and other 'homelands'/Bantustans, whose principal form of integration with the capitalist development of mining and manufacturing (and agriculture) was as a source of migrant labour. Colonial Bechuanaland (Botswana) was also integrated in the regional labour migration economy of southern Africa, with the development of agricultural commodity production within its territory limited to a class of livestock accumulators (of chiefly status) and a relatively small (white) settler presence. In contrast, colonial rule in Mali brought stability to the Samori, which had lost population during the two previous centuries of insecurity as a frontier zone between Mossi and Fulani states, and opened the way for resettlement of the area by immigrant farmers. Of the four areas, the Sourou valley in Bankass exhibited most clearly the prevalence of dryland cultivation for subsistence, with the principal linkage into commodity relations also through periodic labour migration. There, if to a lesser extent than in Venda and rural Botswana, such migration is a long-established and important economic activity for young men, and increasingly now for young women too.

More recently, three of the four areas experienced significant population growth, to which immigration made major contributions. Many cultivators (Kikuyu, Kamba, Chagga) have settled in Kimana since the 1950s, attracted by the availability of wetland and, since the growth of commercial horticulture, by opportunities of agricultural wage employment. In 1948, Kimana was inhabited exclusively by Maasai, who now account for little more than half the population. In the Samori, immigration by Dogon farmers following colonial 'pacification' has been given new impetus with the annual flooding of the Sourou valley since 1989. Recent immigrant farmers in satellite 'hamlets' now outnumber original inhabitants in the more northerly villages of the valley. The influx of immigrant cultivators to the Samori, as to Kimana, has stimulated tendencies to the commoditization of irrigated farming and of access to the land and water it utilizes. Population growth in Venda was driven by another dynamic, of course, namely the forced relocation there of rural Africans, mostly resident on farms in the 'white' countryside of South Africa's notorious 'deep North' (Northern Transvaal), through the socio-spatial engineering of apartheid. Even here, some immigrants were able to secure plots on the Tshiombo scheme when it was established, and it is principally immigrants who have exploited limited opportunities for specialized commodity production in the more remote reaches of the lower Mutale valley. The exception to these patterns of demographic growth is Mmutlane with its stable population of about 1,000; the point about labour – and permanent – migration from rural Botswana is illustrated by the contrast between Mmutlane and Mahalapye, a town some 30 km away on the main north–south rail and road route between Francistown and Gaborone, whose population has grown by 3.5 per cent annually over the last 20 years or so.

Patterns of commoditization

Production systems: resource use

All the farming in our case-study areas centres on foods destined for local and national/regional circuits of consumption (with the exception of some high-value horticultural export commodities in Kajiado), and can be classified by its approximation to 'subsistence' production and 'low' and 'high' commoditization. 'Subsistence' refers to production of staples and/or supplementary foods for own consumption. 'Low' commoditisation refers typically to production of staples, often regarded as 'subsistence plus' farming, that is, with the objective of producing in excess of consumption needs for market exchange (hence not to be confused with production of lower-value staples for own consumption and higher-value staples specifically for exchange as 'cash crops', e.g. combinations of cassava and maize, sorghum and maize, millet and rice). 'High' commoditization refers to more specialized production for exchange (most obvious in relation to commodities with little or no use value to their producers, like most of the 'classic' export crops of African farmers). In terms of this simple classification, the Samori is broadly characterized by subsistence production and 'low' commoditization; Kimana by subsistence livestock (and some grain) production, juxtaposed with specialized ('high') commodity production of vegetables; Mmutlane and Venda by subsistence grain production only exceptionally sufficient for consumption needs ('sub-subsistence'), with pockets of specialized commodity production of vegetables and livestock, some of it on a relatively significant scale.

This classification suggests differential 'room for manoeuvre' that peasants may have in planning their farming strategies, and income strategies more generally, according to specific forms and patterns of commodity relations. Thus, for example, the 'high' commoditization manifested in production of tree crops for export markets allows less room for manoeuvre than annual arable cropping, other things being equal. Conversely, 'low' commoditization of food grain production from seeds from own stock allows more room for manoeuvre than the need to purchase hybrid seeds, other things being equal, and so on. Otherwise, room for manoeuvre in farming strategies – as in income diversification strategies more generally – is likely to be distributed extremely unevenly across different classes of the peasantry. However, while useful in the descriptive sense illustrated here, such classifications are potentially misleading if they are believed to specify 'degrees' of 'market integration', for several reasons, which the theoretical framework of commoditization suggests.

One reason is that any possibility of agricultural production exclusively for own consumption by African farmers/farming households today requires that they engage in commodity economy in other ways to satisfy the needs of reproduction (and how, and how successfully, they do so is likely to affect the nature of their 'subsistence' enterprise, including the option of hiring labour for it). The same applies, by extension, to the conditions of 'low' commoditization. Secondly, this point is reinforced when the conditions of 'subsistence' farming itself are subject to commoditization in more or less direct, more or less evident, ways – for example, the monetary costs of establishing new farming households (intergenerational reproduction) and other 'entry' and/or input costs of subsistence production, including payment – 'formal' and 'informal', in money or in kind – for access to land for cultivation or grazing and/or to water for purposes of 'subsistence' production, of which there are clear examples in the Samori, Kimana and Mmutlane studies. Once again, such costs of entering and maintaining 'subsistence' production suggest the internalization of commodity relations in the simple reproduction of farming enterprises/households, even with apparently 'customary' forms of resource access and reciprocity and cooperation (widely remarked also in relation to 'traditional' or 'communal' work groups, for example, which conceal the effects of class differentiation (Mamdani, 1987; Berry, 1993:154)).

Commoditization of access to land and water

The thesis that in generalized commodity production (as defined earlier) the conditions of 'subsistence' farming, and 'low' as well as 'high' commodity production, become commoditized (albeit unevenly and in contradictory ways) indicates links between resource use and access to means of production as a condition of farming. The case-studies provide instructive comparisons and contrasts in relation to three aspects of access to 'wetlands': mechanisms of access and allocation; the intensity of demand for (and competition over) wetlands; and the entry/reproduction costs of farming enterprises of different kinds ('subsistence', 'low' and 'high' commodity production).

All the case-studies suggest the salience of claims to land through descent/inheritance, and the role of 'customary' tenure and its authorities in allocating land (access to and command over labour is touched on below). Underlying this observation, however, and especially as it applies to the Samori and Kimana, are dynamic and contested processes.

In Mmutlane and Venda, there appears to be little demand for or competition over land (including wetland), for several reasons: most fundamentally, the (principal) sources of livelihood and income for almost all rural people are outside farming; the availability of wetland is extremely limited; and the entry costs of (self-financed) irrigated farming (and commercial livestock production) are beyond the reach of most people. In the lower Mutale valley, immigrant 'strangers' with the desire and means to invest in irrigated farming on river-banks were able to secure the permission of local chiefs to do so with apparent ease (and perhaps with appropriate gifts), an index of a lack of local demand for land and/or the means to engage in its more intensive cultivation. In Botswana, access to water by sinking boreholes is strongly regulated by government land boards and, on village lands, is generally proscribed for the purpose of watering cattle. In short, in both cases there appears to be little or no active exclusion from land (dispossession), despite situations of scarcity of arable land and pasture (upper Mutale valley) and *a fortiori* of water resources and the means to access them (generally throughout Venda and Botswana), although range fencing policies in Botswana and the debates of dam groups in and around Mmutlane point to processes of *de facto* enclosure and 'privatization', whether individual or corporate.

The situation in the Samori and Kimana is much more dynamic, with keen demand and competition for wetlands for purposes of 'subsistence' (dry-season grazing in both areas), 'subsistence plus' farming (rice in the Samori) and specialized commodity production (irrigated vegetables in Kimana, extensive maize and bean farming in higher-rainfall areas of Kajiado). In the Samori, demand for and competition over land and water are pursued through the institutions and practices of (*de facto*) 'customary' right, claims and allocations: between and within resident lineages; between resident farmers and immigrants (including seasonal cultivators); between crop farmers and livestock herders; and between villages (boundary disputes). Here there is evidence of the processes and effects highlighted by Berry (1993), namely, struggles for advantage that contest and negotiate interpretations of customary tenure, right and precedent, and from which some gain at the expense of others (differentiation effects). Examples include changes in sharecropping and loaning practices, and emergent notions of 'rent' as an explicitly economic transaction, interestingly represented by analogy with the urban housing market. And, in the Samori, the limits of flood-plain rice cultivation within present conditions of management (or non-management) have largely been reached, which is likely to intensify competition for rice land. While those competing will seek to exploit the fluidity and ambiguities of 'customary' claim and counterclaim, farmers able to combine relative economic power and socio-political status (lineage heads who have accumulated from the rice 'boom') are in a stronger position to consolidate, and perhaps expand, their control of land and production on it.

Access to and control of land, and especially wetland, is most contested in Kimana, where it has a longer history marked by changes in *de jure* property regimes, both corporate (Maasai group ranches) and individual (registration of land titles and sales), and *de facto* exercise of private property rights. Formal and informal mechanisms of access to and use of (wet)land are complex, and transacted and contested through the institutions of governance of collective property (group ranches, furrow associations) and land sales and rental, including sharecropping. These also exemplify some of the dynamics emphasized by Berry (1993), notably those centred on the politics of patronage, of mobilizing followings and forging alliances, to which the case of Kimana adds processes of intense struggle within and between the structures of Maasai social organization (clans, subclans, age sets) and connections with party and bureaucratic politics, which have their own ethnic and clan dimensions and linkages to the arenas and networks of national politics. These processes are also permeated by the dynamics of commoditization, not least its differentiation effects, as manifested in concentrations of economic and political power and influence (and their often fragile conjunction in the circumstances of Kimana). If much of this is 'fluid, dynamic and ambiguous', in Berry's formulation, it seems clear that in Kimana this works more to the pursuit of advantage by the 'winners' (and aspirant winners) of socio-economic processes of commoditization (and their politics) than by the 'losers' (see also the important paper by Peters (1999) for a more general reflection on this point). 'Active' exclusion from access to resources appears more evident in Kimana (and Kajiado generally) than in our other case-study areas, recalling the strategic qualification to Berry's thesis: that a key index of rural differentiation in processes of commoditization is often between farmers and non-farmers – those who lose or otherwise lack the means to farm 'on their own account' (or are only able to do so in ways that provide a marginal contribution to their liveli-hoods). We return to social differentiation in agrarian change below.

Sustainability and environmental change: resource management

In terms of the 'forward' linkage from resource use to resource management or regulation (the issue of 'sustainability'), the intensification of farming (above all, in the Samori and Kimana) and its commoditization (in Kimana and, in more limited ways, in the Samori and Venda) have not led to the widespread resource depletion or degradation claimed by 'crisis narratives'. Rather, the evidence suggests that aggregate production has increased substantially in these three case-studies. There are, however, signs of environmental change, which need to be addressed if production gains are to be sustained or increased further. Further expansion of rice cultivation in the Samori will require some form of investment in flood control, and future productivity of the floodplain will be threatened by the establishment of weeds and pests characteristic of long-term rice-growing areas. Perennial weeds, in particular, will reduce yields substantially without investment in more sophisticated tillage and water control. The soil and water regime of Mmutlane seems to be stable, within the strong constraints of rainfall patterns and given the lack of pressure on resources from demographic growth or any significant expansion of commodity production. Kimana is experiencing swamp desiccation resulting from upstream furrow irrigation and abstraction for distant water supply, and the clearance of swamp land for cultivation is inappropriate to its (alkali) soil type, leading to severe productivity problems. The pollution of watercourses by largely unregulated pesticide use may also prove to be a danger. In Venda, pressure on the flow of the Mutale River from upstream use (notably large-scale commercial farming) is reducing water availability, manifested in loss of water by 'tail-end' plots on irrigation schemes. The expansion of 'informal' irrigation in the vicinity of Tshiombo and in the lower Mutale valley (where unregulated water use and bush clearing are eroding river-banks) may be reaching its limits.

In short, it is possible to suggest specific instances of how management and regulation could improve the reproduction of soil and water resources and/or enhance the productivity of their utilization. The possible exception, and ironically so, is Mmutlane with effective (if not optimal) regulation exercised by the local land board. Otherwise, the case-studies reveal little in the way of resource 'governance' generated by the dynamics and capacities of rural community, market or state in circumstances of intensified resource use and commoditization. 'Indigenous' communal institutions do not appear to act on matters of (long-term) resource management as distinct from (current) allocation, and the same applies to furrow associations in Kimana, dam groups in Mmutlane and factions of (discontented) irrigators at Tshiombo (none of them strong contenders for the status of 'civil society' formations). Government institutions, where they exist, as at Tshiombo, are largely ineffectual (with the exception of Botswana's land boards, and the very different instance of the Kenya Wildlife Service, which brokers agreements between tourism interests and group ranches in Kajiado); otherwise, there is a lack of institutions responsible for and capable of resource 'governance' on a scale adequate to the need for it, e.g. at the level of a catchment or catchment section, as in the Samori and Kimana/Kajiado.

Social differentiation and change

The generation of social differentiation by processes of commoditization was noted earlier, with specific reference to the general tendencies to dissolution (and recreation) of petty commodity production and to the 'complex variations' manifested by specific historical trajectories of commoditization. Issues of differentiation were a pervasive underlying dimension (that started to surface) in the previous discussion of commoditization, now addressed explicitly.

Issues of access to land are located within three general processes, which, of course, manifest their own specificities in different places. First are historical patterns of population and settlement (including those prior to colonialism), and how they influence subsequent settlement and demographic change in the course of uneven processes of commoditization and colonial and postcolonial state formation. Those processes stimulate particular types of movement by (particular types of) people in and out of different rural areas, which links to the second general process. This is how people in 'peripheral' areas experience the effects of commoditization, which introduces (and internalizes) the need for money and new consumption goods (initially mostly satisfied through labour migration and wage employment in our case-study areas), as well as the experiences of agrarian commodity relation that immigrants to those areas bring with them (notably in Kajiado and Venda, and to some extent in Samori). The third general theme is that of 'customary' tenure (and its mutations), that is, claims to land based on descent and how they are adjudicated.

Clearly, the last is not an unambiguous or unproblematic given. As Berry (1993) and others show, the institutions of descent (kinship, lineage, 'community', 'tribe') are characterized by fluidity and ambiguity, which both reflect and give rise to negotiation and contestation. Mamdani (1996) argues that 'customary' land tenure and allocation are one of the pillars of the 'decentralized despotism' of the colonial state form that constituted rural people in Africa as (political) subjects on the basis of ethnicity ('tribe'). This can then become a factor of differentiation when demand for land increases with pressures on, and new opportunities for, sources of livelihood, as immigration to the Samori and Kajiado illustrates. On the one hand, ethnic identity or status functions as the marker of claims to land against the claims of others, when different 'ethnic' groups occupy or converge on the same area, and especially perhaps when they represent different types of resource users, such as cultivators and pastoralists. On the other hand, the structures of shared 'ethnicity' can provide a basis for pursuing competing claims to land and water by corporate or quasi-corporate entities within them, such as villages and lineages (the Samori) or clans, subclans and age sets (Kimana). Such competition within (as well as between) groups with claims of descent (and precedence) is likely to intensify in circumstances of either or both growing pressures on livelihoods/reproduction linked with population growth and/or pressures on reproduction, combined with opportunities for accumulation generated by commoditization (and social differentiation).

If such competition is one aspect of access to land through the claims of descent, another source of differentiation within the institutions and social dynamics of descent is gender and generational relations. There is a general assumption that women have weaker rights to land than men in patrilineal societies and the case-studies show that this can be compounded or compensated in various ways. There is evidence suggesting that women are more vulnerable than men to changing practices of land loaning in the Samori, although many women retain rights to farm individual (*djonforo*) plots on lineage land. In Kajiado (as elsewhere in Kenya, noted by Berry, (1993)), women's groups have initiated other ways of accessing land in response to their exclusion from 'customary' allocation. There are some women cultivators of 'informally' irrigated land in the lower Mutale valley, but plot-holders on formal irrigation schemes in Venda are overwhelmingly men. In Mmutlane, there is no evidence of discrimination against women in access to land.

Generational tensions within patrilineal insitutions of land tenure and allocation (hence between male generations) were observed in the Samori and Kimana. In the Samori, the subordinate position of male cadets may be enhanced by the strongly patriarchal hierarchy and authority of lineage organization, but well-placed younger men are able to control considerable resources. In Kimana generational tension is manifest in the efforts of better-educated younger Maasai men to wrest control of the governance structures of group ranches, given the strong trend to enclosure/privatization of ranch land (and especially better land) and its implications for their future inheritance. In Venda (as in other former Bantustans in South Africa), contestation of the authority of 'tribal' administration and chiefs by 'civics', led by younger men, is not so much over access to land as over control of local government and the resources it makes available, and echoes the distinctive (self-)celebration of 'the youth' (typically meaning male youth) in 'the struggle' (against apartheid).

Access to land is only one condition, however vital, of agricultural production, as remarked several times, and the relative ease or difficulty of securing its other conditions is a useful index of the effects of commoditization and its forms of social (class) differentiation – and how they intersect or combine with gender and generational differentiation. Those other conditions centre on command over labour and ability to mobilize other means of production – farm equipment and other inputs. All four case-studies suggest that satisfying the means of ('own account') farming through both 'customary' social relations/networks and those of market exchange (wage employment and business) is generally more difficult for women (and often for younger men). In short, the great majority of successful farmers, and *a fortiori* of those accumulating, are men of middle age and older, and especially those able to combine the claims of their status in the arena of 'customary' relations (patriarchy) with means of investment and command of resources derived from market activity (the latter typifying immigrant 'investors', as in Kimana and Venda, who may be able to 'buy into' customary allocation, literally or figuratively).

This then connects differentiation in the conditions of access to land with differentiation of resource use. Accumulation in rural areas is typically the result of sequential or simultaneous 'straddling' of commodity relations in and outside farming (strongly marked in Mmutlane, Kimana and Venda, if less so in the Samori). By 'sequential' is meant the mobilization of savings from careers in wage employment and/or business, which are then invested on 'retirement' in full-time agricultural commodity production (on land often farmed or managed by wives up to that point). Simultaneous 'straddling' refers to the diversification of activities, income sources and investment, in 'portfolio' accumulation. While diversification is often emphasized as a livelihood/reproduction strategy – especially in rural areas characterized by risky environments and/or market conditions (and the generalized social insecurity of

Africa's protracted crisis of development) – it is subject to class differentiation generated by commoditization. Diversification by those whose 'portfolios' combine agrarian commodity production with investment in and incomes from shops, transport, crop and livestock trading, equipment hire and other service provision has a very different (if connected) dynamic from the imperative of diversification as a 'survival' strategy in the face of poverty and insecurity.

Processes of accumulation and diversification thus amplify our observations of the linkages between land and other resources used in farming and the wider circuits of commodity economy in which agricultural production and producers are located. If social differentiation affects the conditions (and prospects) of establishing and reproducing farming enterprises (whether for 'subsistence' or for 'low' or 'high' commodity production), the location of those enterprises in commodity circuits and social divisions of labour itself contributes to their differentiation (if in typically uneven and sometimes precarious ways).

Tendencies to inequality in access to land and water and in the mechanisms of access commonly combine with inequalities in command of other means of production, such as irrigation pumps and tractors (Mmutlane, Kimana, Venda) and ploughs and plough oxen (the Samori). Ploughs and other agricultural implements and machinery increase the productivity (and potentially the scale) of cultivation by their owners and are available for hire to those who lack them, another practice typical of the commoditization of farming. Also of note here is the prominence of larger-scale cultivators as owners and accumulators of cattle in areas with substantial pastoralist populations (most evidently Kimana but also the Samori).

It is also clear that labour hiring is common to all four case-study areas, if more widespread in the Samori and Kimana than in Mmutlane and Venda (where farming is much more constrained by environmental and social conditions). Labour hiring (allowing for the wide range of variation in its forms and extent) is a surer signal of commoditization than an unambiguous index of differentiation, as already noted: hired labour may be used in 'subsistence' production and is critical to the 'low' commoditization of rice farming in the Samori; more generally, it is quite common for (some) farming households to both hire in and hire out labour. None the less, seasonal labour hire at least is a condition of the larger agricultural commodity enterprises in the four areas, especially those specialized in the labour-intensive production of higher-value crops (vegetables in Mmutlane, Kimana and Venda).

Other things being equal, it is reasonable to expect that these dynamics of enterprise differentiation will lead over time to the concentration of land and water resources under private ownership and control. However, other things are rarely equal in the complex socio-economic (and political) processes of commoditization in sub-Saharan Africa, as Berry rightly emphasizes (Berry, 1993). Her argument that the strength of customary claims to land is the principal obstacle to the 'enclosure' and concentration of landed property in rural Africa, despite pervasive commoditization, appears best supported by the Samori among our case-studies. This is also the area where access to a productive and highly prized new wetland resource is most recent, and where struggles over access are fought within and along the boundaries of customary institutions and their demarcations of space, ecology, ethnicity, lineage, property right, gender and generation, expressed in changing meanings of 'tradition' and 'custom', status and entitlement, in the process.

In the other three cases, however, it is likely that aspects of commoditization and differentiation may themselves inhibit the concentration of landed property: the marginality of farming as a source of livelihood for most rural people in Mmutlane and Venda; the linkages between farming and the wider circuits of commodity economy, and their effects for different social categories; the diversification of 'port-folio' accumulation, rather than exclusive investment in the expanded reproduction of agrarian commodity enterprises. Also of note is the presence of quite different interests in land and water resources, mainly illustrated by wildlife tourism in Kimana among our case-studies, which can restrict the spaces available to farming and/or present other economic opportunities, including that of rent.

Having said that, there is one critical aspect of differentiation, indicated earlier but which is commonly neglected, namely, the effective exclusion from farming of some rural people by the increasing entry and reproduction costs of agricultural enterprise (and without any necessary concentration of landholding or formation of large-scale agricultural commodity production). Studies of socio-economic conditions in rural areas, and even of socio-economic change, rarely identify and consider the 'losers' from processes of commoditization and social differentiation, especially if their exclusion is followed by emigration, but even when they remain in their native areas as a residual presence, the most marginal of 'resource-poor' farmers or simply non-farmers (*pace* Berry, 1993). There is an interesting expression of this in the Maasai notion that 'the poor are not us', that is, those without cattle are redefined as non-Maasai *qua* non-pastoralists (Anderson and Broch-Due, 1999). In Botswana, subsidies to plough and plant give possibilities to cultivate to those otherwise unable to farm on their own account (because they lack oxen, ploughs or tractors, or the means to hire them without payment of subsidies). At the same time, the differentiation manifested in unequal distribution of means of production is strengthened, arguably, by how those subsidies confer compound benefits on those with the means to plough their own – and others' – fields.

Concerning resource management or 'governance', there is little to add here to the observations at the end of the previous section, except to note that any institutions that exist or may be established for this purpose – whether by the central or local state or by 'civil society' – are likely to manifest the strong presence or other influence of the (mostly) modest rural petty capitalist class, identified above as accumulators: older men who combine customary (patriarchal) statuses with personal wealth, and often political connections and positions of patronage as well. The implications of this for policies seeking to promote 'sustainable natural resource use' are explored in Chapter 7.

Conclusion

The challenge to 'conventional wisdom' on African environments and environ-mental change and policy is much needed but incomplete in its intellectual framework and agenda. This may usually be the case in the initial phase of any counternarrative: that its analytical field of vision is fixed and limited by the characteristics of the discourses it seeks to contest. So, for example, assumptions of the intrinsic incapacities of African farmers to utilize the resources of their environments with skill and prudence are contested by findings of 'the logic and rationality of "indigenous" knowledge and organization in natural resource management' (Leach and Mearns 1996:5) (study of which, importantly, generates new understanding of the ecology of those natural resources itself). Similarly, the threat of resource degradation/depletion from demographic pressure, asserted by neo-Malthusian 'crisis narratives', can be assessed and often refuted by the kinds of research promoted by the alternative approach.

However, issues of the intensification of resource use – not least of scarce and highly prized wetland resources in dryland environments – are not exhausted by recognition of the ('local') knowledge and skills of farmers and how they are applied and adapted in conditions of population growth. This chapter has argued that the rich diversity of people's historical interactions with particular environments in modern sub-Saharan Africa is permeated and shaped by specific dynamics and patterns of commoditization and the specific forms of social differentiation they generate. In particular, the following points have been emphasized and illustrated:

1. That it is necessary to theorize commoditization as a 'general theme' in order to be able to investigate the 'complex variations' of its historical trajectories and current patterns and tendencies.
2. That the spaces, social relations and practices of 'subsistence' farming are shaped by commodity relations, and that the conditions of 'subsistence' farming (access to and command over land, pasture, water, labour, inputs) are themselves subject to commoditization.
3. That 'non-market' social relations and networks are also permeated by commodity relations, as Berry's emphasis on the need to 'buy into' them (literally as well as metaphorically) suggests.
4. That the class dynamics intrinsic to commoditization are not necessarily manifested in empirically (or phenomenally) evident classes: the formation of the latter in the countryside may be inhibited by certain patterns of commoditization, or experienced in 'invisible and unarticulated ways' (Peters, 1994:210).
5. That the prevalence and/or 'persistence' of 'middle peasants' (relatively stable and prosperous 'small farmers'), where they exist, is the outcome of processes of differentiation associated with commoditization, rather than an index of the lack of social differentiation.
6. That changing patterns and practices of resource use, and not least intensification, are inflected by specific trajectories/patterns of commoditization and the pressures they exert on many, as well as the opportunities they present to some.
7. That, in short, the effective study of environmental change needs to incorporate, and indeed to start from, questions of whose environments/resources, and whose livelihoods are generated from access to, use and management of them, in what ways and with what effects (both social and environmental).

References

Anderson, D.M. & Broch-Due, V. (eds) (1999) *The Poor Are Not Us. Poverty and Pastoralism in Eastern Africa.* James Currey, Oxford.

Berry, S. (1980) 'Rural class formation in Africa'. In: Bates, R. and Lofchie, M. (eds) *Agricultural Development in Africa: Issues of Public Policy.* Praeger, New York, 401–24.

Berry, S. (1993) *No Condition is Permanent. Social Dynamics of Agrarian Change in Sub-Saharan Africa.* University of Wisconsin Press, Madison.

Bharadwaj, K. (1985) 'A view on commercialisation in Indian agriculture and the development of capitalism'. *Journal of Peasant Studies* 12 (4), 7–25

Carney, D. (1998) *Sustainable Rural Livelihoods. What Contribution Can We Make?* DFID, London.

Chambers, R., Pacey, A. & Thrupp, L.A. (eds) (1989) *Farmer First: Farmer Innovation and Agricultural Research.* Intermediate Technology Publications, London.

Cowen, M.P. (1981a) 'The agrarian problem'. *Review of African Political Economy* 20, 57–73.

Cowen, M.P. (1981b) 'Commodity production in Kenya's Central Province'. In: Heyer, J., Roberts, P. and Williams, G. *Rural Development in Tropical Africa.* Macmillan, London, 121–42

Gibbon, P. and Neocosmos, M. (1985) 'Some problems in the political economy of "African Socialism"'. In: Bernstein, H. and Campbell, B.K. (eds) *Contradictions of Accumulation in Africa. Studies in Economy and State.* Sage, Beverly Hills, 153–206.

Gilsenan, M. (1982) *Recognizing Islam.* Croom Helm, London.

Guyer, J. (1981) 'Household and community in African studies'. *African Studies Review* 24 (2/3), 87–137.

Guyer, J. (1984) 'Naturalism in models of African production'. *Man (NS)* 19 (3), 371–88.

Hardin, G. (1968) 'The tragedy of the commons'. *Science* 162, 1243–8.

Kitching, G. (1980) *Class and Economic Change in Kenya. The Making of an African Petite-Bourgeoisie, 1905–1970.* Yale University Press, New Haven.

Leach, M. & Mearns, R. (eds) (1996) *The Lie of the Land. Challenging Received Wisdom on the African Environment.* James Currey, Oxford.

Leach, M., Mearns, R. & Scoones, I. (1997) 'Challenges to community-based sustainable development: dynamics, entitlements, institutions'. *IDS Bulletin* 28 (4), 4–14.

Mackintosh, M. (1989) *Gender, Class and Rural Transition. Agribusiness and the Food Crisis in Senegal.* Zed Books, London.

Mamdani, M. (1987) 'Extreme but not exceptional: towards an analysis of the agrarian question in Uganda'. *Journal of Peasant Studies* 14 (2), 191–224.

Mamdani, M. (1996) *Citizen and Subject. Contemporary Africa and the Legacy of Late Colonialism.* David Philip, Cape Town.

Moore, H. & Vaughan, M. (1994) *Cutting Down Trees. Gender, Nutrition and Agricultural Change in the Northern Province of Zambia, 1890–1990.* James Currey, London.

Murray, C. (1992) *Black Mountain. Land, Class and Power in the Eastern Orange Free State, 1890s–1990s.* Edinburgh University Press, Edinburgh.

Peters, P. (1994) *Dividing the Commons. Politics, Policy and Culture in Botswana.* University Press of Virginia, Charlottesville.

Peters, P. (1999) 'The limits of negotiability: security, equity and class formation in Africa's land systems'. Draft paper (cited with author's permission).

Phillips, A. (1989) *The Enigma of Colonialism.* James Currey, Oxford.

Scoones, I. (1998) *Sustainable Rural Livelihoods: A Framework for Analysis.* IDS Working Paper No. 72, Institute of Development Studies, Brighton.

Williams, G. (1985) 'Taking the part of peasants'. In: Gutkind, P. and Wallerstein, I. (eds) *The Political Economy of Contemporary Africa.* 2nd edn, Sage, Beverly Hills, 144–80.

7

Governance
& the Environment
Politics & Policy

DAVID HULME & PHILIP WOODHOUSE

Introduction: governance and the state

This chapter explores the political dynamics of access to and use of the 'wetland' resources in Africa's drylands and the governance of these areas. It makes particular reference to the four case-studies presented in earlier chapters to explore a number of interlinked themes that recur in policy debates on natural resource governance in Africa: the role of customary authority and right; the 'modernization' of production methods; and the decentralization of control and management of natural resources. Our understanding of governance (Chapter 1) refers to the structures and processes of power and authority, cooperation and conflict that govern decision-making and dispute resolution. A fundamental issue underlying analysis of governance is the way the state is conceptualized. In the wake of the 'pathology' of the African state promoted by the World Bank and others over the past two decades (Chapter 1), it is essential to avoid the pitfalls created by two stereotypes that dominate much thinking about Africa.

At one extreme is the 'end of history' school of thought, which assumes away African histories and specificities and, through a normative analysis, argues that governance must be along the lines of an idealized notion of western democracy allied to a Weberian bureaucracy. African states are thereby viewed as 'in transition' to this universalized western democratic model. In this view, multiparty elections and an 'efficient' state will ensure accountable decision-making and management of natural resources that is both effective and socially just.

At the other extreme are variants of African exceptionalism. In its pessimistic version, this perspective sees Africa as a 'dark continent', in which primordial iden- tities and cultural predispositions incline people to 'irrational' violence and chaos is a norm. According to this view, governance in Africa – national, local, of natural resources – is a mess and is likely to remain that way (Chabal and Daloz, 1999). In its optimistic variant, African 'traditions' offer hope of a more equitable and sustainable society if they can be freed of the distortions of colonialism and the corruption of the post-independence African state (Dia, 1996).

As in earlier chapters, the concern of this research is to set out processes of governance encountered in the case-studies before attempting to draw more general conclusions. These show both important contrasts and similarities in the nature of the state.

In all of our four cases, colonial rule combined expropriation of land and colonial administration with an element of indirect rule through 'customary' or 'tribal' authority. Botswana and Kenya followed the classic model of indirect rule in British colonial Africa, of which South Africa's Bantustans under apartheid may be regarded as a logical extension (Mamdani, 1996). The case of Mali indicates that, even under French colonial administration, key administrative tasks (tax collection, recruitment for the army and supply of labour for public works) were delegated to *canton* chiefs with authority over groups of villages. While varying in important ways (discussed below), the post-independence state manifests this historical similarity in the four cases through the existence of three agencies important in natural resource management in all of them: government agencies, political parties and customary authorities.

Government agencies include principally the 'prefectoral' officials (*commandants de cercle* and *arrondissement*, district commissioners and officers) with general administrative responsibilities, and technical officials of organizations concerned with the direct management of resources claimed as 'national' state property (the Kenya Wildlife Service (KWS), Botswana's Department of Wildlife and National Parks, Mali's Direction National des Eaux et Forêts (DNEF) and South Africa's Kruger National Park). Political parties and multiparty electoral politics feature in all the case-studies, although the latter is only recently established in Mali and South Africa, following constitutional change, and has returned in Kenya only since 1992. In the case of Botswana, multiparty elections have been held since independence, but only one party has held power in the national government.

In all cases, customary authorities continue to have a role in the local judicial system and, to a greater or lesser extent, in allocation of land rights. Understanding the interplay between government, party and customary authority is particularly important, therefore, to conceptualizing the nature of the state and its policies on land and water.

One common and striking aspect of the relationship between formal political parties and customary authorities is that, in the immediate aftermath of independence, the ruling political party in each case-study country mounted an assault on the power of customary authorities. This assertion of authority by the 'national' African leadership, through the new institutions of the independent state, over the existing African authorities of indirect rule under colonialism was an important element of 'nation-building' and was frequently couched in the populist rhetoric of the anticolonial struggle. However, the assertion of national authority over customary authority took different forms in specific countries, with important consequences for the relationship of customary authorities to the formal politics of the state. Since one of the most important powers of customary authorities under colonialism was control over land allocation, the evolving post-independence relationship between customary and formal political power has a crucial impact on governance of land and water.

Mamdani (1996) distinguishes between 'conservative' African states, which incorporated customary authorities within the new national government structure, and 'radical' states, which sought to exclude them. In our four cases, the distinction only partially holds. In Kenya, a classic 'conservative' state in the sense of retention of 'tribal' identities – and by extension authorities – the post-independence role of customary authority was heavily circumscribed by its integration into the market economy. In this case, the control of land by customary authority had been weakened under colonial administration by land expropriation for the settler economy. Rather than seeking restitution through reinstating customary authority over land, the KANU leadership sought it through the market and individual land titles. While customary authorities were, and continue to be, essential to provide legitimacy for this process – through advising on conflicting claims to title or land sales – they are firmly enmeshed within a logic of commercial opportunities, whereby their position in the customary hierarchy is turned to individual material gain through trading influence (votes) or access to resources (land and water) with political and commercial interests.

In Botswana, a different 'conservative' state incorporated customary authorities into the 'public sector' through the post-independence Tribal Land Act, which stripped chiefs of their control over land but retained them in an advisory capacity in government land boards established to administer 'tribal land', redesignated as a 'commons' for the use of all Batswana. Any loss of formal control by chiefs was more than compensated, however, by their greatly increased capacity for individual material accumulation: as senior political or administrative leaders in the independent government; as beneficiaries of the government's support to the livestock industry; and as owners of private water resources (boreholes) with pre-emptive claims on neighbouring grazing areas. In this case, just as the incorporation of customary authorities strengthened the legitimacy of the state, a transition to individualized property ownership by the customary chiefly élite was legitimated by 'impartial' government policy.

In Mali, an initially 'radical' post-independence state sought to extinguish customary authority in the name of more egalitarian access to land for all citizens of the new state, rather than local customary affiliation. However, unlike Botswana, Modibo Keita's one-party state in Mali's First Republic sought to exclude customary authority rather than to incorporate it within the formal political processes of the state, establishing instead a parallel party structure reaching down to village level. Under Moussa Traoré's Second Republic, a similar party structure developed by the Union Démocratique du Peuple Malien (UDPM) provided the channel for patronage and reconciliation between local customary hierarchies and the ruling politicians at national level. Part of this reconciliation was the Second Republic's recognition of the existence and (qualified) legitimacy of customary land rights, an accommodation between party and customary authority at local level contrasting strongly with the tensions growing between government agencies and the rural population, most notably over the government's repressive and predatory administration of natural resources through the state forestry service (a hallmark of the 'centralized despotism'

Mamdani (1996) argues is characteristic of 'radical' African states). The advent of multiparty democracy in Mali following the 1991 coup has clearly disturbed the simple articulation between governing party and customary authorities in two ways. It has, first, introduced oppositional electioneering at village level, which our case-study suggests has a potential to fracture customary authority into factions. Secondly, it has introduced for the first time elected local government (*conseils communaux*), with notional, but poorly defined, responsibilities in the management of natural resources.

In the case of South Africa, an initially conservative stance by the post-apartheid state on customary authority owed much to the African National Congress (ANC's) strategy of forging an alliance with the chiefs (Conference of Traditional Leaders of South Africa: CONTRALESA) in an attempt to prevent splits in the anti-apartheid vote. As a consequence, customary authority remained in control of land within the ex-Bantustan areas, while elected authorities were established down to local level. By 1998, continuing pressure for a more radical, redistributive, policy on land revealed widespread discontent with chiefly control of land in the ex-Bantustans. In response, the publication of the Land Rights Bill set out proposals for the registration of individual or group users' rights on customary land, which would effectively restrict, and in some areas extinguish, the allocational control of customary authorities.[1]

In reviewing these aspects of state power in the case-studies, a number of general themes can be identified. First, under the banner of populist nation-building the 'modernizing' states of post-independence Africa have sought to reform customary authorities inherited from the colonial period. Reforms have involved greater capacity to engage with markets (at least for a minority), as well as calls for more egalitarian access, from both 'socialist' and 'communitarian' perspectives. In every case, there is evidence of compromise in such reform projects, whereby customary authority over land has survived, or where customary rights have been translated into 'modern', commoditized forms. Our fieldwork points to the weaknesses of common stereotypes of governance in Africa. Rather than a universal model that can be imported, it needs to be recognized as the product of continuing historical processes (which may be viewed as progressive or regressive), and attempts to impose 'western multiparty democracy' on African states are likely to produce variants as dysfunctional as the regimes they seek to reform.

At the other extreme, the evidence our case-studies identified of conflict (and sometimes violent conflict) as an important aspect of local-level processes of access to, and use of, natural resources does not support stereotypes of African society as chaotic and irrational. First, as we argued in Chapter 6, the tensions associated with competition in resource use can be understood in terms of intensifying use of land and water and the socio-economic dynamics of commoditization and differentiation. Secondly, the case-studies demonstrate that changing resource use is achievable within local 'indigenous' institutions (as in the Samori), which may generate new organizational forms, such as the furrow associations to manage water for irrigation in Kimana. In

---

[1] The Land Rights Bill no longer featured in policy statements made by the Minister for Land Affairs in February 2000, indicating a change in emphasis in South African government policy on land tenure reform. However, the details and political significance of this change were not yet clear at the time of writing.

these ways, as Bayart (1993:1) argues, African societies and political processes are 'ordinary' but must be understood in terms of their specific histories and contexts.

One further observation that can be made of the stereotypes of the African state is that they all fail to encompass the relationship of the African state with the wider international economy and politics. In the era of structural adjustment, when international funding agencies dictate macroeconomic policy to many African governments, stereotypes neither mention nor question this as a critical element of African states. From this standpoint, universalizing stereotypes of 'western democracy' may be regarded as the corollary of the removal of barriers to the integration of African societies into global capital markets, while the more optimistic variants of African exceptionalism emphasize a reconstitution of African tradition and past as a basis of social solidarity within rural communities. It is evident that the two stereotypes do not necessarily preclude one another, the second providing a possible counterweight to the first. However, both imply a subordination of the African state to the 'international community', not only through indebtedness to its financial institutions, but – of particular importance here – in terms of global environmental priorities, in which Africa figures principally as a 'pristine' environment (for recreational and biodiversity assets) and as a threatened source of refugees from a rural landscape ruined by 'desertification'.

The particular weight given to environmental conservation in African countries' international relationships shapes the role of the state in governance of land and water in important ways. At the macro-level, policies and plans that African governments adopt are often for external consumption, rather than internal implementation, and national environmental action plans tend to be sectorally segregated, commonly assuming a single specified use for a natural resource (e.g. irrigation for agriculture, pasture for grazing) by a distinctly 'rural' population. These are of limited use in the many African realities where resources have multiple uses and/or, as in the cases of water and wildlife, are mobile, and where resource users have strong social and economic ties with the urban economy. Failures to implement policy cannot be attributed solely to the lack of financial and human resources, which is routinely offered as the failure of the Weberian model in Africa (although the case of Botswana suggests this may play a part). Fundamentally, it is a failure to understand the logic and dynamics of resource use. We now discuss in more detail the political dynamics in our case-studies that is relevant to an alternative policy approach.

The political dynamics of resource access: statutory, customary, commercial?

The key institutions that are the focus of the political dynamics of access are those of property and the authority to allocate rights to land and water. In our field studies, as across most of Africa, these institutions have experienced profound change, as demand for land and water has intensified and as colonial and postcolonial public policies have sought to reform institutional frameworks, creating a historical legacy that shapes contemporary processes (Mamdani, 1996).

For our four cases, the institutions of property involved various forms of 'customary' tenure abutted to 'modern' tenure. These mixes had roots embedded in the social histories of their residents and had also been shaped by the attempts of governments to transform systems of property rights. In the early colonial period, two particular processes had an impact on pre-existing systems. First, the colonial preference for 'indirect rule' led to the formal codification of custom through the identification of distinct 'tribes', under the leadership and fixed territorial jurisdiction of (state-sanctioned) chiefly authorities. These policies entrenched the tribal unit and tribal identity as key social features for the future; they also concentrated power in the hands of recognized 'chiefs' and their offspring and associates. The second process concerned the alienation of land for white settlement and the forced relocation of black African populations. This was of particular importance in the Kenyan and South African cases, where it led to a loss of indigenous rights and the creation of a latent set of property reclamation rights that could be activated at moments of regime change (i.e. independence in Kenya and the end of apartheid in South Africa). The decades following the Second World War saw different emphases and, in particular, the encouragement of the concept and practice of individual land ownership (often by freehold), as in Kenya under the Swynnerton Plan, and the alienation of areas to the state for conservation – as at Amboseli in Kenya, Makuya 'national park' in Venda and the proposed *forêt classée* in the Samori.

The authorities involved in allocating land and water rights vary greatly between our case-studies, being a product of the specific institutional histories of these localities. In Samori and Venda, where forms of 'customary' tenure predominate, allocative authority is largely devolved to village and lineage chiefs, appointed to a greater (Venda) or lesser (Samori) degree by the state. This contrasts sharply with Shoshong, where 'customary' rights over land and water (digging wells and sinking boreholes) are allocated by a government-appointed land board, which merely consults the local customary chiefs. In Kimana, access is determined by elected group-ranch committees on the group ranches – an attempt to create a modernized customary institution – or through a land market in areas where land ownership has been individualized. It seemed likely in Kimana and the surrounding area that the group ranches would soon be broken up into individual holdings, thus elevating the role of the land market as the prime allocative mechanism. In all cases, a trend towards the increased use of commoditized transactions for both customary and individual holdings was observed (Chapter 6).

The challenging of property rights is a widespread phenomenon across rural Africa, particularly in places where demand has been intensified through demographic or use changes, as in the Samori and Kimana examples. The notion of 'customary rights' has proved not only flexible but also ambiguous, so that commonly the nature of custom is contested. A key issue is the extent to which processes of commoditization of access to land and water (analysed in Chapter 6) are contested or accepted as part of customary tenure.

In all four cases, 'customary tenure' is formally excluded from land markets, but can be arranged along a continuum of the extent to which commoditized access to land is accepted as part of 'custom'. In Kimana, where a land market and individual freehold title predominate, market norms prevail even within 'communal' group-ranch land, and allocation of plots for individual members to lease out to share-croppers is commonplace. In Botswana, government land boards administer customary tenure in the form of a 'national commons' and the extent of formal freehold tenure of land is limited. However, private property in water in the form of boreholes and dams is leading to *de facto* private control of access to grazing. This is mirrored on a small scale in the village of Mmutlane, in terms of increasing registration and fencing of uncultivated 'arable' lands. In Venda and Samori, the commoditization of land allocation by local customary authorities is more contested. This is evident in Samori, where the introduction of sharecropping of flooded rice by landholding lineage leaders is contested by other village residents as contrary to custom. In Venda, allocation of irrigable land by customary chiefs in the Mutale valley has been largely to individuals, not necessarily from local communities, with the capital to develop commercial irrigated production. Much of this privately developed 'informal' irrigation is on previously uncultivated land cleared from bush, and, although one attempt to register permanent private title to the land was resisted by tribal leaders, about half of these irrigators have reinforced their claims by having their plots surveyed by the Department of Agriculture and obtaining a 'Permission to Occupy' registered with the local administrative authority.

In Chapter 6, we set out the dynamics of increasing demand for wetland resources. This includes demographic pressure, particularly resulting from immigration, and the greater productivity and income achieved through changing land and water use. Increased demand was leading to greater competition for access, particularly in Kimana and Samori, and the institutions involved in the resolution of disputes about access were facing problems. Widespread perceptions of unfairness led to strong emotions about access. In both areas, physical violence had occurred over land disputes, and at Kimana Group Ranch (Chapter 3) riot police had been deployed on one occasion because of the likelihood of a group ranch meeting becoming an open battle. In the Samori (Chapter 2), an intervillage dispute had escalated to violent confrontation, resulting in armed intervention by government to confiscate the harvest and prohibit further cultivation on the disputed area. The available evidence indicated that, when disputes cannot be settled by local institutions and are transferred to official courts, these bodies may be poorly equipped to resolve the disputes. A lack of capacity for constructive intervention reduces the role of formal government to that of maintaining order, while disputes run their course through informal channels, often for extended periods of time.

The linkage of formal political activity to access to land and water was manifest at both local and national levels. In Venda, there was conflict between elected and customary authorities about control of local government generally. Land issues were generally of less immediate importance than more urban concerns of housing and services, but land issues threatened to become part of the struggles as discontented members of Tshiombo irrigation scheme sought representation for their demands for improved water supply. In Samori, the local administration had become involved in intervillage disputes and in defending pastoralists' grazing areas and transit corridors from encroachment by cultivators. However, it was in our Kenyan case-study that the politics of access was most evident. Political parties were a powerful 'behind the scenes' force in trying to ensure that the group ranch committees were controlled by members of their respective parties: the KANU party sanctioned 'ethnic cleansing' in the subdistrict – frightening off the non-Maasai by threats and sometimes beatings –

as part of its effort to win the 1992 and 1997 elections; and patron–client networks stretching down from Nairobi to local residents shaped the competition to install trusted individuals in positions of authority at the subdistrict level.

Three main points emerge from our cases with regard to the political dynamics of access. The first concerns the way in which the wider political environment conditions the processes of local access. For example, in both Samori and Kimana, factionalism within as well as between ethnic groups was fuelled, and drawn upon, by allegiances to national parties in electoral contests. In this way, the role of ethnicity in local contests over access to resources was traceable to factional allegiances forged in party politics at the national level. In the Kenyan case, the move to multiparty politics at the national level had led to party political competition to control local institutions that grant access to resources. Political parties seized on lineages as a means of advancing their interests and, as a result, interlineage competition to control furrow groups developed.

The second point is that, in all of the cases, there was evidence that a small number of individuals were able to combine their economic wealth, social status and political influence to gain control over an increasing proportion of local resources. While market-based accumulation was part of their individual strategy, this was often combined with claims to status through customary identities and by the use of political connections with local and national politicians and bureaucrats, to ensure preferential treatment by publicly controlled allocative institutions. The importance of commoditization of relationships of land and labour and the evolution of a 'middle peasantry' was discussed in Chapter 6. Here it is important to note the role of commoditization in dissolving the boundaries of 'community' relationships of access to land and labour. In particular, members of 'local communities' may hire labour from outside the community and may equally rent land (e.g. through sharecropping) to 'outsiders'. Processes of individual accumulation may thus involve the simultaneous transformation of 'customary' economic ties and the reinforcement of customary status and identity politically.

Finally, and closely related to the previous point, in all four cases, there was clear evidence that, either by design or by default, access is increasingly drifting towards an emphasis on exclusive individual rights. The consequence of this for the institutions that allocate access rights is that market-based exchange is becoming an ever more important component of institutional frameworks. In Kimana, the group ranches are being individualized; in Samori, sharecropping and renting land have become an element of 'customary tenure'; in Shoshong, rights to water are increasingly purchased from private boreholes and dams; and, in Venda, a *de facto* market for irrigable land under customary tenure has developed.

These findings raise important questions about recent policy proposals that privilege 'customary' land rights as the basis for both sustainable resource use and social equity. Whereas such proposals are premised on the association of commoditized access to land (and water) with 'statutory' control of land and the introduction of 'modern' tenure regimes, our case-studies suggest that commoditized access to land is inherent in 'customary' tenure where land values (productivity) rise and/or competition for land increases. It is important to note that commoditized access to land and water is not suggested here as a requirement of increased productivity in agriculture, as many land registration and titling policies assume, but rather as a consequence of increasing demand and/or productivity. Where policy proposals acknowledge this, for example, in relation to peri-urban areas as well as wetlands, these are claimed to be 'exceptions' to the more general rule that customary tenure should prevail (IIED, 1999). This implies a formula that governance of land and water should rely upon customary tenure until their value rises, that is, until 'development' takes place. The evidence from this study suggests that commoditization of access to land and water under customary tenure well before any establishment of formal markets in land, and the attendant processes of social differentiation (and potential for marginalization), means that governance of land by customary tenure cannot be regarded as any guarantor of access to land or water for the poorest.

The political dynamics of resource use: 'productivity and modernization' versus 'sustainability and livelihood security'

In all of our case-studies – as across dryland Africa more generally – there has been an intensification of water use in response to varying combinations of demographic pressure and new economic opportunities. These changes in resource use were associated with higher levels of productivity and, for some users, higher incomes. The changes varied with the specific nature of resources, the opportunities available and patterns of population growth. In Kimana (Chapter 3), a pastoralist system that used wetlands for dry-season pasture and water became diversified into irrigated vegetable production, wildlife tourism and rain-fed maize and beans. In Samori (Chapter 2), open woodland and seasonal pasture had been converted to flooded rice production. In Venda (Chapter 5), informal and privately financed irrigation was being rapidly introduced and rain-fed agriculture was in decline. In Shoshong (Chapter 4), cattle ownership had polarized, goats were becoming more common, cattle were being brought into 'the lands' and irrigation was being practised around boreholes intended to water cattle.

The political dynamic of resource use is most evident through state involvement in planning and regulating land use and the provision of services to encourage change in systems of production. It operates at a variety of levels, from the local to the international. The important role of the latter, noted earlier, is illustrated by the role of the 'northern' conservationist discourse in funding priorities. As a consequence, the Traoré regime portrayed its punitive policing of tree cutting in Mali to international funding agencies as prudent environmental conservation, and the KWS at Amboseli gained support from American and European aid agencies when 'northern' publics became concerned about the future of the African elephant. Here we focus on national- and local-level public policy and service delivery issues.

While the political dynamics varies between cases, there are a number of tensions that were revealed in all of them: in particular, the relative emphasis on agricultural modernization and scientific management in pursuit of higher productivity, as against local knowledge to achieve more ecologically sustainable resource use and (by implication) more secure rural livelihoods. The case-studies show this dichotomy to be almost wholly misplaced. The increases in productivity through intensification in water use were the result of local initiative, not government projects. To the extent that they involved 'modern' technology (e.g. irrigation), this had been adopted and adapted by local knowledge. The critical technologies were boreholes in Botswana and irrigation in Kimana and Venda. In the latter case, it is important to note that the dynamic, expanding land use was informal irrigation (of which agricultural officials were almost entirely ignorant), rather than the existing government-run 'formal' irrigation. In the Samori, the adoption of rice cultivation in uncontrolled flood conditions owes less to 'scientific' agricultural technology, except that the flood itself was a by-product of such technology in the construction of a dam in Burkina Faso.

Three points can be made about these local changes in land use. First, they involved transfer of technology from elsewhere, and in this the role of immigrants was significant, or even (in the case of Chagga and Kikuyu in Kimana) fundamental. Secondly, the importance of local initiative underlines evidence that the capacity of government services to deliver technical support in the areas studied was weak (in Kimana and Venda) to non-existent (in Samori). This was in part owing to weakness in state budgets, as the contrasting strength of government services at local level in Botswana highlights, and more generally owing to low levels of capacity in the public sector. However, the Botswanan case also raises the third reason why local initiative appears to be the dominant dynamic in resource use, which is that, even where available at local level, the support offered by government services may not be appropriate. In Shoshong, the government technical services were devoted to an unsustainable policy of subsidizing rain-fed arable agriculture, whose sole beneficiaries were owners of tractors and oxen. More broadly in Botswana, the technical basis for government policy towards agriculture is questioned by the contradiction between the scientific estimates of carrying capacity regulating grazing pressure on ranches, and ranchers' practice of seasonal release of cattle on to the unfenced commons. The evidence of these case-studies suggests that government attempts to regulate use, and particularly to reduce cattle numbers and convert pastoralism to ranching, have proved ineffective. Despite group ranch boundaries, tracking (Scoones, 1994) remains important for the Maasai when pasture is scarce. Indeed, the tendency of governments to see dryland policy exclusively in terms of cattle has led to a lack of recognition of the significant increases in the numbers of goats (or shoats) in Samori, Shoshong and Kimana, and the consequences this might have for resource use, and, until very recently, of the contribution that wildlife tourism or hunting might make to livelihoods (Hulme and Murphree, 2001).

Similar observations can be made about the zoning of the Loitokitok Division in Kenya as a 'semi-arid' area, which means that government extension officers tend to be livestock specialists and have little training in horticulture. As a consequence, the use of pesticides, locally available through private traders, poses serious hazards to producers and consumers of vegetables. In Mali, also, research focusing on rice with controlled irrigation has little relevance to the 'floating rice' (grown on a rising flood) cultivated in the Sourou valley.

The most significant contribution of state activity in dryland areas has been infrastructural development, particularly of main roads and feeder roads, which has facilitated trade and the import of new ideas. The impressive rhetoric and documents of national and district development plans should not obscure the evidence that most changes in land and water use have come about from local initiative. The case of Singh, who is credited with introducing irrigated agriculture to the Loitokitok Division (Chapter 3), provides a vivid illustration of such indigenous agricultural revolution, to use Richards's (1985) term. Similar informal processes of innovation can be drawn from our other cases: the rapid switch to swamp rice production in Samori, the success of private irrigation schemes in Venda and the use of boreholes, which are officially to water cattle, for irrigation in Shoshong.

These findings may appear to support a 'minimal state' formula, emphasizing only the provision of education and infrastructure by the public sector. This is a simplistic interpretation, however, which ignores significant outcomes in terms of socio-economic differentiation and marginalization (noted above) and also the absence of any institutions for environmental regulation or management. We now consider the second of these in relation to decentralized and community-based resource management.

The political dynamics of resource management: sustainability, decentralization and community-based natural resource management

Earlier in this chapter, we argued that the weight and substance of environmental policy in many African countries is heavily influenced by the way 'Africa' is perceived by those setting the international environmental agenda. In particular, we suggested that this prioritizes the conservation of resources (e.g. wildlife and forests) with recreational or biodiversity potential, and the 'sustainable' use of resources (land, water, forests, fisheries) needed for 'rural livelihoods' (i.e. to maintain communities in rural areas). In many respects, these priorities coincide with those of colonial administrations (see Chapter 1) and the African national states that succeeded them, which typically included concerns over land degradation (or, more recently, environmental degradation), attributed to growth in numbers of people and livestock. In dryland areas, much public policy was premised on the need to regulate cattle numbers, cattle movements or water extraction.

Despite international funding, implementation of national environmental policy has tended to be weak, exemplified in our case-studies by Kenya. In Nairobi, a National Environmental Secretariat and a 14-volume National Environmental Action Plan, ratified by Cabinet, provide a blueprint for cross-sectoral coordination. At subdistrict level, in Loitokitok, departmental coordination is virtually non-existent and a central element of the culture of government agencies is sectoral autonomy (what is known in India as 'rock departmentalism').

The evident ineffectiveness of many environmental policies formulated by central government ministries has provided an important impetus to alternative approaches emphasizing decentralization of resource management to local communities. These alternatives are now strongly represented in 'mainstream' environmental policy-making, such as the Convention to Combat Desertification (see Chapter 1). What do our case-studies tell us about the opportunities and constraints of decentralized natural resource management?

First, we need to emphasize that, as described in the previous section, the case-studies indicate that land and water management is already decentralized in the sense that innovation by local resource users has driven changes in resource use. However, local initiative and entrepreneurship have emphasized increased productivity over concerns of long-term sustainability. As observed in Chapter 6, the case-studies found a lack of institutions at local level responsible for or capable of regulating land and water use on the scale needed. Important exceptions are the KWS and the Botswana land boards, which we discuss again below, but for the most part the absence of institutions concerned with conservation or management contrasted with the ready identification by local resource users of instances where improvements in land and water management are needed. These include threats to the continued productivity of the land, such as the proliferation of perennial weeds in the rice fields of the Sourou valley, and threats to human health, such as pesticide contamination of water in irrigation channels and streams from vegetable growing in Kimana. Other environmental management problems concern conflicts of interest: upstream diversions of streams are causing desiccation of the Kimana Swamps and a reduction in grazing and water for group ranches relying on wetlands downstream of Kimana. Similarly, in the Sourou valley, the expansion of rice cultivation encroaches on grazing areas and obstructs pastoralists' access to the river to water their herds.

The nature of these environmental management problems is that they are integral to sustaining productivity under changing land and water use. However, these local concerns may diverge considerably from the sustainability agenda of aid donors and non-government organizations (NGOs). This is evident particularly in relation to conservation of wildlife (in Kimana) and woodland (in Samori), with which local resource users only engage when they perceive it may strengthen their incomes or claims to property rights. The latter is illustrated by the establishment of the Kimana Community Conservancy when members of the group ranch, under the influence of KWS and the African Wildlife Foundation (AWF), set aside land for wildlife on the understanding that this would give them access to the tourist trade. In the Samori, village authorities' concern in woodland conservation is to restrict outsiders' use of trees (e.g. for timber, animal browsing and fruit).

The political dynamic regarding the ways in which changes in resource use prioritize short-term productivity over long-term sustainability (however that is defined) continues, therefore, to reflect tensions between international concerns and local preferences. Bilateral and multilateral development agencies and international NGOs highlight the importance of sustainability (Adams and Hulme, 2001). National governments and national NGOs repeat this mantra and, to varying degrees, attempt to influence changes in resource use. At the local level, resource users highlight the importance of productivity enhancement.

In all four countries studied, policy discourse highlighting decentralization is popular with the incumbent regimes and other political parties – with its imagery of 'power to the people' – and is a priority policy for aid donors. For the latter, it fits in with the concept of 'good governance' and also with ideas about the desirability of local participation in natural resource management. However, with the exception of Botswana in our case-studies, the capacity of local government agencies to regulate resource use was found to be relatively weak, once the (politically unsustainable) option of excluding people from the resource is relinquished (e.g. the forestry service in Mali following the 1991 coup). Decentralization proposals commonly favour elected local councils as the primary institutional form to achieve more 'responsive' and locally accountable resource management. However, in Kenya and Botswana, where local councils have been long established, they have little autonomy in revenue or staffing and are overshadowed by the processes of national politics: the private sector and political patronage in the case of Kenya; the central government ministries in the case of Botswana. In both cases, decentralization has followed a pattern of 'deconcentration', with district-level government officials remaining accountable to their ministerial headquarters, rather than to elected district councils. In South Africa and Mali, elected local councils have only recently been introduced, in both cases the principle of decentralized government being an important element of constitutional reform. In both cases, there is an expectation that local councils will play a role in natural resource management, which, in the case of the *communes* in Mali, is explicitly anticipated to contribute to the revenue they need to provide services. In both cases, however, the relationship between elected councils and customary authority is unclear, particularly in relation to management of natural resources. In Venda, uncertainty of this kind results in discussion of land and water becoming a terrain for a more general power struggle between civics and chiefs, as in the case of the Makuya Park discussions (Chapter 5). In the Samori, assertions of the 'domain' of natural resources (particularly woodland) to be managed by the *communes* have yet to be tested against the realities of customary village jurisdictions.

The response advocated to such complex and ambiguous institutional situations is often to seek pluralist solutions of 'partnership' or 'comanagement'. One example from our case-studies that may fit this description is the Kimana Wildlife Conservancy, established by Kimana Group Ranch in order to generate revenue from commercial tourism. Here a government agency, the KWS, played the role of broker between a 'community' (group ranch) and the private sector. A second example, from the Samori, is the proposal that the government forestry service (DNEF) formally contract village associations to regulate the use of woodland. In this case, NGOs acted as the 'broker' for the deal between government and 'community'. The role of broker in these two examples is instructive. In both cases, the organization acting as broker was relatively well resourced, in both financial and human terms, presenting a credible and well-informed party to the deal. It is too soon to judge how effective these arrangements will be in regulating and conserving natural resources, but potential lessons are considered further below.

For proponents of 'community-based' natural resource management, the decentralization problem is more that of needing to re-establish 'self-governing' non-state regulatory institutions that build on social capital or coherence within local communities – widely believed to be inherent in customary authority. As argued earlier in relation to customary tenure, our case-studies provide little evidence that community institutions will regulate and conserve land and water in 'wetlands in drylands'. Apart from the emphasis among land users on increasing productivity, discussed earlier, it is apparent that most village- or 'community-level' institutions are insufficiently inclusive of the different types of user groups to be able to address some of the most important land and water management problems that arise between 'communities': intervillage land disputes (Samori); conflicts between pastoralists and cultivators (Kimana, Samori); and problems of increasing scarcity of water arising from more intensive use (Venda, Kimana, Mmutlane). Moreover, initiatives to reinforce 'village-level' resource management, such as the *Programme de Gestion de Ressources Naturelles* (PGRN) in Mali, may accentuate the problem by formalizing village natural resource management committees that exclude key resource users, such as pastoralists.

As we observed at the beginning of this chapter, simple dichotomies between 'central' and 'local' government agencies or between a notional precolonial heritage of customary authority and a central state built in a colonizer's image are no more helpful than that between the nation-state of the African independence movement confronting in a straightforward way customary authority as colonial construct. What this research suggests is that control of access to land at a local level is substantially mediated by customary authorities, who even in an 'advisory' role may have a decisive influence. Further, 'customary tenure' is dynamic and appears to operate increasingly according to market rules, even where there are no formal land markets. Customary tenure appears to present no obstacle to local initiative and entrepreneurship driving innovation and increasing productivity, but with no guarantees for long-term resource conservation or equitable access to resources.

In this sense, decentralization that seeks to build on 'customary institutions' needs to examine critically the realism of expectations of equity and sustainability. This is not, however, an analysis that leads to an argument for greater state control, whether local or central, of natural resource use. Such approaches not only have failed in the past, but also are unrealistic in terms of the resources that most African states can deploy. There appear to be three main lessons to be drawn for policy: in relation to social analysis of resource use; in relation to institutional change; and in relation to the deployment of state resources.

First is the need for a more critical approach to the understanding of the underlying dynamics of social and economic change in Africa. The normative 'transition' models of modernization and the conservative assumptions of populist and communitarian discourse are inadequate to address the clear evidence in all our cases of commoditization of access to land and water (as well as labour – see Chapter 6) and economic differentiation under conditions of increasing productivity. The accumulation of property and/or rights of access by limited numbers of individuals (or households) and the growing numbers of rural residents who are functionally landless or who lack assets, such as cattle, by which they might access resources mean that economically based hierarchies of management (e.g. owners over managers over supervisors over labourers) are displacing more socially based forms of labour organization (e.g. fathers over sons or husbands over wives). These may be accentuated by the large numbers who migrate in search of better productive opportunities. For growing numbers of the residents of the areas that we studied, wage labour for others or other non-agricultural income is either the primary source of income or an increasingly important aspect of a 'multiple livelihood' (Murray, 1999). The process of commoditization is an important general theme of the profound economic, political and social changes taking place in our case-study sites and has great implications for the future. However, these processes play themselves out in different ways. At Loitokitok, the early irrigation initiatives placed a proportion of irrigated lands under the control of non-Maasai agriculturalists. Political processes in Kenya in the 1990s have reversed this trend and shifted control of irrigated land (and of the institutions of water management) to those who can claim to be Maasai. Conversely, at Samori, there is a preference to share cropland with 'stranger' farmers, because of the fear that co-ethnics might convert less commoditized loan agreements into claims for permanent access rights. In our Botswana case, where cattle ownership has become increasingly polarized, private control of surface water by individuals or groups has begun to follow the earlier-established principle of private borehole ownership, and implies the further spread of privatization of grazing on rangeland.

A second lesson is that, although community-level management in the drylands has weakened, particularly with regard to pastoralist institutions, this does not mean that community-based natural resource management has ceased. As mentioned earlier, the Kimana example illustrates the way in which tracking pasture and water outside group ranch boundaries occurred in the drought of 1994. More importantly, new institutions for collective management have evolved. Furrow groups manage water on the new irrigation schemes; a community conservancy has been registered to gain group ranch members access to the wildlife resource; and there are signs that new federated units are emerging in the form of the Loitokitok Group Ranch Association. While some forms of collective management are eroding, new forms (related to new resource uses) are constituting themselves. To the extent that these changes take place within a dynamic of socio-economic differentiation, they will incorporate processes of exclusion and conflict.

From the perspective of state policy, a priority may be to promote regulatory institutions that achieve a wider representation of interests than customary authorities. The land board model of Botswana offers a precedent for bringing together customary authority with statutory regulation. Land boards offer a flexible approach to the registration of individual (customary) land rights, which responds to land users' perception of the need for such registration. However, interests represented are quite narrow (excluding, for example, non-Batswana) and regulation is dominated by rigid 'scientific' criteria, which are of contested validity. It remains to be seen whether such a model could be used for broad representation of different resource use interests and for a dialogue between 'scientific' and 'artisanal' criteria on sustainable resource use. One important opportunity offered by such an institution is that customary criteria of precedent could be tempered by allocational criteria based on constitutional rights and social goals. Since these are in the realm of the politics of the state, 'land boards' could constitute local forums for the negotiation of social outcomes by decentralized institutions of land and water management. The extent to which these are likely to address the interests of disadvantaged social groups would, our case-studies suggest, depend directly on the nature of national politics. In this regard, the experience of South Africa in pursuing redistributive reform of access to land and water will have much to offer.

Finally, and despite the citing of group ranch collaboration above, the evidence from our cases points to the weaknesses of resource management institutions beyond the local level, with particular regard to water. The problems arising from water extraction for those downstream at Loitokitok and Venda and for those needing to water livestock at Shoshong – and the implications of damming a river for those upstream at Samori – reveal that the multitiered forums necessary to ensure representation of relevant interests and the coordination of resource management at large geographical scales are weak or non-existent. The water bailiffs of Loitokitok have not resolved the problems of irrigation schemes drying up in Kuku as more water is diverted from Kimana Swamp. The management of conflicting resource use appears to be ignored, until it results in physical violence, as at Samori, but then is contained, rather than resolved. The implication for state intervention is to put fewer resources into blueprint national conservation plans or in populating a complex local administrative apparatus. Rather, scarce resources might be used to build capacity through conflict mediation and resolution. A supra-local organization focused on understanding and mediating in the conflicts over natural resource use inherent in social changes could build not only a capacity to mediate conflict and avoid violence, but also an understanding of socio-economic dynamics, which could inform policy-makers and provide a basis for designing interventions to combat rural poverty or promote more sustainable resource use.

Conclusion

In this chapter, we have drawn on the four case-studies of 'wetlands in drylands' to reflect on policies for the governance of land and water. A theme running through the chapter has been the way development discourse, whether of the prevailing neoliberalism or the 'alternative' counternarrative, omits key factors in the political dynamics of land and water management. This operates in basic ways, which avoid any questioning of the 'pathology' of the African state: by failing to acknowledge the historical specificity of the formation of states in Africa and by failing to acknowledge the international financial relationships that dominate environmental policy for many African states. From these omissions stem misunderstandings about the reasons for 'failure' of environmental policy in Africa and about the role statutory and customary authority play in governing land and water.

In relation to the latter, we argue that customary authorities, articulated within the modern state in various ways, play a larger role in determining access to land and water than is often acknowledged. Further, and contrary to the convention that market-based access to land is associated with introduction of 'statutory' control over land, trends towards commoditized access to land and water are evident under customary tenure, irrespective of the formal existence of land markets. Moreover, as observed in Chapter 6, such trends apply to production for 'subsistence', as well as to more commercial production, where 'wetland' resources are increasing in productivity and value. These processes of commoditization of land and water have important repercussions for the meaning of 'customary'. One is that social differentiation within communities will involve accumulation by more powerful individuals, who are able simultaneously to dissolve their 'customary' economic ties to the community in favour of market-based forms of exchange, while also developing and consolidating their customary ties politically, in terms of customary status within the community. The specific ways in which such processes determine social outcomes, and particularly the extent of marginalization of the more disadvantaged from access to land and water, are critically dependent upon the influence of wider (national) political goals and processes (e.g. ethnic factionalism in Kenya, 'modernization' in Botswana) on the discourse through which local competition for resources is conducted.

While the 'centre' matters critically in political terms, it is evident that the 'local' is where 'development' initiative and entrepreneurship are most dynamic. Our studies demonstrate technical innovation by land- and water-users, including adoption of 'modern' irrigation technology, often in the face of government services that are inappropriate, ineffectual or entirely absent. New patterns of resource use are related to the demise of some community institutions and the creation of others, but, on the wetland resources we studied, local innovation in resource use does not appear to be matched by local institutions to regulate resource use (other than through controlling access) in order to sustain their long-term productivity.

These findings do not lead straightforwardly, however, to advocacy of 'community-based natural resource management', on the one hand, or to 'capacity-building' for government extension services, on the other. Rather, it suggests a need to recognize the limitations of current narratives of rural development in Africa and to stress the importance of critical analysis of the social and economic dynamics of land and water use and the trajectories of social change with which they are associated. This may be uncomfortably complex for a policy debate more at ease with simple models of development, but the use of simplistic models of 'community', even as a 'strategic' counternarrative to neoliberalism, can create an obstacle to the understanding of the dynamics and trajectory of social change through critical examination of the relationships between state, market and 'custom'. Without such an understanding, it will be difficult to use recent ideas of 'comanagement', 'institutional pluralism' and 'partnership' to achieve environmental conservation or poverty eradication. The processes that propel social differentiation and marginalization under current regimes of resource tenure (whether labelled customary or statutory) will continue to operate under 'comanagement' or 'partnership' arrangements, unless specific efforts are directed at changing them.

References

Adams, W. & Hulme, D. (2001) In: Hulme, D. and Murphree, M. (eds) *African Wildlife and Livelihoods: The Promise and Performance of Community Conservation.* James Currey, Oxford.

Bayart, J.-F. (1993) *The State in Africa. The Politics of the Belly.* Longman, London.

Chabal, P. & Daloz, J.-P. (1999) *Africa Works. Disorder as Political Instrument.* James Currey, Oxford.

Dia, M. (1996) *Africa's Management in the 1990s and Beyond: Reconciling Indigenous and Transplanted Institutions.* Directions in Development Series, World Bank, Washington, D.C.

Hulme, D. & Murphree, M. (eds) (2001) *African Wildlife and Livelihoods: The Promise and Performance of Community Conservation.* James Currey, Oxford.

IIED (1999) *Land Tenure and Resource Access in West Africa: Issues and Opportunities for the Next Twenty-five Years.* International Institute for Environment and Development, London.

Mamdani, M. (1996) *Citizen and Subject. Contemporary Africa and the Legacy of Late Colonialism.* James Currey, Oxford.

Murray, C. (1999) *Changing Livelihoods: The Free State, 1990s.* Multiple Livelihoods and Social Change Working Paper 4, Institute for Development Policy and Management, University of Manchester, Manchester.

Richards, P. (1985) *Indigenous Agricultural Revolution.* Hutchinson, London.

Scoones, I. (1994) *Living with Uncertainty: New Directions in Pastoral Development in Africa.* IT Publications, London.

Index

The following abbreviations have been used in the index for the case-study countries: (B) Botswana, (K) Kenya, (M) Mali, (SA) South Africa

Acacia 21
Accelerated Rain-fed Arable Programme (ARAP) (B) 128, 131, 132, 144, 128, 149
accumulation 209–10, 211, 217, 222, 228, 231; (K) 110, 112, 117; (M) 206; (SA) 171, 187
acquired immune deficiency syndrome (AIDS) 12
afforestation (SA) 185
Africa 1, 2, 3, 5, 9, 16, 17, 196, 197, 201, 212, 215, 216, 218, 219, 223, 228; 'crisis' 9, 12, 18, 21, 195, 207, 212, 213, 230; history 2, 3, 200; 'transition' 16, 216; 'wild' 73, 74
African Land Development Board (ALDEV) (K) 76, 85
African National Congress (ANC) (SA) 157, 173, 188, 218
African Wildlife Foundation (AWF) (K) 226
Afrikaners 121
age grades (K) 74, 80–8, 90–2
age sets (K) 74, 82, 83, 84, 90, 91, 92, 111, 206, 208; (M) 43–4
Agenda 21 (UNCED) 1, 13
agriculture, in colonial society 3, 6–7, 10, 11; in independent Africa 8, 223; (K) 74, 81; (M) 33, 39; (SA) 156, 157, 169
agricultural services (B) 128, 131, 137, 143, 147, 148, 224; (K) 76; (M) 57, 60, 66, 67; (SA) 166, 178, 179–81, 186, 188–9, 224
aid, foreign 2, 7–8, 13, 16, 17, 195, 219, 223, 226; (B) 130, 150–1; (M) 60, 67
alienation, land 11, 18, 220; (K) 76; (SA) 202
Alliance pour la Démocratie au Mali (ADEMA) (M) 35, 65
Amboseli National Park (K) 82, 85, 101, 106, 112, 220, 223
aménagement de terroir/gestion de terroir (AT/GT) (M) 67, 68, 69
anticolonialism (K) 7, 9, 76; (M) 52, 60
apartheid (SA) 155, 156, 157, 180, 189, 190, 202, 203, 209, 216, 220
arable farming 204; (B) 128, 132–3, 136–7, 139, 140–1, 144, 148, 221, 224; (M) 41; (SA) 166
Arable Lands Development Programme (ALDEP) (B) 128, 132, 137, 140, 144, 148, 149
arid and semi-arid lands (ASAL) (K) 74, 76, 77, 79, 101, 113, 224
Arusha, cultivators (K) 100
Association pour le Développement des Villages du Panadougou (ADVP) (M) 50, 58

badisa (overseers) (B) 130, 133, 145, 146
Bambara kingdom (M) 33, 39
Bandiagara plateau (M) 31, 36, 41, 57
Bangwato (B) 123, 128, 133
Bantustans (SA) 155, 202, 209, 216
baobab (M) 37; (SA) 161
Baralong (B) 149
Batalaote (B) 123, 126, 127, 133
Batswana (B) 121, 127, 217, 229
beans (K) 205, 223; (SA) 175
Bechuanaland 121, 202
beer (B) 140; (K) 103; (SA) 175
Belgian Congo 7
Bellah, pastoralists (M) 48, 59, 61
Berry, Sara 3, 198, 200–2, 206, 210, 212
'betterment' planning (SA) 7, 166, 171
biodiversity (K) 112–13
'black' (SA) 151, 157
Boipelego dam (B) 134–5, 143
boma (Maasai encampment) 83, 84
Bonwapitse River (B) 123, 132, 135, 141, 144
Bophutatswana (SA) 156
boreholes (B) 121, 126, 130, 132, 133, 134, 136, 139, 141–2, 144, 145, 146, 150, 205, 217, *passim*; 229; (K) 76; (SA) 178, 184

Botswana 8, 10, 17, 20, 22, 202, 203, 205, 216, 217, 219, 220–1, 224, 226, 227, 229
administration 127
economy 121–3, 139–42
geography 119–20
history 120–1, 123
land and water: access 131–3, 135–6; management 130–1, 142–6; use 124, 126, 136–9
politics 123, 146–51
settlement 120, 123–4
Botswana Agricultural Marketing Board (BAMB) 149
Botswana Democratic Party (BDP) 123, 129, 146, 148, 149
Botswana Meat Commission (BMC) 137, 138, 139
Botswana National Front (BNF) 123, 148
boundaries, communal (B) 145; (K) 101; (M) 51–2, 64
boundaries, conceptual 196–7
Bretton Woods institutions (IMF, WB) 6, 9–11
bribery (K) 87, 101; (M) 62
bureaucracy 215; (B) 122; (K) 114; (SA) 189
Burkina Faso 29, 31, 41, 42, 50–1, 58, 224
bushveld (SA) 161

CAMPFIRE programme 15
'capacity-building' 10, 230, 231
Cape colony 121
capitalism: in Africa 3, 5; in Europe 5; models of 196, 198–200
'carrying capacity' 7; (B) 150, 224; (K) 107
case-studies (in this book) 1, 20, 22–5, 197, 202, 203, 205, 207, 215, 216, 217, 218, 222, 223, 226, 227, 229; (B) 144, 149, 150, 151; (SA) 188, 191; *see also* 'dynamics'
cash economy 204, 208; (K) 100; (M) 56–7; (SA) 178, 186; *see also* commoditization
cassava 204
cattle (B) 121, 122, 130, 137–9, 140, 143, 145, 146–7, 150–1, 223, 224; (K) 74, 81–2, , 87, 99, 100–1, 103, 107, 110, 112–13, 210; (M) 53, 54, 55, 57, 210; (SA) 161, 176–7, 178, 179, 181, 182–3, 184; *see also* livestock
'cattle posts' (B) 126, 133, 139, 141, 142, 144, 145
central planning 7, 8, 13
centralization 25
Chagga, cultivators (K) 87, 100, 104, 105, 203, 224
charcoal (K) 108
chef de village (M) 44, 45, 50, 60, 63, 64, 66
chickens (B) 136; (M) 179, 184
chiefs, tribal 3, 4, 5, 6, 8, 203, 217, 220; (B) 121, 128, 129, 130, 150, 207; (K) 86, 97, 98, 109; (SA) 156, 165, 167, 172–3, 187, 189, 218, 227
children (SA) 156, 177, 183
Chobe River (B) 119
Ciskei (SA) 155
civics (civil associations) (SA) 170, 171, 173, 174, 187, 190, 191, 209, 227
civil society 10, 13, 177, 207, 211
clans 199, 201, 206, 208, 212; (K) 84, 92–5, 111
class formation, Africa 5, 212
class society (SA) 175
clientelism 200; (K) 90, 91, 222; (SA) 167, 170
climate change 21; (K) 94, 107; (SA) 158
cocoa 4, 49, 200, 201; (M) 33
Code Domanial et Foncier (CDF) (M) 61–2, 64
coffee 49; (SA) 186
Collectivités Territoriales (CT) (M) 63–4, 66, 68
colonial period, Africa 4–5, 13, 225; consolidation 2, 3–6; late 2, 3, 6–7
colonial state, 208

233

colonialism, French (M) 33, 38, 44, 61, 216
comanagement 15, 19–20, 227, 231
Combretum 37, 28
Comité Villageois de Gestion de Ressources Naturelles (M) 67, 68
'commercial' agriculture (SA) 181, 182, 188, 221
commercialization 202
commoditization 2, 4, 11, 20, 23, 24, 195–6, 197–202, 203–5, 206, 207–8, 209, 210, 211, 212, 218, 220, 222, 223, 228–9, 230; 'high' 203–4, 205, 210; 'low' 203–4, 205, 210; (B) 145; (K) 88, 89, 103, 108, 109, 110, 112; (SA) 181–5
commons, 'tragedy of' 13, 196; (B) 149; (SA) 167
communal land 4, 7, 11, 12, 18–19, 204, 217; (B) 130, 131–2, 133, 144, 145, 147, 151, , 224; (K) 86, 87; (SA) 156, 165, 168, 185, 189, 191
'community' 1, 5, 10, 13, 14–15, 23, 197, 227, 231; (B) 149
community-based natural resource management 13, 14–15, 19, 225–30, 231; (B) 151; (M) 69–70
community conservation (K) 85
Compagnie Française pour le Développement des Textiles (CFDT) (M) 7, 33
Compagnie Malienne pour le Développement des Textiles (CMDT) (M) 33, 34, 62, 65
compensation, land (B) 132
competition, land etc. 24, 205, 222; (B) 132; (K) 89, 108; (M) 48, 63, 205–6; (SA) 170
Conference of Traditional Leaders of South Africa (CONTRALESA) 218
conflict resolution 22–3, 221, 230; (M) 70
conservation 2, 5, 7, 9, 11, 14, 19, 197, 219, 225, 228, 231; (B) 146–7, 149, 150; (K) 85, 87, 107; (M) 62; (SA) 186, 188
consumer goods 208; (K) 100, 103; (M) 56; (SA) 177–8
Convention to Combat Desertification (CCD) 13–14, 225
Cooperative for American Relief to Everywhere (CARE) (M) 69, 70
cooperatives (B) 147; (M) 67, 69; (SA) 179–81
corruption 216; (K) 77
Côte d'Ivoire 49
cotton (M) 33, 41
Cowen, M.P. 5, 202
cowpea (B) 126, 137; (M) 37
credit facilities 5; (SA) 180–1, 192
crop damage (B) 142; (K) 106; (SA) 177, 179
customary law/rule/tenure 3–4, 5, 7, 8, 13, 15, 17–19, 22, 24, 204, 205, 206, 208, 209, 210, 215, 216, 217, 218, 220, 222, 227, 228, 230–1; (B) 127, 128, 150, 220; (K) 90, 101; (M) 45, 47, 49, 50, 58, 60–3, 69, 217–18; (SA) 165
customary institutions/organizations 228; (B) 127; (K) 88, 90, 95, 112

Dafing (M) 39, 46, 52–3, 54
dairy/milk (B) 136, 138, 139; (K) 100; (SA) 183, 185
dams 22; Burkina Faso 41, 42, 58; (B) 132, 133, 135, 139, 143, 207, 221, 222; (M) 58, 230; (SA) 165, 185, 205
debt, African 9–11
decentralization, in Africa 8, 10, 13, 14, 15, 16–18, 19–20, 215, 225–30; (B) 129; (M) 35, 63–8, 69
deconcentration 16, 17, 227; (B) 119, 128, 131; (M) 63
deforestation 195
democracy, multiparty, in Africa 16, 17, 215, 218, 219; (B) 122, 123, 216; (K) 77, 95–6, 216, 218; (M) 63–5, 70, 216, 218; (SA) 157, 216
Democratic Party (K) 94, 96
Department of Agriculture, Northern Province (SA) 166, 167, 170, 191
Department of Environmental Affairs, Northern Province (SA) 168, 174
Department of Wildlife and National Parks (B) 216
Depression, Great 2, 5, 6; (M) 33
desertification 11, 13, 195, 219; (K) 107, 108, 113; (M) 40
detribalization 5

devaluation 10; (M) 36
development 2, 6–7, 12; (B) 128–30, 151; (K) 77; (M) 58; (SA) 191–2
developmental 2, 6–7, 8, 12, 16, 195, 196, 197, 223, 230, 231
differentiation, social 14, 23, 24, 196, 197, 198–9, 201, 205, 206, 207–11, 212, 218, 223, 225, 230, 231
Direction National des Eaux et Forêts (DNEF) (M) 66, 70, 216, 227
disease control (K) 226; (SA) 178; cattle (B) 139; (K) 99
dispossession, land 205; *see also* 'exclusions'
District Focus for Rural Development policy (K) 85
district councils (B) 128, 129, 130–1; *see also* local government
diversification 209–10
djonforo (plots) (M) 39, 55–6, 57, 209
Dogon, cultivators (M) 36, 38–9, 40, 44, 46, 48, 49, 50, 54, 59, 203
donkeys (B) 133, 137, 138, 140, 141; (M) 39, 56; (SA) 179, 180, 181, 182
drought 9, 12, 21; (B) 121, 122, 123, 130–1, 137, 138, 140, 141, 142, 144, 148; (M) 34, 35, 61; (K) 74, 79, 85, 86, 99, 107, 108, 109, 229; (SA) 158, 177, 178, 180, 183, 184, 186; *see also* desertification
dryland farming 12, 223, 225; (M) 35–8, 39, 60, 223, 224
dry-season farming (B) 136, 141, 144, 223; (K) 77, 92, 101, 114, 223; (M) 47, 53; (SA) 161, 174, 176, 182, 185, 223
'dynamics', in the case-studies 23, 205, 219, 224, 228

East Africa 21, 74, 80
education (B) 121, 131; (K) 103, 113; (SA) 177, 178, 183
elderly, the (SA) 156, 173–4, 187
elders (K) 82, 83, 84, 91, 103; junior 91–2; senior 91–2
elections (K) 97–8, 221–2
élites 17; (B) 121, 217; (K) 77, 91, 98, 111, 112; (SA) 174, 188
enclosures 2, 19, 205, 209, 210; (B) 149; *see also* fencing; subdivision
entrepreneurs, African 5, 18, 226, 228; (K) 82, 114
environmental change 1, 2, 5, 9, 11, 12–20 *passim*, 23, 25, 195, 196, 207, 212, 225; (B) 142; (K) 73, 103; (M) 62; (SA) 157, 185–6
Ethiopia 9, 12
ethnicity 208, 222; (K) 77, 95, 96, 111, 112, 221–2, 231; (SA) 170–1
evictions (M) 49, 50, 51
'exceptionalism', African 12, 215–16, 218, 219
'exclusions' 206, 211, 227

'Fabian colonialism' 5
Fallon, Leland 86
famine 11; (B) 99, 130; (K) 79, 109; (M) 38, 45, 56; *see also* food
fencing (B) 119, 131, 132, 133, 135, 136, 140, 141, 143, 145, 147, 148, 205, 221; (K) , 89; (M) 45, 62; (SA) 178
fertilizer (B) 137, 142; (SA) 174, 180, 181, 186
fishing (M) 40, 41, 51, 61; Niger 61
flooding 21; (B) 141, 142; (M) 41, 47, 53, 54–5, 58–9, 70, 207, 224; (SA) 176
Fonds d'Equipment des Nations Unies (FENU) (M) 59, 70
food/food security 11; (B) 122, 130, 148; (K) 82, 109, 111; (M) 39, 46, 56, 62
forest (M) 38, 40–1, 45, 61, 62, 64, 66, 69, 70
fôret classée (forest reserve) (M) 38, 45, 61, 66, 218, 220, 227
foroba (M) 39, 48, 55–6
'fragile ecosystems' 4, 11, 12
freehold tenure 8, 18, 220, 221; (B) 131, 220–1; (K) 8, 86, 220; (M) 220; (SA) 220
fruit (B) 136; (M) 36; (SA) 186
Fulani state (M) 33, 61, 203
furrow groups (K) 92–4, 96, 105, 106–7, 206, 207, 218, 222, 229; (SA) 175

Gaborone (B) 136
Gazankulu (SA) 157, 169
gender relations 208–9; (SA) 171
generational relations 208; (K) 209; (SA) 171, 173–4, 209
gestions de terroir villageois (M) 67–8, 70
Ghana 4, 200, 201; empire 31
globalization 19
goats (B) 138–9, 223, 224; (M) 47, 224; (SA) 161, 176, 179, 182, 183, 184, 224
governance 1, 10, 14, 16, 23, 207, 215, 216–17, 218, 226; (K) 77
grass, thatching (B) 140; (SA) 166
grassland 20; *see also* savanna ecosystem
grassveld (SA) 158
grass roots 17; (M) 58
grazing (B) 17, 121, 131–3, 142, 144–5, 147; (K) 90; (M) 61, 62
grazing, rights (B) 133, 135; (K) 100–1; (SA) 166, 178, 187
Great Lakes 21
gross domestic product (GDP) 8; (B) 122
groundnut (B) 137; (M) 37; (SA) 174, 175
groundwater (B) 136; (M) 41; (SA) 178, 185
group ranching (B) 146, 147; (K) 77, 85, 86–7, 89, 90, 91–2, 94, 95, 97, 101, 103, 107, 109, 111, 112, 206, 209, 220, 221, 222, 224, 226, 230
Guinea 8; Guinean vegetation (M) 30–1

hameaux de culture: see 'hamlets'
'hamlets' (M) 45–6, 47, 48, 50, 54, 56, 66, 203; *see also* villages
hand cultivation (M) 39, 54, 55; (SA) 176, 180
Hardin, G. 11, 196
'hardveld' (B) 119–20, 123, 137, 151
harvest-sharing (M) 49, 63; *see also* sharecropping
headman (B) 127, 128, 129, 132, 141, 143; (SA) 156, 166, 167, 173, 187–8
Hill, Polly 4
historical materialism 198–200
homelands (SA) 155, 156, 157, 165, 170–1, 180, 188–9, 191, 202
horticulture: *see* market gardening
household production 197, 198, 199
household structure (M) 39; (SA) 166, 184
hunting/gathering (B) 7; (M) 46
hydro-electric power: Burkina Faso 41; Ghana 41

illiteracy (M) 40; (SA) 157; *see also* literacy
ilmurran (Maasai youth) (K) 90, 91, 111
immigration 209, 224; (K) 80, 105; (M) 46, 70
independence, African 2, 6, 7–9
'indigenous' narrative 10, 13, 17, 195, 207, 212, 218
indirect rule 3, 5, 6, 7, 16, 17, 19, 216, 220
industrialization (SA) 155, 156
inequality 15, 196, 210; (B) 123, 144, 145; (K) 97, 111, 113; (SA) 155
infant mortality (B) 122; (SA) 157
infrastructure 7, 224–5; (M) 58, 59
inheritance 205, 209; (SA) 171
Institut pour l'Economie Rurale (IER) (M) 57
institutions, state 216, 217; (B) 128–30; (M) 66; (K) 85–6, 88; (M) 66; (SA) 189
International Fund for Agricultural Development (IFAD) 12
International Institute for Environment and Development (IIED) 14
International Monetary Fund (IMF) 9–11; (K) 77; (M) 34
irrigation 8, 203, 207, 219, 221, 224, 231; furrow (SA) 161, 173; sprinkler (SA) 161, 164, 167; (B) 136, 141, 142, 149; (K) 80, 91, 92–3, 95, 103–7, 108–9, 110, 112, 229; (M) 57; (SA) 161, 166, 167, 168, 170, 171, 173, 175, 181, 182, 184, 185, 186, 189, 192, 221, 222, 223, 225
ISCOR (SA) 169

KADU (K) 96

kagisano (harmony) (B) 151
Kajiado District (K) 22, 73, 77, 78–9, 80, 85, 86, 99, 205, 208, 307, 208, 209
Kalahari desert (B) 119, 120
Kalenjin (K) 96
Kamba (K) 89, 203
KANU (K) 78, 93, 94, 96–8, 112, 217, 221
Keita, Modibo 33, 217
Kenya 7, 8, 10, 22, 200, 201, 216, 217, 220, 221–2, 227, 229
  administration 83–9
  economy 81–2
  geography 74, 78–9
  history 74–5, 82, 84–6
  kinship and lineage 74, 90–5, 96–7
  land and water: access 88–98, 109–11; management 82–8, 107–9; use 98–1-3, 103–7
  politics 95–8, 111–12
  settlement 74, 76, 84–6, 201
Kenya Livestock Development Project (KLDP) 86
Kenya Wildlife Service (KWS) 85, 207, 216, 223, 226, 227
Kenyatta, Jomo 96
Keynesianism 2, 6
Kgalagadi (B) 120
Kglata (B) 121
kgotla (Tswana village assembly) 127–8, 133, 143, 146
Kikuyu (K) 80, 89, 96, 97, 100, 102, 203, 224
Kilimanjaro, Mount 73, 79, 80, 103, 108, 109, 112
Kimana Community Conservancy (K) 226, 227, 229
Kimana/Tikondo Group Ranch (K) 74, 91, 92, 94, 97, 101, 105, 106, 107, 109, 203–10 *passim*, 218, 220–4 *passim*, 226, 227, 229
Kimana Swamp (K) 22, 98, 103, 108, 109, 226, 230
kinship (B) 127; (K) 84, 92–4; (M) 43, 45, 47
Kisonko, clan (K) 84, 92
Kitching, G. 202
Konaré, Alpha Oumar 35
Kruger National Park (SA) 158, 165, 168, 169, 178, 216
Kuku Group Ranch (K) 92, 108, 109, 111, 230

labour, hiring 24, 200–1, 204, 210, 222; (B) 140; (K) 102, 113; (M) 55–6, 63; (SA) 155, 172, 183–4
labour, migration (B) 119, 121, 122, 144; (M) 33; *see also under* migration
labour-based relief programme (LBRP) (B) 130, 131, 140, 141, 144
Land Adjudication Act (K) 86
land allocation 216–17; (SA) 166, 167, 173, 174 .
land boards (B) 128, 129, 130, 131–3, 135, 136, 141, 142, 146, 150–1, 205, 207, 217, 220, 226, 229; *see also* subordinate land boards; (K) 90
land clearing (B) 140, 141, 148; (K) 108, 202, 207; (M) 29, 37, 42, 46, 47, 54–5, 58, 60, 61, 65, 70; (SA) 167, 168, 170, 221
land disputes 216, 220, 221, 228; (B) 132, 144; (K) 89–90, 91, 92, 94, 221; (M) 48, 51-2, 59, 62, 64, 66, 221, 228, 230; (SA) 167, 170, 173, 174
Land (Group Representatives) Act, 1968 (K) 77, 86, 90, 112
land loans (M) 47–8, 50, 54, 59–60, 63, 206, 208, 229
land market 4, 5, 7, 23, 25, 220, 223, 228; (K) 88–90, 111; (SA) 169
land ownership/tenure 8, 11–12, 14, 18–19, 20; (B) 146; (K) 76, 77, 84, 88–90, 107, 111, 217; (M) 45, 48, 61; (SA) 157, 165–6, 169
land registration 222; (B) 132, 142, 221, 229; (K) 76, 77, 87, 89, 97, 103, 111, 206; (M) 50, 62
Land Rights Bill (SA) 218 & n
land use management (K) 82–8 *passim*; (M) 59, 62; (SA) 166, 187
land use planning 7, 11, 12, 13–14, 222
landlessness 228; (SA) 166, 169, 170, 171, 172, 188
'lands' (B) 124, 126, 127, 132, 139, 142, 144, 145, 223

Lawrence Mission (K) 86
Leach, M. & Mearns, R. 195, 196
leasehold tenure 24; (B) 147; (K) 89, 97; (SA) 167
Lebowa (SA) 157
'legitimacy' 17; (K) 111, 217; (M) 69–70
Lemba 171
Lenin, V.I. 3, 200, 201
Liberia 9
Limpopo River 20, 119, 123, 131, 158, 168, 173
lineage (K) 84, 222; (M) 43, 44, 47, 48, 49, 50, 65, 66, 208
literacy, adult (B) 122–3
livestock 204, 225; (B) 120, 128, 133, 137–8, 217, 230; (K) 73, 76, 77, 81, 82–8 passim; (M) 33, 34, 52–4; (SA) 168, 176, 178, 184, 191; see also cattle
local/local government 6, 10, 13, 14, 15, 16, 18, 20, 22–3, 197, 202, 212, 221, 222, 226–7, 231; (B) 128–30; (K) 88; (M) 43–4, 67–8, 218; (SA) 156, 157, 173, 187–8, 190, 204, 208, 221
local state 16, 211
'localities' (K) 82–3
Loitokitok Division (K) 73, 78–9, 80–2, 85, 88–100 passim, 224, 225, 229, 230
Loitokitok Town (K) 80–5, 103
Loitokitok Group Ranch Association (K) 229
Love, R. 149
Luvuvhu River (SA) 158, 161, 165

Maasai (K) 73, 74, 79, 80–1, 82–9 passim, 90–5, 96–8, 100–4, 105, 107–8, 111–12, 202, 203, 206, 211, 229
Maasailand (K) 84, 85, 86, 87, 96, 99, 107, 109
Madimo corridor (SA) 158, 168, 191
mafisa (cattle-borrowing) (B) 138; see also oxen
Mahalapye 131, 135, 141, 203
maize 204, 205; (B) 137, 149; (K) 109, 223; (M) 51; (SA) 174, 175, 176, 186
majimboism: see regionalism
Makuya Park (SA) 167, 168–9, 186, 220
Makuya Park Forum (SA) 169, 174, 190, 227
Makonde (SA) 164, 167, 170, 171, 180, 187
Mali 8, 30–1, 33–6, 216, 217–18
    administration 43–5, 63–8, 227
    economy 33–6, 39–41
    geography 30–1
    history: precolonial 31, 33; French colonial 33, 61, 203, 216; First Republic 33, 44, 217; Second Republic 33, 35, 61, 217, 223; Third Republic 35, 63–8, 218
    kinship and lineage 43–4, 47–8, 49–51, 60
    politics 60–70
    religion 43–4
    settlement 38–9, 45–6, 48
malnutrition (SA) 157; see also food
Malthus, T. 11
Maluleke (SA) 169
Mamdani, M. 3, 4, 8, 208, 217, 218, 231; 'centralized despotism' 217–18; 'conservative states' 8, 217; 'radical states' 8, 217, 218
marginalization 231
'market', the 10, 11, 13, 15, 18, 19, 20, 197, 200, 217, 218, 222, 228
market gardening 10, 203; (B) 136, 141–2, 144; (K) 81, 103, 105, 110, 113, 224; (M) 41; (SA) 175, 183
marketing, agricultural produce 22; (SA) 175, 176, 181, 182, 184
Marx, K. 198
massa (lineage head) (M) 44, 45, 50, 60, 66
Mbirikani Group Ranch (K) 95, 109, 111
mechanization (M) 54
medicine, traditional (SA) 166
members of parliament (B) 127; (K) 94, 95, 97–8, 112
men, and land (K) 90, 207; (M) 209; (SA) 166, 171, 183, 187
méthode acceleré de recherche participative (MARP) (M) 68
mfecane ('scattering') (SA) 4, 120

'middle peasants' 199, 201, 202, 212, 222
migration (internal) 14; (B) 122, 140; (M) 34, 39, 46; (SA) 166, 169
migration, labour 5, 6, 14, 203, 208, 228; (B) 140; (K) 73; (M) 33, 34, 38–9, 49, 57, 70; (SA) 156, 165, 169–70, 171, 186, 202
military land (SA) 158, 168
millet (M) 29, 37, 39, 46, 47, 60; (SA) 164, 175
mining 3, 31, 195, 201; (B) 114, 122, 130, 148, 149; (SA) 155, 168, 169
Ministry of Agriculture (MoA) (B) 128, 131, 135, 137, 148, 150
Ministry of Finance and Development Planning (MFDP) (B) 128, 129, 130
Ministry of Local Government, Lands and Housing (MLGLH) (B) 128, 129
Ministry of Mineral Resources and Water Affairs (MMRWA) (B) 128
'Miombo' grassland 20
Mmutlane (B) 123, 126, 128, 131–2, 133, 135, 136–9, 141, 142, 144, 149, 150, 203, 204, 205, 209, 201, 211, 221
Mmutlane dam (B) 134, 143, 144, 145, 207
'modern' (land tenure) 6, 18, 19, 24, 219, 222; (K) 76, 101, 112; (M) 61, 63
modernization 196, 197, 215, 218, 223, 228; (B) 148, 231; (K) 76; (M) 61, 63; see also development
monetization (K) 102–3
mopane woodland (SA) 20, 101
morafe (Tswana states) (B) 121
Mozambique 7, 8, 9, 20, 158, 168
'multiple livelihood' 205, 209–10, 228; (K) 82, 114; (SA) 182, 188
Mutale River (SA) 22, 155, 157, 158, 161, 164–9 passim, 171–9 passim, 181–8 passim, 203, 206, 207, 209, 221
Mutele (SA) 164, 167, 170, 171, 175–6, 181, 185, 187

Namibia 20
'narratives' 1, 12, 13–14, 23, 195, 196
'nation-building' 7, 8, 197, 216, 218
national action plans (NAPs) 13–14, 219
National Conservation Strategy (B) 151
national development plans (B) 146, 147, 148, 197
National Environment Secretariat (K) 225
National Environmental Action Plan (K) 73, 225
National Parks Ordinance, 1945 (K) 85
National Policy for Agricultural Development (NPAD) (B) 144–5, 147, 148
national parties, African 9; (K) 76, 93, 94
Native Land Act, 1913 (SA) 165
'native policy' 5
'native reserves' (B) 121; (K) 76, 84–5, 100; (SA) 155, 165
Native Trust and Land Act, 1936 (SA) 165
natural resource access 23–4, 199, 204, 205, 219–23; (K) 98
natural resource management 1, 23, 24, 25, 196, 198, 206–7, 211, 215, 216, 225–30; (B) 128, 146; (K) 82–8, 107, 108; (M) 50, 54, 63–8, 218; (SA) 168–9, 185–8, 189
natural resource use/users 1, 15, 16, 24, 198, 199, 203–5, 211, 212, 219, 223–5, 226; (B) , 139, 146–7, 151; (K) 98–107 passim, 113; (M) 66, 68; (SA) 188–9, 190–1
'nature' 4, 15, 199
Near East Foundation (NEF) (M) 69
neo-Malthusianism 11, 12, 13, 195, 212
'networks' 200, 202
Ngwato (B) 123
Niger 31
Niger River 30–1, 33, 39, 47, 53, 54, 57, 59, 61, 62
Nigeria 8, 31, 200
non-government organizations (NGOs) 10, 17, 23, 195, 226, 227; (B) 130; (K) 88, 109, 110; (M) 29, 59, 60, 64, 67, 69–70; (SA) 190, 191
Northern Province (SA) 22, 157, 158, 174, 189–90, 203
Northern Sotho (SA) 170–1

Northern Transvaal Cooperative (NTK) (SA) 176, 181
Nyerere, Julius 3

Odo-mungi clan (K) 84, 92–4, 95, 98
Office du Niger (M) 33, 34, 59
oil, imports 9
oil seeds (M) 33
Okavango swamps (B) 119
Organization of Petroleum-Exporting Countries (OPEC) 9
Orok-kiteng clan (K) 84, 92–4, 98
ostriches (B) 136
overgrazing (B) 121, 142, 143, 144, 149, 150; (K) 96, 107; (SA) 186, 195
oxen (B) 137, 138, 140, 211, 224; (M) 49, 55, 57, 210; (SA) 180
parastatals 6, 7, 9; (K) 88, 98; (M) 33, 34; (SA) 179
'partnership' 10, 20, 231
party politics 206, 216, 222; (B) 146, 148–9; (K) 77, 95–8, 111, 112, 221; (M) 63–5, 70, ; (SA) 221
pastoralism 4, 7, 12–13, 21, 25, 208, 210, 215, 219, 229; (K) 73, 76, 82, 87, 98–9, 102, 108–9, 112, 210, 223, 228; (M) 38, 39, 47, 50, 52–4, 61, 66, 69, 70, 221, 228; (SA) 186
patron–client networks (K) 95, 112, 221; (SA) 170
patronage 200, 206, 227; (K) 90, 91, 111; (M) 217; (SA) 173, 187
peasants 4, 6, 198, 199, 204; *see also* 'middle peasants'
pensions (SA) 182, 188
'people', the 197, 226
'peripheral' areas 208, 211; (M) 38
'permission to occupy' land (SA) 167, 221
pesticides 16; (K) 224, 226; (SA) 174, 180, 181
Peters, P. 146, 150
petty commodity production 6, 198–200, 201, 208, 211
Peulh, pastoralists (M) 38, 39, 44, 51, 52–3, 54, 58, 59
pigs (SA) 179
'pioneers' (B) 139, 141; (K) 103, 104–5, 225; (SA) 184–5, 187
planning, state 225; (B) 128; (SA) 166, 173, 189
plot-holders (M) 49, 50, 55–6; (SA) 166, 167, 170–6 *passim*, 180, 181, 183–4, 187, 190, 207, 209, 221
ploughing (B) 131, 136–7, 138, 139, 140, 144, 145, 148, 211; (M) 54, 55, 60, 210; (SA) 174, 179, 181, 182, 192
pluralism 4, 16, 227, 231; (M) 69–70
'political ecology' 13, 15
pollution 16; (K) 207, 226
population growth 1, 12, 13, 195, 208, 212, 223; (B) 136; (K) 73, 77, 80–1, 107; (M) , 38, 39, 40, 46; (SA) 155, 157, 169, 171, 185, 186
postcolonialism 9
post-independence, Africa 16, 216–17
poverty, rural 1, 8, 11, 12, 15; (B) 123, 130, 146, 151; (K) 77, 82, 109–10, 113; (M) 39–40; (SA) 157, 188
primary production 7
'pristine' environment, African 4, 197, 219
private ownership, land and water 11, 196–210 *passim*; (B) *see under* boreholes, dams; (K) 77, 84, 86, 113, 206; (M) 61, 62; (SA) 165, 171
privatization, land 2, 10, 13, 19, 200, 205, 209, 221, 229; (K) 95, 111
productivity 1, 11, 223–5, 228, 230; (K) 113
Programme de Gestion de Ressources Naturelles (PGRN) (M) 67–8, 228
'progressive farmers' 6–7; (SA) 169–70
property rights 5, 11–12, 18–19, 24, 217, 219–23; *see also* private ownership; state ownership
public/merit goods 8, 10, 200; (K) 113; (M) 50, 58, 64; (SA) 164, 173, 189, 221
pumpkins (SA) 174, 175
pumps, water (SA) 167, 176, 184, 185, 200

rainfall 20–1; (B) 119–20, 123, 130, 137, 142; (K) 74, 99, 101; (M) 30, 33–4, 40, 57, 58; (SA) 158, 161, 164, 178, 186
rain-fed farming: *see* dryland farming

Rambuda (SA) 166, 167, 175
rangeland 145; (B) 121, 147, 149; (K) 76, 77, 85, 86, 90, 102, 107, 108, 112
'rational' economic behaviour 15, 195, 196, 212
regionalism (K) 96
remittances (B) 140; (M) 34–5; (SA) 156, 182
removals, forced 220; (K) 84–5; (SA) 180–1, 187, 203; *see also* apartheid
rents (K) 111; (M) 62–3, 206; (SA) 167
resources: *see under* natural resources
Rhodesia 121
rice (M) 29, 33, 41–2, 46, 47–8, 49, 50–1, 52–3, 54–60, 65, 70, 204, 206, 207, 221, 223, 224, 225, 226
Rift Valley Province (K) 77, 96
rinderpest (B) 121; *see also under* disease control
Rio Summit, 1992 1, 13
river lands 21, 22, 205; (M) 38, 54; *see also* rice; (SA) 170, 186
Rombo Group Ranch (K) 87, 92
rural development (B) 123, 140; (K) 80, 85; (SA) 155
rural-dwellers 2, 8, 11, 12, 18, 19, 230; (K) 109; *see also* poverty, rural

Sahara 30, 43; *see also* Sahel
Sahel 11, 12, 21; (M) 35, 39, 40
Samori (M) 22, 38, 39–40, 44, 45, 52, 58, 62, 70, 203–10 *passim*, 218, 220–9 *passim*
sandveld (B) 120, 121, 133, 151
Sankara, Thomas 58
Sarwa/San (B) 120
savanna ecosystems 20–2; (K) 73, 79; (M) 30, 37–8; (SA) 161; *see also* 'wetlands in drylands'
seasonal labourers (M) 57, 63, 70
'sections' (K) 80, 82, 85, 92
seed, agricultural 204; (B) 131, 137, 148; (M) 57–8; (SA) 174, 180, 181
Senari (SA) 164, 167, 170, 171, 173, 175–6, 181, 187
Senegal 8, 33
Serowe (B) 123, 128, 131, 135
services: *see* public/merit goods
Services des Eaux et Forêts (SEF) (M) 40–1, 61
settlement patterns 24, 208; (M) 38–9, 40
Shangaan (SA) 170–1
sharecropping 24, 206, 222; (K) 105, 220; (M) 49, 57, 61, 63, 221
shea nut (M) 37
sheep (SA) 179
shifting cultivation 4, 12
Shoshong (B) 123, 131, 132, 134, 142, 143, 220, 222, 224, 225, 230
Shoshong Brigades Development Trust (SBDT) 142
Shoshong Hills (B) 22, 119, 123, 138, 149
'small farmers' 198, 212; *see also* 'middle peasants'
smallholders 16; (M) 33; (SA) 166, 169; *see also* plot-holders
'social capital' 15, 227
soil 7, 13, 20, 195, 207; (K) 74, 107; (SA) 158, 161, 185–6, 187
Somalia 9
Songhai empire (M) 31
Soninké (M) 31
sorghum 204; (B) 126, 137, 149; (M) 39, 51, 55; (SA) 164, 174, 175, 176
SOS Sahel 29, 60, 69, 70
Sourou River (M) 22, 31, 36, 38, 41, 44, 46, 49, 51–2, 54–5, 57, 62, 65, 203, 204, 226
sourveld (SA) 161
South Africa 20, 22, 127, 142, 149, 202, 216, 218–20, 227, 229
    administration 156, 165
    economy 157, 182–5
    geography 157–8, 161m 164–5
    history 155–6, 157, 166
    land and water: access 165–9, 169–72; management 185–8; use 174–81

politics 172–4, 188–92
settlement 155–6
South African Agricultural Credit Board 180
South African Native Trust 165
standpipes (B) 133
state, in development 2, 4, 8, 9, 13, 15, 18, 19, 20, 196–7, 200, 211, 215; post- independent 216, 217, 219, 228; (B) 122
state ownership, land 8, 216; (K) 112; (M) 61, 66
state withdrawal 10, 19, 225
'strangers' (rural migrants) 201, 205; (M) 29, 48, 55, 61–2, 226, 229; (SA) 187
structural adjustment 2, 3, 9–12, 219; structural-adjustment lending (SAL) 10–12
subclans (K) 93, 94–5, 98, 208
subdivision, land (B) 129; (K) 76, 87, 89, 90, 94, 110
subordinate land boards (B) 130, 131–2, 135, 136, 142, 145, 19, 150
sub-Saharan Africa 3, 10, 20–2, 196, 197, 201, 210, 212
subsistence agriculture 197, 198–9, 203–4, 205, 210, 212; (SA) 157, 171, 182, 183
sub-subsistence agriculture 204
Sudan/Sudanian vegetation 9, 12, 20, 21, 22
Sudano-Sahelian vegetation 21, 30, 31, 33, 36
surface water (B) 127, 129; (M) 41
sustainability 10, 14, 19, 23, 25, 211, 225–30; (B) 151; (K) 112–13; (M) 57–60; (SA) 189
Swynnerton Plan (K) 7, 76, 220

tamarind (M) 37
Tanzania 8, 20, 74, 80, 87, 105
taxes (B) 121, 146; (K) 100; (M) 33, 45, 64, 66, 68
tea plantations (SA) 165, 185, 186
terroir (community space) (M) 67, 68
Thengwe (SA) 167
thornveld (SA) 158
Thohoyandou (SA) 158, 161, 176, 189
Tikondo: see Kimana/Tikondo
Tombouctou (M) 33
Toucouleur empire (M) 33, 38, 44, 61
tourism (K) 73, 77, 81–2, 103, 106, 223, 226; (SA) 169, 191
'tracking' 21; (K) 100–3, 107, 224, 229
tractors (B) 137, 138, 140, 144, 210, 211; (K) 210; (SA) 170, 174, 176, 179, 180, 182, 184, 186, 192, 210
'tradition'/traditional institutions 5, 13, 14, 18, 204–5, 215–16, 219; (SA) 157, 167, 168, 171, 172, 174, 187, 190
transhumance (B) 124–5; (K) 100–1, 107, 110; (M) 33, 39, 47, 53
Transkei (SA) 155
Transvaal (SA) 20, 120, 157, 203
Traoré, Moussa 33, 35, 61, 62, 66, 217, 223
trees 13, 20, 21; (M) 37–8, 39–40, 54–5, 223
Tribal Authorities (B) 128; (SA) 156, 158, 165, 167, 169, 170, 171, 172, 173, 187, 188, 190
Tribal Grazing Lands Policy (TGLP) (B) 128, 147, 148, 149
Tribal Land Amendment Act (B) 142
Tribal Land Act, 1968 (B) 129, 217
'tribes'/tribalism 3, 4, 5, 8, 14, 216, 217, 220; (B) 129, 131, 146, 147, 150; (K) 74, 76; (SA) 171, 172, 219
tsetse fly 21
Tshandama/Makonde (SA) 161
Tshikondeni mine (SA) 168, 169, 184, 186, 189, 191
Tshiombo Cooperative (SA) 180–1, 190
Tshiombo irrigation scheme (SA) 155, 158, 161, 165, 166, 167, 170–5 passim, 177–85 passim, 187, 203, 207, 221
Tswana (B) 120, 121, 139, 146
Tuareg (M) 33, 35, 61

underdevelopment 8; (SA) 156, 157, 164, 188
underground water (B) 127

unemployment (M) 35; (SA) 171, 192
Union Démocratique du Peuple Malien (UDPM) 33, 35, 65, 217
United Local Government Service (ULGS) (B) 129
United Nations (UN) 13; (M) 59
United Nations Commission on Environment and Development (UNCED) 1
United Nations Development Programme (UNDP) 60
United States Agency for International Development (USAID) (K) 86; (M) 34
urban–rural links 219; (B) 140; (M) 34, 57, 62
urbanization (B) 122, 126, 140, 144, 148; (M) 34, 57, 62
usufruct 13; (SA) 165

Vaughan, M. 3
vegetables 204, 205, 210; (B) 141, 142, 210; (K) 81, 105, 210, 223, 226; (M) 36; (SA) 167, 174, 175, 176, 183, 210
Venda (SA) 22, 155, 156, 157–8, 167, 168, 170–9 passim, 186, 187, 189, 190, 191, 202–11 passim, 220–5 passim, 227, 230
Venda Agricultural Corporation (Agriven) 167, 179–80, 181
Venda Farmers' Union 191
villages/village administration 14, 219; (B) 127–8, 131; (M) 43–6, 50–1, 52, 58, 60, 63–8, 69, 208, 227; (SA) 164, 187
village development committee (VDC) (B) 128, 131, 143
'villagization' 8

wage labour 199, 208, 209, 228; (SA) 172
'wasteland' (SA) 167, 170, 172, 175
water 2, 12, 13, 20, 21, 33, 223–5, 228, 230; see also irrigation
  access (B) 131–3, 135–6; (K) 88–98, 109–11; (M) 46–54; (SA) 165–9, 169–72
  management (B) 130–1, 142–6; (K) 82–8, 107–9; (M) 57–60; (SA) 185–8
  use (B) 124, 126, 136–9; (K) 98–103, 103–7; (M) 54–7; (SA) 174–81
Water Apportionment Board (WAB) (B) 136
watermelons (SA) 174, 175
Weber, M. 215, 219
weeds (B) 137, 140, 148; (K) 107; (M) 39, 54, 59, 60, 207, 226
welfare policy 6, 10, 26, 19; (B) 123; (K) 73, 113; (M) 40, 64; see also public/merit goods
wells (B) 123, 127, 132, 134, 136, 220; (M) 53; (SA) 186; see also boreholes
West Africa 7, 8, 16, 21, 201; (M) 33, 62
wetland 22, 205, 215, 221, 222, 230, 231; (K) 109, 112–13
'wetland in dryland' 2, 20–2, 202–3, 212, 227, 230; (B) 123–4, 126, 202–3; (K) 73, 77, 78–9, 103–7, 109, 112–14, 202–3; (M) 36–42, 203, 210; (SA) 202–3
'white' (SA) 155, 179, 180, 184, 203, 220
wildlife 12, 15, 219, 224, 225, 229; (B) 151; (K) 73, 77, 81, 85, 98, 103, 106, 112, , 223, 226; (SA) 168, 169, 178, 186
Williams, G. 199
women 201, 208–9; (B) 140; (M) 69; (SA) 156, 157, 166, 171, 183, 184, 187, 192
wood, fuel 12, 13, 226; (SA) 166, 195; see also forest
working class, African 5–6
World Bank (WB) 9, 11, 12, 17, 18, 20, 215; (B) 150–1; (K) 77, 86; (M) 34, 67
World Development Report, 1997 10
World Vision (K) 109

youth 103; (K) 90–1, 92, 95, 110–11; see also ilmurran; (M) 43–4, 50, 56, 58; (SA) 173, 174, 188, 192, 209; see also civics

Zambia 7, 20, 200, 201
Zimbabwe 15, 20, 127, 142, 158]
Zulu (SA) 120